Napoleon the Fourth

Col. (Retd) Digby Hague-Holmes

The author has asserted his rights, under the
Copyright, Designs and Patents Act, 1988,
to be identified as the author of this work.

British Library Cataloguing in Publication data

A catalogue record for this book is available
from the British Library

ISBN 978-0-907077-70-1

First published in 2016 by St Michael's Abbey Press
Farnborough Abbey,
Farnborough, Hampshire GU14 7NQ

www.farnboroughabbey.org
www.theabbeyshop.com

St Michael's Abbey Press is a division of
St Michael's Abbey Press Ltd (reg. no. 326241)

Printed and bound in the Republic of Slovakia

Contents

Acknowledgements — vii

Chapter I
Le Petit Prince — 1

Chapter II
The Glory of Empire — 13

Chapter III
A Baptism of Fire — 33

Chapter IV
The Journey to Albion — 55

Chapter V
A Confident Young Man — 77

Chapter VI
The Child of France — 103

Chapter VII
Sword in Hand — 129

Chapter VIII
The Long Voyage — 161

Chapter IX
A Chilling Prediction — 193

Chapter X
His Face to the Foe — 213

Chapter XI
A Crown of Thorns — 245

Appendix A — 285

Appendix B — 287

Bibliography — 289

Index — 293

Acknowledgements

Firstly I would like to acknowledge, with grateful thanks, the gracious permission of Her Majesty the Queen to make use of all the material in the Royal Archives. During my frequent visits to Windsor, the Deputy Registrar, Miss Pamela Clark, and all her charming staff made every effort to answer my various queries, and I am deeply indebted to them all. Needless to say, the Royal Archives have been the source of much new and hitherto unpublished material relating to the Prince's period in this country and to his time in South Africa.

All Crown copyright material relating to Lord Chelmsford's dispatches and to Captain Carey's Court Martial, held in the Public Record Office, is reproduced by kind permission of the Controller of Her Majesty's Stationery Office.

I am also indebted to Brigadier Ken Timbers, secretary of the Royal Artillery Historical Trust, and to Mrs de Lee, Deputy Curator of the Royal Military Academy, Sandhurst Collection, for background information covering the Prince's studies at Woolwich, for access to memorabilia, and for information relating to his brief attachment to the Royal Horse Artillery at Aldershot. Thanks are also due to the late Very Reverend Dom Magnus Wilson, OSB, Prior of Saint Michael's Abbey, Farnborough, for personally showing my wife and myself around the abbey church and crypt, answering all our queries, and permitting photography of the Prince's bust and tomb.

This book could not have been written without close reference to Katherine John's own full-length biography of the Prince Imperial, published in London, 1939, by Putnam. This seminal work has proved invaluable, particularly for the Prince's boyhood years. Regretfully, at the time of writing, it has not been possible to obtain copyright acknowledgement for all the many quotations given in these pages, and I would welcome any opportunity in the future to correct this major shortcoming. And whilst every endeavour has been made, where appropriate, to obtain copyright approval from publishers and authors quoted in the narrative, should there be any further notable omissions, an appropriate acknowledgement will be made immediately upon notification. I have also been unable to trace the present whereabouts of Mr Stanley G. Hutchins, who in April 1973 produced the critique of the Prince Imperial, which is reproduced at Appendix B.

A special word of thanks to my friend of many years, the late Lieutenant Colonel Ronnie Cole-Mackintosh, who so generously gave so much of his time, skill, and advice in producing all the diagramatic maps and sketches. A special thanks to my three children who maintained the momentum with their constant encouragement and to my dear wife who has 'lived' with the Prince longer than she would care to remember, yet has always provided sound practical advice at every stage.

The final acknowledgement must go to the Prince Imperial himself. When I joined the Royal Military Academy course in 1951 he was almost the first person to catch my eye. Standing then — as he does today — on his plinth, gazing firmly across the grounds of New College, he was a constant presence on those early morning 'hoxters'. Over the years it was always my intention to one day bring him back to life in the pages of a book. And now I hope the reader will conclude with me that he was indeed an unusual young man — a truly heroic figure, whose brief life was full of interest and adventure, and who deserves to stand as a role model for all generations.

Col. (Retd) Digby Hague-Holmes

THE IMPERIAL LINE

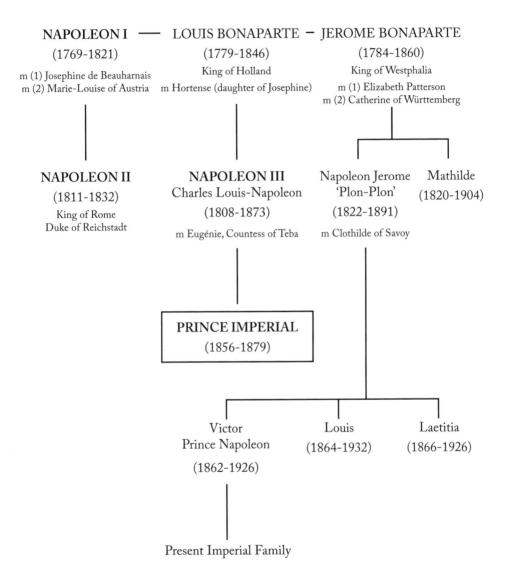

NAPOLEON I —— **LOUIS BONAPARTE** – **JEROME BONAPARTE**

(1769-1821)   (1779-1846)   (1784-1860)

m (1) Josephine de Beauharnais   King of Holland   King of Westphalia
m (2) Marie-Louise of Austria   m Hortense (daughter of Josephine)   m (1) Elizabeth Patterson
     m (2) Catherine of Württemberg

NAPOLEON II   **NAPOLEON III**   Napoleon Jerome   Mathilde

(1811-1832)   Charles Louis-Napoleon   'Plon-Plon'   (1820-1904)

King of Rome   (1808-1873)   (1822-1891)
Duke of Reichstadt

m Eugénie, Countess of Teba   m Clothilde of Savoy

PRINCE IMPERIAL
(1856-1879)

Victor   Louis   Laetitia
Prince Napoleon   (1864-1932)   (1866-1926)

(1862-1926)

Present Imperial Family

Chapter 1

Le Petit Prince

In the early hours of 16th March 1856 the sleepy peacefulness of Paris was to be rudely shattered by the rhythmic pounding of cannon booming from out of the courtyard of the Tuileries. Tradition required a salute of twenty-one guns for a daughter, and a hundred and one for a son. There was a slight pause after the twenty-first salvo had been fired — during which the awakened citizens held their breath — before the resumption of cannon fire signalled the joyous news, now being echoed by every church bell in the city, that shortly after 3 o'clock that morning a son and heir had at last been born to the Emperor Napoleon the Third and his Empress, Eugénie.

In the year 1856 Sunday the 16th March also happened to be Palm Sunday — surely a good omen for any child at the start of life. Yet had the birth taken place only four days later, the Prince Imperial would have entered this world on the same day as his young uncle, the ill-fated King of Rome, only son of the Great Napoleon. But the Empress's pregnancy had been difficult enough without the complications of an extended birth.

Whilst Eugénie lay back exhausted from the forty-eight hours of agonising labour, Louis-Napoleon, ecstatic with delight, temporarily discarded his usual imperial dignity and undemonstrative demeanour. Quite out of character, he now dashed along the corridors of the Tuileries, pausing only to embrace everyone he met, regardless of their status, in an emotional display of exuberant happiness he was rarely to show again. In an impulsive gesture he announced to waiting press reporters that he and his wife would become honorary godparents to all legitimate children of France likewise born on that day — some 3,500. As a further expression of his pleasure, an amnesty was also declared for all those who had been exiled or imprisoned as a result of their opposition to his *coup d'état* of 1851. A sum of 100,000 francs was immediately made available for distribution to the poor of Paris. And to honour the army, Generals Randon, Canrobert and Bosquet were simultaneously appointed Marshals of France.

Louis-Napoleon had every reason to feel ecstatic; at last he had founded a dynasty of his own. No longer would the heir-presumptive be his difficult and jealous cousin, Prince Jerome Napoleon — nicknamed by the press and known to everyone as 'Plon-Plon' — son of the ailing King of Westphalia, the Great Napoleon's youngest brother. In the same vein the majority of the French people could likewise share their Emperor's delight, for this child would ensure a legitimate and orderly succession and hopefully bring to an end the era of destabilising social upheavals which had so scarred the body politic of the Empire. Only the exhausted Empress, with that ingrained sense of drama which was so much part of her character, would have perhaps brooded over the realisation that historically the Crown of France for more than two centuries, from the accession of Louis the Fourteenth, had never been passed directly from father to son. This fear was to haunt her in the years that lay ahead more especially after she had been advised, at the risk of her life, not to bear any more children. Thus, in this only child lay all the hopes of an Imperial dynasty and the peoples of an Empire.

In 1856 Napoleon the Third was at the zenith of his quite astonishing career. Not only had he now secured the succession, but France's recent victory in the Crimean War had more than avenged the humiliation of her 1812 defeat at the hands of the Russians. At the same time it had brought her once more to the very forefront of military prowess in Europe. The fact that the subsequent Peace Congress had assembled in the city of Paris was viewed as international acknowledgement of France's established pre-eminence. When the Empress went into labour the Congress had temporarily adjourned as a mark of respect and on the morning of the birth, various plenipotentiaries and diplomats had dutifully filed past the ornate golden, boat-shaped cradle in which lay the unusually large baby. One of these was a giant of a man, towering over the cradle, across which the red ribbon of the Grand Cross of the *Légion d'honneur* and a crucifix had now been draped. Who then could have foreseen that this junior plenipotentiary from Prussia, Otto Von Bismarck-Schoenhausen, would likewise dominate the later fortunes of the Second Empire and thus woefully influence the future life of the plump baby who now lay gurgling up at him?

The *Légion d'honneur*? This had been instituted by Napoleon the First in 1802, and since that time had continued to be bestowed, without disruption, on the most illustrious of Frenchmen. When the Prince Imperial was twelve years old, the Abbé Deguerry, *curé* of the Madeleine, explained its significance: "*Mon cher petit seigneur*, do you know that I paid you my first visit with many grown-up gentlemen when you were still not quite forty-eight hours old?...You had the red ribbon already. Now, what had you done at two days old to have deserved the grand cross of the *Légion d'honneur*? You had been given the cross, not for services you had rendered, but for those you will one day have to give. The cross is the symbol of sacrifice. The one that was placed in your cradle meant that you had been marked out from your birth to devote yourself to the people."[1] These stirring words had such an impact on the child Prince that, years later, he was able to recall practically every word. Indeed they had become the sub-conscious foundation of that personal sense of destiny which was to dominate his whole life.

Two days after the birth, on the morning of 18th March, a delighted Louis-Napoleon addressed the assembled senators and deputies, introducing his new-born son to them as: 'The Child of France'. He explained: "This is a revival of the usages of the *ancien régime*. It is not, for that reason, a meaningless or antiquated term.

---

1   FILON, p. 4.

For truly, gentlemen, when an heir is born to perpetuate a national institution, that child is the whole country's son: and this name will remind him of his duties."[2] Not surprisingly this renewal of the old Bourbon tradition of *'fils de France'* was to infuriate the Legitimists. But whilst so mystical a title might be invoked on formal ceremonial occasions, it was nonetheless in the days of misfortune that lay ahead to invite not a little ridicule from many quarters. The popular name everyone gave the child — *'le petit Prince'* — was the affectionate title by which he would always be acclaimed by the mass of the people, but when that too persisted in following him through every year of his life, even into young manhood, he began to find its connotation equally as irritating, undermining his sense of dignity and manliness.

Amongst the worthy citizens of Paris who were permitted to file past the cradle was a delegation of ladies from the newly-built market place — *Les dames de la Halle* — and one of them, a large sturdy fishwife, Madame Lebron, asked permission to be allowed to kiss the baby. This was granted. As she leaned over the golden cradle little could she have guessed that, eighteen years later in England, she would remind that same Prince, now a handsome young man, of her gesture. Only then was he able to return that kiss.

A few weeks after the birth, on 30th April, the peace treaty concluding the Crimean War was signed. Basking in popular approval the Emperor now added to the general relief by solemnly declaring: "France breathes more freely by the birth of this child. She associates her future with his destinies when he will reign over this Empire, the Nineteenth Century having reached its extreme period will gather the fruits of the productive seed which has been sown by our generation in the present." And, as if recalling the fate of recent heirs to the French throne, he added confidently, "If I hope that my son will be more fortunate in the future, it is mainly because I rely on God whose protection I cannot doubt when I see how, by a combination of extraordinary circumstances, He has restored all that was overthrown forty years ago as though, in spite of former sorrow and misfortune, He would bless this new dynasty chosen of the people... We must not abuse the favour of fortune, a dynasty has only the possibility of continuing if it remains loyal to its origin and protects the public interests for which it was founded. This child, whose cradle is consecrated by Peace, by the blessing of the Holy Father which arrived by telegram an hour after his birth, by the unanimous cheers of the people whom the 'Great Emperor' loved so dearly, will I trust prove worthy of the high vocation which awaits him."[3]

At the same time, in a less exalted manner, he wrote privately to Queen Victoria expressing the wish that his newly-born son would develop those same 'rare qualities' as the Queen's own children. 'I hope,' he added, 'that my son will also inherit my feelings of sincere friendship for the Royal Family of England and of affectionate esteem for the great English nation.'[4] Ironically, of all the many effusive prophesies then being made for the infant Prince, this personal wish addressed directly to the Queen of England was the only one which was to be fully realised.

---

2   KURTZ, p. 92.
3   TURNBULL, p. 122.
4   ARONSON, p. 75.

From the day of his birth he was to be surrounded by a wet nurse and three French governesses. The most senior of these was Mme Bruat, wife of an admiral; the other two were widows of distinguished officers killed in the Crimea. But the person who was permanently in attendance on the baby Prince, day and night, was the rather tall, austere English nurse, Miss Jane Shaw. This capable and strict lady, with firm ideas on how to bring up children, had only been accepted by the Empress into the imperial household after repeated promptings from Queen Victoria herself. But there was more to this acceptance than the influence of the Queen. As a child, Eugénie had herself been largely brought up by a comparable English governess — a Miss Flowers — and she was to loyally remain with the Montijo family for over fifty years.

The Empress was well aware of the differences between the English and French approach to this vexed matter of child-care. She clearly preferred the English method; calmness allied to strictness, in preference to the French attitude with its tendency to pampering and over-indulgence. Miss Shaw — 'Nana' as the Prince always called her — was to guide her young charge through into his teenage years; she taught him English and, in the opinion of her many critics, always tried hard to ensure that *'le petit Prince'* would eventually be transformed into the stereotyped English gentleman. Her total ignorance of the French language always gave her immunity from such criticism; in any case, she always enjoyed the one thing that mattered — the complete confidence of the child's parents.

To commemorate the birth presents poured in from all quarters. Paris, for example, had produced the golden cradle, a superb creation, involving all the goldsmiths of the city. It had been shaped in the form of a Norman boat, surmounted by the figure of Paris herself holding a gold crown surrounded by eagles, sirens, and sea deities. Congratulatory addresses likewise arrived from all corners of the Empire. One newspaper journalist, reflecting on the event some years later, commented: 'A Prince Imperial meant that the continuity of the Empire was assured. It meant also the setting aside of Prince Napoleon ('Plon-Plon'), and in the opinion of many the second advantage was at least equal to the first.' In fact the setting aside of 'Plon-Plon' (this strange nickname had been derived from the family pet-name of 'Plom-Plom' since he too had been a large, round baby) had started from the moment of the imperial birth. In disgust at the news that the child was a boy, he had sulkily refused to sign the gilded register as a witness to the *acte de naissance*, but then, after being publicly ridiculed by his sister Princess Mathilde, reluctantly signed with a bad grace. In anger he deliberately left a great ink blot on the document beside that signature, as if to symbolise a lifelong distaste for both mother and son.

The British press was to offer its own congratulations. 'The same fortune,' pontificated *The Times*, 'which has raised Louis-Napoleon from an exile to a Sovereign has now presented him with an heir, on whom may devolve vast acquisitions, and who will at any rate have as good a claim as any other Frenchman to the throne of the first nation of the continent...The Napoleon born last Sunday morning may be crowned the fourth of his line: or may add one more to the Pretenders of France.'[5]

5   JOHN, p. 31.

Napoleon the Third knew a great deal about Pretenders to the throne of France. He had spent most of his childhood in exile in Holland and Switzerland, and only returned to France when he was old enough to usefully engage in intrigues against the restored Bourbon monarchy. As the third son of Louis Bonaparte, the younger brother of the Great Napoleon, he was not only a nephew — but through his mother, Hortense de Beauharnais — he was also the grandson of Josephine de Beauharnais, the Great Napoleon's first wife. Consequently he was always to maintain that, in addition to descending from a distinguished family, he was also the natural heir to an illustrious name, even though that interpretation of his position was not to be universally accepted.

Political intrigue and plotting were his favourite preoccupations as a young man. At the age of twenty, he and his brother had offered their support to the *Carbonari*, the secret association pledged to unite Italy and transform it into a truly independent country. Their various revolutionary activities finally resulted in both of them having to be personally rescued from Italy by their mother, Queen Hortense, at which time her eldest son, Napoleon Louis, fell ill and died from measles. Despite her personal grief she managed to smuggle her only surviving son across France to the safety of England, where Louis-Napoleon was to begin the first of his three periods of exile in this country.

After the sudden demise of his brother, and the untimely death from tuberculosis in 1832 of the Great Napoleon's only son, the King of Rome, Louis found himself the oldest surviving male Bonaparte of his generation, knowing that all realistic hopes of any Napoleonic restoration now rested solely with him.

In 1836 he made his first abortive and quite farcical bid for power in France. The plan centred around the assumption that those officers of the army who had fought under the Great Napoleon would automatically rally to his cause — which relied for its appeal almost entirely on the putative magnetism of his dynastic name. But, to his surprise, the first garrison he approached in Strasbourg immediately denounced and arrested him. Most of the soldiers he tried to rally found it difficult to believe that this rather unimpressive 28 year old was actually the nephew of the Great Napoleon! However, because he had virtually acted alone in his attempted *coup* and no lives had been lost the authorities simply deported him, without trial, direct to the United States.

His next attempt, in 1840, was almost as farcical as the first. This had been timed to coincide with the return of the Great Napoleon's body from St. Helena. As before, he launched his bid for power from the sanctuary of England. On this occasion, assisted by about fifty supporters, he hi-jacked the routine paddle-steamer from Gravesend to Boulogne. His colleagues added to the farce by producing a tame, but somewhat bedraggled vulture, which they then chained to the mast, ostensibly representing an eagle to give the expedition a truly Napoleonic flavour! But the first military garrison they entered in Boulogne finally declined to rally to the Bonapartist cause; in frustration, Louis-Napoleon then fired off a pistol in the air, the bullet ricocheted from the ceiling, wounding one of the soldiers. The plotters fled, but they were all soon detained whilst desperately rowing back to the safety of the steamer. This time the authorities decided to act. King Louis Philippe was no longer prepared to indulge this hyperactive Pretender to his throne; Louis-Napoleon was tried and condemned to life-imprisonment in the fortress prison of Ham in Picardy.

Over the next five and a half years he made the most of the enforced seclusion and inactivity to widen his reading. As a consequence he was to become one of the best educated rulers in Europe; in later years he frequently referred to his prison as 'Ham University'. From his cell he produced a pamphlet on the eradication of poverty which was to gain him some popularity amongst the working classes. He also wrote erudite papers on such diverse subjects as electricity and sugar beet; for the military, he published a technical treatise: *Études sur le passé et l'avenir de l'Artillerie* (Studies on the Past and Future of the Artillery) which was to be much praised by many artillery experts. In 1843 he even devised a completely new scheme for the mobilisation of France in time of war which was not unlike the Prussian system which, many years later, was to bring about his own downfall. He also spent time in reassessing his future. 'I believe,' he wrote from his prison, 'that there are certain men who are born to serve as a means for the march of the human race...I consider myself to be one of these.'[6]

After five and half years, disguised as a workman, he succeeded in escaping from the fortress. Eventually he found his way to London, where, on arrival, he casually booked into a hotel as though he were a French tourist, thus beginning a further period of exile in England. On this occasion he acquired an English mistress; he also, for the first time, extended the ends of his moustache and had them waxed — as in the famous 1859 Winterhalter portrait. In the years to come he was often to boast (even to Queen Victoria) about the fact that, during this particular period of exile, he had once enrolled as a special constable — one of 170,000 — to protect London on the occasion of the threatened Chartist march on Westminster.

He finally returned to France in 1848 at the age of forty in the wake of the revolution which had resulted in the sudden abdication of King Louis Philippe. This time he made no attempt to seize power by force, but chose instead to take whatever advantage he could of the nation-wide political turmoil. In that same year he stood as candidate for the Presidency of the new Republic, and relying on the power of his name, and on funds provided by his English mistress, managed to obtain about three-quarters of all the votes cast. But the position of President had little executive power; the term of office would expire in 1852 and, under the new Constitution of 1848, he would then be automatically barred from standing for a second term. But Louis-Napoleon was only interested in achieving supreme power and then retaining it for life.

Three years later, on 2nd December 1851 (the anniversary of Austerlitz and the Coronation of Napoleon the First), he made a concerted bid for that power. Even though he was relying on the ineptitude of his rivals, and the readiness of the people for constitutional change, this time his own life was truly at stake. For if this attempt failed he could only expect to be tried for treason, having deliberately broken his oath to preserve the 1848 Constitution. That morning, many leading

---

6   ZELDIN, p. 511.

deputies, journalists and other figures were arrested; the National Assembly and other public buildings were occupied; once more people surged out on to the streets. The loyalty of the army's senior officers had been assured — by direct bribery, the promise of promotion, the lure of the Napoleonic legend. And with the army's support, resistance in the streets was ruthlessly crushed — in the ensuing exchange of fire some four hundred civilians lost their lives, with many totally innocent bystanders caught up in the confusion. The needless bloodshed of that day deeply disturbed Louis-Napoleon, and the memory of it was to trouble his conscience for the remainder of his life. Despite his lust for supreme political power, at heart he also abhorred violence and genuinely disliked the use of force. Nonetheless his opponents, many of whom were now to go into exile, always sought to have him finally brought to justice for these unlawful killings during his *coup*.

But having gained supreme power, he now proceeded to persuade the nation to proclaim him Emperor and establish a second French Empire to replace the Second Republic. He judged the moment well; excited at the prospect of a second Bonaparte ruler, more than 7 million Frenchmen voted for him, with only 650,000 dissenting. Consequently, on 2nd December 1852 (once more the anniversaries of Austerlitz and Napoleon the First's Coronation, and now the first anniversary of his own *coup d'état*) this dreamy, but ambitious man finally assumed the title of Napoleon the Third, Emperor of the French, maintaining that his great uncle's son, the young but now deceased King of Rome always had title to Napoleon the Second. The same Act which established the new Emperor also authorised his succession by any legitimate family, on the 30th January 1853, as though to publicly emphasise the heir. And should there be no legitimate heir, Louis-Napoleon was further empowered to nominate any descendant of Napoleon the First to succeed him. Additionally, no member of the new imperial family could marry without his personal approval. He also reimposed the Great Napoleon's original edict that every male member of the family should carry his name

To consolidate his imperial elevation and ensure a legitimate succession, he now began, at the age of forty-four, to search in earnest for a suitable consort. By nature a sensuous man his list of mistresses was legendary, and there was much gossip as to which amongst them might now be elevated to Empress Consort. Initially he contemplated making a straightforward political marriage for which a strong candidate was one of Queen Victoria's nieces, the eighteen year old Princess Adelaide of Hohenlohe-Langenberg. But he finally decided to follow the dictates of his heart.

In January 1853, after a somewhat frustrating courtship (for he was not accustomed to conditional conquests) he married Eugénie de Montijo, a twenty-six year old Spanish lady whose mother was the daughter of a Scottish wine-merchant, and whose father was an impecunious Spanish hidalgo, Don Cipriano, Count of Teba, but who, nonetheless, had always been a staunch supporter of the Great Napoleon. Nonetheless there was widespread critical comment that their new Emperor had chosen neither to marry an aristocratic Frenchwoman nor even into a European Royal Bonaparte restoration, the couple rode to their wedding in Notre Dame in the same coach used by Napoleon the First and Josephine for their own coronation in 1805, and as a crown, the new Empress wore a magnificent diadem which had formerly belonged to Josephine. Thousands of curious sightseers flocked to Paris to applaud the spectacle — the first wedding by a reigning monarch since Louis the Fifteenth's in 1725.

Despite the fact that, by 1856, the Second Empire had reached the height of its glory and popularity, neither of these two — as Sovereigns — were particularly confident in their respective roles. Because of their less than regal lineage and the dubious origins of their political power, the established Royal and Imperial Houses of Europe were initially reluctant to accept them as equals.

As far as Queen Victoria was concerned, this self-proclaimed Emperor of the French could only be regarded as a *parvenu*. For a long time she considered that he had exploited the difficulties of her former friend King Louise Philippe, and was genuinely appalled to hear of his attitude towards many of her other French Royalist acquaintances. She was particularly offended to learn that he had compelled the sale of all property belonging to the Orleans family in France and confiscated the former King's private fortune — only to divert the entire proceeds into welfare schemes for the poor.

Prince Albert shared her views about this new Emperor. In principle he was opposed to any second French Empire, headed by yet another Bonaparte, in direct contravention of agreements made by the Allies at the Congress of Vienna. He had noted the duplicity behind Louis-Napoleon's ruthless seizure of supreme power in 1851, and thus always considered him to be untrustworthy. He was not alone in these views. For many people this unexpected and illegal *coup d'état* had raised once more the possibility of renewed French expansionism, which could only destabilise the peaceful Europe which had been the greatest gain from that hard-won victory at Waterloo some forty years earlier. The new Emperor had tried to allay such fears in a major speech in Bordeaux during the 1852 referendum: 'There is,' he declared, 'one anxiety to which I must refer...Some people say, The Empire means war. But I say, the Empire means peace. It means peace because France desires it, and when France is satisfied, the world is peaceful.'[7] But such words placated no-one. The widespread distrust persisted.

However the Crimean War was soon to significantly change public, if not private attitudes. Now that England and France found themselves in alliance against Russia in support of Turkey, the British Royal family could no longer keep their social distance. In 1854 Prince Albert and Louis-Napoleon had a preliminary meeting at Boulogne, where the Emperor was reviewing troops embarking for the Crimea. Prince Albert, expecting to meet a blustering tyrant, was agreeably surprised to encounter a rather quiet, undemonstrative and calm individual, who further surprised him by speaking fluent German. But in private Albert deplored Louis-Napoleon's incessant cigarette smoking, his evasive manner and his total obsession with politics — to the exclusion of almost any other topic. He was particularly disappointed to realise that the new French Emperor had little interest in the arts, a philistine trait characteristic of all the Bonapartes and which continued with the

---

7   RIDLEY, p. 318.

Prince Imperial. And Louis-Napoleon's well-deserved reputation for philandering did nothing to attract the personal admiration of the stern Prince Consort.

Nonetheless the following April it was decided to invite the imperial couple to make a State visit to London and Windsor — ostensibly to co-ordinate war strategy, but in reality to persuade the Emperor to forego his growing wish to take personal command of all the allied forces in the Crimea. Privately Queen Victoria viewed the prospect of such a State visit with considerable distaste. But at her first meeting with the Empress much of this was soon dispelled. She quickly warmed to the beautiful and gracious Eugénie.

At that time Eugénie was still recovering from a second miscarriage. The Queen was quick to take advantage of that situation, giving Eugénie so much intimate, private advice about child-bearing that, when '*le petit Prince*' was finally born the following March, Victoria almost considered herself to have been personally responsible for the child's safe delivery. This first meeting between Queen and Empress was to lay the foundation for a personal rapport which was to deepen with the years, and which was to become particularly close during the sad period of Eugénie's fifty-year long exile in England. Throughout their relationship the two sovereigns always conversed and communicated with each other in the French language, for Eugénie never acquired an adequate fluency in English. More surprising perhaps, on this occasion, was the Queen's gradual softening in her attitude towards the Emperor. By the end of the visit, she was to write, 'He *is* a very *extraordinary* man, with great qualities, there can be *no* doubt — I might almost say a mysterious man...He is endowed with wonderful *self-control*, great *calmness*, even *gentleness*, and with a power of *fascination*, the effect of which upon those who become more intimately acquainted with him is most sensibly felt.'[8] Queen Victoria was not the first woman to be captivated by his undoubted sex-appeal. But the conquest was not all his. In return the Queen flattered this *parvenu* Emperor, finally persuading him not to take command in the Crimea on the spurious grounds that his own life was far too precious to be placed so needlessly at risk! After she had invested him with the Order of the Garter at Windsor Castle, the Emperor was to whisper in her ear, "*Enfin — je suis gentilhomme.*"

His baby son however was to be spared such *arriviste* banter — whatever the prevailing doubts about the legality of his parents' position, Louis was always, from the day of his birth, to be accepted and acknowledged as a Prince of France. His legitimacy in this regard was never questioned — even by those who mounted the most scurrilous personal attacks against him as he grew to manhood.

Later that year a return State visit took place. Paris was holding its first *Exposition Universelle* — a blatant copy of London's Great Exhibition of 1851 — under the presidency of Prince Jerome Napoleon ('Plon-Plon'). Thus half-a-million visitors to the city, in addition to Parisians, cheered the Queen everywhere she went. But Victoria considered the most important event in their busy programme was not their visit to the Palace of Industry, nor to the other pavilions of the Exhibition, but their solemn attendance on the remains of Napoleon the First.

8　JOHN, p. 24.

On the instructions of King Louis Philippe the ashes of the Emperor had been returned from St Helena in 1840, but the marble tomb had still to be completed. For the moment the coffin lay in a side chapel, covered by black velvet. Above it stood a great bronze eagle and at the foot lay the hat worn at Eylau and the sword the Emperor had carried at Austerlitz. 'I stood,' she wrote in her journal, 'at the arm of Napoleon the Third, his nephew, before the coffin of England's bitterest foe, I, the granddaughter of that King who hated him most and who most vigorously opposed him.'[9] Whilst they stood gazing at the coffin a violent thunderstorm raged outside. Indeed the Queen was so moved by the atmosphere of the occasion that she motioned the Prince of Wales — then only fourteen — to kneel before the coffin so as to; 'respect a departed foe, and wipe out old enmities and rivalries'; and as her eldest son knelt and bowed his head, the watching battle-scarred veterans from Wagram and Waterloo could scarcely contain their tears.

On 24th August the Queen attended a special review, on the Champ de Mars, of about forty thousand French troops, symbolic of the military alliance which was now actively engaged in the Crimea. But despite this spectacle of imperial grandeur the Queen also shrewdly sensed the precariousness of the present Napoleon's hold on power — for example, she even noted how the streets of the capital had now been surfaced with macadam, 'to prevent the people from taking up the pavement as hitherto.'

She also observed at first hand the behaviour of the Emperor's two cousins, Prince Jerome Napoleon ('Plon-Plon') and his sister, Princess Mathilde. They both had the same dark-eyed, swarthy appearance so characteristic of most of the Bonaparte family. At the start of his reign, in keeping with his desire for the closest ties with France's former adversary, Napoleon the Third had actually tried to marry 'Plon-Plon' to Queen Victoria's cousin, Princess Mary of Cambridge. Needless to say, Victoria had swiftly blocked the whole idea — and Princess Mary was to be safely married instead to the Duke of Teck, thus becoming the mother of Queen Mary. Now that she had actually met Prince Jerome, Victoria was thankful for her decision — for, apart from his bloated appearance, she also found him difficult, contradictory and quite lacking in normal good manners. She noted: 'He seems to take pleasure in saying something disagreeable and biting, particularly to the Emperor, and with a smile which is quite satanic.'[10] And when, out of protocol necessity, she had to invest him with the Order of the Bath, she noted: 'he was rude and disagreeable in the highest degree.'

During their nine day visit the Royal couple stayed with their hosts at the Palace of Saint-Cloud. Away from official duties, Queen Victoria and the newly pregnant Empress were able to spend many private moments together, often taking carriage drives through the park. Perhaps the Queen harboured thoughts of actually becoming a godmother to the expected child, even though, on religious grounds alone, she well knew that this would neither be acceptable to her hosts nor approved by the Church. But she did the next best thing by persuading Eugénie to accept the English Miss Jane Shaw as the child's head nurse.

---

9   MARTIN, Vol. 3, pp. 337-8.
10   ARONSON, p. 62.

"His baptism will be the prelude to his Coronation,"[11] proclaimed Napoleon the Third, ever mindful of that fact that he himself had never been crowned. Indeed his chances of ever been crowned by anyone other than himself were always slender. After the embarrassing public spectacle of attempting, but failing to crown Napoleon the First, no Pope would now willingly run the risk of a possible repeat humiliation trying to crown his nephew!

Owing to the Empress's extended recovery from the birth the official ceremony of baptism had to be delayed for three months — until 14th June 1856. In fact, as a precaution against the sudden infant mortality so prevalent at the time, the Prince had been privately baptised immediately after his birth. But this was not allowed to detract from the splendour of a public ceremony. Pope Pius IX had already agreed to be godfather, by proxy, and the Queen of Sweden, formerly Princess de Beauharnais of the late Empress Josephine's family, agreed to act as godmother. The order of the baptismal service was to be the same as that used for the last Dauphin of France, that abused little boy who had died so tragically in the Concierge after being cruelly separated from his parents, the executed King Louis the Sixteenth and Queen Marie-Antoinette. Ironically, precisely the same form of service had also been used at the baptism of Napoleon the First's own son, the King of Rome, who likewise was to die young.

The ceremony took place in Notre Dame at six in the evening. But the celebrations had started much earlier. At two o'clock that afternoon, three hundred balloons had been launched over the city, and an hour later these were followed by a large hot-air balloon expelling some four hundred little parachutes holding sweet bags adorned with the colours of the Pope and the Queen of Sweden. The crowds were then able to enjoy the spectacle of a procession of resplendent coaches, where even the horses were covered by drapes of gold, slowly making its way to Notre Dame. The writer Prosper Mérimée described the scene in a letter to a friend: 'The Empress was in great beauty and wore a diadem of diamonds worth no doubt two or three kingdoms. The Emperor also looked very impressive, and when after the ceremony he held up the child in his arms to present him to the multitudes, the enthusiasm was genuine and great. Those who know about such things find the boy enormous for his age while I, who know nothing, noticed that Mme Bruat, who was carrying him, clearly found this hard going. Everything went off very well, but, typical of our heroic nation, some details were muddled. The Archbishop was beginning to preach a sermon in Latin, when the music and the cannon outside cut him short.'[12]

The christening was witnessed by six thousand guests, including representatives of all the crowned heads of Europe, by Cardinal Patrizzi, on behalf of the godfather and by the Grand Duchess Stéphanie of Baden, in the absence of the godmother. The child was formally named Eugène Louis Jean Joseph Napoleon. After the baptism and blessing the Emperor triumphantly held out his son to the view of the large congregation, whilst an aide-de-camp solemnly called out three times: '*Vive le Prince Impérial!*'. This invoked an applause so thunderous that it seemed to those

---

11   BIBESCO, p. 28.
12   KURTZ, p. 98.

present that the building would start to shake. On their return to the Tuileries, Louis-Napoleon confided to his wife: "The baptism has done more for us than a coronation."[13]

That evening there was a grand banquet at the Hôtel de Ville. The following day was declared a public holiday. The people of Paris were treated to military displays, open air performances by troupes of clowns and concerts of joyful music; even the theatres were free, throwing open their doors to the public. During the evening the Emperor personally started the firework illuminations which were to bathe Paris in a blaze of cascading light. One of the city's theatres was to be re-named *Théâtre du Prince-Impérial*, and elsewhere, throughout country, many boulevards and avenues of towns and cities were to be re-titled to honour the new Prince. A little medallion, bearing on one side profiles of the Imperial parents, on the other a bust of the child and the date 14 July 1856, were distributed to every child attending school in Paris and its environs. The future for the resurgent Napoleonic dynasty seemed to be bright indeed.

And only a few weeks after the christening, Eugénie was writing to her sister, Paca: 'My little boy is very pretty, his eyes especially are superb, blue like the sky and with long black eye-lashes. Already, he has a most intelligent smile.'[14]

In December 1856, when he was only nine months old, '*le petit Prince*' was entered formally on the roll of commissioned officers of the 1st Imperial Guard Regiment. Two years earlier Louis-Napoleon had completely reconstituted the former Imperial Guard, partly to emulate his uncle but principally to raise troops whose loyalty to their Emperor could be guaranteed. It was therefore entirely appropriate that his son should now join this elite regiment. And although he could barely stand up straight, '*le petit Prince*' was now to appear in public, dressed in the conspicuous white uniform of the Guard Lancers, wearing over his head the bearskin of the Grenadiers of the Guards. Even before he could walk, the child would be regularly strapped to the saddle of a Shetland pony, which had been a present from Queen Victoria and taught to ride under the supervision of M.Bachon, the Emperor's chief groom. This somewhat uncouth and harsh Gascon had once been the master of a riding-school in Holland, but had subsequently served Louis-Napoleon for many years. The Emperor relied on Bachon to fulfil his dearest wish — that his son should become the most proficient horseman in France. The Empress, likewise, required that the Prince excelled in his equestrian duties. A superb horsewoman herself she instinctively knew that the French people would always expect their rulers to pose majestically on horseback. Curious Parisians therefore were delighted to observe how, behind the railings of the Tuileries, the Prince was taken out daily on a pony which was no larger than a dog, secured to the saddle by straps, with Bachon holding the bridle and Miss Shaw striding purposefully behind. By the age of two, thanks to the groom's firm tuition, the child was able to attend a military review, in uniform, mounted on his own pony, much to the pride of his parents. By now he was even trained to formally return military salutes.

---

13   Ibid., p. 99.
14   Ibid., p. 101.

Chapter II

The Glory of Empire

THE POLITICAL PHILOSOPHY behind what has now come to be termed 'Bonapartism' has always caused some puzzlement amongst historians and political analysts. At heart, Louis-Napoleon was always more of a political opportunist than principled ideologist. With characteristic vagueness he once wrote: 'The Napoleonic idea is not an idea of war, but a social, industrial, commercial and humanitarian idea' — without offering any explanation as to what that idea was. Nonetheless, Bonapartism could at least be described as standing for some of the post-revolutionary ideals of the Great Napoleon, for Louis-Napoleon certainly held his uncle in the deepest admiration. Yet, at the same time, Bonapartism equally strived to uphold the greatest achievements of the French Revolution. To that extent Louis-Napoleon did significantly differ from the various Royalist factions in France who, at heart, would have much preferred to dispense altogether with the Republican Tricolour and the ideological symbolism which was associated with it. Louis-Napoleon tried, not always successfully, to preserve some of those hard won gains — for example, the abolition of privileges for particular social classes and corporations, and the establishment of a society which, in theory if not always in practice, provided opportunities for talented people, treating everyone on an equitable basis. And he genuinely sought to improve the miserable lot of the French working man. In his political judgements he always sought to be well-intentioned, trying to balance the fundamental political issue which has faced every French ruler throughout history — how to make significant progress in developing society whilst, at the same time, maintaining social stability.

Napoleon the Third was to rule France, either as Prince-President or as Emperor, without a break for a total of twenty-one years, easily surpassing that of his famous uncle. Indeed, the length of his particular reign has never been exceeded even in the country's most recent history. Yet, although he always had the support of a strong coterie of enthusiastic and influential supporters, he never felt it necessary to found a distinctive political party of his own. He held to the vision that he had been elected to be the ruler of all Frenchmen and thus of all parties. And there were certainly many of these. There were the Legitimists, who sought to bring Louis-Napoleon down and replace him with their own Bourbon candidate, the exiled Comte de Chaubord. Other factions included the Orleanists, who deplored the overthrow of King Louis Philippe; Socialists; embryonic Communists; Catholics; Liberals; Conservatives; the Anticlerics. But the largest single group by far — and the one most threatening to the Emperor — comprised the many and various activists who could be collectively labelled 'Republicans'. And nearly all these different political parties sheltered extremists, even fanatics, many of whom were quite prepared to resort to political violence to achieve their ends.

In the absence of any clearly-defined ideology the majority of Louis-Napoleon's political ideas had, inevitably, to be largely opportunistic. Throughout his long reign he constantly wavered between authoritarianism and liberalism, without really settling for either. The only consistent strategic vision which could be said to have animated his whole political outlook was that of '*La gloire*'. And behind that patriotic imperative was a determination to somehow erase the national humiliation of 1815 and restore France to its rightful pre-eminent place in Europe. These objectives he pursued through selective military interventionist policies; through gigantic international exhibitions (two were to be staged in Paris in the short space of eleven years) and by the clearing and reconstruction of many of France's major cities. Thus, through the potent image of an imperial grandeur — a glittering Court, frequent State visits, lavish social spectacles, extravagant military displays — he sought both to dazzle and distract his subjects, whilst invoking all the glories of the greatest days of any previous French Monarch. In order to sustain such imperial grandeur France had to become an economically prosperous nation, and in this particular pursuit Louis-Napoleon was to be strikingly successful. That his reign was so long and comparatively stable owed much to the growth and subsequent buoyancy of France's economy. After his abrupt downfall in 1870, perhaps the greatest regret about the passing of the Second Empire was the equally abrupt collapse of that widespread prosperity.

During the 1850s France had made strenuous efforts to catch up with Great Britain in the building of factories, railways, steamships and telegraphs. Development schemes were financed through a mixture of private investment and government funds. Under Louis-Napoleon's economic patronage and centralised direction, France was indeed to greatly prosper. But the achievement was neither uniquely Napoleonic nor particularly French. Such prosperity was to be paralleled in many other European countries, all likewise benefiting from an industrial revolution from which corporations and individuals alike could rapidly make fortunes. Even so France was soon to establish herself as one of the world's leading industrial powers. In time this led to a marked population growth which, by 1866, had reached 37 million. During this period the layout of the city of Paris likewise was to be transformed — and in others, such as Lyons, Marseilles and Le Havre, large central areas were to be similarly cleared to make way for grandiose buildings and squares. During Queen Victoria's State Visit in 1855, Prince Albert had constantly marvelled at the speed, for example, with which the spacious new *boulevards* of Paris had been laid out by Baron Haussmann.

But in his foreign policies Napoleon was to be much less successful. His election promise of peace inevitably foundered as he sought to restore France's prestige in Europe, and with a shared victory in the Crimea, and later in Italy, that objective slowly began to be realised. But whereas in economic matters he was comparatively well-advised and supported, in foreign affairs the Emperor tended to act alone and unpredictably, even if much influenced by the promptings of his wife. Indeed, throughout their reign, Eugénie was to constantly prod him towards a greater authoritarianism, whilst at the same time, in her pious way, she also wanted him to show an unquestioning deference to the wishes of the Roman Catholic Church. Ironically, in time, it was the Empress herself who was to become the more authoritarian, whilst Napoleon's often idiosyncratic and ill-conceived foreign adventures, none of which were conducted with the firm resolve of his uncle, were to prove his final undoing. He never recovered from the Mexican fiasco of 1865, and that setback was to followed only a few years later by the catastrophic war with Prussia.

After the final collapse of the Second Empire in 1870 Bonapartism nonetheless continued to be a significant political force and a party organisation was quickly re-invigorated under the leadership of Eugéne Rouher, one of the Emperor's closest supporters, a lawyer who had helped engineer the *coup* of 1851. But almost from the moment of its inception internal squabbles were to keep the Imperialists divided. In fact the party never succeeded in formulating an attractive political ideology with which to effectively oppose socialism, republicanism and other powerful radical groups. And the early death in exile of the Emperor in 1873 removed overnight the one person who might possibly have succeeded in holding the Bonapartists together. Thereafter, saddled with a party more obsessed with the past than the challenges of the future, the young Prince Imperial found it almost impossible to develop a viable political platform, relevant to the changed conditions in France prevailing throughout the 1870s. A people who had been chastened by the humiliation of the Franco-Prussian war, and the traumas of the subsequent civil insurrection in Paris, were now to be less concerned about 'La gloire' as championed by a discredited and exiled Bonaparte Pretender, preferring peace, internal stability and economic reconstruction. In any case, Bonapartism had always drawn most of its support from the rural classes, but the widespread effects of the industrialisation and urbanisation which had been deliberately encouraged by Louis-Napoleon were gradually eroding that support. During the early years of the Third Republic which followed the Emperor's fall from power, many of the party activists in France needlessly expended their political capital and energy in trying to forge patchy alliances with the various royalist and revivalist factions, and others opposed to radicalism. This confusing situation could only highlight the fact that Napoleon the Third had singularly failed to formulate a viable political philosophy which could be continued and developed by his heir. He naturally assumed that, in due course of time, he would simply be succeeded by his son, who would then be expected to follow his own brand of political opportunism. Thus, there was no definable legacy through which the young Prince could reasonably hope to attract the enthusiastic support of a majority of his fellow-countrymen. His problems in this respect were not helped by the fact that the party elders in France largely disregarded his own sensible political recommendations, considering him to be more of a youthful mascot than a leader in waiting. And what little influence he had would always remain diluted so long as he lived abroad, in exile, excluded from any political activity within the country itself. It is not surprising therefore that, after the Prince Imperial's untimely death,

Bonapartism gradually faded from the French political scene. Indeed, after 1879, it ceased to be a factor of any significance.

Knowing that his wife had been advised to avoid further pregnancies, the Emperor simply returned, with renewed vigour, to his former philandering ways thus causing Eugénie much deep personal distress. She was aware of the fact that he had already fathered two illegitimate children during his captivity in the fortress of Ham, and that, under the Empire, both these boys had now been made Counts. But she soon learnt to live with his constant infidelities since the Emperor always had a horror of unruly domestic scenes and simply refused to discuss such matters in her presence, even on those occasions when she taunted and scolded him over his behaviour. He once explained his rationale, in confidence and in the simplest of terms, "*J'ai besoin de petites distractions.*"[1] Nonetheless, he always continued to treat his wife kindly, calling her by his pet name 'Oogenie', whilst both of them always referred to their son in private as 'Lou-Lou'.

But these outward manifestations of affection were not enough to conceal the deteriorating nature of their personal relationship. At no time — since her marriage or before — had she ever been deeply in love with the Emperor, but nonetheless she was always very fond of him, appreciating his good qualities, his calm determination and how, in his own strange way, he was still infatuated with her. The truth was that Eugénie, despite her fiery Spanish and Scottish ancestry, was always, at least in her love life, to be somewhat cold and distant. Nonetheless, even in the absence of genuine passion in their relationship they were always to be united in their faith in the future of their only child.

Augustin Filon, who was to become a tutor to the young Prince, recorded his first impressions of the Empress in his published recollections, finding her entirely different physically, mentally and morally, from the person he had expected to meet. He pointed out that she never struck a pose: 'she seemed to think no more of playing the part of a pretty woman than of assuming the role of Empress.' Indeed, she impressed him not as: 'the flawless beauty who reigned like a fairy queen in the midst of theatrical splendour, but as a woman of both brains and heart, who inspired him, as she did everyone around her, with a passionate loyalty.' He also pointed out that, because she was a Spaniard, the French always assumed that she would be superstitious whereas, in truth, he considered the Emperor to be the more superstitious of the two. Filon maintained that; 'her religious practices were moderate, and at no time of her life did she surround herself with priests. She was just a good Catholic — and no more.'[2] But these personal views by a loyal and devoted servant were not shared by the majority of the public. It has often been said that three lies were spread about Eugénie every day of her life — one by her friends, and two by her enemies. Maxime du Camp, a prominent journalist of the time, produced a very different assessment: 'Never did a more futile creature bring a more mediocre intelligence to the service of a reckless ambition...cold, unresponsive, both miser and spendthrift, with no other emotion than vanity, she dreamed of playing

---

1   JOHN, p. 69.
2   FILON, Augustin, *Souvenirs sur l'Imperatrice Eugenie*, p. 16.

great star roles...I do not believe she ever had a serious idea on anything whatever.'[3] Although greatly exaggerated, such views were held by many.

Her closest friends in the later years of the Empire were Richard and Pauline Metternich, the Austrian Ambassador and his wife. He was the son of the great statesman who had stabilised Europe after Waterloo, and the Empress regularly sought his company for serious political discussion. His wife, who was also his niece, became one of the best-known personalities of the Second Empire and one of Eugénie's closest friends. Although very ugly — she once remarked, 'I may look like a monkey, but at least I am a fashionable monkey'[4] — she was, like the Empress, both strong-willed and capricious, but with a warm and loyal personality. In Pauline's company Eugénie was always able to indulge her ever youthful sense of fun. Whilst on holiday together at Biarritz, they would roll up napkins and run around the villa, banging unsuspecting people on the head! It was even rumoured that the two of them had once dressed up as men and ridden incognito around Paris, on the top of a horse-drawn omnibus! However, despite her apparent frivolity, the Empress was always to be very prudish in sexual matters; she would simply become exasperated at people's alleged indiscretions and infidelities. "Why? Why?", she would often exclaim, half-hinting at her husband, " *Qu'ont donc tous les hommes. Do they think of nothing but that?"*[5] Whilst she may have been prudish that did not inhibit her from enjoying risqué stories and jokes, listening with relish to Pauline's often bawdy songs and to outspoken gossip about the scandalous behaviour of people at court.

As a child, and as a young woman, she had often been capricious and tomboyish, with a streak of irresponsibility in her character. These characteristics she was to pass on, in abundance, to her son. On one occasion, albeit before her marriage, she had, on a sudden whim, climbed on to a billiard table and performed some wild Spanish dances much to the delight of her many suitors. The Emperor was always embarrassed by such behaviour, and by the candid and often autocratic way in which she frequently expressed herself. And there were many other differences in their personalities. She loved chatter and gossip regardless of the hour, day or night; whereas he often preferred to remain silent, keeping his own counsel. Louis-Napoleon rarely acted on impulse over anything. Every action had to be calculated and weighed carefully before he would even approach the burden of making a decision. And getting him to make any decision at all was often a major undertaking. Indeed, in many of the great political crises of his career, he had often avoided making any clear-cut decision at all, waiting patiently until events subsequently move to his advantage. As this happened on more than one occasion, giving him immense personal satisfaction, endless procrastination was soon to become a substitute for policy. There was always an air of mystery about him. As the years passed he confided less and less in people; sometimes he would decline to speak at all and on those occasions when he did, his eyelids would be often be half-closed, adding to a reputation for general inscrutability. Indeed, it was largely

---

3   NORMINGTON, p. 202.
4   KURTZ, p. 140.
5   JOHN, p. 70.

because of the boredom of his final exile in England, that Louis-Napoleon took time to discuss affairs of State with his son and heir.

But in her general unhappiness over her husband's constant infidelities, Eugénie was to write to her sister Paca; 'I am so revolted by life with the empty past, its present so full of reefs, and perhaps with so short a future (at least I hope so) that I often ask myself if it is really worth while carrying on struggling, and my courage falls from me.'[6] This letter shows something of that flair for the dramatic which she had shown from early childhood and which never entirely left her. And her premonition that she might, perhaps, not have long to live was almost to come true.

On the evening of 14th January 1858, as the imperial coach drew up outside the Paris Opera, a group of Italian fanatics, led by a man called Orsini, threw three bombs, killing eight people and wounding another hundred and fifty, mainly onlookers and innocent bystanders. Miraculously, the imperial couple escaped almost unharmed. Yet, despite the outrage, the gala performance went on as planned, with both of them being rapturously received. Invariably after such incidents the French people would instinctively rally around their Emperor, despite growing murmurs, even as early as 1858, that his star might now perhaps be on the wane. During his long reign there were to be many attempts on Louis-Napoleon's life — by radicals and socialists within France, as well as by so-called Italian patriots, disgruntled at their putative champion's failure to persist in his efforts to bring about their independence!

The Prince was soon to become aware of all these tensions — those which now openly existed between his mother and father, and those which emanated from the constant fear of sudden assassination. He learnt the lessons well. In his mature years he was to be very circumspect in all his personal relationships with the opposite sex and seems to have given his heart to no-one in particular. Nonetheless, all his life, he mixed happily with the ladies; even as a boy he enjoyed teasing and flirting with them and they, in turn, were attracted by his youthful good looks and his irrepressible swashbuckling manner. In his youth his name was to be linked to an assortment of eligible ladies and, at one time, it was even rumoured he might marry Queen Victoria's youngest daughter, Princess Beatrice, or possibly the Danish Princess Thyra, sister of the Princess of Wales. But the Prince knew better; at twenty-three he considered himself far to young to have his 'wings clipped by marriage.'[7] And although, in conformity with the manners and customs of the age, he always had close and intimate friendships with a number of young men, there is no evidence to indicate any inclination towards homosexuality.

In fact throughout his life he always managed to steer a successful middle course between philandering and boorish prudery. From an early age he had become aware of the accusations of 'dissolution' and 'debauchery' which were frequently levelled against his father, and although he knew these to be deliberately exaggerated he also realised that such remarks were not entirely without foundation. But the charge of 'dissolution' could only refer to the womanising — Louis-Napoleon was never addicted to such 'dissolute' activities as drinking and gambling. The Prince always went to great pains to try and safeguard his own personal moral reputation,

6   TURNBULL, p. 153.
7   FILON, Augustin, *The Prince Imperial*, p. 188.

considering this to be the only sure defence against all the smears and accusations which his opponents would constantly level at him. And he learnt to live with the prospect of sudden injury or outright death at the hand of some deranged fanatic; but he steadfastly maintained that only death in battle could ever be acceptable to a Napoleon. Ironically, he was to become the first of his family to die in combat and, whereas his father was to die from ill-health at the comparatively early age of 65, his mother was to live on, seemingly for ever, after the First World War until 1920 — her 94th year!

For his third birthday a solemn Mass was offered at the Tuileries. At the subsequent reception, special gifts were presented to the chubby little boy by a number of European ambassadors. Most of these gifts were quite enchanting, and the cosmopolitan nature of the list gives testimony to the legitimacy which the child Prince enjoyed in the Courts of Europe and beyond. The Pope sent a gold rosary; the Tsar of Russia a real stuffed bear mounted on castors; the King of Prussia a rattle; the Queen of Sweden, in her capacity as official godmother, a little sledge harnessed to a reindeer; Princess Metternich, in the name of the Emperor of Austria, presented a picture book which had once belonged to the young King of Rome; the Queen of Spain sent him a game in the form of a miniature bullfight; the ambassador of the Sultan of Turkey brought a live monkey on a leash — and Queen Victoria sent the child a large rocking horse.

That year *'le petit Prince'* also became one of the first claiming to be cured by the miraculous power of Lourdes. Whilst holidaying at Biarritz, he had succumbed to sunstroke, confined to bed with a fever. But, to Eugénie's great surprise and excitement, had suddenly recovered after drinking a phial of holy water drawn from the nearby grotto of Lourdes — at the very time when Bernadette was publicly recounting her visions of the Virgin Mary.

That same year, 1859, was likewise to be prophetic in the foreign affairs of the Second Empire.

From his early twenties, when he had become an active supporter if not member of the secret *Carbonari*, Louis-Napoleon had always wanted to promote the unification of Italy (at that time split into eight states) under a king from the royal house of Sardinia. In April 1859 Austria unexpectedly declared war on Sardinia and Louis-Napoleon immediately offered the Italians his support. Count Cavour, the champion of Italian unity, secretly agreed to transfer Nice and Savoy to France, provided the Emperor helped to drive the Austrians out of Italy and thus enable the formation of a new kingdom centred around Sardinia. This particular arrangement was then cemented by the bizarre marriage of the middle-aged, atheist and dissolute 'Plon-Plon' to Princess Clotilda, the deeply religious teenage daughter of the King of Sardinia, Victor Emanuel. Through this marriage, a Bonaparte of the present generation would, at long last, be linked into a truly royal dynasty.

For the Italian campaign the Emperor decided to take personal command of the French Army in the field, feeling that it was incumbent on him as the heir to the Great Napoleon to likewise lead his troops into battle — his earlier desire so to do having been frustrated during the Crimea War. But, at Eugénie's insistence, French troops were not to be involved in fomenting revolution against the Papal States, for, apart from the wider political implications, she was to remind him that the Pope was actually godfather to their son. She privately feared that if King Victor Emanuel attempted to occupy Rome, the Pope might then excommunicate the whole of the imperial family in the same way as he had already excommunicated both the King and Cavour. She also told friends of her concern that some divine retribution might likewise fall on the Prince Imperial. Consequently, French intervention was limited to campaigning in Lombardy, in alliance with the Piedmontese forces of King Victor Emanuel, against the somewhat inept Austrians.

But in military matters Louis-Napoleon showed not one trace of that second insight into campaigning which is the hallmark of true military genius, an insight which his uncle had shown to a remarkable degree during his own lightning campaign in Italy in 1796 — a campaign which *'le petit Prince'* was to study in depth during his childhood and which, ironically, he was to be discussing with a colleague only minutes before losing his life.

Although in his youth Louis-Napoleon had joined the Swiss Militia and was eventually promoted Captain, in truth he had little experience of warfare. Indeed, the only discernible military affinity between the Great Napoleon and his nephew was a fascination for artillery — in this subject Napoleon the Third was quite an expert as evidenced by the artillery manual he had produced from his fortress prison in Ham. He had also helped in the design of the heavy 12 pounder *Napoleon* field gun which had been successfully employed on both sides during the American Civil War. He had even presented a suitably embellished and polished commemorative field gun to Queen Victoria and Prince Albert, and this splendid piece can still be seen today in the Rotunda of the Royal Artillery museum at Woolwich.

But the reality was that, unlike his dynamic uncle, he hated the actualities of war. Indeed, in the same way as he always avoided personal squabbles with individuals, he also had a private aversion to violence. Most international disputes involving France he much preferred to settle either by secret negotiation or public conferences. Throughout his long reign he never actually campaigned in the field for very long. Despite an early flush of victories in Italy he was quick to negotiate a peace settlement with the Austrians, and in the early months of the Franco-Prussian War of 1870, he was soon to surrender his person, despite the fact that substantial French forces remained uncommitted and thus undefeated. His imagination, often intuitive and successful in political affairs, simply did not extend to matters military. Indeed his military philosophy, in so much as he had one, could be simply summed up as engaging the enemy in battle as briefly as possible, with as many forces as possible, in the hope of achieving a rapid victory.

Yet in Italy, at the battles of Magenta and Solferino, whilst showing no concern for his own personal safety, he had spent most of the time on horseback, smoking nervously, with little effort on his part to bring these two thoroughly bloody encounters to a swift and decisive conclusion. At Magenta he unwisely split his forces and had to be rescued by General (later Marshal) MacMahon. At Solferino, on 24th June, after appalling carnage, the French had finally emerged with a sort of victory. But the losses on both sides had been appalling — the French; 11,670 killed, wounded and missing: the Piedmontese; 5,521: the Austrians; 22,537. The plight of the wounded was so terrible (with the medical services from both sides being quite unable to cope) that Henri Dunant, a Swiss philanthropist, who had witnessed the bloodbath, was subsequently moved to found an international organisation to help the wounded in times of war. Not surprisingly Louis-Napoleon, along with many other European rulers, was to give his personal support to the subsequent conference in 1864 which formally established the International Red Cross.

Yet barely three weeks after his victory at Solferino the Emperor asked for a meeting with the Austrian Emperor, Franz Joseph. By now he was becoming concerned over the general alarm his intervention in Italy was causing throughout Europe, as well as the concerns of his own Catholic supporters in France at the putative threat to the Papal States. And within the army there was great disquiet at the mounting losses. Many of his senior commanders were becoming totally disenchanted at the military ineptness of their Piedmontese allies, who had been quite content to let the French do most of the fighting. Thus, without any prior consultation with King Victor Emanuel, Louis-Napoleon, as early as 11ᵗʰ July 1859, abruptly signed an armistice between France and Austria. Despite this unexpected but welcome cessation of hostilities, there was great resentment elsewhere, particularly in Great Britain, that the Emperor had now suddenly acquired, through covert diplomacy, the key provinces of Savoy and Nice.

But when Eugénie informed her son of his father's victory at Solferino, the three year old could only brightly exclaim, "What only one? My great uncle won a great many more!"[8]

There was a further outcome to the Italian campaign — a political innovation within France which, in time, was to have fateful consequences. A month after the Prince's birth it had been decreed that, in the event of the Emperor's death or incapacity, the Empress would assume the powers of Regent, until her son came of age which was fixed as eighteen years. With the Emperor's enforced absence in Italy it had been agreed that Eugénie should temporarily assume his powers as Empress-Regent and in this capacity she had presided for the first time in 1859 over the Council of Ministers. Most of them were to be surprised by her knowledgeable grasp of State business, her sound judgement and the decisive way she resolved a number of problems. Her new duties offered a welcome opportunity to disarm all those many critics who always considered her to be somewhat 'frivolous' and 'coquettish'; critics who enjoyed reminding her that like Marie-Antoinette (whose fate had always obsessed Eugénie) she too was a foreigner, whose true commitment to the affairs of France must always be suspect. It haunted her that a Paris mob could, at any time, take up a cry: 'That Spanish Woman!' with the same ease with which, in former revolutionary times, it had yelled for: 'That Austrian Woman!' And so, when the victory at Solferino was celebrated in July 1859 by a solemn Te Deum in Notre Dame, the Empress, as acting Head of State, took great satisfaction in the unexpected and demonstrable glow of public approval. 'Le petit Prince' accompanied his mother in her carriage, sitting on her knee, dressed in Highland dress in the manner of Queen Victoria's own sons (but then the Empress was the daughter of

---

8 Ibid., p. 11.

a Kirkpatrick of Closeburn) quivering with excitement, occasionally clapping his hands and spontaneously blowing kisses to the tumultuous crowds. Later she was to write about her own reactions to their reception on that day: 'I had the glorious certainty that God had designed for my child the task of crowning his father's labours.'[9]

The Italian campaign did however temporarily sour relations with Queen Victoria. At odds with her government in this matter, she refused to be taken in by the Emperor's constant claim that: 'his Empire stood for peace' and she was to describe him in a letter to her uncle, King Leopold of the Belgians, as: 'the universal disturber of the world.'[10] Not surprisingly Prince Albert agreed with his wife. Indeed, there was a growing conviction amongst the upper and middle classes in Britain that, despite the Emperor's current adventuring in Italy, France might now be contemplating a surprise invasion of England. There was no credible evidence for this but the growing fear was widely exploited by those concerned at the poor state of Britain's defences and the marked inferiority of the Royal Navy compared to the recently modernised French fleet. Volunteer regiments were to be raised throughout the country; coastal defences around the Navy's main bases were to be significantly improved; and HMS 'Warrior' — the first iron-clad battleship — was to be specifically designed and launched. But even when the scare had finally subsided France's long-term intentions continued to be viewed with the gravest suspicion in many quarters of English society.

Abroad there could only be disquiet at the triumphalism accorded to the troops returning from Italy to Paris. On 14th August to the cheering of thousands the Army of Italy marched, regiment by regiment, displaying their trophies and tattered banners, along the new boulevards, across the Place Vendome under the watchful eye of the Great Napoleon at the top of his column, whilst his great-nephew reviewed this endless march past accompanied by his young son on a pony. For Louis it was a defining moment in his brief life. From the experiences of that day he formed three opinions which remained unshakeable for the rest of his life — that his father was a hero; that the French Army was invincible; and that nothing could compare to the calling of a soldier.

At six years old 'le petit Prince' was able to ride a full-sized horse. Augustin Filon wrote in his memoirs: 'He was a horseman at heart, if I may say so, uniting agility with suppleness with that noble French horsemanship of which we were justly proud before the invasion of English methods.'[11] The Prince grew to love hunting; indeed the chase was his greatest pleasure. It included everything which appealed to him — the excitement of an unknown quarry; fast movement on horseback, with the added thrill of possible danger. In time, the Prince was to become a superb horseman; so much so that at the end of his two and a half year course at the Royal Military Academy Woolwich he was to win outright the top prize for equestrian skills and yet, tragically, when he was in dire peril, alone with his horse in South Africa the day on which he was killed, all these skills were to be of no avail.

---

9   TURNBULL, p. 171.
10   ARONSON, p. 99.
11   FILON, p. 9.

Augustin Filon was to become a conscientious, devoted, if somewhat indulgent tutor, but who nonetheless frequently felt obliged to bridle the intense militarism which always seemed to surround his charge — a militarism which was deliberately fostered by the Emperor. Whilst he may have privately abhorred war, Louis-Napoleon also sincerely believed that the best protection for the imperial legacy would be for his son to be seen demonstrating a genuine enthusiasm for all things military, for then the mass of the French people might reasonably deduce that their *'petit Prince'* could, one day, pursue that same glorious path for France which had been taken, only a lifetime ago, by his illustrious great uncle. Yet, contrary to popular belief, the Second Empire was not a particularly militarist one. Indeed there was always an uneasy relationship between the army and society. Louis-Napoleon knew instinctively that his interests would always be best served by keeping the troops and the people firmly apart. He was ever mindful of the fact that, at any time, these same soldiers might be required to open fire on rioting crowds, on their fellow citizens and it was vital that, in the event of any uprising or attempted *coup d'état*, such orders must be loyally obeyed. For the same reason he also felt it prudent to encourage the closest possible relationship between his son and the military. And the Prince, all his life, perceived the army as the backbone of France, knowing it to be the one stabilising factor in society, the base from which the Bonaparte dynasty had always drawn its ultimate strength.

'Plon-Plon' always disliked his cousin, his cousin's wife and most especially their 'little brat'. And yet he was a man of real intelligence, energy and ability, whose considerable gifts were to be thoroughly undermined by his constant lack of tact and self-control. From his youth he had always been an outspoken rebel who loved deriding the actions of others. He had few friends. Politically, he was anticlerical, a freethinker, who nonetheless also considered himself to be a sort of Republican! Whilst he too had great reverence for their uncle, Napoleon the First, he frequently disagreed with his cousin and even more so with Eugénie. There is a view that she may have spurned his amorous overtures long before her marriage to his cousin. He disliked her Spanish pride and bearing; in particular, he always deplored what he rightly perceived as her autocratic interference in many of the affairs of State. And since successfully acting as Regent during the Italian campaign she had gained in self-confidence and was now exercising considerable influence over her husband. Inevitably, the very sight of the 'little brat' aroused his deep distaste. He frequently told people that the child was 'idiotic' and an 'imbecile'. During his many uninvited visits to the imperial family he always managed to treat the child with unconcealed contempt — until Louis would become quite unnerved, despite the fact that his parents constantly impressed upon him the need to be polite and always respectful to 'Prince Napoleon'. He was to be an *eminence grise* to the Prince Imperial throughout his life; a sort of malevolent godfather to the one person, who, so he thought, always stood between him and supreme power.

Louis was but seven when he encountered a disillusionment which, to him, was far more serious than any family antagonisms. Out shopping one day with a governess, he was smiling as usual to everyone, gracefully acknowledging the many gifts offered to him by shopkeepers but which, following his mother's specific instructions, he always politely refused to accept. When a group of young people pointedly declined to salute him, (deliberately keeping their hats on their heads), he asked his governess for an explanation. She quietly pointed out that not everyone in France loved his father. For a moment he seemed bewildered and then made a childlike remark which was to be both characteristic and prescient; "We must let them know that I love them dearly, that I love them all."[12] This ill-concealed love for all his fellow-countrymen ran deep in his pysche. Regardless of the later widespread opposition to his very existence and the needling criticisms over his every action, he always believed that it was his sacramental duty to honour all his subjects whatever their political views.

The Prince's seventh birthday was celebrated by a huge military spectacle staged by many of the young sons of Paris's soldiers. With the aid of special pyrotechnics over three hundred children re-enacted the battle of Marengo. 'Le petit Prince' excitedly watched the play with his parents from the imperial box but it was impossible for him to remain there for very long. An observer reported: 'How great was everybody's joy when between acts the dear child was seen leaving the imperial box and going down alone to the little boy soldiers, with whom he began to talk and fraternise in the gayest possible way. All the spectators got up to see him better, and applause broke out everywhere. The Emperor and Empress followed him with eager eyes, but let him do as he pleased.'[13]

In the early 1860s the Emperor, urged on by Eugénie, had instigated French military intervention in Mexico, the official purpose of which was to bully the Mexican government into paying its due debts but which really aimed to establish Archduke Maximilian, the brother of the Emperor of Austria, as Emperor of Mexico! With Maximilian in power, maintained by French troops, it would thus be possible to reassert both a French and Catholic influence in the New World — an influence which had been largely lost after the sale of Louisiana to the United States by the Great Napoleon. From 1861 onwards, and under various pretexts, the Emperor had dispatched some 40,000 French troops across the Atlantic, to be followed by the Archduke himself, assured by a solemn undertaking by Louis-Napoleon to support the new Empire regardless of events elsewhere in Europe. But once again he had miscalculated. With the American Civil War finally over, the victorious Unionists followed the Monroe Doctrine, and refused to tolerate any French presence on the North American continent and soon added to the pressure on the Emperor to withdraw his troops — particularly now that Prussian militarism was starting to threaten French interests in Europe. Consequently the last French soldier left Mexico in early 1867, and the Archduke was abandoned to his fate — execution by firing squad. In France the fiasco caused widespread disquiet. Louis-Napoleon had reneged on a solemn undertaking to the Austrian Imperial family — and French troops had been needlessly exposed and finally humiliated. The stability of the Second Empire was now becoming precarious.

However, the first-known letter by the Prince to his father, written when he was only nine years old, relates to the activities of the French troops soon after they

12   Ibid., p. 12.
13   Ibid.

had disembarked. This letter, although factually incorrect, shows clearly the child's enthusiasm for the Emperor's military adventurism:

> My dear Father,
>
> I congratulate you on the taking of Mexico, I am delighted at it. Yesterday I went and told the soldiers in the guardroom that Mexico had surrendered, and everyone was delighted.
>
> Your devoted son,
> Louis-Napoleon.
>
> P.S. This morning my horse had a fit of kicking, but I sat tight and did not fall.[14]

In appearance the nine year old boy had features which might have been envied by any girl — delicate skin, long eyelashes and slender bones. The Empress would often show friends a photograph of him at that time which she would then go on to describe, with some amusement, as *'Ma fille, la Princesse Impériale!'* As he grew up these girlish characteristics were to largely disappear, but the sallow Mediterranean complexion, so characteristic of the Bonaparte family, was to remain. Yet despite his mother's jests there was nothing particularly feminine about his character. Thanks to the strong influence of Miss Shaw, he had been moulded, right from babyhood, with all the attributes of an English gentleman. Consequently, although always mindful of his position and protective of his dignity, he was invariably very friendly to everyone, sociable and chatty, without any trace of arrogance. He had an instinctive tact, graceful social manners and a genuine anxiety to please and accommodate others. Yet he was always ready to speak his mind.

The great idol of his life at this time was undoubtedly the Emperor, whom he worshipped and who, in turn, adored him. He once caught his son choking on an orange. Instead of snatching it away himself, he instructed one of the nearby courtiers to do it for him. "I could not do so. He would not love me if I did,"[15] he explained rather sadly. But the child also deeply loved his mother, even if she was the only person, besides Miss Shaw, who would regularly say "No!" to him. And at other times she often seemed to him as distant and aloof. But nearly all the other people who were close to him, and who influenced his life, were invariably to be a great deal more indulgent over his occasional misdemeanours.

From his father he inherited a sense of dynastic destiny — but devoid of the same ruthless ambition. In later years he was also to exercise the same seductive personal charm as his father, a charm which struck the ageing Queen Victoria as being just as appealing. The Prince also inherited much of his father's political imagination, even if at times, both father and son were to live in dream-like fantasy worlds, leading them to adopt quite obsessive viewpoints on many issues, attitudes which were often difficult to change. But the Prince was always to be a great deal more decisive and resolute in political matters than his father. And his interests and

---

14   Ibid., p. 16.
15   JOHN, p. 54.

tastes were to be a great deal more catholic even if just as philistine. Whereas Louis-Napoleon was by nature inscrutable, an instinctive plotter and schemer; an autocrat by inclination if not always in practice, the son was to become much more open and direct, even if perhaps less liberal in his political outlook. But, in marked contrast to his father, the Prince always disdained trying to seize power in France through intrigues and *'coups d'état'*, by the ruthless use of force, techniques which had come so naturally to Louis-Napoleon. In exile he soon concluded that either he had to be freely elected to power by the majority of the French people or not at all.

From his mother he was to acquire a nervous excitability, together with a strong sense of the dramatic. Like her, he had a highly-strung nature. And as with so many people of nervous disposition he could be moody, subject to fits of exasperated impatience and occasional irritation. As a young boy he often displayed a streak of irresponsibility and mischievousness which never entirely left him. But he also inherited many of Eugenie's more commendable qualities — sincerity, honesty and loyalty, a passion for ideas and an innate belief in the tides and traditions of history — qualities which came more and more to the fore with every year of his life. He also inherited her unshakeable sense of integrity.

He was always to draw much inner strength from the close family circle in which he had spent his formative years. In the custom of the age he retained a touching affection for the mementoes of his childhood — keeping the little chairs on which he used to sit, and for many years he even cherished a handkerchief that had belonged to 'Nana', placing it on his pillow every night before going to sleep.

Intellectually, however, he was to prove a disappointment. Not by nature bookish, he found it difficult to concentrate on any subject which did not particularly interest him; all too often his mind would be distracted by trivialities and diverted by outbursts of sheer mischievousness. His tutor has described how, when faced with study, 'his blue eyes would become vague and lustreless, and assumed that look of unhappiness which comes from lack of understanding.'[16] But the vagueness would evaporate whenever his mind turned to contemplating the next escapade. The particular afternoon, for example, when he suddenly cantered, without warning, on his little pony up the main staircase of the Tuileries and then somehow managed to get the animal into bed between the sheets, was to cause quite an uproar! The Emperor was privately amused; his tutor at that time simply pretended to ignore what had happened; only Eugénie harshly chided the boy over his bravado. Such rebukes, particularly from his mother, would often make him resentful but not for long. And although he was often impish in character, he was never truculent or downright disobedient.

Neither the Emperor nor Empress could be described as being endowed with a strong sense of humour, but they both enjoyed practical jokes, games of charade, even theatrical farces. The Prince, on the other hand, loved drawing caricatures which, in time, he was to develop into a fine art. One day the question arose — which of his parents did he most resemble? The tactful answer was both — equally. "So then," said the Prince mischievously," it's pappa on the right, and mamma on the left?"[17]

16   FILON, p. 32.
17   Ibid., p. 48.

And, on the spot, he then quickly sketched his own rendering of that situation — drawing his father's impassive face, half-closed eyelids, whilst twiddling with an imaginary extended waxed moustache; and then alongside, sketching his mother's somewhat assertive maternal face, but one which was seemingly all sweetness and light! There was much laughter and great applause! He had shown himself to be a shrewd observer, as well as quite an artist. As he grew older, he took an active part in the seasonal pantomime and amateur dramatics which were an integral feature of court life even though these were only witnessed by family and friends. This however did not develop into a particular passion for the theatre or for any of the performing arts. Unlike so many contemporaries, for example, he never learnt to play a musical instrument although he enjoyed singing, particularly military songs.

Whilst, as a boy, he may not have shown much intellectual promise, he did, from an early age, show a marked talent for drawing. This he had inherited from his grandmother, Queen Hortense, who drew and painted competently all her life. Pencil in hand he loved to sketch everything, mainly military figures and events, but often people such as his tutor and school friends. Once in order to shock 'Nana', he secretly drew a large chamber pot at the bottom of the page of an English text-book which he knew she was about to read to him! In fact he drew so well that, for fear he might turn professional, it was decided early on not to give him any formal instruction. His first professional lessons therefore were to be those in military field sketching during his training at Woolwich and it was a subject in which he naturally did well. Many of his sketches have survived, including early efforts from childhood as well as more mature drawings such as caricatures of his brother officers. Indeed, during the years when the Prince was attached to the Royal Artillery, some of these excellent caricatures drew a general comment from his contemporaries that; 'He might have been an Emperor, or an artist.'[18] Most poignant perhaps are a number of field sketches, signed by the Prince, which he drew during operations in South Africa shortly before his death.

Inevitably he experienced many of the disadvantages which stem from being an only child. He often felt lonely, burdened by the early realisation that, on him and him alone, rested all the dynastic hopes of his parents and all their many supporters. And his parents inevitably focused all their aspirations on to him and, at times, that likewise made him feel over-protected, even resentful. Unusually for elevated and engrossed parents in late Nineteenth Century society, both the Emperor and Empress always found time, amidst their own hectic lives and private disagreements, to give their only child ample personal attention. Even at the Tuileries where most State business was conducted, the Prince would always see them for several hours every day and in their various other residences he was almost permanently in their company. They always took a close interest in everything he said and did. From an early age he had become conscious of the fact that he was really the sole factor keeping his parents together and that, without his presence, they would probably have long since divorced — for the Emperor, like his uncle before him, would always have need of a male heir. On the other hand, despite his father's general indulgence

18   Article by maj-gen sir Richard BANNATINE-ALLASON, KCB, CMG, Colonel Commandant, RHA — dated 2 June 1919.

towards him and the Empress's natural maternal concerns, he could not be dismissed as just another 'spoilt brat', even though this was the common basis for much of the early criticism about him. He neither expected nor demanded to be allowed his own way in everything. And he was also sensitive to the thoughts and feelings of others, and always made due allowance for them. From early boyhood he would always show a special consideration towards those he liked and trusted. One evening, after dinner, the Emperor told Louis that an officer, with some friends, would give him a magic lantern picture show. He immediately insisted that 'Nana' likewise be invited; and then personally conducted her into the room, proudly taking her to the first row, in front of a group of officers who were much amused.

There was much discussion about the Prince's education. Whilst many considered that, like the sons of King Louis Philippe, 'le petit Prince' should publicly attend one of the *lycées* in Paris, the Emperor was adamant that he should not. With some justification, he feared that his son might become the object of derision and even bullying by the many sons of prominent Republicans who were always present, often in large numbers, in all these schools. Eventually it was decided that he should be instructed privately to the same syllabus and sit precisely the same examinations as his contemporaries in the city's schools. To that end he was theoretically placed in the seventh form of the *Lycée Bonaparte* — he had a 'phantom' position in that class, moving up and down in exactly the same way as all the other pupils. He was even instructed in the names and family backgrounds of these other pupils even though he was never personally to get to know any of them. From time to time masters from the *Lycée* would come to the imperial schoolroom to assist Filon in teaching the national syllabus.

On one occasion the Prince actually won a form prize for mathematics. But even that achievement could not disguise the fact that, at heart, he was a slow learner who never really kept up with the pace of the others. Apart from this backwardness, no-one seems to have considered the deeper implications of this somewhat bizarre way of educating the future ruler of France. Throughout those critical formative years the Prince was, in effect, being denied the stimulus of healthy competition; the experience of mixing with other boys less privileged than himself; thus getting to know other people in French society who simply did not share the political views of his parents and their supporters. These shortcomings in his upbringing were later to become severe handicaps. But the problem went much deeper than this. His greatest longing was to do the same things as other boys, but always on an equitable basis so that the final results would be judged solely on merit and ability. If there was going to be any acclaim then it had, in his view, to be based entirely on his own attainments and not simply because of the position he occupied. His early education did not help him to achieve this and it was not until he became a Gentleman Cadet at the Royal Military Academy Woolwich that his yearning in this respect became a reality. But, by that time, he discovered there was a great deal of catching up to do.

His boon companion — at this time and for the rest of his life — was Louis Conneau, the only son of the Emperor's old adviser and personal physician, Dr Conneau. The doctor had, in fact, been an intimate friend to the whole of the Emperor's family for many years; he had attended his mother, Queen Hortense, when she lay dying from cancer. He had also shared the Emperor's long captivity in the Ham fortress, even helping him to escape. In fact their two sons were virtually to be brought up together. For daily lessons they had twin desks, side by side. But, despite their lifelong affection for one another, they occasionally quarrelled and had fights. When at Saint-Cloud during the leisurely summer months the two boys often ran off together to play soldiers, simulating pitched battles, after which one or the other would invariably emerge cut and bleeding. It was usually 'le petit Prince' who suffered the injuries for, more often than not, it was he who would lose control and start playing rough. Other children with whom he was, from time to time, permitted to play eventually nicknamed him with a variety of titles — 'Runabout'; 'Whirlwind' and 'Mr Quicksilver' — simply on account of this unpredictable impulsiveness.

In his memoirs, the tutor, Augustin Filon, described this as due: 'to an excessive nervousness that never allowed his limbs or imagination an instant's repose. His body and mind alike had a dread of quietude...Where this restlessness became a matter for uneasiness was when he was playing with comrades. Then we could not control him and he could not control himself. Once started off, he would have gone through a glass partition, a closed door, or jumped out of a window; he lost every notion of the real or possible. Even in cold blood, danger courted willingly and deliberately was the greatest pleasure he knew, and there was hardly a day when he did not submit his poor tutor to the most grievous trials by this taste for the most difficult and perilous games.'[19] Everyone was to comment on this restlessness and excitability, on his desire to deliberately court danger. As if to overcome any feelings of fear within himself, he would frequently scale the balustrades of the windows at Fontainebleau and then calmly step along the cornice which ran around the Château. On one such occasion the Empress, returning unexpectedly from a drive in the forest, was appalled to see him walking nonchalantly along so high up. She stopped the carriage and called for him to come down at once. But, as he tried to reassure her by waving his hand, he suddenly lost his grip and fell heavily onto the forecourt. Unconscious for a while, he was taken back to Paris by train on a special stretcher and was made to convalesce for the next three weeks. He was only eleven years old.

The imperial court divided its time between a variety of residences. For most of the year the Emperor and Empress conducted State business from the Tuileries in the heart of Paris and they would always be there for Christmas and the New Year. A few weeks of each summer would be spent at Fontainebleau; some of the spring and autumn at Saint-Cloud; and most of the winter months at the Château of Compiégne, north of Paris. But they usually spent the whole of August every year at Biarritz, where the Empress owned a private summer villa, named after her, within sight of the Spanish border. On these occasions they would often be joined by her two lively nieces, Marie and Louise Stuart, nicknamed 'Marquinita' and 'Chiquita', the daughters of her late sister, the Duchess of Alba. These pretty girls would often tease the young Prince, challenging him to devise even bigger and better pranks — the surest way to his heart.

---

19   FILON, p. 29.

Yet there is one well-documented incident, early in his life, which shows that he was fully aware of his own limitations. Whilst staying at the Villa Eugénie, a courtier once deliberately threw him into the sea from a boat — in this manner he would have to teach himself how to swim! When he finally emerged from this spartan treatment to reach the safety of the beach, he, for once, appeared to be thoroughly shaken. As his mother asked how it was that, whereas he had always managed to tolerate with equanimity the thunder of cannon, he seemed to be afraid of the sea, he not unreasonably replied, between his chattering teeth, the tears rolling down his cheeks; "Well — *I'm* in command of the cannon — but, I'm *not* in command of the sea."[20]

On another occasion, likewise at Biarritz, the Prince and his mother went for an afternoon's sail in a naval dispatch vessel, the *Chamois*. A sudden storm blew up. Driven off course the ship finally ran aground on the rocks at the entrance to the harbour of St. Jean de Luz. The imperial party were soon rescued but it was the Empress herself who recalled her son's behaviour. As wave after wave crashed over the vessel, even washing overboard some members of the crew, Eugénie grabbed the boy and for safety hugged him to her; " — Don't be afraid, Lou-Lou," she had whispered. "But," Louis had answered firmly and calmly,"A Napoleon is never afraid."[21] And yet, at the same time, the Empress recalled how fiercely his little heart had been beating.

Just before his ninth birthday he fell ill with measles. The recovery was slow, aggravated by the Prince's determination to pursue a normal active life as soon as possible. One afternoon he fell from a beam in the gymnasium, complaining for a long time afterwards about the pain in a hip. Finally it was decided to drain the abscess which had formed in the joint. True to his character the boy welcomed this opportunity to demonstrate his manliness, looking forward to the operation which he considered to be the nearest equivalent to being wounded in battle. He even tried to persuade the famous surgeon, M.Nélaton, to operate without chloroform — a plea which was simply ignored. On an earlier occasion, after a minor operation, the surgeon recalled asking the Prince if he had hurt him. Louis immediately replied, "No! Not at all — but you did startle me!" In the case of the hip operation the Prince was not pleased to learn that the operational scar would only be visible from the rear, and not from the front. A brave man, he argued, must always have his wounds to the front, otherwise people might think he had run away. That same thought was clearly uppermost in his mind when, fourteen years later, whilst fighting for his life, it transpired that the Prince had manoeuvred quite deliberately to prevent any of his foes striking him from behind.

At the time of his hip operation, there was some concern that he might perhaps emerge with a permanent limp and 'Plon-Plon' was not alone in wondering if France would ever acknowledge an Emperor who had to hobble around permanently on crutches. In the event the operation was entirely successful, and there were no lasting effects. But he had to spend an almost totally inactive year at Saint-Cloud slowly recuperating.

---

20   JOHN, p. 55.
21   FILON, p. 27.

In 1866 Miss Shaw was to witness a little incident which confirmed to everyone just how deep an impression the cult of Napoleon had made on his young mind. She always slept in a nearby room to the Prince's and one night, prompted by some intuition, she awoke only to find his bed empty. Whilst searching along the empty corridors of the Tuileries she eventually saw him through the door of his father's study, kneeling before the glass case which contained the Great Napoleon's personal relics. Coming up behind him, she noticed that he had already removed the sabre carried at the Battle of Austerlitz, and resting his head against the old soiled grey greatcoat — almost as if in some trance — he kept repeating, "Dear God — let his memory protect me!" This particular sword had been bequeathed to his father by the Great Napoleon's son in July 1832; many years later, it was to be retrieved from the Tuileries and sent to the Prince in his exile by the Duc d'Elchingen, a close friend of the Emperor, who was directly descended from the famous Marshal Ney. Louis took it with him to South Africa; but at the moment of his greatest danger, it had already slipped out of its scabbard and, lying in the dust, could no longer protect him.

Chapter III

A Baptism of Fire

H E INVARIABLY ATTENDED MASS PUBLICLY with his parents every Sunday but, as a boy, he showed little piety. Indeed in religious matters he seemed to be more puzzled than instructed. When the Abbé Deguerry prepared him for his first Holy Communion (which, following the tradition of the Dauphins of France, was to be held with due solemnity in the chapel of the Tuileries) he showed no reaction whilst listening to the sufferings of Christ. "Aren't you grieved, *mon cher petit seigneur,* to think how these wicked men behaved to Our Lord?" "Well," responded Louis, "if He was all-powerful, why did He let them?"[1]

On 8th May 1868 the walls of the chapel were draped with crimson velvet which had been made fragrant by lilacs and roses. In the presence of his parents, relatives and courtiers, the young Prince knelt to receive his first Holy Communion at the hands of the elderly Archbishop of Paris, Monsignor Darboy. Afterwards, towards the end of his address, the Archbishop was to utter prophetic words about the Prince's future: "Your youth touches me, your future fills me with concern; beyond the peace and felicity of your early years that now unfold tranquilly amid genius and courage, grace and kindness, your destiny appears to me with some of its storms and conflicts."[2] Later that same evening, at a private ceremony, the Archbishop further administered the sacrament of confirmation.

Whilst the Prince may not have been particularly pious in his youth he was always curious about the Catholic faith. For example, he wanted to know whether, in the hereafter, his dog Nero would be waiting for him. As the Abbé Deguerry contemplated whether to tell him how, in the eyes of the Church, animals were not considered to have souls like human-beings, the boy pointed out that Nero was both good and clever, only lacking in the power of speech — and it was surely speech, the Prince argued, which had led human beings into all kinds of vices, particularly vanity! But vanity was the one vice that could not be levelled against *'le petit Prince'*. When the Emperor had commissioned the well-known sculptor M.Capeaux to fashion a statue of his son, the Prince insisted that Nero must also be represented, standing beside him. Otherwise he felt that he had done nothing to merit a statue purely of himself. Eventually the joint statue was to be reproduced in thousands of Sèvres and Barbedienne replicas which adorned many a Republican as well as Royalist home. And for years after her son's death, the Empress kept the Capeaux

---

1 JOHN, p. 76.
2 FILON, p. 40.

statue in the corridor beside the Prince's room in her house at Farnborough. Today it is on display in the *Museé d'Orsay* in Paris.

But there was no fear even in his religion. Whenever as a small child he had behaved badly, it proved pointless to suggest that the offence might be displeasing to God. The most effective way to bring his restless spirit to order was to alternatively interpret the offence as a 'disgrace to the uniform' he often wore. And should it prove necessary to punish him further the sentries would be instructed not to salute him at all on that particular day.

Later in his life he was to become a great deal more spiritually aware. The horrors he witnessed during the Franco-Prussian War; the ensuing national and personal humiliations as well as the frustrations of a protracted exile in England, all helped to give his faith a fresh and deeper significance. And whilst he was never known for particular piety, he always conscientiously fulfilled his religious duties as a Roman Catholic and tried to live up to its moral obligations. This particular prayer, composed by the Prince personally, (although strongly in style to the private prayers of his mother) and found after his death in his private prayer book indicates the tenor of his inner spiritual life. Today it can be read, inscribed in French, on one side of the plinth bearing his effigy in St George's Chapel, Windsor.

> My God, I give you my heart, do you give me faith. Without faith there can be no fervent prayer and prayer is necessary to my soul. Do not take away, I pray you, the obstacles that stand in my path, but give me the opportunity to overcome them. Do not disarm my enemies, but help me to conquer myself. The only satisfaction I seek is that which lasts for ever which a quiet conscience gives. Then show me always O God where my duty lies; give me the strength to fulfil it all times.[3]

But unlike his mother and the various Catholic factions in France, he never allowed his religious faith to significantly influence his political opinions. Indeed, during a private audience with the Pope in 1876, the young Louis made it very clear to the Holy Father that he considered the Church should keep out of politics altogether and, in particular, not identify herself with any national political party.

As a child, he usually attended evening prayers with his mother in the little chapel which adjoined her bedroom at the Tuileries. Here there was just enough room for both of them to kneel before the reliquary containing the Emperor Charlemagne's talisman — a fragment of the True Cross. This priceless relic had been hurriedly offered to Napoleon the First on his triumphal entry into the city of Aachen by the terrified monks guarding the Holy Roman Emperor's tomb. He, in turn, had passed it on to the Empress Josephine who had then bequeathed the reliquary to her own daughter by her first marriage, Queen Hortense, the Prince Imperial's grandmother. Eventually the Emperor Louis-Napoleon handed it over to his devout wife who finally placed the holy relic on her private altar. Throughout history the legend surrounding its ownership had been used for a political vision —

---

3   RA. R5/89 — Translated from the original French.

a Europe united under French law — as indeed it had been under Charlemagne, the Emperor canonised by the Church.

In the autumn of 1867, when Louis was eleven, the Emperor nominated his military staff — one general, three senior army officers and a naval commander. Whilst this number may appear somewhat excessive for the needs of one youngster, the Emperor's own personal military staff totalled sixteen — fourteen permanent and two honorary aides-de-camp and of these, ten were generals of division, five generals of brigades and one an admiral. The most senior — General Frossard — was also Vice-President of the Committee of Engineers. This distinguished sixty year old veteran was now to be placed in overall control of the boy's education, assuming the title of military governor to the Prince. The army officers appointed to assist him were Lieutenant Colonel the Marquis d'Espeuilles (a brilliant cavalry commander who became a general), Commandant Comte de Ligniville of the Imperial Guard and Commandant Lamey, himself an engineer and thus General Frossard's right hand man. The naval aide was Commander Charles Duperré, a close personal friend of the Emperor, who had just completed a tour as the captain of a frigate and who, many years later, was to rise to admiral rank. The four aides amusingly often referred to each other as '*quatre-z-officiers*'.

General Frossard personally selected a new academic tutor for the Prince — the twenty-five year old teacher and author, Augustin Filon. Professor of Rhetoric at the *Lycée* of Grenoble, he had been originally proposed by the Ministry of Public Instruction. Filon records his surprise at being asked by the general at the initial interview if he planned to marry! It later transpired that a previous candidate had recently married and was wrongly assuming that he could continue living at home, attending the Prince daily. The general required that any appointed tutor must devote himself exclusively to the Prince's upbringing. Filon therefore agreed to stay for as many years as were necessary to complete all aspects of the Prince's education and moral instruction. To that end, he also acknowledged that it would be preferable to remain single, making it easier for him to live permanently alongside the Prince in the various imperial residences. In fact Augustin Filon was to spend the next seven years and a half in close association with Louis, an association which was to profoundly affect them both. In time he was to become the Prince's closest associate and advisor. He also shared most of the Prince's exile in Great Britain and even continued to advise him during the long military course at Woolwich. The tutor was also to establish a particularly close rapport with the Empress and, in later years, acted as one of her personal secretaries. Not surprisingly, he was to be devastated by the Prince's early death and in 1912, although almost blind, compiled his own tribute in the form of memories, documents, photographs and letters, under the generic title *Le Prince impérial, souvenirs et documents*. This book subsequently appeared in English, but the translation is clumsy and Filon's true sentiments distorted as a consequence.

However initially Filon was quite unimpressed by his charge, sharing General Frossard's view that the boy was probably both lazy and unruly, and that his education required a completely fresh approach. As the general was himself something of a martinet, he readily acceded to the Empress's instructions that her son needed stricter discipline and, above all, a proper daily routine. This was to be Filon's first task and an appropriate schedule was soon devised.

The Prince was now expected to rise about half-past six at which time the tutor would supervise his morning prayers. After a light breakfast, he would study until half-past eight. At that point Filon and the military officer on duty would take him out for a short walk in the gardens of the Tuileries. At nine he would bid a formal 'Good Morning' to his parents and then go back to the school desk until luncheon, which he would always eat with Filon and frequently with Louis Conneau. At two o'clock he would ride, usually accompanied by Bachon, for a couple of hours. Sometimes, during the winter months, he would even go with his parents to skate in the Bois de Boulogne. And after a number of early falls, he also became a very keen cyclist — a sport then coming rapidly into fashion. From four until half-past six there were more lessons. Whenever possible he would then join his parents at dinner and afterwards, perhaps after a party game such as hide and seek, Filon would see the young Prince to bed. This routine was seldom changed and, in time, it was to become an important factor in stabilising the Prince's natural restlessness. All his academic lessons were personally supervised by the tutor, frequently supplemented by masters drawn from the *Lycée Bonaparte.*

At the same time the newly-appointed military staff began to further indoctrinate the young officer who continued to hold a commission in the 1st Imperial Guard Regiment. Louis would listen enraptured to their tales of adventure, of derring-do, of battles fought and won. Filon observed with some disquiet the way in which the military were gradually creating in the child's mind an all-embracing fantasy world of glittering uniforms, beating drums, colourful banners and parades, the boy marching in his imagination with his great uncle and his *Grande Armée* across the whole of Europe. Indeed, he was to become so indoctrinated that it was not long before he could hum or whistle, almost to order, the marches and tunes of every single regiment and brigade of the French Army, and usually did whenever Filon was endeavouring to teach him about the real world outside. And yet the most demanding aspects of any military career: studying the principles of strategy and tactics; the complexities of staff work; the fundamentals of leadership and morale — these had no place in the creation of this fantasy world. When, in later years, the Prince experienced the horrors of the Franco-Prussian War and the rigours of the comprehensive military training at Woolwich, he was quite unable to entirely shake off this highly-romanticised view of war — a view which sadly was to make its own contribution to the various military misjudgements which collectively were to lead to his tragic death.

The Emperor loved staging military reviews. They were invariably a feature in the set-piece programme for any important State visit. He instinctively perceived that the publicity surrounding these resplendent displays was almost the equivalent to a victory gained in battle and could only add to the splendour of his Empire. On these occasions the Prince would always appear on horseback in uniform beside his father. Sometimes these reviews took place in Paris to honour a visiting Head of State or alternatively in one of the great military conurbations, such as the recently enlarged base at Châlons-sur-Marne. This had been inaugurated by the Emperor in 1857; it covered an area of about 140 square kilometres and unusually for a military camp of the period included cafes, theatres, even garden allotments for the garrison of some 40,000 soldiers and their families. The Emperor and his son often spent a fortnight there at the end of each August, staying in the simple and rather spartan imperial quarters which had been erected specially on the brow of a hill overlooking the whole base. During these visits many of the barracks and tents would be colourfully adorned with huge banners bearing slogans such as *'Vive l'Empereur' 'Vive le Prince Impérial'*.

Already the Prince was nursing ambitions that, one day, he might perhaps be allowed to enrol at France's own prestigious military academy, Saint Cyr. But Louis found it difficult to apppreciate that such a project was as fraught with the same concerns which had determined the course of his general education. He could never recognise that the presence of so many of the sons of his father's political opponents in the academy would have made his attendance there far too problematical, even dangerous, for his parents to have ever given their consent.

In addition to a new routine Filon also arranged more companions for the Prince's daily lessons. Beside Louis Conneau and the occasional presence of the two lively nieces, he now included the sons of a number of court officials. Tristan Lambert, the son of Baron Lambert, was some years older but had very definite ideas about monarchies and their importance to the nation-state. Lambert was also a very devout Catholic who exercised a wholesome influence on the Prince. One of Louis's own cousins, the young Prince Joachim Murat, grandson of the former King and Queen of Naples (Marshal Murat and the Great Napoleon's youngest sister, Caroline), had now come to live in the Tuileries, but unlike the courtiers' sons who always responded respectfully to the Prince's every whim, he, being family, more often than not actually contradicted and upstaged this 'Child of France'. At first nonplussed the Prince soon learnt how to counter-attack and the experience did him no harm. In time he became very friendly with 'Chino' as young Prince Murat was always nicknamed within the family. But none of these young and privileged companions — Jean Espinasse (who became his best friend after Conneau, and who, like his father, rose to general rank in the army), Maxine Frossard (son of the governor), Pierre Bourgoing (son of an equerry to the Emperor), Simon Corvisart (son of Baron Corvisant, the deputy chief physician) — could give the heir the one thing he needed most — communication and friendship with ordinary young people from all social classes away from the narrow confines of the imperial Court. But Prince Murat, Conneau, Espinasse and Corvisart were all to remain friends for life; they accompanied the Prince from time to time during his exile in England and they were all present on that sad morning at Portsmouth when the Prince's coffin returned from South Africa. And, apart from financial legacies, in his last will Louis also bequeathed various items of his personal arms and uniforms to each of them by name.

His father had always made his own way in the world, gaining supreme power through a combination of intrigue, political opportunism and sheer good fortune. In the process he had experienced bouts of poverty, danger, imprisonment, as well as frequent exile abroad. He therefore always considered himself to be uniquely experienced in many of the hardships also experienced by his subjects. Yet inexplicably Louis-Napoleon seems to have deliberately shielded his young son from any meaningful experience of that same harsh and brutal world in which he would eventually have to make his own way. Filon in particular noted how the Prince appeared to live in a state of dream-like illusion. One day the Empress said to the tutor, "Has he any idea of wretchedness? Does he even know what a poor man is?"[4] The Empress herself knew only too well. Apart from the experiences of her own somewhat impoverished upbringing she also, in her devout way, made a regular practice of visiting the poorest quarters of Paris but, on grounds of security, General Frossard constantly vetoed any suggestion that the Prince should occasionally accompany her. And so he was to be kept in ignorance of such matters, despite the fact that his father might be assassinated at any time thus possibly requiring him to succeed to the throne at an early age. But the Franco-Prussian war in 1870 abruptly destroyed the prospect of any such succession. This was a totally unforeseen development for which his education and upbringing had ill-prepared him.

Ironically, Louis-Napoleon was probably the greatest self-publicist in the France of his day, yet his heir for many years appears to have been unaware of its critical importance towards creating the right populist image. For example, the Emperor quickly perceived the propaganda advantages to be gained through the skilful use of photography — he was, in fact, the first European ruler to do so. The peoples of the Second Empire were to be constantly entranced by a stream of photographs of the imperial family, taken in a variety of poses, all mass-produced specially for public consumption. These ranged from intimate family portraits to ceremonial scenes. But the Prince did not photograph particularly well. In later years many of the formal photographs tended to unduly flatter his appearance, causing some disappointment to those who subsequently met him. Additionally, for many of the official photographs, in keeping with the expectations of the time, he had been persuaded to adopt a stiff, almost imperious pose, quite contrary to his true nature. These tended to emphasise the melancholic, even priggish side of his personality. It was always the informal snapshot which showed him at his natural best.

In 1865 the fourteen year old Prince Arthur, Queen Victoria's third son, had paid his first official visit to Paris and was formally received at the Tuileries by the nine year old Prince Imperial. Major Elphinstone, Prince Arthur's governor, wrote to Queen Victoria that the Prince Imperial seemed to be a delicate child who had 'a very intelligent pleasing face, a face that would gain upon one, for it has a sweet expression.'[5] Prince Arthur returned to Paris two years later in 1867; this time he reviewed the *Garde Impériale*, wearing the dark blue uniform of a Gentleman Cadet of Woolwich, adorned with the light blue Garter Ribbon. Afterwards the Prince Imperial showed him round St Cloud and Major Elphinstone informed the Queen, 'He does not appear to have grown much since 1865 and he is very small for his age, but very nice, and with perfect manners.'[6]

---

4   FILON, p. 57.
5   RA. Add. A15/645.
6   RA. Add. A15/1091.

In the summer of 1869 the young Prince was to experience, for the first time, the nature of the political opposition with which he would eventually have to grapple. Because he was, in theory at least, a pupil of the *Lycée Bonaparte* it was suggested that he should present the prizes for the *Concours général* at the Sorbonne. This was always a great public occasion, as well as being the most important ceremony in the life of the students of the Paris University. Since he had already previously dined with the fellow pupils of his particular class at the *Lycée*, without incident (indeed, aided by the vintage champagne generously provided by his father, the Prince, by all accounts, had become the life and soul of the party!) trouble was not anticipated. Unfortunately, it had not been appreciated that amongst the prize-winners was Godefroi Cavaignac, son of the Emperor's bitterest political opponent who, as Republican candidate for the Presidency, had been defeated by Louis-Napoleon in 1848 and subsequently imprisoned after the *coup d'état*. The Empress accompanied the Prince Imperial as far as the Sorbonne, from whence he was escorted into the hall by General Frossard and Filon. Dressed in his usual black velvet suit, adorned with the red ribbon of the *Légion d'honneur*, this was to be the first public duty carried out by the Prince in his own right. The prize-giving went well enough until the name of Godefroi Cavaignac was called. All eyes in the hall soon turned towards where the young Cavaignac was sitting alongside his mother. The Prince smiled down on the assembly, holding the prize in his hand, patiently waiting. When the boy stood up in anticipation everyone immediately broke into applause. Was it possible that a sensational event was about to take place in front of everyone? A public greeting and embrace between the son of the Emperor and the son of his bitterest Republican opponent? Suddenly, Madame Cavaignac was seen to pull her son down back on to his seat. The applause slowly died away, but not before many piercing shouts of *'Vive Cavaignac!'* and *'Vive la République!'* had resounded through the hall. Embarrassed, the Rector quickly read out the next name on his list and the Prince continued, outwardly unmoved, with the rest of the prize-giving. But his looks were deceptive. Privately he felt totally humiliated, not on his own account, but for his father. On the journey back the tears poured down his cheeks. He just could not understand how the French people whom he had sworn to love — how they could treat his adored father like this.

The Emperor took the news quietly, saying that, "Some time or other Lou-Lou was bound to come up against opposition,"[7] whilst privately admiring his son's reported composure, but the Empress immediately fell into one of her hysterical outbursts, running to her suite where she had to be attended by a doctor. Later that evening at dinner, having eventually recovered, she dabbed her eyes, murmuring, *'Mon pauvre petit garcon.*[8] She had rightly perceived that, after the Mexican debacle and the government's evident inertia after Prussia's recent victory over Austria at Sadowa, the people's love for their Emperor was now beginning to fade. Considerable disquiet about the imperial family was now being expressed almost daily in many newspapers. Only in her darling 'Lou-Lou' could she find consolation for that betrayed love and now he, too, had been publicly humiliated The fact that her son,

7   JOHN, p. 139.
8   Ibid.,

in his thirteenth year, had shown such commendable self-control and restraint, in contrast to her own hysterical response, was no compensation. At that time she would not have appreciated these commendable comments made by Saint-Beuve in a letter to Princess Mathilde: 'In such situations one needs tact, intelligence and character, It is impossible to become practised in these things too early. The whole incident is a most happy augury.'[9]

Only the previous year, 1868, the Prince had reiterated to no less a person than Bismarck his feelings about the French people. The two had met again in the Tuileries where the towering Prussian Chancellor — now a dominant figure in European politics — was in Paris for the second Great Exhibition. He came across Louis playing chess and after watching for a while, himself became involved in a brief game which the youngster lost, but not overwhelmingly. "I was wrong in trying to save my knight," mused the Prince, adding with a smile, "In French we call it *un cheval* and I like horses too much!" Bismarck affably acknowledged the comment and then, as if to show off his own knowledge of French, he quoted the proverb: "'Unlucky in play, lucky in love!' I hear Your Imperial Highness is beloved by the French." Quick as a flash came the answer: "You are wrong, sir, — it is I who love them."[10]

In 1869, on the occasion of the centenary of the birth of the Great Napoleon, mother and son made a special pilgrimage to the island of Corsica. The Emperor himself was ill and could not make the journey. His absence did not inhibit almost the whole population from turning out to cheer '*Le petit Prince*', conspicuously ignoring 'that Spanish woman'. He was to be escorted in triumphant procession to the modest birthplace where, alone, he finally knelt and lit a candle in the actual room where his ancestor had been born. Outside the huge crowd pressed at the doors and windows until the escort officer warned the Prince that the mass of surging onlookers might soon become uncontrollable and put his life in danger. To the officer's dismay, he simply stood up and called out in a loud clear voice for everyone to hear: "Pooh! let them come in, they belong to the family!"[11] At that the crowd went delirious and the Prince was only extracted from the building with the greatest difficulty. Scenes such as these contrasted oddly with this scathing commentary about the Prince, written about this time by the well-known English journalist, Archibald Forbes:

> Almost in vain does one range through the records of the Second Empire in a quest of but a glimmer of naturalness. There is a boy in the story, it is true, and surely, hopes the enquirer, some trait of nature is to be recognised in him. But no; he was a buckram boy from his swaddling clothes, poor little toy and tool of sham Imperialism. No trace is discernible of him as a boy in the fashion of other boys; he is ever found a mere padded clothes-horse, or rather, clothes-pony. Now attired in the cumbrous uniform of the Compiégne hunt, with a *couteau de châsse* and a huge hunting horn hung about the poor melancholy little chap; now bedight in military garb, with a

9   KURTZ, p. 230.
10   TISDALL, p. 22.
11   FILON, p. 62.

puny bit of a sword dangling about his shins, and his gloved hand raised in the frequent formal salute...The boyhood of this unfortunate child was as unreal as the fantasy of which it was the victim.[12]

There has to be much irony in the fact that Prince was to spend the last evening of life talking to this same Archibald Forbes in South Africa and that the journalist who had written of him so sarcastically was, at his request, to post the Prince's last letter to his mother.

After the Mexican fiasco of 1865 the Second Empire was starting to unravel. Louis-Napoleon was now into his sixties but felt and looked a great deal older. In recent years he had suffered the loss, through natural death, of some of his most able advisers. His own health too was poor and deteriorating with every year. He suffered dreadfully from increasing pain caused by the large stone which had formed in his gall-bladder. This situation was aggravated by the fact that the Emperor had a deep distrust of doctors and surgeons, indeed with the whole business of medicine. Accordingly he demurred from having the sort of corrective operation which might conceivably have prolonged his life. But, with some justification, he also feared that he might die under the surgeon's knife whilst his heir was still a vulnerable child. For the same reason, abdication on health grounds was also out of the question. There can be little doubt that Louis-Napoleon's deteriorating health does much to explain the rather inept manner in which the affairs of France were now conducted; indeed, the sequence of events which led to the final collapse of the Second Empire can, in large part, be traced back to this physical and mental decline. Knowing that he was seriously ill his overriding concern now was to secure the Empire for his son. Losing his appetite for power, the sick man even devised a secret scheme whereby the Prince would automatically succeed him on the day of his eighteenth birthday in 1874, at which time both Eugénie and himself would quietly abdicate and go into retirement.

To give himself a measure of popular approval the Emperor had, on two previous occasions, submitted political alternatives to the wishes of the people. Now, in 1870, he decided to hold a third plebiscite. With his wife abroad attending the inauguration of the Suez Canal, he took the opportunity to offer the people of France a more liberal style of government (the most liberal then on offer anywhere in Europe) in return for a decisive affirmative vote of popular approval, which could also prepare the way for his son's succession as Napoleon the Fourth. Although confident he would win this somewhat meaningless exercise in self-aggrandisement, he was less sure about the size of any 'No' votes. Leaving nothing to chance the government made strenuous efforts to ensure the maximum turnout. After widespread polling the first results came as something of a shock — Lyons, Marseilles, Bordeaux, Toulouse — these great cities had all decisively rejected the proposals. The subsequent rejection by Paris herself only deepened that disappointment. But when all the results from across the whole country were announced the situation was suddenly transformed. Louis-Napoleon had finally secured his majority approval. Eighty-two percent of

---

12   JOHN, p. 158.

the electorate had made their choice. Of these, sixty-eight percent (7.3 million) had voted 'Yes'. In fact, this approval figure was only slightly less than the two previous plebiscites. But it seems that only the young Prince observed the true significance of the results; namely, that another fourteen percent (1.5 million Frenchmen) — a sizeable proportion — had actually voted directly against their Emperor and thus, by implication, for a Third Republic. There had also been 1.8 million Frenchmen who had deliberately abstained.

On 21st May 1870 the results of the plebiscite were formally presented by the *Corps législatif*. The Prince appeared for the first time dressed in the uniform of a second-lieutenant and the Emperor publicly expressed his pleasure in seeing his dynasty so firmly established: "Today more than ever we may contemplate the future without alarm."[13] But the most disturbing fact about the vote as a whole had been deliberately withheld from the Prince; namely, that a large number of 'No' votes had actually emerged from the army's own ballot boxes. For the first time, Louis-Napoleon sensed that the army, particularly after the Mexican fiasco, might now be turning against him. But in his growing isolation the Emperor would not have appreciated that any dissatisfaction within the army probably arose more from its own internal problems — complaints about inadequate pay, chronic equipment shortages, poor conditions of service and low morale — than mere loyalty to the Commander-in-Chief.

Yet in the next few weeks the sick Emperor was to allow himself to be so out-manoeuvred diplomatically by Prussia that he was left with no alternative but to go to war — a war which in a matter of weeks was to bring about the total disintegration of the Second Empire and the final exile of its Emperor, this time with all his family, to the shores of Great Britain. It was a defining event, which was also to bring about a marked transformation in the character and personality of the young Prince Imperial.

The causes of the Franco-Prussian war are complex. Throughout the 1860s nationalism was in the ascendancy throughout Europe and in Prussia, under Bismarck's political leadership, there was undeniably a strong movement for German unification. To that end Prussia went to war with Denmark in 1864, acquiring Schleswig-Holstein. This also prepared the way for the Austro-Prussian war two years later. In 1866 the Prussians, in a lightning campaign of only seven weeks, finally crushed Austria at the battle of Sadowa.

There was now a serious threat to the stability of the whole of Europe and thus to the security of France. It was this threat which had encouraged Louis-Napoleon to acquiesce to American diplomatic pressure and withdraw French troops from Mexico — despite his undertaking to Archduke Maximilian of support, regardless of events elsewhere in Europe. People began to grow more and more concerned that Chancellor Bismarck, by bringing the Bavarian states into military alliance with the Prussian-led North German Confederation, would create an all-powerful German entity and, were that to happen, France would have no option but to concede the loss of its hard won pre-eminence in Europe. Towards the end of the 1860s French

---

13   Ibid., p. 163.

public opinion was becoming increasingly fatalistic about the prospect of a war with Prussia, and this corrosive feeling of inevitability undoubtedly helped to precipitate the events of 1870.

Sensing the public mood the ailing Louis Napoleon tried, in vain, to secure allies and friends to stand with France against this menacing growth of Prussia power. But the price of the Emperor's previous inept foreign adventures now had to be paid. Having always sponsored Italian unity he now had little moral authority to lead any European coalition seeking to block Prussia's own quest for full nationhood. And Austria, mindful of his abrupt withdrawal from Italy and his equally abrupt desertion of the Emperor's brother in Mexico, determined to lay down a specific condition before offering support — that France must now successfully invade and occupy Southern Germany. Denmark likewise would only join after France had first secured a major victory. Italy, still smarting from being abandoned by France in 1859 (losing Nice and Savoy in the process), would do nothing to help as long as French troops remained in Rome — a guarantee for the Pope which Eugénie consistently and stubbornly refused to have withdrawn. Russia remained coldly neutral and after the Mexican fiasco, the United States likewise refused to become involved. Any chance of British support had been abruptly dashed by Bismarck's crafty release (to *The Times* newspaper) of an earlier secret French proposal in which the Emperor had offered to give Prussia a free hand in Southern Germany in return for a tacit Prussian agreement for France to annex Belgium!

Matters came to a head when the Prussian royal family — the Hohenzollerns — had reluctantly agreed, but only after much prompting by Bismarck, to provide a candidate for the throne of Spain which had become unexpectedly vacant after the abdication of Queen Isabella. For decades France had always regarded Spain as being within its own particular sphere of influence and therefore an already sore public opinion was to become further inflamed at the prospect of Prince Leopold Von Hohenzollern becoming its ruler.

The French Ambassador to Berlin, however, managed to convince Kaiser Wilhelm the First to agree that Prince Leopold could now tactfully withdraw his nomination. In fact this apparent reversal was not too difficult since William himself had never been particularly enthusiastic about the proposal in the first place. But, goaded by increasing public bellicosity, there was mounting pressure on the French government to take the whole matter a stage further in an attempt to pull off a great diplomatic coup — to erase the national humiliation of the Mexican fiasco. Not content with Prussia's tacit agreement to withdraw their 'volunteer nominee', the French ambassador was further instructed to now obtain a cast-iron guarantee from the Kaiser, then on holiday at Bad Ems, that the Hohenzollern candidacy would never again be revived. This, not surprisingly, William refused to do; in his irritation at being accosted on this matter during his private daily walk, he also refused to grant the ambassador any further audiences during his holiday. He notified these developments to Bismarck in Berlin. When he received the telegram the Chancellor quickly released an abridged, but skilfully edited version to the press — the famous 'Ems telegram'— which highlighted the Kaiser's implied snub to the ambassador, in the hope of provoking France into yet another ill-considered response.

But the truth was that neither Louis-Napoleon nor his cousin, 'Plon-Plon' really wanted war with Prussia. Unlike most senior French generals they had both drawn the inevitable conclusions from Prussia's awesome victory at Sadowa — that the French army was simply in no fit state to guarantee Prussia's defeat. The cousins may not have had the dazzling insights of their illustrious uncle but they were both sufficiently experienced in military affairs to perceive the superiority of the Prussian war machine and the certain prospect of a French defeat. On this matter they were in rare agreement.

In foreign affairs Louis-Napoleon normally showed little concern about public opinion particularly when that opinion conflicted with his own views. During the earlier military interventions in Italy and Mexico he had acted alone, often contrary to sound advice, but neither seeking nor particularly encouraging public support. But this was no longer possible. In the wake of this perceived diplomatic snub to their ambassador the French press proceeded to whip up a national hysteria which soon threatened to engulf the entire government. The sick Emperor was now under greater pressure than ever to declare war; from the Chief Minister, M. Ollivier; from many of his Council, including the heavy-handed Foreign Minister, the Duc de Gramont (he nursed a personal grievance — Bismarck had once described him as the 'stupidest man in Europe'!) and not least from Eugénie who pointing to the Prince Imperial declared, in her usual dramatic way: "this child will never reign unless we repair the misfortunes of Sadowa."[14]

But such posturings hardly justified plunging the whole nation into war. Nor was the 'Ems telegram', despite Bismarck's skilful editing and its implied diplomatic insult, a credible *casus belli*. Paris was celebrating Bastille Day, 14th July, when news of the telegram first came to public notice. An outraged press immediately issued a clarion call for war and the crowds greeted the customary military parades through the city with even greater enthusiasm than usual, as though willing the army to recover the nation's honour. At noon that day the Council met at Saint-Cloud when the Emperor tried his best to avert war, proposing instead to call an international conference or request Great Britain's mediation to settle the dispute. It was to no avail. The Council determined to issue the declaration, and at the same time, by 247 votes to a pitiful 10, voted the necessary war credits whilst endorsing general mobilisation, with some troops starting to move that same day towards the frontier. Yet the declaration, when despatched to Berlin four days later on 19th July 1870, was not underpinned by any clear national objectives or by any coherent military strategy — it appeared to have no other purpose than to retaliate against a presumed diplomatic insult. Leon Gambetta, the leader of the Republicans, perhaps summed up the rhetoric when he publicly declared: 'The aim of this war is to settle, once and for all, the question of supremacy between the French and German peoples'. During his final years of exile Louis-Napoleon was always held personally responsible for starting the war, a view with which all his opponents, including Gambetta, now predominant in the new Third Republic, vociferously concurred. However the overwhelming evidence is that, until the very last minute, he did his utmost to thwart

---

14   HORNE, p. 36.

the declaration now being served on Prussia. But with his authority diminished after the Mexican war and his health undermined by debilitating illness, he no longer had the power or the will to single-handedly direct France's affairs. Not unexpectedly, from that day onwards, France was to find herself entirely alone, without allies or friends and without much sympathy. 'The liberal Empire goes to war on a mere point of etiquette' enthused the *Illustrated London News,* sarcastically summing up the feelings of most people in Europe.

Meanwhile Paris grew delirious at the prospect of a lightning campaign which would swiftly break Prussian power and arrogance. When the departing Prussian military attache travelled by cab to the station, the driver refused point blank to accept any fare: "*Adieu, monsieur,*" he laughed, "One doesn't charge a gentleman to be driven to his own funeral!"[15]

But who amongst the excited public could have known that the French army was so ill-prepared for a major war in Europe? Whilst the soldiers were formidable enough in battle they were, on the whole, poorly led, trained and administered. And apart from the geographically limited Italian and Mexican campaigns, the army had, during most of the last thirty years, been largely engaged on operations in North Africa in circumstances far removed from the complex terrain and climatic conditions of Europe. The reality was that it really lacked the experience, the material resources and the modern equipment to fight a major war in Europe. It was utterly ludicrous, for example, for the Minister of War, Marshal Leboeuf, to pompously advise the Emperor: "*Sire,* your army is ready down to the last gaiter button!"[16] Some wits later maintained that this was largely true — since there were no gaiters available in store anyway!

In numbers the French Army could only muster a force of about a quarter of a million against a German mobilisation scheme which, in the short space of a fortnight exploiting the extensive rail network, could produce over four times that amount. It is true that, compared to the Prussians, the French had the more colourful uniforms, the louder fanfares with their troops led by dashing young officers, all brimming with self-confidence and *élan*. But it was the sort of boastful confidence which resulted in all the maps, now being issued for the forthcoming campaign, to be restricted to coverage of Germany — excluding France! The French did have one significant advantage in their cartridge-firing *chassepot* rifle, which had nearly twice the range of the Prussian equivalent and a further advantage in another new weapon, *la mitrailleuse*, a bundle of twenty-five barrels which was really a prototype machine-gun. Had there been enough of these two new and formidable weapons, and had all French soldiers, regular and reservist, been properly trained in their use, the outcome of the war might have been different.

But these were really the only French advantages. In most other respects, the Prussians were superior. In their steel breech-loading cannon (as mass produced by the famous Krupp family) they had an artillery weapon of superior range and destructiveness to anything the French could field. Their leaders, particularly at senior rank, were far better trained and experienced, being less subject to centralised control

---

15   TISDALL, p. 28.
16   Ibid., p. 28.

than the French. Whereas, in peace time, Louis-Napoleon regularly intervened in military affairs and during war functioned as the supreme Commander-in-Chief, the Prussian king largely remained a titular figure, leaving the preparation and conduct of war to his professional generals. And they had already learnt a great deal from their recent campaigns against Denmark and Austria. More flexible than the French in their tactics they were also much better supported logistically. Indeed, almost unnoticed by the rest of Europe, they had practically revolutionised the whole concept of war through the creation of a highly professional General Staff — a body of well-trained officers who could systematically plan and prepare for every aspect of war and who, in their present Chief of Staff, General Von Moltke, had a military craftsman of the highest calibre. Baron Stoffel, the perceptive French military attache in Berlin, had long since warned his government that the Prussian General Staff would: 'constitute the most formidable element of superiority in the Prussian Army.' But no-one in Paris paid any attention.

On its own France's centralised and bureaucratic mobilisation system succeeded in reducing the army to near total chaos — long before a single shot had ever been fired. There was no regional system of call-up. Reserves were initially sent to a regimental depot to collect their equipment and then further dispatched to join their parent line regiment, which was probably at the other end of France. In July 1870, for example, no less than 65 out of 100 line regiments were billeted in towns far distant from their depots. But there was at least some justification for this apparent anomaly. By constantly moving regiments from garrison to garrison (on average, once every two years) soldiers would, it was considered, be better insulated from local seditious influences and thus kept continually apart from the general populace. Consequently, reservists called up from Dunkirk had to travel to join their regiments at Strasbourg by way of the depot at Perpignan! Zouaves from the North of France were sent down to Marseilles, then across to Oran and then back again to Marseilles, and from there, on to Alsace! Thus, thousands of soldiers were travelling aimlessly all over the country, trying to reach their respective depots and regiments.

There were chronic shortages of equipment and supplies. Regiments would join their divisions without tents, blankets, lacking even basic cooking utensils. There were no harnesses for many of the horses. Wherever guns assembled there was usually no ammunition. Depots even lacked adequate supplies of food; it was therefore not surprising that many of the hungry, disorientated soldiers soon fell into drunkenness and ill-discipline. Emile Zola summed up the sheer ineptitude with which the dispirited legions of France's Second Empire went out to meet the finest army in the whole of Europe: 'Germany ready, better commanded, better armed, sublimated by a great charge of patriotism; France frightened, delivered into disorder...having neither the leaders, nor the men, nor the necessary arms.'[17]

On the day of the declaration of war the imperial family remained secluded at Saint-Cloud. They could not hear the people of Paris openly singing the forbidden *Marseillaise* in the streets — nor the cries of 'A bas la Prusse! -A Berlin! A Berlin!' The Emperor, dispirited, tired and ill, walked around as if in a trance. The Empress,

---

17   HORNE, p. 43.

who had actively pressed for war, now fell silent. The only person excited at the prospect of combat was 'Le petit Prince'. He would never forget the morning when his father quietly informed him that the two of them, together, would be controlling the forthcoming campaign. Louis was in his seventh heaven; for what other boy of fourteen, in the whole of France, would have the opportunity to go to war with his father? Louis Conneau, for one, tried but failed. "My son," explained the Emperor, rejecting the boy's entreaties, "is not joining the Army to play at soldiers, but to learn his *métier de souverain* (profession of being a sovereign)."[18]

The Prince now wore uniform all day long. He was even seen inserting the fingers of his left hand between the buttons of the blue jacket, in the manner of the Great Napoleon leading his *Grande Armée*. Filon just looked glum, much to his pupil's disappointment, but the tutor was becoming more and more disturbed at the excited way in which the boy approached the whole prospect of war — as if it was simply going to be some thrilling adventure.

The Empress relayed her private feelings in a letter to her mother, the Comtesse de Montijo:

> Louis has sent you a lock of his hair; he is full of spirit and courage, and so am I. There are names which oblige, and his are heavy to carry, he must do his duty therefore, and he will do it, I have the sweetness of thinking so. You are very fortunate to have only *daughters*, for often I am like a wild beast, I could take my baby and carry him away to the wilderness, and tear everyone who tries to lay hands on him. Then comes reflection and prejudice, and I tell myself it would be better to see him dead than without honour. In short, I feel myself a prey to so many contrary ideas that I dare not think of them. And meanwhile I work Louis up — not that he needs it![19]

From an early age an ex-dragoon, Xavier Uhlmann, had been acting as a sort of valet and bodyguard to the boy Prince. From Alsace the former soldier was a large man, somewhat serious, but totally reliable. From now on he was to accompany the Prince everywhere he went.

Every lieutenant in the French Army was allowed one black tin trunk in which to carry all his personal kit. Uhlmann brought the regulation trunk, *cantine*, for the Prince to pack. In fact, Louis had amassed enough gear to bedeck the commander of an army, far more than he could possibly squeeze into the black box. Uniforms, shirts and other linen, a soldier's holdall (with needles and thread with which to sew on any badges of rank that might be ripped off in the tumult of battle), a box of medical dressings in case (as he perhaps secretly hoped) he was slightly wounded, spare whips for his horse and so on. He also included his diary, a silver crucifix (which his mother had given him), a prayer book and some cuff links made from the stones of olives which had been planted by the Great Napoleon during his exile on Elba. He was hoping to wear these on his father's triumphant entry into Berlin. The public were deliberately kept well-informed of these preparations for the Prince's

18   JOHN, p. 175.
19   Ibid., p. 176.

participation in the war. A special photograph was taken of Louis in his uniform and widely distributed. Newspapers described in detail how his hair had been shorn of its locks to conform to the regulation army haircut and how the Empress had personally supervised his packing. These same newspapers repeated the Emperor's reference to Louis in his parting declaration to the Parisians: 'I am taking my son with me notwithstanding his tender age. The life of camps is unsuitable for youth; but with a name which he bears he cannot, and must not, be absent from my side.' But, like the majority of his fellow countrymen, *'le petit Prince'* had not the slightest awareness of the nation's general unpreparedness for war with Prussia.

No mention however was made in the press about the Emperor's health. On 1st July he had been secretly examined by the surgeon, M.Nelaton and four other doctors. One of them — a young surgeon called Germain Sée — had urged an immediate operation on the gall-bladder stone, but when the others demurred, he had insisted on putting his recommendations in writing, handing them over in a sealed envelope to Dr Conneau. This envelope, still unopened, was to be found amongst the Emperor's papers by Eugénie in 1874. But it did not require doctors to pronounce the Emperor ill; it was obvious to everyone who came into contact with him. After war had been declared, Princess Mathilde bluntly told him that he was not in a fit state: "to ride a horse or even endure the jolting of a carriage — let alone take command of an army." On the eve of their departure from Paris, he could only confide in his old friend Marshal Randon, "I'm too old, much too ill — and quite unfit to go campaigning."[20] Even the thought of having to canter around the battlefield was enough to fill him with dread since, by now, the pain from the stone in his gall bladder was almost constant and excruciating. One therefore wonders why he felt impelled once more to take personal command in the field, to engage in the violence he hated so much. Was this to be the apotheosis of the Napoleonic destiny? Was it to trust all to good fortune — to produce a stunning lightning victory which would restore all his fortunes? Or was it simply to pacify Eugénie? In her ignorance about his true medical condition, she had attributed much of his frequent depressions, general inertia and listlessness, his spasms of acute pain to mere hypochondria and far from making her sympathetic towards her husband it had merely increased her impatience over what she perceived as his continual ineffectiveness. She now goaded him into activity.

The Empress was formally nominated as Regent on 26th July 1870 and two days later — nine days after the declaration of war — the Emperor, in the uniform of a Lieutenant General of the Empire, the Empress and their son, Second Lieutenant His Highness the Prince Imperial, came down to the main entrance of the Palace of Saint-Cloud — behind them followed 'Plon-Plon', in the uniform of a general of division with a retinue of aides and personal staff officers including two doctors. Privately, the young Prince was somewhat disappointed at the restrained manner of their departure; he assumed they would travel first of all to Paris, from whence they would ride off, escorted by the resplendent imperial cavalry — the *Cent-Gardes* — with bands blaring, drums beating, banners unfurled, pursued by cheering crowds.

---

20   Ibid., p. 179,

After all, this is how his father had set out for the 1859 Italian campaign. Instead, on health grounds, the Emperor had chosen to drive in carriage direct to the little railway terminal by the Orléans Gate of the Park and then go by side train to join the main line to Metz. At the station, Eugénie took her son into her arms, making the sign of the cross on his forehead with her thumb-nail — a Spanish custom which she always followed — and pressed him into the carriage alongside his father. As the train began to glide away, she shouted some last words to her emotionless and almost inert husband; perhaps they were also intended for her son: *"Louis! Fais ton devoir*! (Do your duty!)"[21]

Later Filon observed that the Empress drove back to Saint-Cloud face in hands sobbing openly. But in her sadness she could never have envisaged that neither husband nor son would ever return to Paris.

The imperial train pulled in to a special siding in the huge military base at Metz at about six o'clock on the evening of 28th July. To the surprise of the troops the Emperor came to his headquarters in a carriage and not on horseback as had been expected. Shortly after entering he issued his first Order of the Day which contained a welcome sense of realism. In it he expressed all his earlier forebodings which had simply been brushed aside by those who considered they knew better. He solemnly warned his troops that they were about to engage one of the best armies in Europe; that the conflict was likely to last for a long time and that each battle would have to be fought over ground which bristled with fortresses and many natural obstacles.

On 1st August at nearby Saint-Avold the Emperor, accompanied by Louis, briefed senior commanders and staff officers on his strategy. Not unexpectedly, it was the very essence of simplicity. Even before French mobilisation had been completed he proposed to advance rapidly eastwards into Germany, to force the Southern German States into neutrality and then persuade Austria to link up with him for the final drive on to Berlin. At the same time he envisaged an amphibious landing on the coast of northern Prussia, through which it was hoped to link up with the Danes and thus develop joint operations against the city of Hanover. But he did not disclose that the Danes had only agreed to this proposal on the condition that the French had first obtained a major victory. The more thoughtful officers listened to this nebulous plan with some incredulity. They were all aware that, even as the Emperor was speaking, there was not a single corps in the army which could be considered fit and ready for such a campaign. Two, under the command of Marshal MacMahon, were still assembling at Strasbourg and there were five more likewise gathering in the Metz district to form the Army of the Rhine, over which the Emperor himself was now to assume personal command. And as the 'Blue Division' of marines lacked the strength and firepower for any effective landing in northern Prussia; it was not long before they were diverted to reinforce Marshal MacMahon's troops.

It was evident to any knowledgeable observer that the so-called Army of the Rhine — ostensibly the finest in France — was really only fit for parade reviews and little else. It lacked sufficient ammunition, transport, supplies; indeed it lacked the

---

21   Ibid., p. 181.

very minimum logistic backing to sustain any strategic thrust deep into enemy-held territory. Even as the Emperor was briefing senior commanders, there were only thirty-six bakers in the whole of the Metz complex to provide a basic bread ration for more than 130,000 soldiers. These were not the only problems. After a period of mobilisation which had now lasted two weeks only about two-thirds of the reservists had been accounted for — and none of them had received any training whatsoever in the use of the new French weapons. As his staff briefed him on the true situation, Louis Napoleon quickly began to despair. Later he relayed his concerns to Eugénie: 'Nothing is ready. We do not have enough troops. I feel any advance is lost already.'[22]

But it would be quite wrong to blame all these inadequacies on Louis-Napoleon himself. After all, it had been entirely due to the Emperor's constant interference and insistence that the superior *chassepot* rifle had finally been issued to the army in the first place. The Artillery Committee had strongly objected — indeed, this same committee had successfully blocked all Louis-Napoleon's efforts to modernise the artillery. Even the *mitrailleuse* would never have been developed had it not been for the Emperor's personal funding of the project, at least in its initial stages. Apart from this obstruction by military advisers on re-equipment, the Emperor had been equally frustrated in his attempts to introduce an efficient mobilisation scheme and a reorganisation of the structure of the whole army. All his efforts had finally come to nought — vetoed, principally on the grounds of cost by his Finance Minister as well as by complacent politicians, particularly those on the Left, who were totally opposed to any further expenditure on rearmament.

But who cared about these issues now? The only thing people wanted was news of an early French victory. The Prussians were mobilising at great speed; they could cross the frontier in force at any moment. At the suggestion of General Frossard (who had now assumed command of 2nd French Corps) Louis-Napoleon decided to make the opening move — to stage a set-piece battle at Saarbrucken, but with such overwhelming superiority that a French victory would be guaranteed.

Saarbrucken was a small fortified town just across the frontier, divided in two by the River Saar. It had one strategic asset — a railway junction on the far bank. In the town itself was a garrison of about 1,000 Prussian soldiers, supported by a few guns, all under the command of a junior colonel. Against them a composite French force of six divisions, totalling almost 60,000 troops, was to be deployed under the command of General Frossard.

Even before the opening battle on 2nd August the Prussian commander had obtained permission from his superiors to withdraw at his discretion, provided he kept the position for as long as practicable. In his enthusiasm for this opening show-down with the French he invited all the many war correspondents who were present to join him: "Hurrah! I go to draw de shoots of de enemy! Come along!"[23] The journalists were even more amused when they noted that many of the outlying Prussian pickets, set up on the ridge on the French side of the town, were generously augmented by stuffed dummies, all wearing the famous *pickel-haubes*!

---

22   Ibid., p. 185.
23   Ibid., p. 188.

Once engaged, the Prussians held out for about three hours without too much difficulty before they skilfully withdrew, in perfect order, across the river Saar. They were not pursued. Later, French troops were marched into Saarbrucken. Shortly afterwards they all inexplicably marched out again. They then took up positions on the high ground overlooking the town but, after two days, these too were finally abandoned and the whole of General Frossard's force marched back to Metz! This was to be the only battle during the whole war in which the Prince Imperial could claim to have personally taken part. Naturally General Frossard was delighted to give his young pupil a realistic demonstration as to how the French Army won its battles. At one stage, towards the end of the day, the Emperor and his son had cantered on to the ridge overlooking the town. In his excitement the Prince had already taken off his *képi*, waving it triumphantly in the air. Later he confessed to his old friend Tristan Lambert that his first thought, as the shells and bullets continued to whistle around them, had been of God and then: 'the noise, the excitement of the soldiers and the smell of powder began to thrill me, and I felt as though it were a review.'[24]

A day later he recalled all the events and general excitement in this hasty letter to his tutor:

> My dear Monsieur Filon,
>
> Thank you for the letter you wrote me, it gave me great pleasure to get it; you asked for some details, I think, on the engagement of Saarbrucken, and complained that our friends do not write often to you. I shall try, if I can, to make up for their neglect which I do not understand.
>
> The Emperor arrived at Forbach at about eleven o'clock in the forenoon. He got into a carriage to wait for his horses at the frontier, that was where we heard the first cannon; some minutes later the Emperor was in the saddle, making for a ridge which was the Prussian's position, and which we had just seized. Their batteries were in retreat and were crossing the bridges over the Saar at full trot, to take up a position a little further away. They were occupying a post, that is to say a wine-shop, on which was written *Zur Bellevue*; we drove them out of it; there were two corpses in it: an officer and a Prussian private.
>
> All I saw were wounded in the head. The Prussian batteries had withdrawn behind the wood that commanded the town; but only two shells reached us. They still had two or three companies in ambush behind a bridge and they were firing on any horseman who showed themselves. Papa chose to look all the same, and we heard several bullets. A splinter of a shell was picked up quite near the Emperor; I heard a noise of old iron over my head, but I only found out what it was afterwards...we are now entering Saarbrucken though we are not occupying it as yet. Please correct my spelling mistakes, of which there are probably a great many (for I have a bad pen and am writing in haste) before you show this letter to the Empress.

---

24   Ibid.

Je vous embrasse de tout coeur,

Your affectionate,

Louis Napoleon

P.S. All the bands played the *Marseillaise*, and everyone was singing it; it was very fine. The Prussians could hear it, I shouldn't think it cheered them up.[25]

But there was one incident that day which the Prince had failed to notice. As the last shots of the battle echoed across the valley, the Emperor had been compelled to dismount from his horse, gasping for breath from pain. The staff gathered round and someone summoned a carriage. But the Emperor waved it away. He walked on slowly, his face contorted by recurring spasms of agony, until the stone in his gall bladder had settled sufficiently to enable him to re-mount.

When the battle had finally subsided the Prince was permitted to gallop around, accompanied by his aides. The soldiers all cheered him, although he was privately irked by their embarrassing and, to him, unmanly cries of '*Petit Prince! Petit Prince!*' That night, as the army encamped around Saarbrucken, Colonel Comte Clary, who had just been appointed as one of his aides, wrote to his wife: 'The Prince was admirably cool and natural in his behaviour...Assure the Empress that I am not exaggerating, and that she ought to be proud of her son's conduct. I am sorry she could not have seen him galloping in the thick of the troops...This little affair at the beginning of the campaign is of excellent omen, and besides, it gives the men confidence.'[26]

That night the Emperor also sent a telegram to his wife: 'Louis has received the baptism of fire. His coolness was admirable. He showed no emotion, and might have been strolling in the Bois de Boulogne.' He then announced the capture of Saarbrucken, describing the feebleness of Prussian resistance: 'even in the front line the balls and bullets fell at our feet' — and then, almost as an afterthought, he added that Louis had picked up one of the spent bullets to keep as a souvenir. 'There were men who shed tears on seeing him so calm.'[27]

At dinner that evening the Empress expressed her private opinion of her son's conduct: "He will be lucky like the Bonapartes. He has come under fire in August which is their month; he has been present at a favourable action. Nothing has happened to him or to any one of his suite. I am sure that he is *sacré*."[28]

Needless to say, the news of the capture of Saarbrucken was rapturously received in Paris and elsewhere. Yet what had, in truth, been no more than a brief skirmish was now to be embroidered into a grandiose title — 'The Battle of Saarbrucken'. But even as people gathered excitedly around headlines which trumpeted: '**Devastating effects of the Chassepot**' — '**Almost no Prussian resistance**' — no-one could have known that, at that very moment, there was not a single French soldier remaining in the town; that there had been no invasion of Germany; that the 60,000 conquerors

25   FILON, p. 70.
26   Ibid., p. 69.
27   Ibid., p. 191.
28   TURNBULL, p. 261.

had now marched back to Metz and that key points, such as the bridge over the Saar and the railway terminus, had not even been demolished and were thus still at the future disposal of the Prussians.

The Emperor's comment about Louis and the spent bullet had been intended for Eugénie's eyes only, but the Chief Minister, M. Ollivier, persuaded her to have it published, arguing that it would have a beneficial impact on public morale. This was a fatal miscalculation which the Emperor, had he been present, would almost certainly have vetoed. He knew better than anyone that publicity derived from an incident like that could be easily misinterpreted. When they heard the news, people burst into laughter, calling Louis by a new nickname — *'L'enfant de la balle!'* — but, in time, this good-natured banter was to turn into a bitter derision. The incident became the rationale for a torrent of sustained abuse which was to follow and haunt the Prince for the rest of his life — for here, it was constantly repeated by his opponents, here was the last Bonaparte, the heir to the imperial throne of France, casually strolling around a battlefield on which so many of his fellow countrymen had shed their blood, when his sole concern had been to pick-up a spent cartridge as a souvenir!

Chapter IV

THE JOURNEY TO ALBION

ON THE 4TH AUGUST, TWO DAYS AFTER SAARBRUCKEN, the Prussian General Staff brought into effect the meticulously prepared orders for the invasion of France. The plan was realistic; its objectives attainable. Noting that the French Army, as an entity, was divided into two by the line of the Vosges Mountains, the Prussians decided to deploy and concentrate their forces in such a way that they could bring an overwhelming superiority against either half.

Consequently, the Prussian Second Army was to strike towards Saarbrucken; the smaller First Army was to advance in line with it on the River Saar; whilst the Third Army, on the left wing, was to drive deep into Alsace. Cavalry was deployed in strength, fanning out in front of each of these armies, confusing the French whilst providing the Prussian Staff with all the information it needed. The first hammer blow fell at dawn on 4th August. At Wissenburg, and later at Woerth, Marshal MacMahon's Army of Metz suffered a serious defeat even though the Prussians, themselves incurring heavy losses, were unable to immediately follow up on their victory.

Two days later, on the 6th August, the Army of the Rhine, under the Emperor's command, was to suffer an equally demoralising defeat at Spicheren, to the left of the Vosges. Again, Prussian losses were heavy and although both these French defeats were far from decisive, morale by now had become seriously shaken. The dominant Prussian artillery always seemed to rip great swathes of casualties through the ranks of the French infantry — long before Prussian troops had even come into the range of their superior *chassepot* rifles. As a consequence Marshal MacMahon's troops began to fall back on the huge base at Châlons, thus splitting the Emperor's overall military capabilities into two. The remainder, under Marshal Bazaine, started to withdraw towards Metz. From now on, and for the rest of the war, the French were compelled to remain on the defensive, whilst constantly having to fall back, deeper and deeper into France. For an army which always performed at its best in the advance and attack, this continuous withdrawal could only add to the general demoralisation.

On 7th August French Imperial Headquarters issued orders for a general withdrawal behind the River Moselle, thus, at a stroke, unwittingly passing the strategic initiative to the hard-pressed Prussians. When this shattering news reached Paris, the Ollivier government fell and General Palikao became Chief Minister. Much of the initial euphoria over the war had now vanished and the pervading air

of gloom was aggravated by the realisation that neither Austria nor Italy intended
to enter the conflict in support of France. On that same day Paris was officially
declared to be in a 'state of siege'.

Amongst his troops the Emperor himself was close to physical and mental
collapse. Nobody seemed to believe in him any more and he knew it. In despair he
telegraphed Paris: 'Our troops are in full retreat. Nothing remains but the defence
of the capital.'[1] Many staff officers considered that the best course would be for
the Emperor to now return to Paris, but the Empress-Regent flared up at the
very suggestion. And more than one member of her Council of Ministers vocally
supported Eugénie's public admonishment: 'The Emperor may lose his throne or
perish, but to leave the army would be dishonour.'[2] Perhaps it was an unfortunate
decision, for had the Emperor returned to the capital and been able to somehow
reimpose his political authority events might have followed a different course. On
the other hand, Eugénie would have sensed that perhaps her husband and her son
would be safer if they continued to remain with the army.

By now Louis-Napoleon had already determined that he was in no fit state
to continue directing military operations in the field. He decided to hand over the
supreme command to Marshal Bazaine. Yet Bazaine had no particular claim to
seniority and no particular claim to military competence. Whilst having undergone
a great deal of active service — in the Crimea, in Lombardy and in Mexico — he
had no experience whatsoever in the command of forces as large as an army group,
and his inadequacy in this respect was soon to become crucial. But, as the Emperor
knew full well, the Parisians adored *notre glorieux Bazaine*; he had risen through the
ranks and his apparent political neutrality made him particularly acceptable to the
Left. And he was, after all, the only French Marshal in the field who appeared not
to have been defeated so far by the Prussians.

At a fateful staff meeting at Metz on 12th August the Emperor formally handed
over command to Marshal Bazaine. The atmosphere at that staff meeting was later
described by one witness as truly 'lamentable'. In effect this decision created far
more problems than it solved. What was the Emperor expected to do now? Clearly,
nobody wanted him — either in the capital or on the field of battle. Whilst he
seemed to have abdicated all military authority what remained of his political
power? And what was the embarrassed Marshal Bazaine expected to do about the
former Commander-in-Chief who still continued as to be his Sovereign? And did
this mean that the Empress Eugénie had herself assumed supreme political and
military direction of the war?

The Emperor was now too ill to be much concerned about any of these
questions. Nonetheless, he was still desperately anxious to make the best decision
for his son, who had now slumped, like his father, into a deepening depression.

The Prince had noted the grim faces of the staff and the haunted looks of
the tired and demoralised soldiers. It seemed to him beyond belief that these same
resplendently uniformed soldiers he had so often proudly reviewed on parade
alongside his father were the same soldiers who were now shuffling up and down

---

1   JOHN, p. 192.
2   Ibid., p. 194.

the roads, their white gaiters filthy, red trousers streaked with mud, many without *kepis*, looking totally dishevelled, disorganised. As he watched them pass — and they saw him standing there — nobody raised a cheer anymore; indeed nobody seemed to show the slightest interest. He felt utterly bewildered and confused; after all, if his father had personally won at Solferino, why were they not winning now? And what about General Frossard? The Prince had always thought his military governor infallible; he had won the battle at Saarbrucken and so why was he now looking so downcast and despondent?

Increasingly worried about his son's safety, Louis-Napoleon felt the best course would be to send him back to his mother in Paris. But Eugénie was under equally great strain. She now took a strange decision. In a coded message, she gave instructions that the Prince Imperial was to remain with the Emperor; she also instructed her husband to send her a telegram, but in clear not in code, saying that he was sending the Prince back to Paris — but, separately, she also privately ordered him to keep the Prince in the battle zone! Whatever her reasons — whether she thought Paris might erupt on his return, or the Prince Imperial would also be dishonoured if he now left the army — on this occasion the Emperor made no attempt to argue with her.

After endless staff discussions over the next military moves, Marshal Bazaine finally decided that the remnants of the Emperor's Army of the Rhine should leave the Metz district on 14th August and start moving westwards, deeper into France, in order to link up with Marshal MacMahon's army, already withdrawn to the huge base at Châlons-sur-Marne.

When the timetables for the order of march were issued the Emperor arranged to leave earlier, independently of the marching regiments. Escorted by the composite squadron of *Cent-Gardes* which accompanied him everywhere — with their blue tunics, red *pantalons*, white cross belts, old-fashioned *chapeaux* (in place of the usual helmet), a large 'N' on every saddle cloth — the imperial carriages moved off in the early afternoon, making their own way out of Metz and along the road to Longueville. Here and there groups of soldiers, covered in dirt and dust, lolling by the road side, watched with total indifference as the imperial entourage party clattered past. When he could no longer stand the jolting of the carriage the Emperor ordered an early halt for the night at Longueville.

However the sleep of both father and son was to be rudely shattered early the next morning by the loud crashing of multiple explosions, all very close to the villa in which they were staying. Louis awoke to see his father shaking him: "Up, LouLou! Up and dress! The Prussians are shelling the villa."[3] Even as he hurriedly dressed there was the overhead whine of yet another shell. It landed very close. Peering out of the window he realised that it had burst amongst a group of officers casually breakfasting in the garden, and as the smoke slowly drifted away he could see that a number of them had been killed and wounded. Father and son quickly mounted their horses, and escorted by aides, galloped away from the villa, without even waiting for their carriages and the escort squadron of *Cente-Gardes*.

---

3   Ibid., p. 196.

That day — 15ᵗʰ August 1870 — they reached Gravelotte where again they halted early for the night. Twenty years earlier a small triumphal arch had been built in the town to celebrate Louis-Napoleon's tumultuous visit to Alsace-Lorraine. But now, in only three days' time, around this very town, the bloodiest battle of the whole of the Franco-Prussian war would soon be taking place. As the imperial carriages entered Gravelotte weary soldiers were being hastily uprooted from the local inn in order to make room for the new arrivals. This caused much grumbling and resentment.

In the evening light Louis-Napoleon wandered around the little garden, dazed and distraught, whilst his cousin, 'Plon-Plon' settled himself on to a kitchen chair and proceeded to read a book, puffing on a cigar. He had much to feel smug about. After all, he had always opposed this war with Prussia for which he considered the Empress to be largely responsible. He had witnessed all the recent events with growing interest — was it possible that the Prussian Uhlan patrols (which could, and often did, appear without warning) might catch up with, perhaps even kill the precious 'brat'? The very thought gave him much satisfaction.

That evening a courier arrived at the inn with information that Marshal Bazaine had finally decided not to try and link up with MacMahon's Army at Châlons. Because of continuing confusion over the precise whereabouts of Prussian forces, he considered that it would be more sensible to now go back to Metz and avoid being cut off. In his message the Marshal also requested the Emperor's opinion on this change of plan, and in reply Louis-Napoleon advised that the army should continue its progress to Châlons: 'in order,' as he put it, 'to provide reinforcements for the troops hastily preparing to defend Paris.' But this argument made little impact. When Bazaine himself arrived in the town about four o'clock on the morning of 16ᵗʰ August, he personally informed the Emperor that he intended to stand by his earlier decision to turn his troops round and march eastwards, back to Metz. Irritated at this blatant disregard of his advice the Emperor informed Bazaine that he personally intended to continue — alone — on his original journey westwards to Châlons-sur-Marne. At the moment of their parting, outside the inn, Louis-Napoleon issued his last imperial edict: "Marshal! To your charge I commit the last army of France. Think of the Prince Imperial."[4]

As the imperial carriages began to move out in the opposite direction to the army, the spreading jeers from the watching soldiers showed just how much they now were blaming the Emperor for their present plight. In their eyes he was simply abandoning them to their fate. Those same jeers also expressed their disgust at the opulent manner in which the imperial party appeared to be travelling — a procession of smart carriages, immaculate cavalry escort and a large number of staff officers, household officials, cooks, servants, and footmen — all resplendent in imperial livery. 'Le petit Prince' just looked on, bewildered — he had never before heard or seen his father being so publicly derided.

To move at a faster pace Louis-Napoleon now summoned up two regiments of *Chasseurs d'Afrique* to supplement the heavy dragoons of the *Cent-Garde*. Of the

---

4   Ibid., p. 197.

two light cavalry regiments the 1ˢᵗ had fought so valiantly in the Mexican campaign that it had become the first ever to be collectively awarded the *Légion d'honneur*, and the 3ʳᵈ, later, was to fight with great gallantry at Sedan. The Emperor knew he could count on the total loyalty of these Algerian troopers with their magnificent Arab horses, led by General the Marquis de Gallifet, a personal friend, to escort them all safely through the expected Prussian patrols, for even the Prussians were well aware of their fearsome nickname — 'The Blue Butchers'. Once the regiments had arrived the large party quickly cleared the long lines of exhausted troops. And although they now moved at speed along the empty by-roads, a patrol of Prussian Uhlans, with their dark blue uniforms and traditional square-topped *czapska* caps, suddenly appeared from out of a wood and started to gallop towards them. The troopers reigned in their Arab greys, drawing sabres and carbines in anticipation of an attack but the Prussians inexplicably halted, turned about and galloped back into the wood. The Marquis concluded that they had probably recognised the imperial carriages and were now withdrawing in order to collect reinforcements. Discounting the idea they might have equally withdrawn at the sight of so many 'Blue Butchers', he ordered the whole column to move at an even greater speed and as their carriage increasingly swayed from side to side the Emperor could only groan with pain, the sweat pouring down his face. Yet, despite the agonies of his father beside him, the Prince sensed a moment of sheer exhilaration. He kept looking back, hoping that perhaps the Prussians would reappear so that they could at least have a pitched battle; one in which he knew the warlike *Chasseurs d'Afrique* would quickly beat off any Prussian attempt to capture them. Indeed, he felt so uplifted by the incident that when the party subsequently stopped at Étain for a belated meal he went off on his own to find the local telegraph office, sending a brief message to his mother: 'Things are going better and better!'[5]

Amidst all the confusing and depressing messages now reaching Paris perhaps this particular one, from her own son, might have given her some room for hope. Indeed the Emperor, when he saw the Prince's copy, was so moved by his son's optimism that, for a while, he even pretended to take it seriously. The whole party rested a while in Verdun only to be abruptly roused by the village *curé* who, bursting into their lodgings at night, shouted that Prussian troops were already in the streets outside. It was just one more false alarm.

The Emperor now felt quite unable to go any further in a jolting carriage over such roughly-surfaced roads; he ordered a special train to transport all of them the remaining sixty miles to Châlons-sur-Marne. But there was no such train in Verdun. All the engines and rolling-stock at the railway terminus had long since been requisitioned for military use. After much searching the authorities in Verdun managed to procure a decrepit old locomotive engine, together with one dilapidated third-class carriage. At the last minute someone managed to find cushions to place over the wooden benches. Because of the limited space most of the military staff and household servants had to travel behind in a line of ordinary cattle trucks. The two *Chasseur d'Afrique* regiments meanwhile quartered themselves in the town.

5   Ibid., p. 198.

Leaving at eleven that night the train finally chugged at dawn on 17th August into the terminal beside the great base of Châlons-sur-Marne, the Aldershot of the French Army.

Through sleepy eyes the Prince looked at the vast expanse of parade ground over which he and his father had, on previous occasions, so often reviewed the regiments. He wistfully recalled how his own name had been officially inscribed on the roll of the Grenadiers of the Imperial Guard, and how his father had proudly shown him off to all the soldiers, walking hand in hand along the ranks. And then there were those huge open-air Masses on Sundays when, with his father and some 20,000 soldiers, they would stand and kneel before an altar specially erected in the middle of the parade ground. Now these same grounds were littered with the discarded debris of a defeated army — broken down carriages, shattered gun limbers, abandoned equipment and stores.

Whilst they rested in their familiar imperial quarters overlooking the sprawling military complex the Prince noted that a large number of soldiers had been gradually collecting together outside. In his naivety he assumed they had gathered to greet their Emperor — but many of these scruffy and disgruntled troops had intentions far divorced from merely offering loyal greetings. The majority had come from the *Gardes Mobiles de la Seine* — troops who, having previously avoided full -time military service for one reason or another, had now been hastily called-up and sent out of Paris specifically to reinforce the Châlons-based army. They were, for the most part, students, shopkeepers, part-time soldiers — Republicans almost to a man. Their shouts filled the air. 'Go home!' 'You have betrayed us!' 'Go back to the armies you have deserted!' 'Go to Belgium!' 'Go to hell!'

The Emperor sat slumped in a chair. No-one had wanted him at Metz and, as was now becoming clear, no-one wanted him at Châlons. He knew the war was lost and in that defeat, the imperial throne and Empire had likewise been destroyed. All that was left now was his son and heir. Later during that morning, still in disbelief, the Prince had wandered around some of the disorganised tent-lines; here and there, some of the soldiers did cheer him, somewhat half-heartedly, but most were embarrassed at seeing him and simply slumbered on or slouched away. At least, this time, no-one was openly shouting abuse. One staff officer was to describe these demoralised soldiers as: 'Vegetating rather than living, scarcely moving even if you kicked them, grumbling at being disturbed in their weary sleep.'[6]

Although he was only fourteen Louis realised that given competent and inspiring leadership these soldiers could still be made to pull themselves together and that, despite the series of defeats, all was not lost. Walking through the lines he reflected on what had been gleaned from various staff officers: that in many of the battles so far, these same soldiers had managed to inflict very heavy casualties on the Prussians, blunting and sometimes even temporarily halting their advances. All that was needed now was the same inspired leadership with which the Great Napoleon had rallied the ragged French army in Italy in 1796. Many years later Augustin Filon was to opine that, had the Prince Imperial been a seasoned officer

---

6   HORNE, p. 47.

in 1870, allowing for all the qualities he was to later develop, he might equally well have managed to rally the army and save it from total collapse.

As it was, the next move came from 'Plon-Plon'. He succeeded in convincing all the senior staff at Châlons that the paramount requirement now was to dispose of the Emperor. He bluntly told Marshal MacMahon that, for an army commander to be burdened with the overseeing presence of his Sovereign was tantamount: 'to going into battle with a plate of soup on your head, and with instructions on no account to spill a drop of it!'[7] At another embarrassing staff conference on 21st August, 'Plon-Plon' produced his own plan of action. An experienced officer, General Trochu (who had been one of the few senior officers to oppose the war) happened to be present in the camp at Châlons but without a specific command. The proposal therefore was that the Emperor should now formally appoint him Military Governor of Paris, and in that capacity, the general should set off for the capital at once — with the Emperor following not far behind so that he could co-operate with the new Governor in organising its defence. Even as he listened to this proposal, Louis-Napoleon could anticipate Eugénie's likely reaction, but after much subsequent discussion he rather feebly explained that he would, first of all, need to consult with the Regent. At this 'Plon-Plon' erupted: "Consult the Regent! Aren't *you* the ruler of France? Trochu must set off immediately!"[8] The weary Emperor could only meekly acquiesce to his cousin's plan and sign the necessary authorisation. At the same conference it was also agreed that Marshal MacMahon should now withdraw the army from Châlons-sur-Marne base altogether and redeploy it westwards in readiness to defend the capital.

In Paris Eugénie found that her so-called Council of War was now beginning to crumble away. The failure of the Emperor to create a cohesive political party of his own was now beginning to tell. The Council contained every shade of political opinion — Republican, Orleanist, Legitimist, Liberal — and at this momentous time they could only acknowledge one thing — that the Empire was collapsing all around them. Only the Regent-Empress determined otherwise; with little sleep or rest she calmly faced the engulfing storm with remarkable courage and honesty. As early as 6th August she had already realised: "The dynasty is lost — we must think only of France now."[9] It was a measure of her patriotism that the country, not of her birth, was now more important than her family.

Her stance gave strength to many. One of her dwindling band of supporters wrote at the time: 'I've seen the Empress twice since all these misfortunes descended on us. She is as firm as a rock. She told me she was a stranger to fatigue. If everyone had her courage the country would be saved.'[10]

Another observer, although an ardent republican, felt obliged to admit: 'During this terrible ordeal, the Empress showed a grandeur of soul, a magnanimous heart, a sterling courage, a noble self-abnegation, a burning love for France. She was as a person respected; one spoke of her with a sympathy bordering on admiration, but

---

7   JOHN, p. 202.
8   Ibid., p. 203.
9   Ibid., p. 206.
10   TURNBULL, p. 261.

that was all. These sentiments did not go beyond her person and did not help the government which she, as Regent, represented.'[11]

As the crisis deepened she issued a rousing proclamation to the country: 'People of France...The war has begun unfavourably for us. We have met with reverses. Be firm in the face of this and let us make haste to repair it. Let there be among us but one party, France; but one standard, that of national honour. I am here in your midst and, faithful to my mission and my duty, you will see me first in the place of danger to defend the flag of France. I adjure all citizens to maintain order; to trouble it is to conspire with the enemy.'[12] There is no doubt that she sincerely meant every word. If necessary, although born a Spaniard, she would rather die for France than submit to Prussia.

Fearing the worst, however, she now took a number of practical steps to safeguard the future. All the art treasures and contents of museums were secretly moved from Paris to Brest; the crown jewels were deposited in a place of complete safety (she sensibly insisted on a comprehensive receipt); additionally, she urged strengthening the fortifications of Paris by strategically emplacing some heavy naval guns. She even insisted that military engineers prepare for the demolition of such key points as bridges and lock gates. Above all, she ensured that proper arrangements were made to establish a skeletal government which could continue to function from the city of Tours, once Paris had become untenable as the nation's seat of power.

But what she dreaded most at this moment was interference by the Emperor, and in this fear she was supported by the newly-appointed Chief Minister, General Palikao. He had already concluded that the army at Châlons, far from moving westwards towards Paris, should now link-up with Marshal Bazaine at Metz — and the Empress and her Chief Minister now unwittingly proceeded to thwart 'Plon-Plon's scheme. Eugénie sent a private message to her husband which indicated that, if he ever returned to Paris as planned, he would, more likely than not, be pelted: 'not by stones, but with manure'. She insisted that he should remain at Châlons for further orders.

Nonetheless all this was too late to prevent General Trochu from arriving in Paris to take up his new appointment, for which he produced a written authority personally signed by the Emperor. Everyone received him either with indifference or hostility. The Empress was called from bed in the early hours in order to receive him. Irritated at this development, she had every reason to be wary. He was known to be a personal friend of 'Plon-Plon', and in close contact with the Liberals; but, at the same time, she also appreciated that his appointment as Governor would be well received by the people of Paris, now becoming more and more agitated about the security of their city. Those who weeks earlier had been enthusiastically calling for a rapid assault on Berlin were now beginning to worry about their own safety. As a gesture of personal loyalty General Trochu also dramatically promised to defend the Empress with his life. "I am a Catholic, I am a Breton, I am a soldier," he told her,

---

11   Ibid., p. 262.
12   Ibid., p. 264.

"before they reach you, Madame, they will pass over my dead body."[13] It had little effect. She deeply distrusted Trochu's posturing and, for the rest of her life, remained firmly convinced that he had always intended from the start to betray her.

The Empress wrote yet again to her husband. This time her harsh words were tactfully toned down by Filon, now acting as her principal private secretary. But the purport was plain — Louis Napoleon could never return to Paris in the present circumstances; and the implication was clear — he must either bring about a decisive victory or else die on the battlefield. Her farewell words on the day he left Paris — *'Louis, fais ton devoir'* — were never more appropriate.

News now began to filter through of Marshal Bazaine's defeat at Gravelotte (despite the fact that he had actually lost fewer men than the Prussians) and that the remnants of his army, including the Imperial Guard and General Frossard's 2nd Corps, were now penned in at Metz — a force of about 180,000 troops. The First and Second Prussian Armies were surrounding the fortress, whilst the Third was moving rapidly towards Paris. Marshal MacMahon appreciated that he would now have to evacuate Châlons-sur-Marne before that, too, was surrounded by the enemy. Inexplicably he finally decided to go neither west (to Paris) nor east (to Metz), but northwards, towards Rheims. Whilst the Emperor was not involved in any of these decisions, he did exercise what was left of his remaining authority in finally getting rid of his troublesome cousin. 'Plon-Plon' was ordered to travel to Italy and try to persuade his father-in-law, King Victor Emanuel, to come to France's assistance by mounting an immediate invasion of Bavaria. It was a forlorn hope but it did at least enable 'Plon-Plon' to conveniently distance himself from the *débâcle* to come. He was content to leave at once. Needless to say his mission proved hopeless, and Italy never did come to the aid of its former champion.

On 25th August the leading elements of Marshal MacMahon's army, with the Emperor still present in the line of march, arrived in Rheims. Waiting for them was a leading figure from amongst the residual band of imperial supporters, Eugéne Rouher, who was so close to the Emperor that he was often referred to as the *vice-empereur*. He had made the journey to personally urge Louis-Napoleon not to return to Paris if a further revolution was to be avoided. At the same time he also beseeched Marshal MacMahon to now link-up with Bazaine at Metz. In a situation which was changing hourly, MacMahon was not convinced that this would be the best course — but when he subsequently received a formal directive to that effect from the Empress he decided to comply.

Within two days, his army had slowly turned around and begun moving eastwards in the direction of Metz. Thus, without anyone realising it, least of all the Empress who had issued the order, the stage was now being inexorably set for the final disaster at Sedan.

Continuous rain now added to the miseries of the weary troops. Rations were desperately short and as they were leaving now the fertile plains of Champagne, plunging further into a region of dense forests, with few farms, food became even scarcer. On top of all their physical deprivations, the troops were seething with

---

13   RIDLEY p. 566.

resentment and anger at the recent turn of events. Just in time, an officer managed to snatch a rifle from one soldier who was kneeling behind a hedge, taking deliberate aim at the Emperor's carriage as it passed. When invited to explain himself, the soldier grudgingly admitted: "I was just going to pick off the *cochon* (pig) who brought all this on us."[14]

The Emperor now took one more crucial decision. It was now imperative to remove the Prince from out of the battle zone, but made no direct mention of this to Louis. It was impossible to explain to him the complex and constantly changing strategic situation which, at this moment, could conceivably lead to sudden death or humiliating capture. But already the Prince had recognised the widespread demoralisation, the spreading atmosphere of defeat and capitulation. Even so, whatever the soldiers' fulminations against his father, there were still occasional cheers for *'Le petit Prince'* as he spent much of his time, in his own boyish way, trying to encourage and raise their spirits. He was now finding it difficult to eat and sleep properly, and although suffering from violent headaches, tried to keep calm and dignified. The condition of his father was causing additional concern. In almost constant agony, the Emperor had become entirely listless; his long, straggling hair had turned completely white, his face beginning to resemble that of a corpse. The constant pain was beginning to sap his will and undermine his powers of decision.

As they journeyed to and fro a few peasants would still call out: *'Vive L'Empereur'* — but as their gaze switched from father to son, they would shake their heads: — *'Celui-ci est trop jeune et celui-la trop vieux* (This one here is too young, and that one there is too old)!'[15] On more than one occasion the Emperor would order the carriage to stop, so that with the help of his son, he could climb out and rest his body upright against a tree, gasping for breath.

Marshal MacMahon's Army halted at Tourteron on 27th August with the imperial party sandwiched in between the straggling columns. It was now time for father and son to part company. The Emperor had long since determined not to consult the Empress over their son's safety. He knew it would only lead to further arguments and confusion. By way of explanation, he simply told Louis that circumstances required that they should now split and go their separate ways; and that he was to submit to this decision with all the obedience, loyalty and discipline expected of any officer of the French Army. There was no argument, no emotion. Louis meekly accepted his father's wish. The following morning they embraced, and the Prince stood back to formally salute his father for the last time. They were not to see each other again for six months. Louis then climbed into a single carriage, now accompanied by his principal personal aide, Commander Charles Duperré of the French Navy. At the start of the war Duperré had been given command of warship in anticipation of the amphibious landing in North Prussia, but when that project was finally abandoned he had hastened to rejoin the Prince. The two other aides — Colonel Comte Clary and Commandant Lamey — mounted their horses, whilst Captain Watrin, the escort commander, ordered his *Cent-Garde* troop to move out on to the road towards Mézières, away from the army's present line of march. The

14 JOHN, p. 219.
15 Ibid., p. 216.

Prince still had no clear comprehension of the scale of the disaster now overtaking France, nor did he seem to have realised that his father was no longer in overall command. With the eager optimism of youth, he still believed that victory could somehow be snatched from defeat.

Meanwhile the Empress had lost track of her son's whereabouts. Her mother had suggested that perhaps he ought to be sent for safety to Spain, but Eugénie had finally declined the offer — in her reply she wrote:

> Of all my trials, the hardest for my heart is to see Louis (the Prince) threatened by all sorts of danger. But I can change nothing; it is his destiny...He must stay in his country, as long as his country will have us. It is impossible to run away in the hour of danger and return when times are good. Believe me, it is not the throne that I am defending, but honour, and if after the war, when there is no longer a single Prussian on French soil, the country does not want us any more, believe me, I will be happy, and then, far from the noise and the world, I can perhaps forget what I have suffered.[16]

On 31st August, the Prussian Third Army finally caught up with the columns — and MacMahon, realising that there was now no hope of breaking through to Metz still sixty miles away, decided to fall back on to the small fortified town of Sedan. With one French army already bottled up at Metz, the second was now likewise becoming entrapped — with its back to the Belgian frontier (only seven miles away) and two powerful Prussian corps quickly sealing all the approaches from the other three sides. There was only enough food in Sedan for a few days, yet the little town was packed with demoralised and wounded soldiers, further swelled by hordes of terrified refugees from the surrounding countryside. From the heights surrounding the approaches to the town the Prussian artillery began a relentless bombardment.

Despite the chaos and pervading sense of doom, throughout 1st September, the French cavalry continually rode out from Sedan to mount repeated suicidal assaults against the bullets and guns of the encircling Prussians. The futility could be compared to the famous charge of the Light Brigade during the Crimean War. Their commander, General the Marquis de Gallifet, was asked if his cavalry would try once more? "As often as you like," the brave Gallifet is reported to have said, "as long as there is one of us left."[17] And when they charged yet again the King of Prussia, who was watching, could only exclaim in admiration: "Ah! The brave fellows!" Such sentiments would have been echoed by the young Prince Imperial had he been there; and these same words of admiration are inscribed on the special monument to the imperial cavalry, erected by the subsequent Third Republic and which stands today on the ridge at Floing.

During these last hours, in brilliant autumnal sunshine, the Emperor, although he had no command, could be seen riding in agony amongst his troops outside the walls, hoping that a Prussian shell or bullet might mercifully put an end to

16   RIDLEY, p. 567.
17   KURTZ, p. 248.

his humiliation. Earlier that day he had powdered his face with rouge to cover up his death-like pallor which otherwise might have been interpreted as fear. On the tunic of his uniform he had pinned all his decorations; he even wore the same gold-braided *képi* from the battle of Solferino.

After a while, as the carnage continued to increase, the Emperor insisted that a white flag be hoisted over the citadel. As, by his own choice, he no longer held any authority over French forces this decision was clearly a personal one. It was resisted for a long time by the Garrison Commander who objected strongly to the Emperor's interference. Marshal MacMahon himself had been slightly wounded and now conveniently detained in hospital was no longer in a position to exercise supreme command. That evening Louis-Napoleon sent a personal message to the Prussian King: 'Since I could not die in the midst of my troops, I can only put my sword in Your Majesty's hands. I am your Majesty's good brother.'

Perhaps he hoped that by making himself a prisoner of war he could persuade the Prussians to allow his 130,000 troops to formally surrender and then march out from Sedan — with full military honours, bands playing, still bearing their arms. But the Prussians were in no mood for such chivalrous concessions. At this moment they only had one concern — to establish precisely what was being surrendered? Was it simply the Emperor as the head of the imperial family; the citadel of Sedan; or was it the government of France?

Louis-Napoleon drove out of Sedan at 5a.m. on 2nd September 1870 to nearby Donchery to discuss these issues personally with the King of Prussia. But Bismarck abruptly intercepted the carriage, seeking to have all these areas of doubt clearly resolved beforehand. But Louis-Napoleon steadfastly insisted that any general peace terms must be negotiated direct with the Empress-Regent and the government in Paris. This was unsatisfactory. Bismarck appreciated that the Second Empire was unlikely to survive the news of Sedan, and that any peace treaty therefore would have to be concluded with whatever administration succeeded it. At this stage therefore he decided to make Louis-Napoleon a prisoner of war. He also required the commander of all the French forces at Sedan to sign a formal instrument of unconditional surrender before any interview with the King would be permitted to take place. After some wrangling, the surrender document was eventually signed; the Emperor then dispatched the telegram to Paris which dramatically signalled the end of his Empire: *L'armée est defaite et captive. Moi-même je suis prisonnier. Napoleon.'*

The way was now clear for the interview which Louis-Napoleon had requested and which finally took place some seven hours later — at noon. An observer noted: 'the contrast between the two sovereigns...the German tall, upright, square-shouldered, with the flash of success from the keen blue eyes from under the helmet, and the glow of triumph on the fresh cheek; the Frenchman, with weary stoop of the shoulders, his eyes drooping, his lips quivering, bare-headed and dishevelled.'[18] After some platitudinous exchanges about their respective families and further courtesies, praising the skills of each other's armies, the King politely informed the Emperor

18   CHRISTIANSEN, p. 155.

that he would now be escorted to Schloss Wilhemshohe in Germany, which had formerly been the seat of his uncle Jerome, the former King of Westphalia. And Louis-Napoleon, in the hour of his deepest humiliation, could only request in return that he should not have to pass through the ranks of his defeated army. Six weeks earlier he had led them to that first victory at Saarbrucken — now, bereft of sword, disgraced and defeated, he wanted to be spared the final humiliation of their jeers. His wish was granted.

Alone, after the King's departure, the Emperor was to write to his wife:

> Ma chère Eugénie,
> You have no idea how much I have suffered and am still suffering. We have carried out a march contrary to all principles of war and common sense. It was bound to bring disaster; and it has done. I would have preferred to die rather than witness such a shameful surrender, and yet in the existing circumstances it was the only way of stopping 60,000 people from being butchered.
> And again, if that were but the end of my torments! I think of you, our son, our unhappy country. May God protect it! What will happen in Paris?
> I have just seen the King. There were tears in his eyes as he spoke to me of the grief he knew I must be feeling. He has put one of his castles near Hesse-Kassel at my disposal. But what do I care where I go? I'm in despair. *Adieu,* I embrace you tenderly.
> Napoleon [19]

But the fallen Emperor was to be mistaken in believing his surrender might somehow bring the whole war to a speedy end. In three weeks the Prussians had surrounded Paris. But the formal peace treaty between Prussia and France was not to be signed until five months later, on 23rd January 1871.

The Prince Imperial's party had no knowledge of these events. They had arrived in Mézières shortly after midday on 28th August. Here, at last, Louis managed to get a decent night's sleep. Early the following morning a courier arrived with a message from the Emperor, instructing the party to leave immediately for Sedan. They reached that fortified town mid-morning — just three days before the decisive battle. To add to the general misery it was now pouring with rain. Ironically, the Prince was lodged in the very same house which would shortly be occupied by his father, but hardly had they started unpacking before there were cries of panic from nearby streets: — 'The Prussians are coming! The Prussians!' Colonel Clary remounted and quickly galloped around to survey the locality. Whilst there were no Prussians to be seen at the moment, the general air of panic and constant rumours that they might not be far away convinced Commander Duperré that the whole party must now re-pack and return at once to the comparative security of Mézières. But as they re-entered that town any sense of security had long since vanished. Now there were indescribable scenes of chaos — streets blocked by fugitive soldiers, with

---

19   TURNBULL, p. 276.

many wounded from the battlefields lying around in doorways. Nearly all the wine shops had been looted. Discipline appeared to have broken down.

The three aides quickly discussed amongst themselves what should now be done. Ignorant of the true situation they finally concluded that it would probably be best to stay in Mézières that night. But, at about ten o'clock, when the Prince was asleep, and the others were preparing to rest, the prefecture was officially informed that Prussian troops were closing rapidly on to the town. All the officers felt that they had no alternative but to leave at once for Avesnes — a town further north-west which, they judged, must still be secure.

However when Commander Duperré went to waken the Prince he was to be very taken aback by his strong reaction. This time Louis refused point-blank to leave. All this constant moving, the sheer indignity of it all, the feeling of utter helplessness, the realisation that nobody really knew what was happening — it had all become too much for the tired, irritated fourteen year old. He resolutely refused to run away any more. Indeed, he now started to argue that they should fortify the building they were in and fight it out, if necessary, to the last man. In desperation Commander Duperré forcefully reminded the Prince that his father would expect him to always obey the officer charged with his protection and safety. And if the Prussians succeeded in capturing the heir to the Empire that would merely present them with yet another propaganda coup, adding to the general demoralisation of the French people. In bad grace, realising that Duperré was probably right, Louis finally capitulated. But this time only the empty carriage with cavalry escort went by road; a special train having been arranged to transport the Prince and his guardians. They finally left at two in the morning on 30th August arriving at peaceful Asvenes about seven hours later.

Eventually lodgings were found in the Maison Hannoye, presently occupied by the President of the local court. Here the whole party enjoyed three clear days of rest and comparative tranquillity. The local fire brigade mounted a permanent guard outside the house; the *gardes mobile* kept watch on the ramparts, whilst Captain Watrin's troopers patrolled the streets and monitored the approaches to the town. As a further security measure the Prince was not allowed to appear anywhere in public — he had to content himself with resting, reading and playing cards with his hosts. Would he have realised that in this same house — the Maison Hannoye — his great uncle, Napoleon the First, had spent some time just before the Battle of Waterloo and that it was from this same house that he had issued that famous last manifesto to the *Grande Armée*?

As the days passed Commander Duperré was becoming increasingly impatient at the lack of any clear instructions about the Prince's final destination. When they had left the Emperor their only orders had been vague in the extreme — 'to protect the heir and avoid scenes of fighting'. On 30th August Duperré, in some desperation, had dispatched a trooper with the sole task of establishing the Emperor's exact whereabouts but he had not returned. On the afternoon of their third day of seclusion at Avenses, 1st September, the naval commander concluded that the Prince must have some fresh air and so took him out for a short drive. As their escorted carriage passed out of the walled town they could hear in the far distance the thuds of constant bombardment coming from the direction of the Ardennes. Unbeknown to the Prince, at that very moment his father was on a slope outside Sedan, hoping that one of the shells crashing around him would bring his life to a merciful end.

Later that evening rumours began to sweep Avenses — somewhere, somehow, there had been an appalling disaster. This was confirmed the following morning when trains rolled into the town full of unkempt soldiers, caked in mud and blood. Those able to walk were now smashing their way into the food shops and wine cellars, terrorising the inhabitants. The Prince was persuaded yet again to clamber into his carriage, even though he continued to believe that the rumours of yet another crushing defeat could not be true.

In the small town of Landrecies, about ten miles to the west, they were pleasantly surprised on the morning of 2nd September to receive a tumultuous welcome. The people, warned in advance of the Prince's arrival and suitably aroused by the ardent and enthusiastic Bonapartist *maire*, ran out into the streets to greet the party. Firemen lined the route; the town band, parading on the square, struck up the Bonapartist anthem *Partant pour La Syrie*; whilst cries of: *'Vive l'Empereur!'* *'Vive le petit Prince!'* could be heard everywhere. A pretty little girl broke away from the crowd and ran up to the Prince's carriage, armed with a posy of flowers, only to be abruptly shooed away by one of the tense escorting troopers. The Prince looked annoyed at the trooper's gesture; immediately halting the carriage, he called the little girl over, stroked her golden hair and embraced her. The crowd cheered and cheered. Later, once he had been installed in the mayor's own villa, in response to constant shouts and applause, he appeared several times on the balcony, smiling happily and waving his thanks, clearly enjoying this brief respite from the traumas of the last few days.

Concerned at the continuing lack of instructions, Commander Duperré determined to travel to Paris himself to discover what exactly he was now expected to do with the Prince. But even as he was preparing to catch the afternoon train, a courier rode into the town carrying official dispatches from Paris, which included this stinging admonition from the Empress herself:

> I do not approve of these wanderings from town to town. You must make a stand where you are. If the town were captured, it would be time enough to hide your charge and get him away secretly. If Avesnes is impossible, go to Laon: that is a fortified place, and in the theatre of war. You have a care more urgent than security. It is that of honour...each of us must sustain, within the limit of our power, the harsh duties which fall upon us. My heart is rent but resolved. I have no news of my husband, nor of you. I am in terrible anguish, but my will is, first and foremost, that each of you should do his duty. Remember this: I could weep for my son dead or wounded, but a fugitive! I should never forgive you. It is, therefore, to your honour as soldiers that I appeal. Act for the best, but act like soldiers. I cover you and take full responsibility. We shall stand firm in Paris.[20]

20   JOHN, p. 227.

Commander Duperré read this ambiguous, rambling letter with some exasperation. What alternative was there to renewed flight, moving from town to town? What was the point of exposing the fourteen year old heir to needless danger by remaining in one location until it was captured? So what exactly was this 'duty' which the Empress expected of them? It was in order to clarify these points that the worried naval officer resolved to resume his journey to Paris, hoping to have an audience with the Empress personally.

He reached the Tuileries about midnight. There is no record of any direct conversation with the Empress herself. It has been said that she declined to see him, but this ignores the fact that, at least, she would have surely wanted to learn firsthand how her son was faring. However he was able to discuss the whole situation with Augustin Filon and together they agreed a special telegraphic code of some thirty words by which they could safely communicate with one another. Commander Duperré started his return journey at three in the morning, having at least got permission to convey the Prince — not to Laon, which was now known to be in Prussian hands — but eastwards, closer to the frontier with Belgium. At that time no-one in Paris knew of the Emperor's surrender at Sedan. But no sooner had he returned to Landrecies and started making the arrangements for their move than a coded message arrived from Paris which instructed him to: 'Await fresh orders where you are.'

He could only feel mounting frustration at this apparent cancellation of a plan which had only been agreed with Filon a few hours earlier. Later that day another telegram arrived for Duperré; this one from the Mayor of Avesnes: 'MacMahon's Army defeated and captive. The Emperor a prisoner.' At first it was difficult to accept this shattering news, but after receiving official confirmation, the aides decided to keep it to themselves and leave at once for Maubeuge, closer to the frontier, travelling by train for added security. But the last train had already left and the horses were considered unfit and unready at that hour for the journey of about twenty-five miles.

During that night the aides prepared a deception plan to protect their departure by train first thing in the morning. To avoid any possible demonstrations in the town it was publicly announced that the Prince would be attending a solemn High Mass in the local church early on 4th September. As a consequence the majority of the loyal citizens were heading for the church just as the Prince was leaving from the station, at the other side of town, on the first train to Maubeuge. When advised of this further move, he made no objections; nor did he ask for any explanation. The dejected boy now seemed totally resigned to his fate. And it was in the town of Maubeuge that the *Cent-Garde* troopers first heard of the surrender, not from their own officers but from railway porters. As the party drove through the town to their lodgings, public handbills with the official notification of France's humiliating defeat were being pasted up on notice boards. Clearly the terrible news could not be withheld from the Prince for much longer.

In their lodgings, in the privacy of his room, Commander Duperré gently told the Prince about the events at Sedan. The boy listened quietly making no comment. He then asked Duperré to leave the room. As the naval officer feared the young

Prince might suddenly commit suicide using the loaded pistol he always wore on his belt, the three aides took turns to keep him under discreet observation through the door, which had been deliberately left slightly ajar. But they had nothing to fear. Louis held his face in his hands and, for the first time since leaving Paris, sobbed uncontrollably. It was a little while before he had recovered sufficiently to come out of the room and join the others. At lunch he ate nothing, but managed to smile and make pleasant conversation with his hostess, Madame Marchand.

Shortly afterwards Commander Duperré was handed another telegram, this time from the Emperor himself, now held in custody at Bouillon. In it he simply asked for news of his son's whereabouts. Suspicious that the Prussians might likewise be interested, Duperré decided to consult Paris before answering.

He signalled Filon: 'We are at Maubeuge. The Emperor has telegraphed from Bouillon for news of us. When giving it we asked for his commands. We should like yours at the same time. Impatiently waiting your reply. Have seen the ministers' proclamation. Duperré.'

The reply came back at once. 'Received your two dispatches; you will have verbal orders before tonight, and a letter from me by courier. The Empress wishes you to pay no attention to communications from Bouillon. The Emperor cannot appreciate the situation. Filon.'[21]

At almost the same time, Commander Duperré received a follow-up communication from the Emperor which ordered him to leave with the Prince at once for Belgium and thence travel to England. Since this was the clearest and most meaningful instruction he had yet received concerning the Prince's future he wasted no more time in making the necessary arrangements. Meanwhile, crowd tension was rising in Maubeuge — in every cafe and shop the imperial family and government were being denounced and chilling cries of '*trahison*' were beginning to echo around the streets.

The three aides felt it prudent to leave at once and, for greater security, one of them discreetly acquired an assortment of civilian clothes. It took a little time to persuade the Prince to take off his uniform, particularly as they declined to reveal to him their final destination. But already he was beginning to sense that perhaps he was now going into a period of exile from France — but, in his deepest despair, he could never have imagined that it would be for the rest of his life.

At five that afternoon a brief confirmatory order came from Filon: 'Start at once for Belgium'.

The officers' carefully prepared exit plan was now put into effect. The *Cent-Garde* escort discreetly covered their departure. Thereafter, Captain Watrin would lead the troopers out of the town to rejoin their parent regiment in the defence of Paris. Louis sadly said goodbye to his hostess. "I'll be back soon!" he promised and then, dressed in a crude peasant's smock, clambered with the others into a small omnibus. But as they were about to drive off he caught sight of Captain Watrin collecting the escort. He leapt out and flung both arms round his neck: *'Allons! du courage;* goodbye, Watrin! Goodbye!" Deeply moved, the young officer bowed and then saluted the Prince for the last time.

Even as darkness was falling the omnibus carriage set off on the short journey to the nearby Belgian frontier. When evening came the lamps, as usual, were lit in the Prince's rooms and Captain Watrin, after making a public display of his presence, standing by the windows in full dress uniform, then went through the motions of dining with the Prince in his room. The townsfolk assumed Louis was still with them — whereas, at this very moment, he had already crossed the nearby frontier and was safely into neutral Belgium.

The imperial family was now completely scattered. The Emperor en route for Germany and imprisonment; whilst the Empress-Regent was herself preparing to flee from Paris to England. Neither father nor son would ever see France again. And it was to be many years before the widowed Eugénie would be permitted to return, as an ordinary tourist mingling incognito with others, to gaze at the rubble ruins of the Tuileries — the scene of her greatest moments of true courage and grandeur.

Those last days were like a nightmare. Her staunch friend, the Austrian Ambassador, Prince Metternich notified his government about the Empress's condition:

> She is worn out with fatigue and emotion. The day before yesterday, she said to me that all night long she had been telling herself she was mad, that all this was not true, was only the working of a disordered brain. The conviction was so strong that on waking she shed tears of despair to find that she was not mad.[22]

It was not until late on 2nd September that Louis-Napoleon's telegram announcing the capitulation reached the Council. The Empress immediately flew into one of her terrible rages. She continued to protest that Louis-Napoleon should have sought death in battle in preference to turning coward and surrendering. It was as if the dam of her pent-up feelings about him — all his past infidelities, his recent political ineptness and military incompetence — had suddenly burst. In her view he had long since betrayed her as a husband; now he had betrayed France; but, even worse in her eyes, he had finally betrayed and ruined their son. Perhaps, in her intuitive way, she had already sensed that there was never going to be a Napoleon the Fourth. In her rage at his cowardice, she finally capitulated to hysteria, retiring to her rooms to weep. In his memoirs, Filon chose to draw a discreet veil over the Empress's precise words on that occasion. Instead he confined himself to describing that; ' her soul stirred to its innermost depths, poured forth its agony in a torrent of incoherent and mad words...what she said then...I shall die without repeating.'[23]

The government kept the news from the people for about eighteen hours until the afternoon of 3rd September, when General Palikao managed to announce the surrender at Sedan without once mentioning the name of the Emperor. Within hours, in the face of widespread political agitation, the government simply

---

22   JOHN, p. 234.
23   FILON, p. 81.

disintegrated. Standing on a window-sill of the Hôtel de Ville, the popular radical, Leon Gambetta, was to proclaim the birth of the Third Republic and General Trochu, still the Military Governor of the city, its first President. And, as in all previous French revolutions, it was the citizens of the capital city Paris who now took upon themselves the governance of France, without any consideration for, or consultation with, the people of the country as a whole.

The Empress was only finally persuaded to flee the country by the Italian and Austrian Ambassadors. Initially she had refused. She was appalled at Trochu's treachery. For the rest of her life she was neither to forget nor forgive this particular individual, whom she always labelled the 'Judas of the Second Empire.' At first she wanted to challenge his unlawful assumption of power. But the two ambassadors argued that, as the legally appointed Regent, she would always carry that legitimate authority with her wherever she went — and that it was now far more important to avoid being arrested and thus politically neutralised. And she remembered only too well the humiliations heaped on the fat Bourbon King Louis the Eighteenth when he had been compelled to leave in haste (he did not even have time to collect his slippers!), and how old King Louise Philippe and his wife had been bundled out of these same Tuileries, leaving their dinner to be finished by the revolutionaries! But any doubts she may have had were finally resolved when some of her servants began to desert and the mobs gathered outside, baying, as she always feared, for 'That Spanish Woman'.

The Tuileries lay open and unguarded. But Eugénie did not panic. She hastily packed a small handbag and flung a heavy travelling cloak over the black cashmere dress she had worn all that week. She took no money, but scooped up most of her personal jewellery and handed the precious pieces to her loyal friend, Princess Pauline Metternich. She sensibly reasoned that, as the wife of the Austrian Ambassador was an immensely popular figure in Paris, she would be unlikely to be molested and robbed. Eugénie then calmly told Filon to go to his room and collect a loaded revolver, but when he returned the Empress had already left.

She had decided not to wait. Perhaps she recalled the fate of previous court ladies caught by revolutionary mobs. To be publicly mocked, humiliated, even violated was more than she could contemplate. She led the two ambassadors, who were now acting as escorts, not on account of their diplomatic appointments but out of personal friendship for the Empress, to a private passage through the Prince Imperial's quarters, which were in the process of being redecorated and repaired during his absence. As they passed through Eugénie stopped briefly to look, for the last time, at the mementoes of her son. They moved on to a side door, slipped outside and then went as far as the Rue de Rivoli. Thereafter, accompanied only by Madame Lebreton, a lady-in-waiting, she finally had to turn for help to her American dentist, Dr Thomas Evans. He did not hesitate; he succeeded in smuggling the Empress out of Paris in his own carriage, explaining to the sentries on the barricades that his sad lady passenger was 'a poor woman on her way to a lunatic asylum.' But despite the general chaos there is no evidence to suggest that the new authorities of the city were particularly interested in pursuing or detaining the fugitive Empress. President Trochu, having personally sworn to protect her, now probably reasoned that his new administration would be far more effective not having to face the additional problems of dealing with a difficult and determined Regent-Empress who might still rally some support. No doubt he would have been quite happy to learn that she was safely out of the country. Throughout the strain of the long and tiring journey to the coast Eugénie maintained her composure and only collapsed into tears when they reached Deauville. Here Dr Evans persuaded an Englishman, Sir John Burgoyne, whose yacht, the *Gazelle*, was already in the harbour, to take the Empress, Madame Lebreton and himself over to England. Burgoyne later described the scene in a letter; 'The Empress was very much agitated and sobbed bitterly on my saying to her, "*N'ayez pas peur, Madame.*" She managed to reply in passable English, "I am safe with an English gentleman."[24]

They sailed at 7 a.m. on 7th September. To add to the misery she also had to endure a wretched and stormy crossing. Indeed, a number of other larger ships actually foundered in the Channel storms of that day. Later she was to write: 'The little vessel was jumping on the waves like a cork. I thought we were lost. Death in that great tumult seemed to me enviable and sweet. I reflected that I was about to disappear, and that, as my crossing to England had been a secret, no one would ever know what had become of me. Thus an impenetrable mystery would have enwrapped the end of my fate.' In this typically dramatic interpretation of her circumstances the Empress appears to have overlooked the fact that Mrs Evans, who had remained behind in Deauville, for one knew all about her whereabouts. Furthermore, from Deauville, she had also sent off a number of personal messages to friends.

Indeed the storm had been so bad that when she finally landed at Ryde on the Isle of Wight early on 8th September a doctor had to be summoned — by a strange coincidence, he turned out to be the same who had attended the seventy-five year old King Louise Philippe after his sudden flight from France in 1848. But as soon as she learnt that the Prince Imperial was safe and staying in the Marine Hotel in Hastings, she quickly recovered, joining him there at once that evening. And it was from Hastings that she wrote to her mother: 'I want you to know that I only left after the proclamation of the Republic and when I was invaded at the Tuileries. So I did not desert my post.'[25]

The Prince Imperial, dressed in the blouse of a peasant boy, seated in a third class railway carriage, arrived at the station at Mons in Belgium on the evening of 4th September. The party of four quietly dined that evening in the Hôtel de la Couronne. News of their presence soon spread through the town, but curiosity was quickly replaced by a widespread fear that perhaps the Prussians might suddenly enter Belgium in pursuit. This unease was heightened when it became known that the Prussians had coolly informed the King of the Belgians that, in order to avoid internal difficulties across Northern France, they intended to take the captured French Emperor under escort the shortest route to Germany, through Belgium.

It is not surprising therefore that the Provincial Governor advised the Prince Imperial's party to move on directly after their meal to Namur. As they drove to the station in the Governor's carriage a large crowd began to gather outside. The

---

24 TISDALL, p. 73.
25 RIDLEY, p. 572.

Prince said nothing. He clambered into the compartment and stared aimlessly in front of him. Belgians took turns to peer at him through the window. One old lady reappeared several times, wiping away her tears with a handkerchief, murmuring sadly, *'Pauvre petit Prince'*.

They reached Namur early on the morning of 5th September. Meanwhile the Emperor, with an escort of Prussian officers, had already entered Belgium where he rested briefly at the station at Verviers on his way to Kassel in Germany. That afternoon, at the Namur hotel, Commander Duperré was to receive a formal communication in which the Prussians signified their permission for the Emperor to meet with his son. Verviers itself was only about fifty miles away. But everyone knew that the young Prince was totally dispirited and travel-weary, quite unfit to face what could only be an emotional and distressing meeting with his father? On balance, Duperré felt it was best not to tell Louis about the message and the boy was sent instead to bed for a few hours rest.

However Colonel Comte Clary was deputed to travel to Verviers and inform the Emperor that his son was safe and well. He found Louis-Napoleon sitting on a bench at the railway station, head in hands, surrounded by Prussian officers. At first the Emperor became upset when he learnt that his son would not be arriving. Clary soon realised why — for the Emperor had originally intended to take Louis with him into captivity at Wilhelmshohe, the Prussians having raised no objections. After some discussion, however, he clearly had second thoughts for his final words to Clary were concise enough: "Take him to England — get him to England immediately."[26]

That afternoon the Prince Imperial, in ignorance of the close proximity of his father, was smuggled through the kitchen door at the side of the hotel into a waiting cab and accompanied by the three aides travelled by a tortuous route to Namur Central Station. But, despite the attempts at secrecy, hundreds of people were still waiting to see him arrive. Police helped to hustle the boy into the station-master's office where he sat quietly waiting for a special train, provided by the King, to take him direct to the port of Ostend, avoiding the Belgian capital Brussels. In the seclusion of the office he once more had a violent fit of tears — but when the carriage of the train was drawn up directly outside the building, he steeled himself to walk out and, with a gracious smile to everyone, climbed into a compartment. But he declined to wave as the train pulled out.

That night the whole party slept at the Hôtel d'Allemagne at Ostend. Then, in the early hours of 6th September, the Prince boarded the Belgian steamer — *Comte de Flandres*. Commandant Lamey said goodbye; he now intended to travel direct to Paris and notify the Empress. Little did he know that his journey would be pointless since she herself was also en route for England. Once on board the Prince remained in his cabin. But when the steamer had cleared the harbour, he came out on deck and sat there, motionless and silent, staring over the stern of the ship as the coast of Belgium slowly receded out of sight. Forty days had passed since that momentous morning when, alongside his adored father, he had jauntily

26   FILON, p. 83.

set out from Fontainebleau to go to war. All that optimism and self-confidence had now vanished; the France of his soul had been crushed and humiliated; his father a prisoner and his mother, he knew not where. At fourteen his whole world had fallen apart. It was a moment of deep bitterness and sadness which the Prince was never to forget, but it was also the turning point of his life — for, from out of these traumatic experiences '*le petit Prince*' was to be transformed into a confident young man.

Chapter v

A Confident Young Man

THE *COMTE DE FLANDRES* LANDED AT DOVER at about one o'clock on the afternoon of 6th September 1870. A large but silent crowd stood in the pouring rain to watch the young Prince step ashore followed by Commander Duperré and Colonel Clary in their ill-fitting civilian clothes. They were met by a discreet Government official who ushered them through the crowd and then escorted them on their cab journey to the railway station to join the train for Hastings. Here they went straight to the Marine Hotel, where two rooms had already been reserved for them.

By early the following morning a small group of people had already collected by the entrance to the hotel, hoping to catch at least glimpse of the Prince and, after a while, he acknowledged their persistence by coming specially down the entrance steps to greet them. Some of the young girls stepped forward and offered him bunches of flowers which he gracefully accepted and afterwards personally carried back in his arms upstairs. But he insisted on having all his meals in the privacy of his room and, for most of the next two days, remained a virtual recluse inside the hotel.

On the evening of 8th September, just as he was about to retire for the night, there was a commotion in the corridor, followed by a loud knocking on the door. Standing outside was a familiar face which he soon recognised as that of the American dentist, Dr Evans. To his further surprise, as he looked beyond the beaming dentist, he immediately recognised the figure of his mother, shrouded in a travelling cloak with the hood pulled over her head, hurrying along the corridor with her arms already outstretched. As she clasped her son they both burst into a flood of tears. Dr Evans, Commander Duperré, and Colonel Comte Clary could only stand to one side, somewhat embarrassed. Still clinging to each other mother and son moved into the privacy of the room; Commander Duperré stepped forward and gently closed the door.

The following morning newspapers in France announced that both the Empress and the Prince had finally been located in the Marine Hotel at Hastings. With this firm news of their whereabouts, many of their supporters and friends now finalised their own arrangements to leave France and join them. Augustin Filon set off for England that same day. The Comtesse Clary rejoined her husband in the hotel on 10th September. The following day, the Duke of Alba, Eugénie's brother-in-law, arrived with his two daughters, 'Marquinita' and 'Chiquita'. The Conneau family travelled with this party as well. On 12th September they were all joined by Princess Pauline Metternich and Eugéne Rouher, the so-called *vice-empereur*.

Miss Shaw, who had left the Tuileries just before the Empress, had now arrived at Dover looking for her 'boy'. Clearly the hotel was finding it more and more difficult to house this constantly enlarging group of French refugees with any degree of reasonable comfort.

As all the Empress's jewels were now safe in the Austrian Embassy in Paris, Princess Pauline Metternich generously offered to provide Eugénie with a large advance of money on their security. She also privately urged Filon and Dr Evans to start searching for a suitable residence in which to house the Empress and her growing entourage. However, Eugénie continued to insist that she was quite content with the present arrangements. At that time she genuinely did not expect to remain in England for any length of time. Already she had written to Louis-Napoleon in his captivity at Wilhelmshohe to suggest that they should all now settle in Trieste. But in his reply the Emperor had insisted: 'When I am free it is in England I should like to settle, with you and Louis, in a little cottage with bow windows and climbing plants.'[1]

Despite the hurt and pain at the humiliation of Sedan her feelings towards her husband were slowly beginning to change. She had softened a great deal since that agonising moment in the Tuileries when she had roundly abused him, in his absence, for surrendering to the Prussians. In her subsequent disgust at the apparent treachery of General Trochu and many others who had ostensibly supported her during those final days, she had gradually come round to the view that Louis-Napoleon might, after all, have been shabbily treated by the nation to whom he had devoted the whole of his life and by certain people who owed their every advancement to him. In the stress of their present misfortunes, she began to develop a genuine compassion for the plight of the man who, now shorn of all power, ill and isolated, was languishing in a captivity that was to last over six months. She finally resolved to try and meet his wishes about their future home, at least in the spirit if not the precise letter.

Dr Evans and Filon enquired around all the local estate agents, whilst many people began writing to the Empress offering to place their own houses at her disposal. Eugénie had always enjoyed a special public favour in England and, as she was now becoming aware, there were many people who greatly sympathised with her plight. A royal equerry arrived at the hotel with a personal message in French from the Prince of Wales, in which he offered Eugénie the use his own residence, Chiswick House, beside the Thames. This impulsive gesture on his part, without regard to the political and propaganda implications, was subsequently to infuriate Queen Victoria. The Foreign Secretary, Lord Granville, was to be equally annoyed at the Prince's presumption, remarking caustically that: 'the only good thing about H.R.H's letter was his French.'[2]

Fortunately, the problem had already resolved itself. The Empress could not have accepted the Prince's generous offer even if she had wanted to. A lease had already been signed for Camden Place at Chislehurst. The suggestion had originally been made by a Mr Nathaniel Strode and after personal inspection by Commander

1   JOHN, p. 248.
2   TISDALL, p. 82.

Duperré and Madame Lebreton, the Empress, on the basis of their glowing descriptions, decided to accept the offer. It may not have been a 'little cottage with bow windows', but, by a strange coincidence unbeknown to Eugénie, the house was already well known to her husband from the period of his second exile. Nor, at that time, was the Empress aware that Mr Strode in fact also knew the Emperor well. Nor was she aware that, nine years earlier, her husband had secretly authorised the payment of 90,000 francs from the Civil List to Mr Strode — a payment which was first made public in 1873 by the new Republican Government as part of its campaign to discredit the fallen Emperor. It is not clear why this payment was made. Theories have ranged from securing Camden Place in advance as a possible retreat — to repaying one of his English mistresses, through Strode's good offices, for loans which had helped finance his earlier political campaigns.

Camden Place today is a residential golf club with only a prominent wall plaque to commemorate its former illustrious tenants. Although only fifteen miles from London, the house, at that time, could genuinely be described as being located in the Kent countryside, on the edge of the common at Chislehurst. A medium-sized Georgian house of red brick, three storeys high, it stood in pleasant grounds surrounded by many trees which secluded it from prying eyes. The rent was several hundred pounds a year. Mr Strode happened to be a keen Francophil and, in keeping with the fashion of the time, had filled the house with costly French furniture and *objets d'art*. But the Empress was more drawn to the house by the fact that it had its own private little chapel. Close to hand, in Chislehurst itself, there was also the small Roman Catholic Church of St Mary.

At the front of Camden Place was emblazoned the Strode family motto — *Malo mori quam foederi*. When he first saw it, the Prince Imperial, seeking to conceal his ignorance of Latin, discreetly asked Mademoiselle Marie de Laminat, a newly-arrived lady in waiting, how it should best be translated. 'Better death than desertion.' she suggested. Louis liked that. 'That's fine!' he cried. 'That's the sort of Latin I like!'[3]

The house was soon to be filled to overflowing. The Murats, the Mouchys, the Duc de Bassano, the Aguados and Rouher families all started to arrive from France to form a Tuileries court in miniature. Additionally, the household included a supporting staff of thirty-two other ladies and gentlemen, plus twenty-three servants, amongst whom was Uhlmann, the Prince's valet. In fact by the time the national census took place in 1871 a total of sixty-two people were registered as being permanent inmates of the house! It could indeed be described as being the imperial court, albeit in exile.

Of necessity, others were soon to be moved into alternative accommodation in the neighbourhood. The Clarys occupied Oak Lodge, a smaller house at the other side of the grounds. Comtesse Davilliers and her daughter established themselves in the village of Chislehurst. The Duc de Bassano (the imperial Chamberlain) and the Aguados family rented houses in Aldborough whilst Eugéne Rouher finally settled with his family in Richmond.

---

3   JOHN, p. 249.

But there was to be an unexpected embarrassment from the moment the Empress first set foot in the house on 24th September. It soon became evident there had been some misunderstanding over the precise terms of the lease. Clearly, Mr Strode was under the impression that, far from renting the house exclusively for herself, the Empress was staying as his personal guest — and the so-called rent money was really no more than a contribution towards the cost of maintaining the house and improving the grounds to an appropriate standard. Eugénie therefore was a bit surprised to learn that Mr Strode and his steward intended to remain in the house; but she started to become annoyed when they appeared at table for every meal. Mr Strode was genial, polite but endlessly boring. And a distracted Eugénie was simply in no mood to be engaged in constant conversation with the talkative Mr Strode at every single meal. To add to all her other discomforts was the news, received just before she left Hastings, that King Victor Emanuel had succeeded in uniting Italy by finally bombarding and then occupying the Holy City of Rome. Thus, at a stroke, all her lifelong exertions to shield and protect the Papacy had also come to nought. This was a bitter personal blow which simply aggravated the vexatious problem of what to do about Mr Strode. Finally, Filon was instructed to somehow resolve this intolerable situation. The tutor must have shown great skill and tact, since the owner and his steward abruptly left without any complaint or ill-feeling, returning to London the following day.

In her new residence the Empress continued to conduct affairs of State. She may have fled the country but she was still legally and constitutionally the Empress-Regent. The Provisional government had tried to open peace talks with the Prussians, but these had been immediately broken off when Bismarck demanded the permanent cession of Alsace and a large part of Lorraine. Jules Favre, the new French Vice-President, argued that as Napoleon the Third and not the French people had actually started the war, Prussia's peace terms should be less harsh. But Bismarck was in no mood for quibbling. He continued to demand the cessation and when Favre finally refused, the Prussian Chancellor threatened to restore the Emperor to power and negotiate the transfer of the two provinces directly with him. In the meantime, Paris, now encircled, was being starved and bombarded into submission.

As Louis-Napoleon consistently declined to negotiate with the Prussians as long as he remained a prisoner-of-war, Bismarck, during October, started to make secret overtures, through Count Bernsdorff his ambassador in London, direct to Eugénie at Chislehurst. He rather hoped that, as Regent, she could be persuaded to instruct Marshal Bazaine to surrender his army which remained totally surrounded at Metz. He even indicated that, if she would agree to cede Alsace and Lorraine, he would consider using Prussian troops to forcibly restore the Emperor. Ever the patriot she steadfastly refused to enter into any such negotiations. She may have been a foreigner, but it was as unthinkable to her as to any Frenchman that France should agree to the permanent loss of Alsace and Lorraine. In desperation she wrote personally to King William of Prussia asking him not to annex these border territories. He replied with his customary courtesy, acknowledging her distress, but politely insisting that possession of Alsace and Lorraine was essential for Germany's future security. At this time she also addressed personal appeals to both the Tsar and the Emperor Franz Joseph, asking for their support in bringing the war to a close.

An unwelcome visitor during those early days at Camden Place was 'Plon-Plon.' He had left his young Italian wife behind in France and was now living openly in London with his famous mistress, Cora Pearl. Inevitably the first meeting ended in acrimony. "If you had been in Paris on 4th September (the day on which the new Republic was declared) you might have been able to give us good advice. But you were absent, as at the moment of danger you have often been — to your regret, I do not doubt."[4] Without a word 'Plon-Plon' immediately left and returned to London.

At the end of October, with the approval of the Prussians, the Empress accompanied only by Comte Clary travelled through Belgium to Wilhelmshöhe to spend three days with her husband. She was agreeably surprised to find him comparatively fit and well. Freed from the burden of responsibility, enjoying long walks, fresh air and relaxation, the Emperor's health had clearly improved. He endorsed her refusal to negotiate with Bismarck. But even as she was on the point of departing news arrived that Marshal Bazaine, after being besieged at Metz for almost three months, had finally surrendered of his own volition — without obtaining the authority of the French Provisional government. In Paris he was immediately denounced as a traitor. Subsequently he was to join the Emperor in captivity and after the armistice was sent back to Paris — to be tried for treason. Although sentenced to death he succeeded in escaping from prison and eventually found political asylum in Madrid.

On return to England she wrote to her husband: 'We are united, united a hundred times more because of our sufferings and our hopes are melted into one on the dear young head of Louis. The darker the future is, the more one feels the need to lean on one another.'[5]

The first members of the British Royal family to officially call on the Empress were the Prince and Princess of Wales. They were soon followed by the Queen's daughters, Princess Helena and Princess Louise. Finally, on 30th November, the Queen herself arrived at Camden Place accompanied by her youngest daughter, the thirteen year old Princess Beatrice.

As was her habit Queen Victoria described the day's events in her private journal: 'At the door [of Camden Place] stood the poor Empress, in black, the Prince Imperial and, a little behind, the Ladies and Gentlemen. The Empress at once led me through a sort of corridor or vestibule and an ante-room into a drawing-room with a bow window. Everything was like a French house and many pretty things about. The Empress and Prince Imperial alone came in, and she asked me to sit down near her on the sofa. She looks very thin and pale, but still very handsome. There is an expression of deep sadness in her face, and she frequently had tears in her eyes...She said how much had happened since we had met at Paris and that she could not forget the dreadful impressions of her departure from there. She had remained as long as she could, but once General Trochu had allowed the Chambers to be taken possession of by the populace, there was nothing to be done but to go

4   Ibid., p. 251.
5   TURNBULL, p. 305.

away. The garden had been already full of people who were entering the Tuileries, and there had been no troops to resist them. The night before she had lain down fully dressed, on her bed. The crossing had been fearful. Afterwards she talked of other things. The Prince Imperial is a nice little boy, but rather short and stumpy. His eyes are rather like those of his mother, but otherwise I think him more like the Emperor... We stayed about half an hour and then left... The Empress again most kindly came to the door. It was a sad visit and seemed like a strange dream.'[6]

A week later, as required by protocol, the Empress and her son made their return call on the Queen at Windsor Castle. 'She (Eugénie) was very nervous when she arrived, and as she walked upstairs said cryingly: *"Cela m'a fait une telle émotion,"* and quite sobbed. I pressed her poor little hand and took her to the Audience Room. The Prince Imperial came in with the Empress. She took an interest in the room which she said she had not seen before, and spoke of Windsor generally. Arthur and Leopold took the little Prince to see the castle... The Empress left at four. What a fearful contrast to her visit here in '55! Then all was state and pomp, wild excitement and enthusiasm — and now?... The poor Empress looked so lovely in her simple black, and so touching in her gentleness and submission.[7]

Such sentiments however would not have been echoed by many of her entourage at Camden Place. Away from the forbidding presence of Queen Victoria the Empress was anything but gentle and submissive. Her favourite lady in waiting, the young Marie de Larminat, recalled the true situation: 'She found it difficult to forgive; a caustic article in a newspaper, an odious insinuation; or a mere nothing would wound her to the quick, and sometimes put her completely out of humour, and we would pass some unpleasant hours. Her impetuous, passionate nature must have made her suffer more intensely than others.[8]

Almost every evening, after dinner, the dreaded subject of General Trochu would arise. Marie de Larminat learnt to hate that name as much as her mistress. His treacherous behaviour had so enraged the Empress that she would often talk about it for hours, losing all track of time. On one occasion, when the hall clock had chimed a quarter to one in the morning, Marie de Larminat could barely suppress a yawn. The Empress interrupted the flow to ask what time it was. "Madame," she explained, "it's forty-five minutes past *Trochu*." Eugénie laughed. "Yes, you're quite right — I talk of nothing else — but then how can I think of anything else?"[9]

Despite their ostensibly close rapport Queen Victoria, in fact, was never to experience Eugénie's personality in the round. The Empress took care to display only those aspects of her volatile and complex character she wished the Queen to see. Nonetheless the shock of the Second French Empire's unexpected and sudden collapse; the Empress's terrifying flight from Paris and now the cruel separation from her sick husband, had deeply touched the widowed Queen and, from now on, their relationship was to develop into something deeper than mere acquaintance. In time Queen Victoria was to become the Empress's staunchest protector and

6   BUCKLE, *The Letters of Queen Victoria*, Series 2, Volume 2, pp. 89-90.
7   ARONSON, p. 141.
8   Ibid., p. 142.
9   JOHN, p. 255.

champion in this country, despite the political difficulties this often created with her Ministers. This generous and steadfast support was to become a decisive factor in the Empress's final willingness to settle permanently in England. And it was not long before the Queen was to exercise an equally influential patronage over the fortunes of the young Prince Imperial.

Filon was able to observe both ladies at close quarters; in his recollections he analysed and compared them: 'The Queen was hardworking and methodical, desirous of housing facts in her brain and marshalling them in good order; the Empress was impulsive like all her race, but incapable of continuing any regular routine, quick to perceive a truth which might have escaped better-trained eyes, yet losing sight of it again after much reflection and discussion: the one woman was very reserved, the other very imprudent, but both were incapable of deceit; they had reached the age when one esteems sincerity above everything.'[10] He might have added that both were strong characters in their own right, with great physical and moral courage.

Of the many problems facing mother and son at this time the least pressing was actually money. Eugénie's financial assets were quite considerable. She personally owned a number of properties in addition to the Villa Eugénie at Biarritz and these had all been quickly sold off. Before leaving France she had also taken the precaution of transferring substantial cash holdings to banks in Spain. Many of her personal jewels were likewise to be disposed of by Rothchilds at auction. By the end of the first year of exile the Empress could rely on a regular income of about £75,000 a year, with even larger sums tied up in capital. Today, income and capital would total many millions of pounds. She was thus quite independent financially and, during their exile, a great deal wealthier than her husband.

Of all the refugees now collecting around Chislehurst it was the Prince Imperial who continued to suffer the most. For many months after arriving in England he seemed to care for nothing. The normally ebullient, enthusiastic young boy was now largely withdrawn and silent. In his memoirs, Filon recorded that when he first saw him again: 'He hardly spoke. His face, in which his impressions were generally reflected with such animation, had grown pale and impassive like the Emperor's. One might decipher it in an immense and grievous fatigue in which his spirit shared, the fatigue of a child who has undergone a physical and mental trial far beyond his years.'[11] Everyone tried unsuccessfully to shield him from the depressing news emanating from France but he soon learnt what was happening from various English newspapers to which he had access. The unauthorised capitulation of Marshal Bazaine, and the continuing siege and starvation of Paris only added to his miseries.

At the tender age of fourteen he was having to face some deeply disturbing truths. The happy innocence of his childhood had now been shattered for ever. For the first time he began to learn the meaning of such concepts such as 'loyalty', 'betrayal' and 'treason'. He felt deeply ashamed about the circumstances of his flight from France — smuggled out in shabby peasant clothes like a common deserter

10   FILON, Augustin. *Souvenirs sur l'Imperatrice Eugénie.* p. 29.
11   FILON, Augustin. *The Prince Imperial.* p. 84.

quitting his place of duty. He re-acted badly to the press suggestions of cowardice, to the accusation that he had abandoned his country at the very moment when so many of his fellow countrymen were continuing to fight and lose their lives. In his misery, he began to wish he had been captured and imprisoned alongside the Emperor.

Now he was exiled, isolated, a refugee in a foreign country whilst his homeland continued its struggle against Prussia. And whilst he could understand the Prussian disparagement of his father, the vilification now being unleashed on the Second Empire by his own fellow countrymen came as a severe shock. It was hard to accept that so many Frenchmen could invent such damaging stories simply to slander and belittle his parents and himself. Until the war the Prince had thoroughly enjoyed his position as the 'Child of France', even if he had largely taken it for granted; now he began to perceive his birthright, not as just a privilege to be enjoyed but as a sacred duty and a point of honour — a birthright which had already cost him much in personal terms — the loss of his home, friends, his beloved uniform and the freedom to live amongst his own people. Deprived of all the things most dear to him he could only feel deeply unhappy, spiritually lost, a stranger in a foreign land. On his fifteenth birthday one of the ladies asked what would really make him happy. He did not hesitate: "I would give my name, rank, prospects — everything I have in the world — only for a commission as lieutenant in the French Army!"[12]

At Camden Place Filon occupied a room next to the Prince; and the faithful Uhlmann often slept across the Prince's door, always at immediate call. The tutor quickly resumed classes for the two boys. 'Tell Louis he must get on with his studies' his father had instructed from Wilhelmshohe. Filon himself taught the majority of the subjects, but engaged outside tutors for mathematics and German. He also reconstituted a library to support their studies. But the Prince considered the continuation of these dreary lessons after all his recent turbulent experiences as a complete anti-climax. He simply could not accept the need to continue his studies when the war, in which he had already been a participant, was still being waged? And now there was no General Frossard to oversee the military aspects of his education and explain to him why so many things had gone wrong. In fact, unbeknown to the Prince, his former military governor had been bottled-up in Metz with Marshal Bazaine and eventually, like him, had gone into captivity. The Prince was never to see him again.

Apart from the routine of formal lessons, he would usually ride with Colonel Comte Clary and Louis Conneau every day from two to four. Bedtime was normally half-past nine. Occasionally, there were other diversions. Suitably escorted he might spend an evening at the theatre or opera — not that he was ever really enthusiastic about the performing arts. Sometimes, instead of riding, he would go on local sightseeing trips with Filon. Princess Pauline Metternich arranged for him to visit the Tower of London; he was also taken to Westminster where the Speaker personally explained to him the workings of Parliament. Later he went to view Brunel's famous steamship, the *Great Eastern*, at Sheerness.

---

12   JOHN, p. 251.

The Emperor finally rejoined his family at Chislehurst on 20th March 1871, four days too late for his son's fifteenth birthday. Almost two months earlier — on 28th January — the Prussians had agreed an armistice to enable the French people to elect a National Assembly which would be capable of bringing the war to a conclusion. Although those in favour of restoring a Monarchy to France secured the majority seats they were to be hopelessly divided over the claims of rival Pretenders. Nonetheless Thiers obtained the necessary authority to negotiate with the Prussians. The terms were unexpectedly harsh. Besides ceding Alsace and Lorraine, France was also required to pay a huge indemnity of 5,000 million francs in gold. Furthermore, a German army of occupation would remain in the country until such time as that sum had been fully paid. And, as if to add insult to injury, only eleven days before, a humiliated France had been made to witness King William of Prussia being proclaimed Emperor of a united Germany in the Hall of Mirrors at the Palace of Versailles. On 8th February, for the first time, the captive Emperor had spoken out publicly, challenging the legality of the so-called Provisional government but by March, the new National Assembly, meeting in Bordeaux, had formally deposed Napoleon the Third, holding him personally responsible 'for all our misfortunes and the ruin, the invasion and the dismemberment of France.' Only five deputies voted against the motion of deposition and they were all Bonapartists. The Emperor protested in vain to the President of the Assembly, Jules Grevy, at the unfairness of this judgement and against the deposition, since it had not been sanctioned by the people who originally elected him. He received no reply.

Under the peace treaty all prisoners were to be freed and on 19th March Louis-Napoleon finally left for England where, accompanied by his doctor, Baron Corvisart and private secretary, Franceschini Pietri, he was met at Dover by his wife and son. To his genuine surprise he was also warmly received by a huge crowd of onlookers. They cheered and applauded. He was bombarded with flowers. It was only with difficulty that the police managed to clear a passage for the imperial family to the railway station. It was the Emperor's first experience of the Englishman's traditional sympathy for a gallant loser and it raised his spirits enormously. In a way he was really coming home. His rise to power had, after all, begun in England and now that the years of glory were over he was simply returning to the start point. Amongst the spectators that day was a reporter from *The Times*. The following morning the newspaper was asking all the right questions about the enthusiastic reception:

> What are we to think, and what will the Germans think, and what will the French people think, of all this effusive and unqualified admiration? What, indeed, will Louis Napoleon, himself, think of it, when the quietude of Chislehurst enables him to review the events of the day?[13]

Perhaps he would ruminate on a strange event which had taken place on the very day of his return. Joining the special train at Dover they had all been surprised — and somewhat embarrassed — to find themselves face to face with the Orleans

---

13   Ibid., p. 252.

family, the sons of the deposed King Louis-Philippe, who were now on their way back to France to stake their own claim to the vacant throne! The Empress hesitated — whilst her husband and son bowed and doffed their hats. The Orleans family likewise acknowledged their gesture and, without a single word passing between them, hurried to the waiting steamer.

A few days after the Emperor had taken up residence at Camden Place, adding to the crowdedness with his own staff (less distinguished members of the suite now had to sleep two or even three to a room), the Prince of Wales arrived with an invitation from his mother for Louis-Napoleon to pay a private visit to Windsor. In making this invitation the Queen simply shrugged off comments about its political inadvisability from her Ministers. The government was not alone in treating the refugee Emperor with coolness — most of the English aristocracy likewise felt it prudent to stand to one side, at least for the moment.

On the day of his visit the Queen observed in her journal that: 'he had grown very stout and grey, and his moustaches are no longer curled and waxed as formerly.' As they talked in the audience room, the Queen found herself once more responding to 'that same pleasing, gentle and gracious manner' which had so captivated her at their first meeting in 1855. Now they discussed his captivity; the deteriorating situation in France; and Napoleon's continuing admiration for Great Britain.

As was customary the Queen returned the visit a few days later. This time she drove from Chislehurst station through cheering crowds and at the door of Camden Place was met by the Prince Imperial — 'looking very much better' — and inside, by the Emperor and Empress. Their conversation was largely devoted to the current situation in Paris, where the civil war — between the revolutionary Communards who had seized the city and troops of the new Republic — was now in full spate. The fighting was to last two months with many atrocities on both sides. In one week alone over twenty thousand people were killed. The spectacle of Frenchmen killing Frenchmen in this way was to cause widespread distress both in this country and abroad, with the Emperor always maintaining that, had he remained in power, this tragedy might have been avoided. By the time the civil war was over almost half of Paris had been totally gutted by fire. The two former imperial residences, the Tuileries and Saint-Cloud, lay in ruins. When the Queen departed from Camden Place she had particularly noted the Emperor's stoicism about all these various misfortunes which had come one after the other. Indeed, this calmness and lack of rancour was to be much commented upon by everyone.

The Empress, in later years, was to pay particular tribute to her husband's great qualities of forgiveness which she tried hard but failed to match. 'I want to tell you how fine he was,' she once recounted to a friend, 'how unselfish, how generous. In our happy times I always found him simple and good, kindly and compassionate: he would put up with opposition and misrepresentation with wonderful compliance... when we were overwhelmed with misfortune, his stoicism and gentleness were sublime. You should have seen him during those last years at Chislehurst: never a word of complaint, or blame, or abuse. I often used to beg him to defend himself, to repulse some imprudent attack or the vile execrations hurled at him, to check once and for all the flood of insults that were endlessly pouring over us. But he would reply gently: "No, I shall not defend myself...sometimes a disaster falls upon a nation of such a kind that it is justified in blaming it all, even unfairly, upon its ruler...A sovereign can offer no excuses, he can plead no extenuating circumstances. It is his highest prerogative to shoulder all the responsibilities incurred by those who have served him...or those who have betrayed him.'" [14]

During these last years, Louis-Napoleon and his wife were to enjoy a close, affectionate relationship, a comforting happiness in their shared misfortune which had hitherto always eluded them. The Emperor, in particular, was full of admiration and gratitude for his wife's conduct as Regent in Paris during those final dreadful days. To her and to others, he described the circumstances at Sedan — how 14,000 soldiers had already been either killed or wounded; that it would have been an act of utter irresponsibility to allow the slaughter to continue when the battle had clearly been lost. But the principal beneficiary from the presence of the Emperor was his son. The prospect of now being able to spend all his days in close proximity to his father gave the fifteen year old a significant boost to his morale. And Louis-Napoleon somehow managed to sublimate all his regrets over past failures into the triumphant future he was constantly prophesying for his son. He had no doubt that one day he would be crowned Napoleon the Fourth and thus carry the Napoleonic succession into the new Twentieth Century.

"You know," he once remarked at Camden Place, "we're a mixed lot here. We belong to all parties. Conneau there is a Republican — always was. Madame Lebreton is an *Orléanist*. The Empress is a *Légitimist* — she thinks the Comte de Chambord so dignified, and even admires his proclamations. And I am Socialist, as we all know."

"But in that case," protested Louis, "who are the Bonapartists?"

The Emperor put an arm round him: "*You* are the Bonapartist, dear child." [15]

The father determined to make up for past omissions by now personally educating his son in all the complexities of French and European politics. The two of them would walk for hours in the grounds of Camden Place, the father with his invalid's dragging step, one hand on Louis's shoulder. Now, for the first time, Louis heard at firsthand the detailed story of his father's lifelong struggle for power, the early abortive plots, the final *coup d'état,* the significance of Bonapartism, the true causes of the recent war, the reasons for the surrender at Sedan and, perhaps most important for the Prince, the prospects of a Napoleonic restoration. One consequence of their many discussions together was that the Emperor now began to appreciate, probably for the first time, that his son, an otherwise indifferent student, really did have the necessary intellectual powers and political imagination to pursue the Napoleonic destiny. All that dreaming, that former lack of concentration and general scholastic backwardness — they all now seemed to have vanished. The boy was displaying an alertness and curiosity, a willingness to listen and learn, which was most gratifying. As a consequence the Emperor chose to include his son at all his regular meetings with Rouher, and with other visitors, whenever serious political matters would be under discussion. In time, helped by his father, the Prince began

---

14   ARONSON, p. 150.
15   JOHN, p. 266.

to see recent events in a much calmer and more balanced way. But nothing could entirely erase his personal distress at the news of the mindless destruction of Saint-Cloud and the ruination of his birthplace, the Tuileries. He was particularly upset to learn that the saintly and distinguished Abbé Deguerry, a personal friend as much as a religious mentor had, at the age of seventy-five, been taken hostage by the Communards. But that distress turned into real grief when he learnt that the Abbé, together with the sick Archbishop of Paris, Monsignor Darboy (who had so gloomily prophesied at his first Holy Communion) and four other priests had been dragged out of prison into an alleyway, where, after the old Archbishop had courageously insisted on personally blessing each of his colleagues, they were all gunned down. Subsequently the bodies were deliberately mutilated with bayonets. The appalling horrors of the civil war in Paris made a lasting impression on the Prince. The fear of any possible recurrence constrained much of his political thinking in the years to come, particularly the forcible seizure of power by *coup d'état* — a course urged upon him more than once by enthusiastic supporters.

Many of these supporters were now themselves refugees from France — and shortly after their arrival in England made their presence known to the Emperor and his family. Amongst those seeking to pay their respects were the Prince of Moscow, the Duc de Padoue, Generals Castelnau and Pajol, the former Minister of the Interior and Baron Lambert accompanied by his son Tristan, one the Prince's closest friends. They all brought some reassuring news — how many people in France now regretted the fall of the Empire. It raised the spirits of the little 'Court of Camden Place'.

Louis-Napoleon, in reassessing his son's potential, now recognised the penalties of his hitherto entirely private education. He now decided Louis ought to meet and get to know ordinary people. Considering that he would be comparatively safe in the disinterested company of English boys the Emperor misguidedly enrolled the Prince, together with Louis Conneau, for unspecified studies at King's College beside Waterloo Bridge. Unfortunately, this ill-conceived decision was taken on the suggestion of an English friend without any prior consultation with the tutor. Filon, not surprisingly, had great difficulty in choosing a suitable course for his fifteen year old *protégés* at an establishment where the majority of students were approaching nineteen or twenty. Thus the two boys spent an entirely fruitless year trying to study elementary physics. Despite the best efforts of their teacher, Professor Adams, they learnt very little. Neither boy had the necessary basic grounding in mathematics or technical English to derive any benefit from such a course. During their disappointing year at the College they were also ignored by most of the other students and thus made no friends of their own. Filon noted that the majority, in any case, belonged to the lower middle classes and, in their religious observance, were strictly Church of England. Indeed, membership of that Church was a prerequisite for admission and consequently a special dispensation had to be made for the two French boys. On their first day they noticed how the majority of the students appeared to spend a lot of their time walking up and down the various corridors — whistling incessantly. Anyone purporting to be a gentleman in the late Nineteenth Century simply did not whistle in public. So the Prince offered his own humorous explanation: "It's not really a school — it's a nest of blackbirds!"[16]

But the experiment was not entirely wasted. During term times Louis thoroughly enjoyed the experience of commuting three times a week into Charing Cross Station and mixing totally incognito with the inhabitants of a great city. The fact that people no longer stopped and stared greatly appealed to him. He soon became accustomed to being jostled by the streams of commuters pouring past him at the station. Peering into shops, sitting in cafes with his tutor and Conneau, enjoying cups of chocolate, mixing with the dirtiest workmen and the smartest city clerks, he slowly began to learn about the real world. During all these exciting new experiences, he constantly bombarded Filon with a barrage of questions about everything he heard and saw.

Queen Victoria also began to take a closer interest in the Prince. She noted how his spirits had risen since the return of his father. Many other leading figures were to become likewise enchanted by the boy's obvious good manners and enthusiasms. Even the austere, severe Mr Gladstone succumbed. They had met, quite by accident, at the railway station at Chislehurst. The Prince had spoken up with confidence and cheerfully told the forbidding statesman all about his course at King's College. Afterwards Filon recorded: 'Mr Gladstone seemed worried at first; his manner was cold and stiff. But gradually his face relaxed and softened, and on parting he looked down on the Imperial lad with a sort of fatherly interest mingled with pity.'[17]

During a royal military review at Bushey Park, to which the Prince had been specially invited, the Queen noted how the crowds cheered him. Many newspapers were to comment on his 'somewhat melancholy grace', whilst the crowds applauded his obvious equestrian expertise. Before leaving the parade ground, the Queen, in front of everyone, summoned him across to her carriage and for quite a while, seated on his horse alongside, he chatted to her in French with an ease and self-confidence which surprised all her entourage. The Queen considered that he looked 'very nice'; and clearly sensed that, with his grace and charm, the young Prince was rapidly acquiring the same smooth sex-appeal of his father. And, in the same way as it had fascinated the young Victoria, it now warmed the old Queen's spirits as well as reminding her of the past.

The family spent a few days in August 1871 at Cowes accompanied by Eugénie's two nieces. The aristocracy, influenced by the Queen's palpable interest, had slowly begun to warm towards the exiles and many of them, likewise on holiday on the Isle of Wight, now offered them generous hospitality. They all went yachting with an American girl, Jennie Jerome, who was soon to become Lady Randolph Churchill, and subsequently the mother of Winston Churchill. She had first been presented to Louis Napoleon in the Tuileries; she was now shocked to see just how 'old, ill and sad' he looked. 'Even in my young eyes,' she was to write later, 'he seemed to have nothing to live for.'[18]

---

16   FILON, p. 93.
17   JOHN, p. 270.
18   RIDLEY, p. 583.

That autumn Eugénie, avoiding France, travelled by sea to Spain in order to see her ailing mother. During her absence the Emperor took his son, Prince Joachim Murat and Louis Conneau, escorted by Comte Clary, to stay for a few days at the Imperial Hotel in Torquay. On the way home they diverted northwards to Bath, spending a day in the city; the Prince Imperial being particularly thrilled by the enthusiastic reception of the people. He wrote to his mother in Spain: 'The Emperor got a terrific welcome: a crowd escorted him from the station to the hotel, and from the hotel to the station, with full accompaniment of hurrahs and handshakings.' In the same letter he also warned her that her last to him had been detained and opened in Paris — 'but I'm only too charmed that *ces messieurs les Républicans* should have had the chance of reading it, for there were only *des sentiments dignes de vous.* They won't publish it you may be sure.'[19]

On their return from Bath to Camden Place, the Emperor gave a first press interview to a newspaper journalist and his comments were to be published internationally. He emphatically denied rumours that he was conspiring to regain power in France. But that did not appease the new government in Paris. Chronically unstable and insecure in the first years, it was always sensitive about various pro-Bonapartist manifestations in Great Britain and made more than one irritable representation to the British government on this subject. There were constant rumours amongst the inhabitants of Chislehurst that secret agents of the Republican government were now living in their midst, even climbing trees in their efforts to peer into Camden Place. The French government even went as far as to formally express its displeasure at the number of people who crossed over from France and collected at Camden Place to celebrate the Prince Imperial's sixteenth birthday on 16th March 1872. On that occasion *The Times* observed that the Prince had been transformed from 'a slight and somewhat effeminate lad to a strong, healthy, well-conditioned youth, an excellent horseman, and in all respects as ruddy and hardy as the majority of English boys of his age. There is in his entire bearing a manly simplicity most engaging, and immediately noticed by all who come into contact with him.'

Daily life at Camden Place soon settled into a routine. As Madame Lebreton described later: 'The Emperor was like an oak tree round which everybody gathered.' Before he entered the course at King's College, under Filon's direction, the Prince would spend every morning at lessons with Louis Conneau. Not until luncheon did the family meet together. The Empress always rose early, and usually passed the morning studying the French and English newspapers. The Emperor invariably got up much later; he would pass the morning in his study; afternoons were often spent granting audiences to a variety of people; otherwise he would often pore over family papers and documents. He particularly cherished all the letters from his mother, Queen Hortense. After the Prince had returned from his customary afternoon ride they would all come together again for tea. In the early evening the family might congregate in the Emperor's little study, when Louis-Napoleon would often read from his mother's letters, pointing out to his son her various shrewd observations

---

19   JOHN, p. 267.

in statecraft. 'Nobody', he often said, 'understood the prodigious mind of your great uncle as well as she.' Sometimes, if the weather was agreeable, all three might then walk together to St Paul's Cray Common. Alternatively, father and son might watch others playing in the billiard-room. After dinner the Emperor would often sit beside the fireplace in the little drawing room. As Eugénie perhaps studied the latest book, Louis-Napoleon would invariably be lost in thought, contemplating the smoke from his cigarette. And from the hall the Prince Imperial might be heard persuading the ladies to play martial airs on the piano, whilst he would often dash up and down, humming the tunes to himself.

The biggest event of the week was the big reception held on most Saturday afternoons. The three o'clock train from London would bring a small army of specially invited guests. Apart from the resident French colony there would many from all strata of British society — not just aristocrats, politicians and military officers, but also scientists, writers, artists, even comedians. On these occasions the Prince and his father would mingle happily with the various groups, making themselves better known to people of influence and standing. At one such reception the Prince was surprised to be handed a packet by a Colonial Officer who happened to be on leave in England. Inside he found a plant. "It is the shoot of a weeping willow," the officer explained. "I have brought it specially from Saint Helena where the tree itself stood right beside the last home of the Emperor Napoleon the First."[20] Louis felt the tears welling in his eyes as he thanked the visitor for his thoughtfulness and generosity. That evening father and son quietly planted the shoot in the grounds of Camden Place, and every week the young tree would be watered by them personally.

But such generous gifts might often be offset by crank mail arriving at the house almost daily. In one letter a young woman, signing herself as 'Marie-Jeanne of the People,' wanted to offer herself to the Emperor so as to give birth to a son who would become the 'Saviour of France'! In another letter a man claimed to be the son of a secret union between the Empress and Comte de Chambord (the principal claimant to the Royal throne of France). He thus considered the Prince Imperial to be his 'half-brother' and invited the Empress to pay his expenses so that he could travel to meet him! Filon himself was to be approached by an American impresario with the offer of a handsome commission were the Emperor to agree to go on display around key cities in the United States! Others wrote insisting that Napoleon was the Anti-Christ as prophesied in the Book of Daniel!

But the public were now to see less and less of the deposed Emperor. Occasionally he might be spotted walking across the common to the Church of St Mary to attend Mass, although he preferred the privacy of their private chapel at Camden Place where the Chislehurst Catholic parish priest, Father Goddard, would officiate. Quite by coincidence the priest had been a former seminarist of *Saint-Sulpice* in France and thus spoke French fluently.

In June 1871 Louis heard a brass band and choir singing *Auld Land Syne* and *God Save the Queen* at the entrance to the grounds, but when he heard the words of *La Marseillaise*, somewhat crudely sung with a strong English accent, interspersed

20   FREREJEAN, p. 176.

with cheers and clapping, he decided he had better go and find his parents. It transpired that the band and choir had been formed from the municipal workers of Greenwich and they were now touring Kent to publicise their annual fete. In response Louis Napoleon walked slowly down to the drive, accompanied by his wife and son, to listen and then thank them. Whereupon one of them boldly stepped forward, doffed his hat and made a short speech. He said that everyone knew the Emperor was a friend of England and expressed the hope that he might soon be restored to his throne. When the Emperor replied that he had always done his best to encourage feelings of friendship between Great Britain and France, the whole group burst into applause and individuals came forward to shake his hand. The family returned to the house profoundly touched.

It was partly the warmth of England's welcome and his continuing popularity that spurred on hopes of a future restoration. But thanks to the intense secrecy with which he surrounded most of his political ventures, the evidence for this last putative *coup* continues to be fragmentary and rather inconclusive. There can be no doubt that he was receiving and dispatching both agents and information to and fro across the Channel. The Republican government genuinely took alarm at the increasing amount of Bonapartist literature in circulation in Paris and elsewhere, and the manner in which the Bonapartists were now organising themselves into a cohesive political force. For example, there were now over sixty Bonapartist newspapers being published throughout France, and of these almost twenty were appearing every day. A number of prominent Bonapartists were known to be journeying to England, spending hours closeted with the Emperor in his study at Camden Plase. 'Plon-Plon' was also in constant consultation with his cousin, and his movements up and down from London were being regularly monitored and notified to Paris.

On 9th December it is believed that a formal meeting of party activists took place in order to finalise all the detailed plans. Inevitably, the restoration was to be conceived in Napoleonic terms, starting with a second legendary 'Return from Elba.' Louis-Napoleon would leave England in secret; join 'Plon-Plon' in Switzerland and together they would enter Lyons, where the area commander was known to be sympathetic to a Bonapartist revival. From Lyons they would march with a number of unspecified loyal regiments on to Paris. All this was confidently expected to be achieved without any bloodshed. It is alleged that the plotters had even chosen their new cabinet in which, amongst others, Marshal MacMahon (later to become President of the Third Republic) would be appointed Minister of War. There is the unsubstantiated claim that they even went as far as to obtain the tacit but secret approval of Bismarck and other European leaders, all of whom genuinely abhorred republicanism and who, for peace of mind, would prefer to see an imperial restoration. Whatever the secret planning and diplomatic overtures there certainly was never going to be a better opportunity for launching a *coup d'état*. France was in a state of political chaos — the Republicans were deeply divided and there was little support for the splintered Royalist factions. Since February 1871 the Bonapartists had managed to win a number of additional seats, discerning a great deal of residual enthusiasm amongst rural communities. This rise in fortune had been crowned by the surprise election, in February 1872, of Eugéne Rouher as deputy for Corsica.

The Emperor now began talking along the same mystical lines he had used in his Ham fortress prison almost thirty years earlier; "I know, I am certain, I am the only solution."[21]

It is not clear whether the Emperor ever discussed his plans with the Prince. The balance of probability is that he did not. Louis-Napoleon, with all his hard-won experience, would surely have recognised that the chances of this final *coup* ever being successful without widespread bloodshed were not particularly high. Indeed, the whole exercise was probably as much to keep Bonapartism in France both alert and expectant than to actually restore him to power. He would also have appreciated that failure, this time, would result in catastrophic consequences for himself and the family. At worst, it might lead to his own execution as an alleged traitor and at best, it would inevitably influence his son's prospects for any legitimate succession. As long as the young Prince remained untarnished by any disreputable past he could always be presented to the French people as an entirely fresh Bonapartist candidate in his own right. It therefore made political sense not to involve Louis; to exclude him altogether from any preparations.

However there is some evidence that Eugénie was busy making plans of her own. With the Tuileries now totally destroyed they would govern from the Louvre. The restored imperial court would be less 'frivolous' and more in touch with the ordinary people who had suffered so much. This time she would eschew politics altogether and devote herself entirely to charitable work. Given good fortune and steady resolve, it might be hoped that Napoleon the Third would be back on his throne by March 1873. The chosen date for the proclamation of the restored Empire was going to be 20th March — four days after the Prince Imperial's seventeenth birthday — a year before his official coming-of-age. But if this plan was to have any hope of success, for which the Emperor would need all his former physical and mental robustness as well as good fortune, he had, first of all, to be fully restored to health. Above all he had to be capable of making a triumphant re-entry into Paris on horseback at the head of his followers without which no restoration, at least in the eyes of the public, would ever be credible. Since arriving at Chislehurst he had only been on horseback three times and on the last occasion had almost collapsed with pain on dismounting. But as he observed to his wife, "I cannot walk on foot at the head of the troops. It would have a still worse effect to enter Paris in a carriage. It is necessary that I ride.."[22] Yet he knew full well that riding now was almost impossible.

The stone in his gall bladder continued to trouble him but this was not the only source of ill-health. He was also suffering from kidney problems. In addition to consulting Conneau and Corvisart, the two French doctors now permanently with him in Camden Place, he sought the advice of Sir William Gull, Sir James Paget and Sir Henry Thompson, the leading British surgeons of the day. Sir Henry Thompson proposed the same stone-crushing operation with which he had been able to cure King Leopold of the Belgians. But first he would need to make a preliminary investigation under chloroform. As always whenever it came to surgical

---

21 TURNBULL, p. 314.
22 FORBES, *Life of Napoleon the Third*, p. 341.

operations the Emperor hesitated. To think it over he took a short holiday at Bognor with Dr Conneau, whilst Eugénie, together with Comte Clary and Louis Conneau, her nephew Carlos, Duc de Huescar and the Duc of Tamames, took her son up to Scotland. This, of course, was the land of her maternal forebears.

Staying at various houses of the nobility they visited many of the famous Scottish sights including Edinburgh, Dalkeith, Abbotsford and the Trossachs. One day they rode up the side of Ben Nevis, climbing the last 3000 feet on foot. Though aged forty-six, the Empress was still fit and sprightly. Everywhere they travelled in Scotland they were received with much warmth, even affection. On the boat journey to the Isle of Skye there were a number of French tourists from Paris — who on return spoke publicly about the manner in which the Imperial party had been greeted. After leaving Scotland the whole family went to Brighton and then to Cowes, where the parents rented Beaulieu House, whilst Louis was ensconced in the nearby villa of Paou Shun together with some teachers. Even so, mother and son were able to bathe and picnic, go sailing and play tennis, away from the oppressive atmosphere of Camden Place. But not every day was given to holiday pursuits. With the assistance of Filon and others, the Prince was also engaged in an intensive crammer course to prepare himself for a new challenge.

Earlier that year a Colonel Manby, known personally to the Emperor from a previous exile, suggested to his old friend that, instead of returning to King's College, the Prince should undergo officer training at the Royal Military Academy at Woolwich. The Emperor enthusiastically supported this suggestion, which eventually obtained the personal approval of the Queen's cousin, the Duke of Cambridge, who occupied the post of Commander-in-Chief of the British Army. The Academy — commonly referred to as 'The Shop' — trained potential officers for the Royal Engineers and Royal Regiment of Artillery. It seemed entirely fitting therefore that Louis, like the Great Napoleon and his father before him, should become skilled at gunnery. Naturally the Prince was ecstatic at the prospect of wearing uniform once more. At the same time, it was accepted that Louis Conneau should also be considered for entry in order to act as a companion, and prepare himself for his own chosen military career in the French Army.

The Governor of the Academy, Major-General Sir Lintorn Simmons, an officer of the Royal Engineers who had rendered particularly distinguished services during the Crimean war, was specially invited to Camden Place to discuss the proposal in more detail. From the outset it was recognised that if the Prince completed the course, he could not, as a French citizen, expect to receive the Queen's Commission. Nor, as the heir to the imperial throne of France, could he be expected to take the customary oath of allegiance to the Queen of Great Britain. Otherwise he would be treated no differently from the other two hundred Gentlemen Cadets at Woolwich. But the Governor also pointed out that no amount of patronage could exempt him from passing the stiff entrance examination, even though other candidates from the British Royal Family had privately been spared the examination. And, in that particular year, there were about five applicants for each individual place at Woolwich.

Now truly motivated for the first time since his arrival in England, Louis began to prepare himself with a dedication and determination which astounded Filon. Additional tutors were engaged. He particularly redoubled efforts to improve his knowledge of mathematics which, he had been warned, would be a major subject during the Woolwich course..

On their return from Cowes the Prince, together with Louis Conneau and Filon, travelled to Woolwich for the entrance examination. They both underwent written tests and individual interviews. The Prince kept calm throughout and acquitted himself reasonably well. The mathematics professor at the Academy even reported that he might possess 'high mathematical powers'; an assessment which caused Filon much surprise! In the event both boys passed — the Prince came 27th out of the 30 other candidates who were also successful, whilst Conneau's own placing was not publicised. The ailing Emperor was to derive immense pleasure from studying the Governor's detailed report which concluded that his son would be eminently suitable for the training. And as the Emperor knew the course took two and a half years, it seems unlikely that he would have agreed to his son's entry if the intention, from the start, was to remove him only a month or so later to participate in that final 'Return from Elba.'

Each year at Woolwich there were two terms; February to June, and August to January. Inexplicably, it was arranged that the Prince and Conneau would not wait until the new January term but enter early in November, towards the end of the second. In October, when his cadet's uniform arrived, the Prince was delighted. He insisted on his mother trying out the new gold and blue pill-box cap, at the correct jaunty angle, and then the busby with its clipped white plume. He even made her struggle into his tight blue and red tunic. The Empress thus pranced up and down the hall like a music hall *artiste,* much to the delight and applause of many of her ladies. There had not been such laughter in the imperial household for a long time.

The Emperor's health now began to further deteriorate. He reluctantly acceded to Sir Henry Thompson's view that a closer investigation, under chloroform, should not be delayed any longer. After a further examination by Sir William Gull and Sir James Paget, Louis-Napoleon wrote to his son who had just started the course at Woolwich:

> My dear boy,
>   The consultation took place today and I am very well satisfied. Sir W. Gull and Sir J. Paget are agreed, and think that with certain not very drastic remedies I shall be cured in a month's time. — I was very sorry at your departure, but as long as you are well and sensible, I shall console myself with thinking of your future career.
>   Je t'embrasse tendrement.
>   Your affectionate father,
>   Napoleon[23]

---

23   FILON, p. 100.

This was to be his last letter to the Prince.

The investigatory operation took place on Christmas Day 1872. Immediately afterwards Sir William Gull could only exclaim in amazement, "Good Heavens! Was that man really on horseback for five hours at the battle of Sedan?"[24] Although the stone was very large, the surgeons still considered that it could be crushed in stages. Now, for the first time, Eugénie was told the true source of the Emperor's constant ill-health.

The first crushing operation took place on 4th January — with a second two days later. After much broken gravel had been successfully removed, Sir Henry Thompson performed a third operation on 7th January. Despite the intense pain Louis-Napoleon bore all these operations with great fortitude. Looking around the room, he once asked, "Where is Louis?" The Empress replied, "He's at Woolwich. Would you like me to send for him?" "No, he's working; we must let him alone."[25]

When his close friend Dr Conneau appeared, the Emperor in a halting voice asked him; "Were you at Sedan?" "Yes, Sire." Louis-Napoleon tried to raise himself up; "We weren't cowards — were we?"[26]

After being further examined by his own doctors as well as by the British team, they all agreed that the Emperor was strong enough to undergo a fourth operation on 9th January. But when Sir Henry Thompson was making the necessary preparations in the bedroom he became alarmed at a sudden change in the Emperor's condition. He immediately sent for Eugénie, who afterwards recounted what happened to Queen Victoria, who, in turn, noted the details in her journal: 'As she came to the door (of his room) Dr Corvisart opened it, calling out 'Father Goddard, Father Goddard,' & she at once saw there was danger. When she entered into the room & kissed the Emperor's hand, they said to him 'Voilà l'Impératrice' but he no longer was able to see her, though he still moved his lips to kiss her. In 5 or 10 minutes afterwards all was over.'[27]

He died at 10.45 a.m. on 9th January 1873. A post-mortem examination, carried out the following day, disclosed that the Emperor had also been suffering from an advanced kidney disease from which he would have probably died in the next few years anyway.

The Prince was in the middle of a trigonometry lesson at the Academy when at ten o'clock he received a message that Comte Clary had just arrived. Louis had last seen his father during the Christmas recess after the first exploratory operation. The Comte explained the latest developments. Camden Place was only twenty minutes away but he was still too late. Rushing through the doorway, he was met in the hall by Doctor Conneau and Baron Corvisart with the sad news. The tearful Empress embraced her son with the dramatic words, "Louis — I have only you now!" With great self-control he knelt at his father's bedside and immediately recited the Lord's Prayer. Filon commented later that when he knelt down he was still only a boy, but

24 JOHN, p. 281.
25 Ibid., p. 282.
26 LACHNITT, p. 177.
27 BUCKLE, *The Letters of Queen Victoria*, Series 2, Volume 2, p. 244.

that when he finally rose to his feet he had suddenly been transformed into a man.[28] That evening, the Clarys took him away from the house to their own home at Oak Lodge.

Queen Victoria was at Osborne House on the Isle of Wight when she received the telegram from the secretary, Franceschini Piétri, '*L'Empereur a cesse de souffrir a 11 heures moins 14. L'Impératrice est dans les larmes.*' She immediately wrote a personal letter of condolence to Eugénie, signing it with all the flourish of the Second Empire, 'Your Imperial Majesty's affectionate sister, Victoria R.' And the majority of the formal messages she subsequently received as Head of State, including those from the German royal family, she arranged to be forwarded to the sixteen year old Prince Imperial — now that he had become Head of the Bonaparte family.

At Oak Lodge the Prince conducted himself with great restraint. Many visitors wished to pay their respects but he would only receive the most important. One knelt before him and kissed his hand, addressing him as 'Sire'. The courtesy irked him; he barely concealed his displeasure. This form of address had always belonged to his father, to hear it now only served to remind that he was no more. Thereafter he took the view that the title of 'Emperor' could only be conferred on him as a result of a majority wish by the people of France. And, despite various representations from his supporters, he always refused to adopt the title — Napoleon the Fourth.

The Empress had gone into deep mourning. She spent most of the time alone, and in tears.

'An enormous name has passed out of the living world into history,' intoned *The Times.* 'Silent, self-reserved and self-controlled, he did not take the world into the secret of his regrets or remorse. If his party raised their heads again, and bragged of a new revolution to their profit while France was struggling still in the social and financial chaos into which they had cast her, we have no reason to believe he gave them encouragement. But the Emperor returned to England, whose life and people he always liked, and lived like an English country gentleman whose shattered health condemns him to retirement and the society of a few inmates.'[29]

Most of the French press, however, thought quite differently. *Le Républicain* described him as 'a man of repression...the adventurer, the vulgar conspirator who did evil.' *L'Avenir* of Rennes commented that if he had died but three years earlier then the lives of two hundred thousand Frenchmen would have been saved; Alsace and Lorraine would still be part of France, and the country five thousand million francs richer. *L'Avenir Nationale* actually regretted his death on the grounds it would no longer be possible to bring him to trial for his illegal seizure of power in December 1851.

On 14th January the body of Napoleon the Third lay in state in the main hall of Camden Place. Over 60,000 people (of whom some 3,000 were French) filed past between midday and ten in the evening, and throughout the following day. Some of the leading figures of the Second Empire appeared to pay their respects — members of the squabbling Bonaparte family; many of the failed marshals and generals; the various discredited Ministers and diplomats. But Marshal MacMahon

28   FILON, p. 101.
29   JOHN, p. 283.

and the Emperor's former Prime Minister, Emile Ollivier, were conspicuous by their deliberate absence. The Emperor lay in a satin-lined coffin with his moustache jauntily waxed and white hair combed forward. They had dressed him in the uniform of a general, adorned with the star of the *Légion d'honneur* and his blue Garter ribbon. Close to his heart lay photographs of the Empress and Prince Imperial. He wore two rings — his own wedding ring, and the ring which had been removed from the Great Napoleon's finger on his deathbed. By his side was the sword surrendered to the King of Prussia.

Next day the body was taken to St Mary's Catholic Church for the funeral. The Prince Imperial and 'Plon-Plon' were the principal mourners, walking directly behind the coffin throughout the thirty minute journey. To many of the onlookers, the young heir looked slight and small — surely he was too small a figure to be carrying such responsibility? But image of *'le petit Prince'* vanished for ever that morning. The 'Child of France' had truly become a man — he walked firmly, his head held high, looking straight ahead, just like any soldier on parade. Everyone admired his composure and firm self-control.

In accordance with etiquette Eugénie herself did not attend the funeral. Nor did Queen Victoria. The French government had already formally requested that the ceremony should not be allowed to become an official one. Although her government tried hard to dissuade him, she was nonetheless represented by the Prince of Wales. Whilst there was only room for about two hundred people in the church itself, over twenty thousand managed to gather outside. The Catholic Bishop of Southwark, assisted by Father Goddard, received the coffin at the entrance. Afterwards the young Prince had to face the ordeal of receiving most of the official mourners. He said a few words of thanks to those he recognised, many of whom broke down in tears. Amongst them was his former nanny, Miss Shaw. Someone in the line called out *'Vive L'Empereur! Vive Napoléon IV!'* This cry was taken up by many others, so that only those closest to the Prince heard his noble and calm response: "No! No! Your Emperor is dead — but France never dies. *Vive la France!*"

Three years later, when Filon lost his own father, the Prince wrote a private letter of condolence in which, with benefit of hindsight, he referred to his own period of mourning:

> When I lost my father, my duty showed itself clearly. From that day, I had only one end in life, and I go always straight on, without looking back. If my feet are on a precipice, I shall fall like an honest man, and perhaps I shall find at the foot all that I have lost in life. If without turning aside from my path, I overcome its obstacles, I shall have the satisfaction of having carried on the work of the Emperor.[30]

Ten days afterwards the Empress wrote to Queen Victoria to thank her for her support: 'If anything in the world could mitigate my sorrow, Your Majesty's kind words would have done so, but my heart is broken with sorrow.' When the Queen

---

30   FILON, p. 102.

asked for some memento of the deceased Emperor, Eugénie sent his travelling clock, together with the message: 'It has marked the happy times of other days and the long hours of moral and physical suffering, both the years of joy and intense grief; but how great a part of them were the latter!'[31]

A few weeks later the Queen accompanied by Princess Beatrice paid her private respects to the Emperor's coffin in St Mary's Church and then called on the Empress at Camden Place. At the door looking pale and sad stood the Prince Imperial. And behind him in deepest mourning 'looking very ill, very handsome, and the picture of sorrow, was the poor dear Empress.' Eugénie took the opportunity of the Queen's visit to inform her personally about one particular event since the funeral. The Emperor's will had been drawn up in 1865. At that time who could have known that he would die, stripped of his titles, a refugee in a foreign land? But, although terminally ill, he still had not seen fit to amend the document or add any codicil to reflect the changed circumstances of the imperial family in the last eight years. Surprisingly, Louis-Napoleon left everything he had to Eugénie, despite the fact that French law required a father to leave at least a part of his estate to his heir. There was nothing for Louis except 'the seal I used to carry on my watch-chain, and which belonged to my mother.' His private money only amounted to £60,000, whereas his wife was worth that sum many times over. Throughout his life the Emperor had spent generously, finding it difficult to ignore any worthy cause. It seems inexplicable therefore that he deliberately chose to deny Louis the financial means to make an independent start in life. At eighteen the Prince would become legally of age, and thus titular head of the Bonapartist party, but officially without a single penny to his name. It was a situation which, later on, was to cause the Prince some embarrassment. In the will the Emperor had written: 'The Empress Eugénie possesses all the qualities for conducting the Regency...I leave to the Empress Eugénie all my private property...I trust that my memory will be dear to her and that after my death she will forget the griefs I may have caused her.'[32] Nobody else was mentioned in the will.

'Plon-Plon' obstinately refused to accept that fact. He could not accept that his cousin had not revised the will in recent months. He therefore insisted on searching the Emperor's study personally for a second testament, which he believed existed and which he believed had been deliberately suppressed. Turning out every single drawer and document he found nothing. From now on he could only rage at a situation which left him — the most senior Bonaparte still surviving and thus nominally in charge of the Napoleonic dynasty — without any acknowledgement or reference in the will.

Despite his behaviour, Eugénie decided, for the sake of family unity, to take this opportunity to resolve all their previous antagonisms. She stretched out her hand: "Listen!', she said. "You know me — I'm not a woman who bears grudges. Let you and I forget our differences. Put your hands in mine, and have done with

---

31   ARONSON, p. 156.
32   TURNBULL, p. 322.

the past." "Madam," he responded, "in a short time I will acquaint you with my intentions."[33]

These were delivered two days later when an aide — Colonel Stoffel — called at Camden Place. The first requirement was that he, and he alone, should assume responsibility for leading the party. But his second caused her to fly into one of her terrible rages. She told Queen Victoria. "He dared, can you believe it? He dared to say that the Prince Imperial must be given up to him — entrusted to his sole guardianship! My son was to leave Woolwich and go to *faire l'aventure* with him abroad!"[34]

For quite some time she continued to feel outraged at the implications of his outrageous proposals. Clearly, he not only considered her unfit to direct the policies of the party (despite the fact that she had several times been Regent of France), but now, after seventeen years, he also considered her unfit to complete the upbringing of her own son. Eugénie's anger was to last for a long time. Ironically, it was so fierce and so obsessive that it served to ease some of the pain of her grief. And by his tactless and impudent demands Prince Jerome Napoleon had finally forfeited any lingering vestige of respect which Eugénie and others might have felt for him. The Prince Imperial was just as furious as his mother. He now came to despise his uncle and was to take a private revenge of his own — at the appropriate time.

After the Empress had unburdened the whole sorry story, Victoria found herself being sympathetically drawn towards Bonapartism. 'The Queen does *not* think the Bonapartist cause will lose by the poor Emperor's death,' she wrote to Prince Albert's biographer, Theodore Martin,' on the contrary *she* thinks the reverse. *For* the peace of Europe, *She* thinks (though the Orléans Princes are her dear friends and connections and some relations, and she would not for the world have it *said* as coming from her) that...it would be best if the Prince Imperial was *ultimately* to succeed.'[35] And the Queen was never to waver from this view over the rest of her long life — and she was to repeat it on the many occasions, particularly in the 1890s, long after the Prince's death, when one crisis after another appeared to rock the very foundations of the Third Republic.

On 4th March 1873 — some weeks after the Emperor's death — the Queen invited Louis to a private luncheon at Windsor. In her journal she describes how 'I met him at the top of the staircase with Lenchen & Beatrice and took him alone for a few moments into the Audience Room. I repeated how much I had felt for him and how I hoped he would try and comfort his poor mother. He had tears in his eyes as soon as he spoke of his father, and thanked me much for my kindness which he said they would never forget. We then went to luncheon... The young Prince has charming quiet manners and reminds me in many ways of his father. His features are a mixture of both parents; the shape of the brow, and eyes, and the mouth and smile are those of the Empress.'[36]

---

33   JOHN, p. 293.
34   Ibid.
35   RA. Y/169/33
36   RA QVJ: 4 Mar.1873

She now proceeded to honour her new *protége* in a special way. Amongst the books in his study at Woolwich the Prince was proud to display two particular volumes: a handsomely bound Shakespeare, and *Leaves from the Journal of Our Life in the Highlands,* each inscribed in French by the Queen's own hand: 'To my cousin the Prince Imperial of France, with many wishes for his happiness...His affectionate cousin, Victoria R. 16th March 1873'[37]

---

37   JOHN, p. 293.

Chapter VI

THE CHILD OF FRANCE

THE PRINCE IMPERIAL, accompanied by Louis Conneau, Filon and Uhlmann, arrived to start his training at the Royal Military Academy at Woolwich on 18th November 1872. At sixteen Louis was almost a year younger than most of his contemporaries. As foreigners, neither he nor Conneau could be granted the official appointment of 'Gentleman Cadet' — on entry the Queen exercised her personal prerogative and appointed them both instead as 'Queen's Cadets.'[1] Although the Academy register today shows the following official entry: 'Not appointed cadet but permitted to go through a course of study with cadets' — in practical terms, however, the Prince was still addressed and referred to as 'Cadet *Bonaparte*'. He was to remain a Queen's Cadet for over two years, finally attaining the honorary rank of 'Corporal' shortly before he graduated on 16th February 1875.

Although there is no military academy at Woolwich today (it was closed after the Second World War), there has been little change to the overall facade. The long dark-brown, principal building still faces a broad parade ground, comprising a tall central block with four distinctive turret-style towers flanked on either side by two lower wings. The gravel parade ground extends forward until it reaches the edge of a large lawn which, in turn, spreads out in the form of a huge triangle, the apex of which touches the Common — marking the site at which the Prince Imperial's memorial statue was first erected after his death. Herbert Road still runs along the southern side of the grounds, past the lodge and main entrance gates, where the Governor's house and staff quarters stood directly opposite. Behind the main building were various gunsheds, store-sheds and further playing grounds. Today, the adjacent bus-stop is still called 'The Imperial' and the nearby link road is prominently signposted 'Prince Imperial Road'.

'The Shop' was, in many ways, no more than a military version of an English public school. It embraced the same type of schoolboy culture, with its distinctive hierarchies, idiosyncratic rituals, harsh punishments and peculiar slang. Even meals were organised to public school routines with 'dinner' programmed for the early afternoon, not the evening. This is not surprising since, up until the mid-1870s, candidates for regular commissions in the British Army were to be largely drawn from the upper strata of Victorian society; young men who were themselves usually products of the public school system, many also the sons of serving or retired officers.

---

1   Obtained from Deputy Curator, RMAS collection (letter 25th September 1995).

The Woolwich Academy was devoted solely to the training of potential officers for the Royal Regiment of Artillery and the Royal Engineers. Consequently much of instruction was highly technical. Indeed the training was so long and demanding that, unlike the Royal Military College at Sandhurst, cadets successfully completing the course were commissioned, without purchase, directly into the rank of Lieutenant, and not as Ensigns or Second Lieutenants. Although the Prince's command of English was adequate he was to find much difficulty in mastering the specialised language of fortifications and gunnery. And yet, despite the fact that lessons were also conducted in both French and German (cadets were positively encouraged to study in another language), the Prince declined to take advantage of these facilities. Thus, Filon was to spend a great deal of his time at Woolwich assisting the Prince with the more difficult subjects in the curriculum, as well as continuing to instruct him privately in French history and politics.

The Company of Gentlemen Cadets was divided into five classes of students — of which the fifth was the lowest. Individuals entered at this level and were referred to as 'snookers' throughout their first term. Additionally, the whole Company was split into three Divisions. 'A' Division contained those in their last term of study; it included all the under-officers and cadet corporals who were on the threshold of being commissioned. 'B' and 'C' Divisions comprised all the others at different levels of training. Traditionally, cadets of the second class always assumed responsibility for initiating any new arrivals into the particular culture of 'The Shop.' Following principles first established by the famous Dr Arnold, Headmaster of Rugby School, the Academy was largely self-disciplined — in that senior cadets, like sixth-form prefects, were both entrusted and empowered to control, correct and if necessary punish the junior 'snookers' as they were called.

As true outsiders the Prince and Conneau could have had no inkling of what was in store for them. Nor did they have much opportunity to find out. Right from the day of arrival they had been effectively cut off from entering fully into the lives of their fellow cadets. The Emperor had insisted, and the Governor had agreed, that the Prince's group would all be permitted to live outside the Academy precincts. As special 'Queen's Cadets' they were considered to be exempt the otherwise strict regulation that all cadets must be billeted within the Academy grounds. On arrival the French party were offered a rather cramped and unsuitable little house in Nightingale Lane. Here the four of them were soon joined by a footman, cook and cleaning maid. The Prince himself appeared totally indifferent to these uncomfortable and unattractive surroundings. But the poor facilities and cramped conditions particularly irritated Filon who considered the Prince deserved better. But, as far as Louis was concerned, it was ample enough recompense to be able to wear a uniform again, even if the drab dress of an English Gentleman Cadet could hardly compare to the colourful dash of a French Second Lieutenant's uniform.

Every day the Prince and Conneau would walk from their house to the Academy. The first parade usually took place at 8 a.m. and, in normal circumstances, they would return to the house about twelve hours later — at 8 p.m. For their use during the day, the Governor had thoughtfully arranged three rooms for them on the first floor of the West-facing tower of the main building — a study, sitting room and small dressing room. Eugénie, correctly anticipating that these would only be fitted out with the most basic items of barrack room furniture, sought to make these rooms more homely by providing special family photographs, pictures and ornaments.

Both boys quickly adapted to the daily set routine with its strict timings:

0645	Hoxters (extra drills)
0800–1000	Drills
1000–1130	Lectures or study
1130–1200	Luncheon break (biscuits and one pint of beer)
1200–1400	Lectures
1405	Dinner parade and inspection
1415	Dinner
1500–1800	Recreation
1800–2000	Lectures

Every Saturday morning the whole Company would parade before the Governor and march to the music of the Royal Artillery band. When that weekly parade had finally been dismissed, everyone was free to change into civilian clothes, doff top hats and depart from the Academy until the following Monday. Thus both the Prince and Louis Conneau spent most weekends at Camden Place — which was barely twenty minutes away.

From the start the Prince determined to be as sociable as possible. But since, unlike the other newcomers, he did not share their barrack room accommodation it took longer than usual to make himself known. This situation was aggravated by the fact that both French boys had entered long after the term had started, and consequently most of their fellow cadets had long since established their own cliques and personal friends. Few in that first term therefore knew that the heir to the French imperial throne was actually living and working amongst them. He noted that the instructors were always polite, even if rather formal in their attitude towards him; he also discovered that the majority of his fellow 'snookers' were friendly, and not the least bit like the indifferent and casual English students he had encountered at King's College. But even though they had joined late, they were not exempt the 'Rosh-Band Night' initiation ceremony which was always programmed to take place at this late stage of the term.

One evening all 'snookers' were ordered to appear in full parade dress in the gymnasium, where the artillery band had already assembled and members of 'A' Division stood around. Although no ladies were present, the new arrivals were required to dance with each other. The compulsory 'snookers' waltz proved to be something of an ordeal since the spectators, without warning, would suddenly step forward and trip them up. But when the 'snookers' lancers was announced, the innocent sets, once formed, were immediately set upon by the second, third and fourth classmen, until everyone finished in an untidy heap in the centre of the floor. Filon was shocked when the Prince and Conneau returned, battered and bruised, their parade dress covered in dust and dirt, still wondering what the whole evening had been about.

It was not long before the Prince personally found himself the subject of bullying by senior cadets. Noticing that some of them wore their pill-box caps with the stiffening removed, and chin-strap swung round to the back of the head, he decided to do the same. No-one had advised him that this rakish rearrangement was the sole prerogative of the senior 'A' Division cadets. On the first afternoon he wore the cap in this manner, a senior from amongst a group of cadets stepped forward, shouting, challenging his right to do so. Without warning, this same senior suddenly leaned forward and, with a sweep of his hand, knocked the cap straight off Louis's head. The others then proceeded to kick it around like a football. The Prince felt his temper rising. Someone asked him if he wanted a 'toshing'. The look of puzzlement across his face was immediately interpreted as dumb insolence. "Go and fill the bath!" someone else shouted. Others ran off at once to the nearest bath house. The Prince meanwhile was roughly grabbed by the arms and legs, and carried off in the same direction. Throughout the incident Louis Conneau had stood silently to one side fearing to intervene; with some apprehension, he now followed the group into the building. But as soon as he saw a bath being filled with icy cold water, he started to remonstrate with everyone, pointing out that their intended victim was His Highness the Prince Imperial. No-one took the slightest notice. Carefully standing to one side to avoid the inevitable splash, and with great shouts of glee, they simply dumped the fully-clothed Prince straight into the icy water. But as they laughed and turned away, all of them were to be suddenly drenched by an even bigger splash — as Louis Conneau voluntarily leapt into the bath and joined his friend. This caused them to pause — who were these two foreigners, who obviously supported one another through thick and thin? As Conneau's irate explanation began to dawn on them they started to apologise profusely; some immediately went off to bring towels and replacement clothes. Later the Prince had great difficulty in dissuading Filon from complaining formally to the Governor about his treatment.

The after dinner 'roshers' were a further ordeal which awaited all 'snookers'. This initiation required the juniors to surmount a formidable obstacle course, specially constructed from various chairs, tables and desks, set down along a corridor. At either side, along the length of the corridor, stood cadets from the second and third classes, armed with canes, horse whips, toasting forks and similar instruments with which to 'encourage' the competitors to greater efforts. Anyone held up by an obstacle could expect little mercy. When the seniors began to organise the 'snookers' for the start, both the Prince and Louis Conneau were discreetly motioned to stand to one side. But the Prince immediately shook his head, insisting that they should be treated in the same way as the others.

From the word 'Go', both of them moved so rapidly down the obstacle course that they suffered only minor 'encouragement'. Indeed they got off so lightly that they were directed to re-run the whole course again! With a nimbleness acquired from constant riding and fencing, both once more ran the gauntlet with the same comparative ease, finally earning the enthusiastic applause of everyone. That night, in the little house in Nightingale Lane, they both wondered why the English should behave in such an eccentric way? Filon listened to their experiences but was as baffled as they were.

They had much more difficulty trying to master the intricacies of British military jargon. The Prince was advised by other 'snookers' that the customary reply to an officer's instruction should always be *'Very good, sir'*. In normal circumstances this would be correct, but unfortunately, Louis chose the wrong occasion to use it. On parade one morning an officer, who did not know the Prince, spotted a white fleck on his blue uniform.

'Fluff! Fluff! — Take an extra drill!'

'Very good, sir!'

'Don't answer back! Take another drill!'

'Very good.'

'Shut up — if you like extra drills so much — take a third — see to it sergeant!'

'Very good, sir!' answered the sergeant and the Prince wondered why his own words had so offended the officer.

As a consequence he now had to get up even earlier to attend his first 'hoxter' — a special punishment parade held at the early hour of 6.45 a.m. On these extra drills one would invariably be booked by the officer in charge for some other minor irregularity, ridiculous offences such as appearing to be 'unsteady' on parade, so that attending 'hoxters' every morning, instead of being an isolated punishment, quickly became the daily norm! Both the Prince and Conneau soon learned to habitually rise and get on parade even earlier each morning.

It had been the Emperor's express wish that his son should not participate in the Academy's usual team games. He considered that daily riding and fencing would be ample enough exercise, and that programme time allocated for team games might more profitably be spent at additional lessons. In any case, team games were a peculiarly English activity which did not feature strongly in the French sporting culture of the period. Consequently Filon would often walk up from the house and join them in their rooms for this purpose after dinner. But late one afternoon the tutor found the Prince bent over his mathematics books, head in hands, a look of despair on his face. "I have entered here too soon. All my school fellows have had at least three years' mathematics; I have had hardly a year."

"But your examination."

"Oh, the examination! We thought too much of that. It was certainly a mere formality. The truth is that I am not fit to take the classes."[2]

Concerned at this sudden development, Filon immediately sought an interview with the Governor and years later recalled what happened:

> Deeply troubled, I explained the situation to him without any reserve. He heard me out calmly and showed no annoyance, nor even surprise. He gave me to understand that there were precedents, and that several young princes had already been through the Academy without taking any pains to become great mathematicians, taking part in military exercises and distinguishing

2 FILON, p. 99.

themselves in cricket and in football. Well, the Prince Imperial would do as they did: he would take the classes — as a Prince.

I answered him that this solution would not satisfy our Prince, whose ambition was to prove himself at all points an efficient pupil, and to go through his officer's training in all seriousness. I saw by his eyes that his sympathy for the Prince was greatly increased by this, and he promised me that the masters would do all they could to help him through all his early difficulties.[3]

With this encouragement, the Prince made even greater efforts. But throughout this first term at 'The Shop' he often felt homesick and unhappy. And by the time he rejoined the course on 1st February 1873 that unhappiness was aggravated by grief at the death of his father. At that time it had been agreed that he would now answer the daily roll-call under a new name: Cadet *Napoléon*. He also decided to change his signature from 'Prince Louis Napoléon' to 'Napoléon' on its own. Thus it would become clear to the Academy hierarchy, his French supporters and to the public at large, that he now considered himself to be the head of the family, and, as such, heir to its dynastic rights. On the left arm of his uniform he wore the customary mourning band of crape. Owing to his father's unexpected death he had missed the usual end-of-term examinations which might have enabled him to move up early into the second class. The Governor generously made allowances for this disadvantage by offering to promote both of them regardless, but the Prince declined. He did not wish to be favoured in this way — he much preferred to start again by completing a first term in full. And so both boys once more became 'snookers', joining the new intake to the fifth class. But this time they knew how to play the 'snooker' game, and could be of immense help to all the others. For their second appearance at the Academy, they were also moved into different accommodation.

The new address was 51 Woolwich Common. Today this house no longer exists, having been destroyed through bombing in the Second World War. In 1873 it was the end house of a row of semi-detached dwellings, all looking alike, facing the end of the Circular Road and, in location, much closer to the Academy. Nonetheless, despite the fact that their new residence was three storeys high, they were just as cramped as in Nightingale Lane for there were only two rooms on each floor. At the front, on the second, was the Prince's drawing room furnished with items from Camden Place, including a piano, whilst his bedroom was on the floor above. Elsewhere the little house somehow accommodated, besides Filon, Conneau and Uhlmann, two maids and a page boy called Charley who years later became butler to the Empress. Filon was being both amusing and apt when he described their new home as a *perchoir de perroquet* (parrot's cage)!

During the afternoons, whilst his fellows were engaged in team games, the Prince would spend much of his time studying modern French history and politics with his tutor. Filon was to derive immense satisfaction from the fact that, after all these years, Louis's intellect had suddenly blossomed. It was if all the nervous energy

---

3   Ibid.

formerly expended in hyperactive physical activity had now somehow been diverted into mental gymnastics. He was to write: 'memorable afternoons, when I watched this intellectual expansion I had waited for so long, that I had vainly tried to hasten.'

And of those pleasant evenings, as winter changed into spring, and spring to summer, the tutor was to recount at length:

> As eight o'clock came near I used to go out to meet him when he was leaving the Academy, and I often found him at the very place where his statue stands today. My weak eyes (Filon was soon to become almost blind) could hardly make him out when night was falling or was already come. I had with me a little black dog, born the very day the Emperor died and very much attached to the Prince. He, with his fine voice that rang out like a bugle, would strike up some of those songs of the African troops that an unknown poet had adapted to our cavalry calls. At the last note he would be at my side, his face lit up with a frank smile, for to find me was to find France once more after his English day. He would come back to the house to sup, with what an appetite! There was no trace of fatigue left in him when we went upstairs to the little green drawing room. A new day began. Sitting or lying on the sofa, playing with the dog or fretting the keys of the piano with one finger, to pick out the notes of some favourite tune, he would ask for news, and we would discuss the events of the day. The most important papers, French and English, friendly or hostile, were on the table.[4]

His friendship with Louis Conneau had likewise matured. The two were virtually inseparable. They constantly compared notes, helped one another over the complexities of technical English, and, together with Filon, tried to retain their essential Frenchness in this strange environment. Whilst they kept close together, giving each other mutual support and strength, they were all gradually becoming used to English ways. And in turn, with that acceptance, their fellow cadets began to respond in kind. The Prince was now becoming better known, and thus better appreciated. It was also recognised that, unlike other Princes attending the course, Louis had sat and passed the stiff entrance examination. Initially, most people had expected him to be off-hand and dismissive but they soon realised that, whilst always self-assured and aware of his position, there was nothing remotely arrogant, disdainful or offhand about him. Even so he made few really close English friends during the Academy course. There were a number of reasons for this. He did not wish to be seen to have favourites amongst his fellow cadets who, in any case, he viewed more as competitors than potential friends. Furthermore, as long as Louis Conneau continued to live in their house and attend the course alongside him, he had little incentive to forge fresh relationships with English boys in his class, many of whom, in any case, were almost a year older.

And he stood out as a foreigner amongst Englishmen precisely because he loved showing off in those particular skills at which he excelled. He was undoubtedly

---

4   Ibid., p. 106.

the best horseman in the Academy and made no effort to disguise that fact. But then no-one else had been taught to ride as soon as he could walk, and then by such a skilled instructor as M.Bachon. But that was but one achievement. No cadet could beat him at fencing either. Unbeknown to the Prince this, in fact, invoked the admiration of the whole Company — for every cadet secretly desired to excel at these two particularly important military skills. He delighted too in other physical feats, comparable acts of bravado and daring. Nonetheless he still preferred not to participate in the various games of the Academy, principally because he realised he would never perform really well in such peculiarly English pastimes as cricket and football, and had long since come to the view that he must now excel at every single thing he tackled. Nonetheless, despite his penchant for showing off, the Prince did not take himself too seriously, nor did he constantly stand on his dignity. He could always take any joke on any subject, always provided it did not reflect adversely on his birthright or mock his country or his family. It was really this more than anything else which so endeared him to others that, by course end, he had become one of the most popular cadets in the whole of the Academy.

Whilst Miss Shaw had bequeathed him a substantial English vocabulary, she had been less successful over his pronunciation and spelling. Sometimes, when taking his turn to bark out commands on the parade ground, his fellows were not quite sure what particular drill movement he had in mind. On these occasions, more often than not, they would simply stand still, perplexed as to what to do next. Then someone would break into a giggle; a wave of laughter would ripple through the ranks, with the Prince himself, out in front, finally joining in the general hilarity.

One afternoon, one of the officers, drilling a group of cadets in one of the inner courts, was startled by a tremendous crash and clattering right behind him. As he turned he saw the Prince tumbled at the foot of a flight of stone steps, with the wreckage of a bicycle nearby. Louis scrambled on to his feet, explaining to the puzzled officer, that he had tried to ride the bicycle down the steps. "Wasn't that very rash, sir?" "Well," replied the Prince, "I cleared it yesterday, and meant to do so again — but, as you see, sir, my steed has thrown me, and broken his back."[5]

He was duly admonished for his recklessness, but incidents such as these soon became known amongst the staff and cadets, earning their amused admiration.

Two of his favourite expressions gradually became known to everybody. Whenever he was rudely taken to task by a superior his only concern was the possible injury to his status and pride, so he would quickly check with others; "Is that an insult?" — for that he would never accept. His second phrase always caused much amusement; it was his usual reaction to any sudden event: "What the divel 'eapened?"[6]

But, there were other clashes with authority from time to time.

His military history instructor found it almost impossible to discourse on the Napoleonic wars without the Prince constantly interrupting. Matters came to a head when the battle of Waterloo came under particular scrutiny. At one point, the Prince dramatically sprang to his feet, trembling with indignation at what he

5   JOHN, p. 304.
6   Ibid.

perceived as a distortion of the facts concerning the movements of French troops on that fateful morning. Irritated at this latest interruption, the instructor personally complained to the Governor, recommending that the Prince Imperial be excused further military history lessons.

General Simmons summoned Louis to his office to explain that, whilst as a Frenchman his views were always worthy of respect, everyone knew that English history was written by Englishmen for Englishmen, and precisely the same was true of the French! He should therefore accept that reality and keep his private views to himself, at least until the end of the class when any disputes should be raised discreetly, and discussed privately direct with the instructor. The Governor likewise gently pointed out that self-control, no matter how provocative the circumstances, was an essential attribute of any leader of men. Louis did not object to the implied rebuke, nor did he harbour any feelings of resentment; he saw the sense of the Governor's remarks, acknowledged the advice and rejoined the class. There were no more interruptions.

By the end of his first full term everyone at 'The Shop' from the Governor downwards agreed that the Prince Imperial — who they now affectionately referred to simply as 'the P.I.' — was out of the ordinary run of Prince cadets. Whilst there was always an element who would always show him social deference on account of his status, many were simply drawn to him because of his own attractive personality, his exquisite manners and genuine interest in their problems. Some of them wondered about his private thoughts. Did he really expect to become Emperor of the French? But whenever they tried to probe his views on this issue, he tended to change the subject. But in franker conversations with others he would sometimes let slip: "When I return to France — I intend to do so-and-so"[7], referring perhaps to the introduction of some useful English method into a particular aspect of French military life.

Sometimes Louis could appear as flippant, even frivolous, but those who knew him well soon discovered that he was, at heart, a thoughtful and conscientious young man who was noticeably truthful and straightforward in everything he undertook. By now he had determined to excel in every subject and in every activity at the Academy. Such resolve really gave him a steely determination which further singled him out from many of the others. Such dedication and professionalism were hardly in keeping with the languid casualness towards military competence so characteristic of many upper-class British officers of the period, but most recognised that, as a French Prince and heir to the Napoleonic legacy, he had his own private objectives — to be achieved in his own way. Thus, most took an indulgent view at his occasional bouts of self-display. After all everyone knew that at the end of the course, unlike them, he was not going to be granted the Queen's commission and therefore had every incentive to conveniently side-step the most awkward examinations and the most difficult challenges. But staff and cadets alike noted how, throughout the course, he insisted on competing on exactly the same terms as everyone else. They were also aware that he had declined to collect the additional marks which were

---

7   Ibid., p. 299.

automatically awarded to those cadets who had a thorough knowledge of a second language. He thus steadfastly refused to compete in French even though, from time to time, he attended some of the lessons conducted in his mother tongue and helped others having language difficulties.

The Prince would usually return to Camden Place most weekends. During one of these he filled in a revealing questionnaire. The most fashionable social game at that time was to 'play confessions', by answering certain pre-printed questions in the pages of a special album which might be placed on display on a drawing-room table. Some of these questions were deliberately facetious, designed to make people look ridiculous and on these grounds many people declined to participate, but not Louis. Filon kept a record of his answers to some of these questions:

What is your favourite virtue?	*Courage*
Your leading passion?	*Patriotism*
Your idea of happiness?	*To do good*
Your idea of unhappiness?	*To live in exile*
Where would you like to live?	*In France*
Your heroes in history?	*Napoleon, Caesar*
Your motto in life?	*Do your duty; do your best*
Your present state of mind?	*Sad*

In many ways his answers to some of these questions simply reflected the virtues expected of any respectable gentleman of Nineteenth Century society, regardless of status, but the sadness expressed in the last was uniquely his. He was reminded of this sadness when a Frenchman called at the Academy on business, and, whenever this occurred, the Prince, as a courtesy, was always notified — for now he wanted to meet as many of his countrymen as possible, regardless of their political views. This particular visitor was duly presented and, in all goodwill and friendliness, the Prince immediately asked which part of France he had come from. The unknown Frenchman folded his arms, staring hard and long at him. Eventually, emphasising the words with marked bitterness, he replied, "From Sedan." At that Louis went rather pale, murmuring, "Well — That's a very pretty district." And as he walked away, the accompanying staff officer could only admire the Prince's forbearance and self-control.[8]

During those hours allocated for team games and leisure Filon continued to instruct him on all aspects of French history. Together they made a detailed survey of the Revolution and the advent of Napoleon Bonaparte, the period when, as Louis personally described it, 'the First Consul threw down on our soil those blocks of granite which were to be the foundations of *la société moderne.*'[9] It was typical of the Prince to isolate from a mass of detail what he considered to be the fundamentals. As he explored more deeply into the history of his homeland he was always on the look out for key truths, around which he could build his own political views.

---

8   JOHN, p. 300.
9   Ibid., p. 305.

For these 'blocks of granite' were the very weapons he needed to demonstrate the inevitability of his return to France.

In June 1873, at the end of term, the Prince travelled to Switzerland to join his mother at the small family chateau of Arenenberg. Although not permitted to travel through France, the Prussian Chancellor Bismarck raised no objection to both of them criss-crossing Germany. Overlooking Lake Constance, Arenenberg had formerly been Queen Hortense's villa where the Emperor Louis-Napoleon had spent much of his youth. Here, accompanied by such long-standing friends as Espinasse, Bizot and others from that Tuileries classroom of his boyhood, the Prince would go climbing over the rocks and ravines, often walking for hours across the mountains. After studying so hard all year, the constant fresh air and outdoor exercise revitalised him. In all these activities, he naturally took the lead with the others following dutifully behind.

In early August, leaving his mother behind at Arenenberg, the Prince returned alone to Camden Place to deliver his first political speech. Eugéne Rouher was now taking an increasingly significant role in the Prince's life. Elected in 1872 to represent Corsica, he now led a small group in the French Chamber. But they no longer called themselves 'Bonapartists' in public; the party had now been re-vamped under a new slogan — 'L'Appel au Peuple!'. In a further change of policy all ideas of attempting to seize power by force were quietly shelved. Instead, the new party aimed to blend the political culture of the Napoleonic dynasty with truly democratic principles. The only way now for Napoleon the Fourth to reclaim his throne would be through the majority will of the people. As the principal political activist, Rouher was dividing his time equally between Chislehurst and Paris. And he had come to the conclusion that it was important to now publicly launch the young Prince as the only Catholic and Conservative Bonapartist who could truly 'appeal to the people'.

Although nominally the head of the party until the Prince's formal coming-of-age, the Empress did not approve of many of Rouher's schemes and decided it would be more prudent if she stayed away from the planned Proclamation ceremony. With her realistic perception of what was politically possible, she had long since come to the conclusion that the party had little chance of ever overthrowing the Third Republic, either by force or by persuasion. Brushing these concerns to one side, Rouher decided it was nonetheless time to start the Prince on his political career by formally presenting him to the public at a mass rally at Chislehurst on 15th August 1873 — the birthday anniversary of the Great Napoleon.

For this occasion about a thousand five hundred Frenchmen crossed the Channel, and of these, only about two hundred managed to crowd into little St Mary's Church, Chislehurst for a solemn Mass, at which Father Goddard preached with great eloquence, praising the whole family, turning at the end to address the Prince: 'Son of the noble lady who has shown us how to bear with dignity the hardest trials and the most cruel sorrows, you can never forget that great souls are nurtured in the school of adversity. You, *monseigneur*, have already developed qualities that prove you worthy of your father and mother. Persevere, and God will reward your services and your virtue.'[10]

Afterwards the visitors were formally received in the grounds and the seventeen year old Prince was persuaded to speak. He declined Rouher's offer to provide suitable words, pulling instead from his pocket a short speech which he had written himself earlier that morning:

"I thank you, in my own name and that of the Empress, for having come to join your prayers with ours, and for your remembrance of the path by which you sought us out once before. I thank also those absent friends who have sent us so many tokens of their love and loyalty. For myself in exile and by the tomb of my father, I meditate the precepts he left me; I find in my inheritance the principle of national sovereignty, and the flag which consecrates it. This principle was summed up by the founder of our House, in words to which I shall always be faithful: TOUT POUR LE PEUPLE ET PAR LE PEUPLE.[11]

There was a prolonged outburst of cheering and applause. The reference to the national flag subtly challenged the Royalist threat, already undermined by one of the Pretenders, Comte de Chambord (grandson of Charles the Tenth), steadfastly refusing in his own manifesto to abandon the *ancien* white flag of Henry the Fourth for the Republican Tricolour. The other Royalist faction — the Orleanistes — centred around the person of the Comte de Paris, grandson of King Louise-Philipe.

And the phrase *For the people and through the people* spelt out very clearly that the only route to power was going to be through a nation-wide plebiscite. A delighted Rouher made sure that this Proclamation, together with an attractive photograph of the young Prince, was widely published and distributed throughout France. The campaign to restore the Napoleonic dynasty by democratic means had officially got under way. That evening Marie de Larminat offered her own private congratulations to the Prince. "Yes," he said quietly and rather sadly, "I was very pleased; it seemed almost as though I were in France."[12]

He resumed the course at Woolwich, having now successfully graduated to the second class. This term he added to his growing reputation for daring by joining the 'Alpine Club'. This was an exclusive body of mountain climbers — an activity then still in its infancy, but one which nonetheless aroused a great deal of admiration, particularly from those who preferred not to participate! To become a member, one was required, during the hours of darkness, to make a complete circuit of all four pointed rooftops around the main courtyard! This was no easy task — the slate roofs could be slippery; the feat required cool nerves and considerable strength. Late one night the Prince managed to slip out of the house without alerting Filon and the others; scaled the high railings around the grounds, and then accomplished the required circuit to the satisfaction of the onlooking club 'officials'. Once accepted as a member there were further challenges, for which there were even mock putty medallions! The ascent of the 'Grand Dome'; the 'Pic de Wettercoq'; the 'Flagstaff Horn'! The Prince succeeded in scaling all of these during the hours of darkness.

---

10 Ibid., p. 315.
11 Ibid., p. 315.
12 Ibid., p. 315.

This empowered him to participate in one of the club's most popular exploits — placing chamber pots on the spires and towers of Woolwich village, as well as 'The Shop', the night before the traditional end of term parade. This splendid passing-out parade, with its backcloth of chamber pots on steeples, would invariably be taken by Field Marshal the Duke of Cambridge, Commander-in-Chief of the Army.

Another 'P.I.' escapade however brought him straight into the Governor's office. An ancient 13 inch mortar stood out in the grounds with a heavy spherical drill shell beside it. The Prince had become involved in a wager with another cadet as to the exact size of charge needed to propel that heavy shell so slowly along the barrel that it could be caught by waiting hands as it plopped from the muzzle! The pair of them had manufactured small charges of varying strengths and then carried them out to the mortar one games afternoon. The Prince had taken the first turn, standing by the muzzle to receive the shell, whilst the other lit the fuse. To their surprise, the heavy shell had barely moved in the massive barrel and soon slipped back again through the puffs of smoke. So they had inserted a stronger charge, and changed places. This time there had been a sudden roar and a great sheet of flame. The heavy shell tore out of the muzzle at high speed, arching its way right across the football field, finally crashing high up on the stonework of a racquet court making a sizeable round hole in the process.

General Simmons had not been amused, and both of them had expected either to be rusticated or even dismissed. The Governor had just glared at them in silence for a while. "Gentlemen," he suddenly shouted, "You have grossly miscalculated the weight of the charge. You are therefore unfit to be trusted with powder — so don't try this again. March out!"[13]

But, despite such incidents, the Prince was making significant progress in his studies. In October 1873 he informed his tutor, temporarily abroad: 'I am writing to you, dear M.Filon, to tell you about my examination. I was fifteenth in mathematics, ninth in fortification, eighth in military drawing. The General came himself to tell me this result which I learned with great pleasure. I thought you would share my satisfaction: that is why I wanted to write to you.'[14]

A massive rally was organised for the Prince's eighteenth birthday on 16th March 1874 — his official coming-of-age. This had been arranged against the wishes of both the Empress and the Prince, who would have preferred any celebrations to be deferred until his graduation from Woolwich. But, as so often in the past, their personal objections were simply brushed to one side. Eugéne Rouher and others took the view that to publicly and formally proclaim the Prince to be of legal age would signal that the Constitutions of the Empire still existed, since these, originally established by plebiscite, had never been subsequently annulled by any comparable vote. Consequently, the Prince was both legally and morally Napoleon the Fourth, Emperor of the French. So many supporters argued that he should now adopt the title of Napoleon the Fourth — which was his constitutional right. But Rouher felt that such a course would be fraught with difficulties — the British government, for one, would certainly refuse to recognise such a title and, as consequence, would

---

13   TISDALL, p. 154.
14   FILON, p. 105.

probably sever all relations; furthermore, the military academy would surely decline to permit someone entitled Napoleon the Fourth to complete the course.

Advertisements summoning all the faithful to Camden Place were placed in the various Bonapartist newspapers. Throughout France there was a massive and free distribution of 300,000 specially printed portraits of the Prince Imperial — and many more were printed in England and Belgium. Preparations were made to run special excursion boats and trains to bring thousands of party supporters from France. The French government became quite alarmed. Whilst they had taken no official action against military and civilian officers attending the Emperor's funeral as a former Head of State, they now threatened to dismiss anyone in their employ attending the Prince's coming-of-age celebrations. Furthermore, no service officers or civil servants would be permitted to go on holiday to England until after 16th March, and those already in England before that date must return by 16th. In fact such irksome and petty restrictions simply made many of them all the more determined to participate.

Three weeks beforehand the Prince gave his first interview to a French journalist. He took the opportunity to explain that he would be announcing his political stance at the celebrations; that he was busy studying at Woolwich and had no immediate plans to return to France. He also took the opportunity to announce that he had no intention of ever trying to come to power by *coup d'état*. And unlike his father on these occasions, the Prince was being utterly sincere.

For the 16th March nearly seven thousand people travelled specially from all over France to Chislehurst. At a time when foreign travel was expensive and when ordinary French people did not often travel abroad this figure reflected an immense interest. For a few days only the French language could be heard in many of the streets of London. The Bonapartist Headquarters in Kings Street, Piccadilly, had only three thousand tickets for the Camden Place celebrations and was soon besieged by many more people likewise hoping to gain access. That weekend every London station had been decorated with huge notices in red, white and blue, proclaiming in French and English: SOUTH-EASTERN RAILWAY — MONDAY 16TH MARCH — MAJORITY OF THE PRINCE IMPERIAL. Special trains were laid on from Charing Cross and London Bridge all that morning, leaving at ten minute intervals. The English likewise turned out in their thousands to watch the spectacle. A local band, and the band of a Highland Regiment, were playing appropriate music up and down the streets of Chislehurst. The bells of both the Catholic and Anglican churches rang every hour. Chislehurst Common, normally empty, began to take on the appearance of a Paris suburb on festive holiday. On the green where today stands the town's memorial to the Prince, there was but a solitary drinks stall desperately trying to cater for needs of the huge crowds.

In the grounds of Camden Place two huge marquees had been erected, one to provide a buffet, and the other to house some three thousand people for the Prince's speech. Those who could not obtain entry simply milled around outside the entrance gates. At the slightest excuse, whenever anyone arrived looking even remotely distinguished, cries would erupt: '*Vive L'Empereur! Vive Napoléon IV! Vive L'Impératrice!*' Many of the Bonaparte and Murat families crossed the Channel for the occasion, as well as sixty-five out of the eighty-seven Prefects who had held office under the Second Empire. Fourteen deputies from the National Assembly of the Third Republic likewise attended. Despite a personal invitation from the Prince, 'Plon-Plon' finally decided to stay away. Ironically his absence gave some comfort to the Republican government since it made strikingly public the deep split within the new Bonapartist party — between the Empress, Rouher and the Prince on the one hand, and Prince Jerome Napoleon and his family on the other. But, amidst all the tumult and chaos, a place had still been reserved for the sturdy Madame Lebon, 77, now one of the oldest and stoutest ladies (*Dames de la Halle)* of the Paris market. Eighteen years earlier she had headked a deputation of workers who had been permitted to approach close to the Prince's cradle when he was born, and he now invited her to a private audience at Camden Place. She told him how, all those years ago, she had leaned over his cradle and kissed him. "Well then, *Madame,*" the Prince laughed, opening out his arms, "I shall return that kiss of yours right now...with interest!"[15] The news of his gallant gesture quickly spread through the crowds and the proud Madame Lebon thoroughly enjoyed recounting all the intimate details to the waiting newspaper reporters.

As before, at 11 o'clock, a select group attended a solemn Mass in St Mary's in the presence of the Empress and the Prince. This time Father Goddard excelled himself. In his perfect French the priest lauded the virtues of Napoleon the Third — 'If the Emperor fell, he fell, not by the act of France, but by the act of enemies of the human race, who dared to undertake the most ill-judged revolt ever known, revolt in sight of a victorious enemy!'[16] This proved too emotive for a congregation largely representing the officialdom and the aristocracy of the Second Empire — for the first time ever, a round of spontaneous applause echoed around St Mary's. In the meantime, hundreds of French and English devotees were being shown round the house by Eugéne Rouher and Dr Conneau. They were thus able to see the room, even the bed, in which their Emperor had actually died.

After the Mass, mother and son triumphantly re-entered the grounds. The Prince now prepared himself for his great speech, the actual words of which were his own, even though the style and rhythm had been discreetly fashioned jointly by Rouher and Filon.

As he stepped forward onto the dais inside the marquee the majority of those present were seeing him for the first time. He was wearing black formal evening dress, coloured by the red ribbon of the *Légion d'honneur.* They observed that he was quite small, and contrary to many of his flattering photographs, not particularly handsome. In fact, to many people, Louis looked more like a Spaniard than a Frenchman. He had the same down-slanting eyes, the same straight nose and firm jaw as his mother. As they watched intently, his face pale and intense seemed to suggest a certain hardness and resolution, but tempered by the same melancholy as his mother. Although a little nervous, he held himself erect, standing alone with his mother close behind. He spoke throughout without notes in a clear and confident voice:

15   FREREJEAN, p. 224.
16   JOHN, p. 325.

Messieurs,

In assembling here today, you have followed a sentiment of fidelity to the Emperor's memory, and for that I desire first of all to thank you.

The public conscience has vindicated that great memory from calumny and sees the Emperor in his true aspect. You, who come from very diverse regions of our country, you can bear this witness; his reign was one constant care for the good of all; his last day on French soil was a day of heroism and renunciation.

Your presence around me, the many addresses that have come to me prove to what extent France is uneasy as to her future destinies...Order is safe under the sword of the Duke of Magenta (Marshal MacMahon), that old comrade of my father's glories and misfortunes. But order in material things is not security. The future remains unknown.

Hence arises the sentiment whose echo you bring to me. A sentiment that draws opinion with irresistible might towards a direct appeal to the nation to lay the foundations of a settled government.

The plebiscite means safety and justice — power restored to authority — an era of lasting security again opening for our country. It is a great national party — with neither victors nor defeated — raising itself above all to reconcile all!

Will France, if she is openly consulted, cast her eyes upon on the son of Napoleon the Third?

This possibility awakens in me distrust of my strength rather than pride. The Emperor taught me how heavy is the burden of sovereign authority, even upon manly shoulders, and how essential are faith in oneself and the sense of duty to carry out so high a mission.

It is that faith which will give me what my youth lacks. United to my mother by the tenderest and most grateful affection, I shall labour without remission to outstrip the march of years.

When the moment arrives — if another Government attracts the votes of the greatest number, I shall bow with respect before the decision of the country. If for the eighth time the name of Napoleon comes out of people's ballot-boxes I am ready to accept the responsibility that the nation's suffrage would lay upon me.

You now know my mind, messieurs! Thank you for coming such a long way to hear it. Take back my remembrances to the absent and to France the prayers of one of her sons. My courage and my life are hers.

May God watch over her and restore to her prosperity and her greatness![17]

The speech was a triumph. It succeeded in arousing all the right emotions. His choice of words conveyed just the right sincerity, maturity and patriotism. But

---

17   TISDALL, p. 157

it was the reference to a plebiscite which had sparked off the greatest applause. Amidst the spontaneous cheering, some people openly wept. No longer could anyone doubt his commitment, his obvious desire to restore France's greatness; people could only admire the way in which his patriotism had been intensified, not in any way diminished, by his long years of exile. Many who had heard nothing but propaganda tales about his physical feebleness, his intellectual ineptness and his moral cowardice, were astonished. Others started to press forward, almost crushing the Prince, who now suddenly found himself being carried shoulder high back to the entrance of the house. Here, when some semblance of order had been restored, he proceeded to shake hands individually with all those who were prepared to queue patiently and long enough to have the opportunity of speaking to him personally. The Prince somehow found a reassuring word, a little to enthuse and uplift each person. Some of them afterwards said that he made them feel that they were, to him, the most important person in the world. Others described what an excellent impression he had made — he seemed to have so much practical common sense as well as a genuine willingness to listen carefully to their views.

As darkness fell, the crowds were reluctant to disperse and continued milling around the grounds. Soon a window overlooking the lawn was opened and the Prince stood there quite alone, facing the people. Despite feeling rather tired and drained, he found the constant cheering and applause buoyed him up. He waved and bowed repeatedly. And then at the end he just stood still, gazing into the night, at the stars above their heads, sensing for the first time in his life the uplifting spiritual surge of his destiny, of the birthright which he felt was now within his power to claim. It was an almost mystical feeling.

Eventually the pilgrims returned to Chislehurst railway station for their long journey back to France, happy to have seen the young Prince in the flesh, and to have heard his stirring words. Augustin Filon in his memoirs referred to: 'his tone. I shall never forget his tone. Men trembled, there were exclamations, oaths, sobs: they were so electrified that they would have followed him anywhere.'[18] People spoke to each other excitedly for a long time afterwards — 'Did you hear him?' 'Would you have believed it?' *Comme il parle, le petit Prince!* Such enthusiasm could only reflect a political reality — that whereas Royalists and Republicans were bound up with dogma and principles, Bonapartism bound people to one individual.

The following day, sympathy for the Bonaparte cause was reflected quite openly in *The Times:*

> As months go by, a feeling seems to be growing in France that the disasters of the last days of the Empire were the misfortune rather than the fault of Napoleon the Third, and that the blame must be thrown in equal proportions on Bismarck and the wickedness of 'traitors'. In Paris they talk more than ever of the Empire and the Prince Imperial. They return unceasingly to the topic as if there were no other political prospect — as if beyond that are only darkness and chaos.[19]

18   FILON, p. 117.
19   TURNBULL, p. 329.

Through private correspondence the Empress was already receiving reports from France which appeared to confirm the newspaper's analysis. One supporter wrote to her immediately after the celebrations: 'The Prince has impressed me very much. I think he is born to inspire real affection and sincere devotion...Public opinion has changed, the uncertainty has turned many minds back to a régime from which the present government are daily compelled to borrow the formula.'[20]

The talk of Paris, more than ever before, was about a new Third Empire — as though it was the only alternative to the present political chaos and the looming threat of a resumed civil war. Yet no-one had the faintest idea whether this new Napoleon was likely to be as authoritarian as his father or as clerical as his mother. People could only envisage a fresh start through some national plebiscite — were it to be allowed to take place. But many of the Chislehurst pilgrims — on their return to France — found themselves discriminated against in all sorts of petty ways by zealous bureaucrats of the Ministry of the Interior. For example, some who had been the local mayors of their towns were abruptly suspended from office. In retaliation, the Bonapartists decided to perpetuate the coming-of-age ceremony by striking special bronze coins (in Belgium), in conformity with the prevalent currency, whilst showing the Prince in profile as *Napoléon IV Empereur* — coins which today are rare and valuable. And the fine portrait of the Prince, by Jules Lefebvre, was put on public display in Paris. This time the authorities declined to take action.

But none of this sudden public interest turned the Prince's head. After the celebrations (for which he had been granted special leave of absence) he quietly resumed his life at Woolwich. But many of his supporters were now beginning to openly question why the Prince was continuing to study at this particularly English military institution — hardly an appropriate place for a future Emperor of the French. Indeed their sole concern now was to judge the right moment on which to formally launch him on his public and political career. At Woolwich, however, whilst everyone was well aware of the celebrations at Chislehurst, few asked him what it was like to be acclaimed a future Emperor. And when they did, the Prince usually turned a serious query into some joke about himself. But the waves of publicity emanating from the coming-of-age celebrations slowly began to affect life for everyone at 'The Shop'. Groups of French tourists could now be seen constantly peering through the high railings trying to catch a glimpse of the Prince at work. Others persistently rang the bell at No 51, hoping to meet him and were only persuaded by Filon with some difficulty to move on. Hundreds of letters were now arriving with appeals, or requests for audiences. Although the Prince made time to read them all, Filon was left with the onerous task of devising suitable replies.

Louis meanwhile continued with his studies as though oblivious to all the recent publicity. One evening he returned to the house with a copy of an essay he had composed that day entitled 'The Duties of an Officer'. Filon recorded some of the paragraphs as being very revealing of the Prince's attitude towards his own responsibilities:

---

20 KURTZ, p. 281.

The regiment then is a great family, the heads of which are the officers. This imposes upon them the same duties as on a father, who in everything seeks the welfare of his children.

On the battlefield, the officer must be penurious of his men's blood, and never sacrifice lives needlessly, merely for his own glory.

In times of peace or after victory, the officer should concern himself with the soldiers' morality, and repress the lower instincts of certain men, who take the occasion of success to glut their appetites.

The men must see that their leader is always alert, sharing their hardships, their privations; he must watch when all the camp is at rest. He must be the first afoot, the first in attack and the last in the retreat; by his own strong spirit he must revive their flagging courage. Such a man will never be abandoned by his soldiers; they will rally round him, knowing that they will find always on the path of honour.[21]

In a few short years, these commendable thoughts were to be put to the severest test in the heat of combat.

The Prince knew that he had only one more year in which to reach the very top of his class. Now he was working so hard that even his devoted valet, Uhlmann, was moved to warn the tutor that, in his humble opinion, his master was practically killing himself with work. "No, no!" Filon argued back, "he won't kill himself. No matter what people say, work never killed anyone."[22]

With typical modesty, Filon laid all the credit for the Prince's sudden intellectual advancement to Louis himself, describing the Prince in his memoirs as: 'a self-made man; he educated himself, like those who rise from the lowest rank to the highest.'

Every evening after the day's work the Prince would read most of the French and English newspaper reports about his activities. He began to experience, really for the first time, the flood of hate propaganda against him now being unleashed by a rattled Republican and Left Wing press in France. He did not particularly mind these attacks provided they were based on fact, reasoned and serious. It was the utter banality and personal ridicule in many of them which he found so hard to bear. He read himself variously scorned as 'The Baby', 'Napoleon Three and a Half,' 'Velocipede IV' (a snide reference to his well-known passion for cycling). Other cynical comments were constantly being made about *L'enfant de la balle* who, at Saarbrucken, had struck 'terror' in the hearts of the Prussians. Some of these so incensed him that he even carried the relevant newspaper cuttings around with him in a wallet to show to others. Other articles labelled him the dunce (*fruit sec*) of his class at Woolwich. It was said that his examination results were so awful that the authorities did not even attempt to give him a place in the class order. It particularly pained him to read that he was so arrogant and boastful that his fellow cadets had finally 'sent him to Coventry', refusing to speak to him. The fact that there was

21   FILON, p. 122.
22   Ibid., p. 123.

little he could do personally to counter these spiteful untruths merely deepened his frustration. Had his father been alive and well, early steps might have been taken to refute such propaganda but the Bonapartists themselves took little effective counter-action. In some defiance, therefore, he arranged for a special photograph (dated 18ᵗʰ June 1874) to be taken of the whole of his class — he is shown sitting happily and at ease with all his fellows — 'those who no longer spoke to him' — and on the copy he gave to Filon, he wryly inscribed the words: 'A *fruit sec* in Coventry!' But even this amusing yet revealing photograph was never disseminated in France.

Anonymous hate letters, disparaging to the Prince, now began to pour into England. Surprisingly, some of these actually came from Bonapartist enthusiasts who were disgusted to learn that a 'Prince of France' was continuing to attend an English military academy. Those not addressed directly to 51 Woolwich Common were delivered to the Governor, the Queen, the Duke of Cambridge, even to the Empress herself. But Eugénie was privately pleased at this latest development. "Their very violence," she happily declared, "assures me that my son is a Power!"[23]

As if to show public solidarity with her son, Eugénie now became a regular and honoured visitor to the Academy during that summer. Her carriage could frequently be seen and heard clattering through Woolwich, sweeping past the Academy gates, across the parade ground to the Prince's study. During one such afternoon, as a cricket game was in progress, a ball came whistling over the parade ground, missing the Empress's bonnet by mere inches! As the players rushed on to the parade ground to apologise the Empress broke into peals of laughter. This strange English game of cricket she had always found highly amusing!

Eugéne Rouher always kept a close watchful eye over the various activities of the Prince. On one occasion he told Filon to obtain permission to conduct a journalist — Léonce Dupont — around the Academy. Dupont was planning to write a book specially for the party entitled 'Napoleon the Fourth'. The journalist therefore was not best pleased, on arrival, to meet the Prince in deep conversation with the French professor of the Academy, M.Karcher. The professor was a notorious Republican — indeed, he had actually been exiled from France for his political activities by Louis-Napoleon. Although the Prince did not take French as a subject, out of interest he had attended some of the classes and thus had got to know the professor well and grew to like him very much. When Léonce Dupont later reported that, bewitched by the personality of the Prince, this renowned Republican might have conceivably turned Bonapartist, Karcher was furious. He complained bitterly to Filon over this apparent slur to his sincere and deeply-held Republican views. When Filon explained that Dupont's silly accusation was based on a grotesque misunderstanding of the relationship the professor gradually simmered down. In the course of the same conversation both men turned to discussing the character of the Prince. Karcher generously volunteered his own opinion: "The Prince is a charming young man. Everybody at the Academy likes him. We have hot debates with each other, but without malice. I should be truly grieved if anything happened to him, and I have real delight in witnessing his progress in every direction, though

23   TISDALL, p. 160.

my destiny is perhaps to fight against him."[24] When the Prince finally graduated he must have recalled this particular incident — his leaving present to the startled French professor was a handsomely bound set of his father's own books! And Karcher was not the only avowed Republican to be personally charmed if not converted by the Prince; others were to be equally impressed in the years ahead.

Early in May it was announced that Tsar Alexander the Second would be paying a formal visit to the Academy. The Governor sent for the Prince and inquired if he wished to participate in the Guard of Honour being formed to salute the ruler of Russia on his arrival. Louis hesitated. The last time he had met the Tsar had been in the Tuileries in 1868, the year of the Paris Exhibition, when he was only twelve years old. "Will the Tsar speak to me, sir?" He could not bear the thought of perhaps being deliberately and publicly snubbed. The Governor could only tactfully reply that, as the Tsar would know of his presence at the Academy, he would naturally expect to see him in the welcoming Guard of Honour.

The Tsar duly arrived on 19th May. After reviewing the Guard, and publicly shaking the Prince by the hand, he later sent for Louis and greeted him most warmly. To the surprise of many, the Tsar then specifically requested that the Prince be invited to accompany him at the Artillery Review to be staged on Woolwich Common the following day and the Governor readily gave his approval. The parade was watched by a large gathering; they cheered at the passing of the Tsar and their own Prince of Wales, but when the solitary Cadet *Napoléon* rode past directly behind them, the applause rose to a crescendo. Many people ran alongside the barriers to shout greetings to the young Prince as he continued on his way. But he kept his eyes strictly to the front, making no sign of any acknowledgement. That evening he was also a guest at the official dinner when Alexander got up to propose a toast '.. to the son of Napoleon the Third, to his good health and future'.[25]

The following month however was less memorable. Louis Conneau was now approaching the age for conscription in France. Although exiled abroad, as a French citizen he was still subject to possible military call-up, and any refusal on his part to formally submit his name would make him liable to prosecution. In fact, as he had already been offered a vacancy at the French Military Academy at Saint Cyr, he decided to leave earlier for France, thus avoiding the question of conscription altogether. The two friends arranged to spend their last weekend together at Camden Place. The parting was painful for them both — for the Prince it was like saying 'farewell' to the whole of his youth, and the feeling of loss was almost as deep as that which had followed his father's death. He returned alone to Woolwich, having now to rely solely on his tutor for close company. And yet, ironically, the Prince now needed his tutorial services less and less, and Filon was already making his own plans to return to France. He formally requested permission to leave his post at the end of the course in January 1875, when he hoped to resume his academic career in France and also to marry, having loyally abided by his original undertaking to General Frossard, keeping his patient fiancee waiting for many years.

---

24   FILON, p. 125.
25   FREREJEAN, p. 227.

At the end of this particular term — the penultimate — the Prince was placed eleventh overall in the examinations out of a class of thirty-four. He was still not satisfied — despite the fact that he had secured commendable individual subject placings: tenth in mathematics, eighth in fortification, fourth in artillery, and fourteenth in military drawing. His low position in drawing was due to a lack of accuracy; in the view of the examiners there was too much freelance 'artistry'. But had he claimed that extra language — French — he would have been placed eighth overall. And now there was only one more term in which to reach the top.

Towards the end of the summer holidays, the Prince and his tutor travelled to Dover to go their separate ways — Louis, via Ostend and Germany, to another short break at Arenenberg; Filon from Calais to Paris, and thence to his home town Douai. In fact he planned to spend a little time in Douai before returning for Louis's final term at Woolwich. As the tutor's boat was the first to leave the Prince went as far as the top of the gangway to say *Au Revoir*. "You are going to France, you are very lucky!" he called out, "My love to everybody!" Then he added, with a broad grin, "... even to my enemies!"[26]

Amongst the spectators at the quayside was a Republican agent who had obviously failed to notice the Prince subsequently leaving the ferry boat just before it sailed. A telegram was soon on its way to Paris with news that the Bonaparte Pretender was en route for France! During the journey to Paris Filon sensed an atmosphere of suspicion noting that, even on the train, his every movement was being watched by strange people loitering in the corridor. At Douai guards had already been posted along the Rue de Fleurus where he lived and during the night, mounted patrols passed regularly up and down. The following day he read suspicions in the press that he was hiding Napoleon the Fourth! The atmosphere only changed when it became known that, after meeting his mother at Arenenberg, the Prince was busily touring Interlaken, Lauterbrunnen and Meyringen.

The Prince and Filon returned together to Woolwich for the final term in late August 1874. He had now been promoted to the honorary rank of Cadet Corporal which entitled him to wear special shoulder straps, known as 'swabs'. Despite this recognition of his worth, the Prince felt unusually tense because, although his final results would not determine any future career in the British Army, a low placing in the final passing-out order would only provide further ammunition to his many critics and detractors. He was determined more than ever to excel — it was now the only impartial yardstick by which the public could measure his real achievements.

At the beginning of this last term the senior cadets had to spend several weeks at practice camp at Shoeburyness. The Prince travelled with his tutor by train to the artillery ranges near Southend. At Tilbury Station, warned that there might be a crowd waiting for him the other end, the Prince insisted that they took their seats in a third and not the customary first-class carriage. When they arrived later that night at Southend, the station was badly lit and the crowd, looking out for the Prince, surged automatically towards the first-class carriage further along the train. The tutor watched in amazement as the Prince now leapt out on to the platform,

---

26   Ibid., p. 12.

and joining the throng from behind, began shouting wildly for the 'Prince Imperial', even imitating a cockney-style accent. He somehow elbowed his way to the front, and personally led the search all along the first-class carriage, before eventually slipping away totally unnoticed to the cab outside!

At the practice camp the Prince proved to be the most enthusiastic gunner of the whole course. He also gained the highest marks for practical gunnery. The Empress was invited down by the Governor, and rejoiced to see him so fit and alert, even if at times, as an ordinary member of a gun team, he had to perform various menial tasks which would, no doubt, have enraged many of his ambitious political supporters. Back at Woolwich he worked at fever pitch for those final examinations. He even refused the distraction of returning home to join his mother at the weekends. She was to write that it would soon be over — *Je suis tres* nervous *comme disent les Anglais'.* (I am very *nervous* as the English say.)

When the final examination results were announced in January 1875, the Prince decided that, after his mother, Eugéne Rouher should be the first to be officially notified:

> I've passed out seventh — but I was first in the final examinations. The Duke of Cambridge, as well as the Governor of the Academy, has been charming to me, and my comrades have bidden me *adieu* in the warmest fashion.[27]

The Prince had indeed finished top of 'A' Division in the last set of papers, a position normally only achieved by one of the under-officers. And he had been graded seventh overall out of thirty-four — this final placing being based on points accumulated throughout the whole course, not only for each subject, but also for non-academic activities such as conduct, character and abilities at games and sports. And this had been achieved despite the fact that he was eleven months younger than most of the cadets in his class. And during the period of intensive training at the Academy he had also suffered the loss of his father, and compelled to assume more and more the responsibilities of family and party politics. As a foreigner he had also started the course with many other disadvantages, of language and culture, yet had managed to overcome all of them. Indeed his instructors considered that, had he been less nervous about the actual examination papers, or had he only agreed to take French as a second language, he could have achieved fourth place. As it was he had also won the top individual prizes for equestrian skills and fencing. Immediately afterwards the Prince, out of curiosity, asked if he might be permitted to sit the French examinations *incognito*, and was genuinely amused to be placed second — after an Englishman!

At first he had felt thoroughly dissatisfied over his final placing at Woolwich. His only ambition had been to come first in every subject, and with perhaps just one further term, he knew that could have been achieved. But his ruffled feelings were quickly soothed on learning that, as a result of that final placing, he had earned for himself a special position within a select band. Indeed it was the equivalent to an

---

27   Ibid., p. 130.

honours degree. The first ten in the Academy lists were always guaranteed a coveted commission in the Royal Engineers, but to the surprise and relief of the eleventh man, the Prince decided nonetheless to stay with the Royal Artillery — for, after all, that would have been his father's wish.

In pointing out to Rouher that his comrades had said farewell in the warmest fashion the Prince was somewhat under-stating the position. His departure from the Academy was an event he remembered with pride and happiness for the remainder of his life.

The Empress was the guest of honour at the Examination Review held in the presence of Commander-in-Chief, the Duke of Cambridge. Delivering his official address in the gymnasium, the Governor made special reference to the Prince Imperial's particular achievements. His words were loudly applauded. In a final written report addressed to the Duke, General Simmons stated: 'The Prince Imperial, by his invariable punctuality and exactitude in the performance of his duties, by his perfect respect for authority and submission to discipline, has set an example which deserves honourable mention.'[28]

In his personal diary, the Duke of Cambridge noted: 'Went to Woolwich for the public day of the Royal Academy. Saw the cadets who drilled and looked well. When called upon, the Prince Imperial drilled them remarkably well. The Empress Eugénie was present throughout the day. She went with me into the gymnasium where the reports were read and prizes given. The Prince Imperial took seventh place in the graduation total of thirty four. A most excellent position for a cadet who is eleven months younger than the greater portion of his class and who also had to study in a foreign language...saw the rides which were excellent. The Prince Imperial took first place — he also passed out first in fencing.'[29]

At the Final Parade the orders were customarily issued by one of the under-officers of 'A' Division but on this occasion the Duke of Cambridge intervened, calling upon the Prince Imperial to step forward and take command of the parade. With great self-confidence he now proceeded to drill the assembled Company of Gentlemen Cadets in a loud and clear voice, pronouncing each word very distinctly. "Very good — could not have been better," the Duke nodded as he dismissed him. Then, in full view of the whole parade, the Duke rode up to the Empress's carriage to add his personal congratulations. Eugénie just sat there overcome with pride, dabbing her eyes.

That evening there was the traditional commissioning ball in the gymnasium at which the Empress was also present. Filon noted how everyone 'from the Governor to the youngest in the school', joined hands at the end and sang *Auld Lang Syne*. This traditional manner of saying goodbye was a totally new experience for the French guests; they found the ritual very moving. And then, suddenly, without warning, the senior cadets surged round the 'P.I.' and, lifting him shoulder-high, carried him in triumph round and round the gymnasium, singing at the tops of their voices: 'For He's a Jolly Good Fellow.' It may have been unexpected, it may have even been

28   MACKINNON AND SHADBOLT, p. 36.
29   SHEPPARD, Vol. 11, p. 53.

undignified, but as she watched the Empress could only shed a few more tears of pride.

Two days later the Prince was the guest of honour at the annual Royal Artillery Banquet held at Woolwich. In response to the Colonel Commandant's warm words of praise, the Prince got up and replied:

> I hope that the officers of the Royal Artillery will allow me still to consider myself as belonging to their Corps. *(Cheers)*. Thanks to the hospitality of England, I have been enabled to carry on the tradition of my family of gunners. *(Cheers)*. Not having been able to complete my education in my native country, I am proud of having had for companions men who have fought with us so bravely on many a field of battle. *(Loud and prolonged cheers)*. At all events I can never forget the two years I have spent in this garrison, or fail to estimate highly the honour of belonging to a Corps whose motto is *Ubique Quo Fas Et Gloria Ducunt* (Everywhere Where Deeds and Glory lead).[30]

The last celebration was a private class dinner at the small '*Blue Posts*' tavern in London, adjacent to what is now Carnaby Street. On this occasion no senior officers were present; there were no formal toasts or speeches; the party was only for the newly-commissioned Lieutenants. Everyone thoroughly enjoyed themselves, the Prince most of all. In a fit of enthusiasm, emboldened by all the beer and wine, he suddenly leapt on to the table and, opening his arms wide, generously invited all his English friends to come over to France one day and be his guests in the Louvre. He promised everyone would receive a personal welcome. They cheered; they banged the table and enthusiastically drank his health. Perhaps the Empress was referring to this particular evening when, years later, she told Lady Simmons that when, on one occasion the Prince had been dreadfully drunk and the news had been leaked to a London newspaper, he promised her that never again would he over-indulge. And he never did.

With all the celebrations over, he finally sat down in his father's study in Camden Place and wrote a personal letter of gratitude to Major-General Sir Lintorn Simmons:

> I told my comrades some days ago that they would always find in me a true friend, allow me to tell you the same and to assure you that I will never forget the Academy nor its Governor, who is loved and esteemed by all the cadets, and who is more especially entitled to my affection.[31]

Queen Victoria took the occasion of the Prince's graduation to write to her cousin, the Duke of Cambridge:

30   RA. J84/104
31   JOHN, p. 348.

I am truly gratified and pleased at the success of the dear young Prince Imperial. Who knows what his future may be, and the Academy will, I am sure, always feel proud that he distinguished himself in their school, and that he should have acquitted himself so honourably, and, above all, *behaved* so well.[32]

In stressing the word 'behaved' the Queen was surely comparing him to her own Bertie, Prince of Wales, who had so disgraced himself with a prostitute during his first attachment to the military in Ireland.

As already arranged the time had now come for Augustin Filon to leave the Prince's employment and return to France. Although sad at the prospect, the tutor could only take great pride in the achievements of his special pupil. Seven and a half years ago he had taken charge of a restless, ill-disciplined, intellectually backward boy, with a wild streak of irresponsibility in his make-up. Much had happened since then. The trauma of the Franco-Prussian war, the humiliating surrender at Sedan, the flight from France, the sudden death of the Emperor may have been devastating set-backs but these experiences had also matured and strengthened him. As the tutor noted in his memoirs: 'My own ideas were on certain points, and not the least points, very different from those which he held and ought to have held. For those alone could inspire him and sustain him in his task. Princes, and still less claimants to a throne, may not pause to await certainties, which sometimes never come, and which events weaken and obscure, instead of strengthening and illuminating. They must act; and to act one must have faith: faith in a just and sovereign power, faith in one's own strength, faith in men's goodness, in their generosity at bottom, in the efficacy of their action, in the final triumph of good in human affairs. Well — the Prince believed firmly and passionately in all of these.'[33]

Now, after almost two and a half years of disciplined military training, when the Prince had determinedly brought himself up to the first rank, the tutor was leaving behind, 'a bold and spirited young man, radiant with intelligence, overflowing with energy, glad to be alive and eager for action.'[34] And Augustin Filon was just one amongst many who never doubted that, one day, the people of France would turn to him for leadership, and whenever that call came the Prince Imperial would be ready.

---

32 SHEPPARD, Vol. 2., p. 325.
33 FILON, p. 142.
34 Ibid., p. 132.

Chapter VII

SWORD IN HAND

B UT THE EMPRESS'S THOUGHTS were more immediate and practical. What was her restless son going to do now? She greatly feared that after the challenges, the intensive studies and comradeship of cadet life at Woolwich, he would soon feel lonely and become bored. She wrote to her favourite niece 'Chiquita': 'Your poor cousin badly wants a change, for he is tired and unwell. I'm afraid Chislehurst will be too lonely for him, without his work. Really, it was heartless of Conneau to desert him, just when he needs a companion of the same age. There's no doubt he is very isolated, poor boy.'[1]

During this period of enforced idleness the Prince was able to give a great deal of thought to his future. He recalled the inspirational words of the old Abbé Deguerry when he had only been twelve — that the *Légion d'honneur,* draped over his cradle, had been the sign that he belonged wholly to France, and that he had been marked out from birth to devote himself to her people.. The Abbé had always stressed that Sovereigns were not in a position to simply live out their own lives as it pleased them. And Louis had always agreed with that view. He felt deeply that, having been sacramentally anointed the 'Child of France', no war, no political resolution, indeed no vote, popular or otherwise, could ever negate that. Nor did he ever consider that his legitimacy was derived solely from his father — sacramentally, it also came from God. His personal sense of destiny therefore was not unduly influenced by the farewell political testament left by his father — which he was to read time and time again: 'Power is a heavy burden, for one cannot do all the good one desires, or hope for justice from one's contemporaries...Therefore, it is necessary to bear in mind that the souls of those you have loved are looking down from heaven, and watching over you. The soul of my uncle has been my own prop and inspiration. It will be the same with my son, for he will always be worthy of the name he bears.'[2]

Whilst the Prince cherished the memory of his father and needed the comfort of his presence, he never sought to emulate his route to power. There was to be no re-enactment of those earlier farces of Strasbourg and Boulogne. Whilst his father may have been outwardly calm, but inwardly lusting for power, he, although seemingly impatient and impulsive, was quietly determined to leave nothing to chance in his attempt to regain the imperial throne. What he needed above all was concrete proof

---

1   JOHN, p. 350.
2   Ibid., p. 357.

that the majority of his fellow-countrymen really wanted to be saved by another Bonaparte. And in this matter there was no lack of advice — but it came from those who had benefited from his father's long reign, many of whom were now elderly, out of touch, some in exile themselves, all with vested interests of their own to safeguard. So keen were they for a speedy restoration there was always the danger that, without his agreement, they might be tempted to launch a pre-emptive political strike before the new Republic had become thoroughly entrenched. France had only officially adopted a Republican form of government on 30th January 1875 — and then only by a majority of one.

But the new 1875 Constitution had been cleverly constructed to diffuse political power away from mere individuals. It permitted various party groups to effectively combine to thwart any single person from putting himself forward as a purely national candidate, as opposed to party leader. In reality, power was now almost totally in the hands of the Chamber of Deputies who could and did make or remove governments, and control the President, without, in any way, being inhibited by party or individual loyalties. That this system appeared to work simply made the Prince's task all the harder. The reality was that under the new administration, however chaotic, France was slowly returning back to a semblance of normality. Incredibly that indemnity to Prussia had now been fully paid and the last German soldier had consequently left French soil, way ahead of schedule. And now Paris was reverting to its old self — becoming prosperous, even a centre of gaiety once more.

But as this prosperity blossomed, almost in spite of the continuing political instability, the Prince knew that judging the right moment to enter national politics was going to be his greatest challenge. If he mis-read the situation, if he intervened at the wrong moment, he could so easily plunge France into further civil strife. And if he misjudged that moment and failed, he could end up the laughing-stock of Europe. Nor was there going to be the luxury of many opportunities. In his heart he knew there was probably only going to be one real chance and that it would be unlikely to be repeated. In his isolation and anxiety he had much to brood over.

Now that he too had reached the age for compulsory military service, he would have to consider submitting his name to the authorities in France for possible call-up. Failure to do so could make him liable at law. On this matter, however, he received conflicting advice. Some suggested he should use this opportunity to return openly to France and launch his political career. Others declared that, as the only son of a widow, he could claim exemption from military service altogether. The Prince himself took a sensible and realistic view, appreciating that it was highly unlikely he would ever actually be called forward. In the event, Eugéne Rouher went to the Hôtel de Ville in Paris and formally registered the Prince's name. Nothing happened. But the gesture did not go unnoticed in France. And his enemies could never claim that he had tried to evade his basic civic duties.

Out of boredom he now determined to rejoin the British Army. Of course many objected, particularly those who constantly urged him to return to France. They reminded him of his coming-of-age pledge:— 'My courage and life belong to France.' How could that be compatible with service in a foreign army? But the Prince insisted that he must have a job of some sort in this country, particularly since current political conditions in France made it unlikely that his services would be required in the short term. Furthermore, Queen Victoria, albeit indirectly, had encouraged him to seek an attachment — she told Lord Cowley (a former ambassador to the imperial Court in Paris): "I am so glad to think that it is in our power to do something for this amiable and interesting young Prince."[3]

He decided to officially request an indefinite attachment to a regiment of the Royal Artillery. The Duke of Cambridge answered the application with a personal letter:

> I have great pleasure in assuring you that there will be no difficulty in carrying out your wishes, and I have obtained the sanction of Her Majesty's Government to your being attached to a battery for the purpose stated, wearing the uniform of an officer of the corps. I can assure you that it affords me great pleasure to see you continuing your military studies, which you have commenced at the Academy at Woolwich in so creditable and highly honourable manner.[4]

But the government's consent had been less than wholehearted. The Prime Minister, Lord Derby, 'did not object to the Prince Imperial being attached to a battery as proposed,' but asked his military superiors, 'not to make more fuss of him than they could help.'[5] Had he known of the Prime Minister's strictures, the Prince would have been furious. He did not want any fuss; he simply wanted to be treated on the same basis as his brother officers. Like all his Woolwich contemporaries now donning officer uniform for the first time, Louis was thrilled to put on the smart blue 'patrol jacket' which would become his daily dress, wearing the customary 'crown' insignia of rank on the collar — denoting his appointment as an honorary Lieutenant. He wrote to Conneau at Saint Cyr that the red stripe down the trouser leg was broader than the cadet stripe, and he expressed the hope that it would not be long before it was so wide that it would soon be transformed into the traditional all-red *pantalon* of a French officer!

On 21st June 1875 at Aldershot the Prince reported himself to Lieutenant-Colonel Whinyates, commander of the 24th Brigade, Royal Horse Artillery. In turn, the colonel presented the Prince's new battery commander, Major Ward-Ashton. Amongst the officers in G Battery were Major Talbot, Captain J R Slade and Lieutenants Roger North and Arthur Bigge. The Prince was placed under the direct instruction of the twenty-six year old Arthur Bigge. The young artillery officer could never have realised just how this chance introduction to the Prince would, in time, totally transform his life. For it was through Louis that the tall, lean young man, from a large and comparatively impoverished lower middle class Norwich family, was to be first introduced to Queen Victoria, at whose wish he eventually resigned from the army to start a fresh career in Royal service. He finally died as

---

3   Ibid., p. 364.
4   Ibid., p. 363.
5   Ibid., p. 364.

Lord Stamfordham, after having served both Queen Victoria and King George the Fifth with great distinction as Principal Private Secretary.

Needless to say, the Prince took an immediate liking to Arthur Bigge. He admired his intellect, his strong sense of integrity and the enthusiasm with which he approached all his military duties, but also his uninhibited sense of fun. In turn, Bigge came to recognise that the Prince's passion for soldiering was genuine and his desire to achieve not motivated solely for personal aggrandisement. And through Bigge, Louis also made two other close friends already serving in the Royal Horse Artillery — Lieutenants Wodehouse and 'Keggie' Slade, both of whom were to have distinguished careers in the Army. Indeed, Slade was to become General Sir Frederick Slade, ending his career as Inspector-General of the Royal Artillery, and Josceline Wodehouse likewise finally retired in the rank of General. These three officers proved to be very different company from the majority of the Prince's contemporaries at Woolwich. Altogether older and more mature, firmly settled into their respective military careers, the Prince never felt obliged to compete against them. With each he was to gradually forge a personal relationship which did much to compensate for the loss of Louis Conneau and other close French colleagues. During the many periods when he was away from Aldershot, he would write to one or other of them almost daily. And they were frequently invited for weekends at Camden Place, where all four would sit up through the night hours, discussing military issues and the events of the day. The Empress thoroughly enjoyed their presence, for she always liked the company of bright, clever young people and positively encouraged Louis to strengthen these friendships. She was particularly drawn to Arthur Bigge. Later, all three officers were to be personally invited to spend their summer holidays with the Prince and his mother at Arenenberg. On these occasions, Louis would take great pride in introducing his new-found English friends to a variety of other house guests.

From these highly intelligent and well-informed young men, Louis was to gradually gain a deeper insight into English political and military attitudes. Up until now, whilst reconciled to a long exile in a foreign country, he had taken little interest in the affairs of Great Britain — his whole being and mind had inevitably been largely focused on the problems of France. But the stimulation of their intellects, and the sincerity of their friendship towards him, greatly enhanced the warm feelings he had already formed about this country during his time at Woolwich. Out of the three, in time, he was to choose the quiet, but thoroughly reliable Arthur Bigge to be the one true friend to whom he could always pour out his deepest feelings and thoughts. And for his part Bigge always honoured that personal trust, developing a deep respect and subsequent affection for the young Frenchman, who was to so greatly influenced his own life, the fond remembrance of whom was to remain with him for the remainder of his days.

Another frequent visitor to Camden Place at this time was the Prince's former Woolwich governor, Major-General Sir Lintorn Simmons and his wife. The General continued to take a close interest in his former pupil and Eugénie, in particular, grew to cherish that support. Gradually, over the years, the Simmons family were to become close friends, and the former Crimean War veteran did much to ease various personal problems experienced by the Empress during the remainder of her long exile in this country.

In G/24 Battery the Prince quickly learnt to join the men on gun drill with the nine-pounder muzzle-loaders, and to ride alongside the drivers of the gun teams. The gunner soldiers soon became amused over the intense enthusiasm with which he so obviously carried out all these activities, no matter how menial. And everyone admired his superb horsemanship. For his part, the Prince greatly enjoyed the many manoeuvres and exercises, particularly living out in the field. He took a particular interest in the welfare of the soldiers, amongst whom he rapidly became a great favourite. One of his letters to his mother indicates the extent of that care, as well as his irrepressible high spirits: 'For the five days that we have been in tents, it has done nothing but rain; nevertheless I find myself very well in this life, a complete novelty to me...Our misfortunes have had no effect on the men's temper; they are resigned to the weather now that they have a French cook to make up for it. The cook is a delightful young fellow, endowed with the most exquisite qualities of mind and body...This cook, as you will have guessed from my account of him, is me! Thanks to a long conversation I have had with Uhlmann, I've managed to make a good soup, sure enough with 'eyes of fat on it', but declared first-rate by the gunners!.'[6]

In her journal the Queen continued to observe the Prince's activities. Whilst noting he had volunteered to serve with the battery at Aldershot, she commented on one particular aspect which was to prove portentous: 'he is quite alone there without a gentleman or even his valet de chambre.'[7] She would have never permitted one of her own sons to serve in the army without appropriate staff.

But he could never really resist the temptation to show off occasionally, usually through some feat of physical prowess. During his first summer camp he attempted to leap, at one bound, over a blazing camp-fire, but during the run-up suddenly slipped into the flames, burning his arm quite severely. Although shrugging off the injury and insisting on riding as planned with the battery through Guildford the following morning, he was already in a fever, his arm now thoroughly swollen. True to character he persuaded the regiment's doctor to make light of the injury. The medical officer, for his part, could not say enough about the Prince's courage in bearing such severe pain without a single word of complaint.

Returning to Camden Place to recuperate, he was further downcast to receive a letter from Louis Conneau in France. His greatest friend had now passed out of Saint Cyr, about to be commissioned as a cavalry officer in the French Army. To commemorate the event he had written, requesting the Prince to personally make a gift of the sword which, from now on, he would always wear and draw in the service of France. The Prince did not hesitate — writing to Comte Clary to obtain a regulation sword of the finest temper, he further instructed him to have it specially inscribed with the words: *'Napoléon a L.N. Conneau. Passavant le meillor'* (Pass before the best). He then wrote a stirring reply to Conneau, ending with the words: 'If I am never to draw my own sword in your company — well, I shall have the satisfaction of knowing that a memento of our close friendship is always with you; that my good

---

6   FILON, p. 136.
7   RA. QVJ: 26 Jun.1875

blade, hanging at the side next your heart, is always ready to prove that heart warm and noble.'[8]

At Camden Place his relationship to his mother inevitably began to change. Any political authority the Empress chose to wield over her son had officially ceased when he came of age and thus leader of the party in his own right. In other circumstances, on reaching adulthood, he would have simply succeeded his father and, with her husband, the Empress would probably have gone into semi-retirement to Compiégne. But, thrown together in exile, that was not possible. By now she had come to respect her son's strength of character, his moral courage and his determination to forge his own career. She was also mindful of the oft-quoted accusation that she manipulated him purely for her own political ends. The reality was that, early on in the exile, she had decided to quit politics altogether; indeed, in the event of a successful restoration she had long since determined to devote herself entirely to charitable works. Now she deliberately refrained from trying to influence him as she had the Emperor throughout his reign. And whilst he was allowed to deal directly with his political advisers without her presence or interference, she nonetheless was always ready with advice, if called for, and she continued to maintain a discreet watch over developments. Eugénie knew only too well that he could so easily be exploited by unscrupulous party politicians. In March 1876 she wrote to her mother: 'He is not ambitious, but he has a strong sense of duty and is audacious. By appealing to these sentiments, they might succeed in making him commit some imprudence or folly...Fortunately, while I am about, they won't succeed easily.'[9] But, on most political issues, they were usually in broad agreement with little dispute between them.

But she was becoming concerned about their personal relationship. Eugénie recognised that, above all, he wanted to keep her happy and not add to her anxieties. Indeed he had once remarked to a friend: "I mean to set an example by always honouring and respecting my mother."[10] But, she often wondered to herself, was he now going to turn out like his father — having undesirable friends, dissolute ways and loose morals? After all, the Emperor had himself started to stray in his personal standards during his first period of boring exile in England. And whilst she made no public comment over the fact that the Emperor had officially left his heir without financial resources of his own, in her anxiety to keep him from straying, she always contrived to keep the Prince short of money. And this was at the root of the growing tension between them.

He was frugal enough in his own personal tastes and did not particularly mind going without. But, without a residence of his own, he could not officially entertain as he pleased. And at the back of his mind he knew that only those guests acceptable to his mother would ever be invited to Camden Place. Consequently, he felt obliged to politely refuse many invitations to private dinners and decline some of the offers of weekends in the country houses of the aristocracy, knowing that it would be difficult, if not impossible, for him to adequately repay such hospitality. There were

---

8   JOHN, p. 369.
9   KURTZ, p. 284.
10   JOHN, p. 374.

even occasions when he was unable to meet personal bills and, rather embarrassed, had to request small loans from friends.

It was rumoured that, on one occasion, there had been to a heated argument between mother and son at Camden Place — that the Prince had expressed his anger at not being provided with adequate enough funds to 'maintain his position and have something of a household.'[11] As soon as the Empress realised that financial restraints were beginning to undermine his social life, thus inhibiting his ability to form relationships with those who might be influential to his future, she concluded that he ought now to be allocated his legitimate share of the Emperor's estate which, in accordance with French law, would normally be half. At the same time she also released a special legacy left to him by Princess Bacciochi (who had been the daughter of the Great Napoleon's sister Elisa, dying as a sole inheritress without issue of her own in 1869) when he was only thirteen, which, with interest, now totalled a substantial sum. Thus, at a stroke, the Prince became a man of means, although few noticed it at the time. There was little evident change to his way of life; nor did he ever establish his own household.

During October 1876 both Eugénie and her son, accompanied by the Clarys, Mme Lebreton, Dr Conneau and Marie de Larminat, left Camden Place in order to winter in Italy. At that time Florence, not Rome, was the capital of the newly-united country. Whilst the Empress and her retinue remained in the rented Villa Oppenheim, Louis accompanied by his cousin Prince Joachim Murat (Chino) and his friend the young Espinasse travelled to Venice and then toured the battlefields of Solferino and Magenta. In the latter town they located the exact spot where General Espinasse had fallen in battle. Meanwhile the Empress had returned the earlier protocol call made in Florence by King Victor Emanuel. But in the audience room of the Pitti Palace she noted with displeasure that, whilst there were many paintings of the German Emperor and other members of the Hohenzollern family, pictures of the King of Bavaria, of Bismarck and Marshal Von Moltke, there was not a single portrait or photograph of Napoleon the Third. As she looked around in some surprise, the King tactlessly asked if she was displeased at what she saw. 'No', was her reply. She was just displeased at what she did not see. As he began making excuses, she abruptly left the room, appalled at this further evidence of the ingratitude shown by her husband's former allies since his downfall.

From Florence, mother and son travelled to Rome where they paid separate calls on his godfather, Pope Pius IX. Afterwards he wrote a personal account of the visit to Tristan Lambert, the most devoutly religious of all his older friends:

Florence, 5th January 1877

I did not go to see the Holy Father with any political aim; I did not go to ask for the support of the Catholics of France. But I went to lay my homage at the feet of a saintly old man, the dethroned Sovereign, but still the all-powerful head of Christendom.

---

11 RA. Add. A12/474 — Letter from Lord Torrington to Ponsonby dated 8 July 1879 relating to dinner-table gossip.

I went to assure the Holy Father that the Third Empire, like the First and Second, would be the protector of all useful liberties, and especially for those that help to do good.

But I gave him to understand that I considered the Church should keep more outside the political arena, and that, on pain of losing her influence and her prestige, she ought not to identify herself with any party.

And this idea, which I permitted myself to express to him, was so much in accordance with his own, that he answered one day to a Royalist who spoke to him of a white flag:

"Sir, you are completely mistaken; we men of God have no other flag than the Cross of Calvary."

The welcome my godfather gave me was most sympathetic; he left me with these words:

I hope that a speedy return will restore you to France; I wish it for the sake of the Church, I wish it for the sake of your country, I wish it for the sake of Europe, for when France is quiet within, calm reigns throughout the world; but when she is agitated by revolutionary passions, the security of the world is threatened.[12]

Meanwhile, in France, Republican propaganda skilfully exploited the Papal audience, pointing out to those who wanted to believe — that Napoleon IV's first act on coming to power would be to go to war with Italy in order to restore the temporal power of the Papacy — that 'waves of blood would be spilt to satisfy the revenge of the cloth.'[13]

That winter in Florence proved a pleasant interlude from life at Camden Place. Italian society warmly welcomed the young Prince and his mother. One of the more agreeable aspects of their stay was to meet with various cousins, and other members of the larger Bonaparte family, many of whom were now permanently domiciled in Italy. They attended parties and social evenings, and went on innumerable sightseeing excursions. The Prince was even persuaded to take a few professional lessons in painting — but he agreed only reluctantly, commenting: "I've too much penchant for art. If I give way to it, I should be drawn in farther than was right, and neglect my calling in life."[14] But, in Italy, he deliberately dampened the high spirits and practical joking for which he was becoming well-known in English society. Perhaps he felt such high jinks would not have been appreciated by the rather touchy Italians and his many distant relatives, many of whom recalled stories of the wild ways of his mother in her youth and were ready to accept that the son would behave likewise.

But there was one event during that Italian holiday which was both needless and painful. The Prince and Augustin Filon had their one and only quarrel throughout their many years of close intimacy.

At the heart of the dispute were their respective interpretations of the Russo-Turkish conflict of 1877. Judging from newspaper reports, Great Britain appeared

12   FILON, p. 139.
13   FREREJEAN, p. 237.
14   JOHN, p. 384.

to be on the verge of war with Russia, having dispatched a naval squadron to Constantinople to deter the Russians from seizing that strategic city. However *The Times* consistently opined that there would be no war and that the tension in the Near East would soon evaporate. In an article in one of the Bonapartist newspapers — *La Nation* — Filon had strongly supported that view, adding that, in any case, England was simply not strong enough, either in naval or military capability, to start fighting a major power such as Russia. When the Prince read Filon's article he became angry; as an officer attached to the British Army he resented the implied slur on the effectiveness of that army. And he believed, in contrast to Filon, that war in the end might be the only solution. Above all he was annoyed that Filon's views might also be ascribed to him as the leader of the party. He complained to Eugéne Rouher, and soon special articles began to appear in every single Bonapartist publication to refute Filon's point of view. But the Prince's ire was really quite pointless. Few people in France, and none at all in England, were even remotely aware of their disagreement, and the Prince's overreaction therefore achieved very little.

Nonetheless he proceeded to write a sharp letter of rebuke to his former tutor, in which he also requested an immediate recantation. This Filon steadfastly refused to do. He sincerely believed every word he had written in the offending article. Nor could he accept the attitude which implied that anything written by him would automatically be interpreted as reflecting the views of the Prince Imperial. Unlike his mother, Louis could be unduly resentful — and this particular dispute lingered on, needlessly, for many months. Filon felt the long estrangement very keenly and remained deeply upset. Fortunately the matter was quickly resolved when the tutor some months later suddenly fell ill, virtually losing his sight as a consequence. Immediately the Prince became aware of his plight he resumed their usual warm and regular correspondence, the dispute now totally forgotten.

During this same Italian holiday, the Prince wrote a long letter to Arthur Bigge. After dinner in the officers mess in Aldershot, they had frequently discussed the British Army and how it could be improved. This analysis, on the selection and training of officers, reveals something of the innovative quality of the Prince's mind as he makes suggestions many of which, in essence, are nowadays standard practice but which, in 1877, were quite radical:

Florence, 20th January 1877

My dear Bigge,
Your kind letter gave me a great deal of pleasure; but I was sorry to hear of the disagreeable accident that happened to you and poor Slade. I hope the fall on your nose hasn't damaged your beauty too much!

I have been to Venice and Mantua; I have visited the battlefields of Solferino and Magenta, and I must say that all the time I have been in Italy I have been deeply interested in everything I have seen. And so I shall have a whole heap of things to tell you when I get back to England; but at this moment I am so busy that I simply don't have the time to give you a detailed account of my doings.

If you will allow me I shall now give you my humble opinion as to the best way of obtaining recruits of a little better social standing, with a view to making military service popular throughout the whole country.

The question is how to get from the country the most capable men. This result may be arrived at by increasing the soldiers' pay, and, above all, the estimation in which they are held in the country. In fact, all men, and soldiers most of all, have their proper pride; and furthermore, on leaving the service, they ought to be able to secure good employment, as in France and Germany.

This is a hard problem to solve. I think the solution is as follows: Firstly, the conditions for the enrolment and advancement of officers must be altered; secondly, a better pension and a government job must be ensured to men who leave the service with a good conduct certificate; thirdly, two or three schools must be established where soldiers' children will find a good education and a military education.

I think it is a great mistake to choose the officers solely by examination. I am wholly convinced that a man may be very learned and highly intelligent, and at the same time a bad officer; and since an examination can only measure the extent of his knowledge, this examination is an insufficient guarantee of his capacity.

I propose to establish in England what I think existed formerly in France, and what actually exists in Germany: a 'Cadet Corps'.

A cadet, in order to become an officer, must go through the ranks and serve for a certain time as a plain soldier, on exactly the same footing as the other men in all the duties of the day, but with power to follow certain classes and to undertake the functions of corporal, sergeant, sergeant-major successively, so that he makes himself completely master of all the details of service. As for the privileges granted to these future officers, I would have very few. They might be exempted from grosser manual tasks, and allowed to dine at mess with the officers when they are invited. After eight or nine months of this regime, their superiors might authorise them to enter for the examinations that admit to the military school: where they would spend about eighteen months, and on leaving receive their commissions.

These would be the advantages of such a system:

Firstly. It would be possible to make a thorough study of the character and moral qualities of the cadets while they were with the regiment.

Secondly. Since practical knowledge would be won before theoretical knowledge, the acquiring of the latter would be simplified and the officer, once he held his commission, would have nothing more to learn.

Thirdly. The intercourse between the common soldiers and men of superior breeding, and the prospect opened to the former of winning higher rank if they succeed in mastering the necessary knowledge, will almost make 'gentlemen' of them, and so enhance the consideration paid to them.

As for the schools for the soldiers' children, they would present great advantages.

Firstly. They would decrease the household expenses of married soldiers, and consequently the expense to the Government. (Free education did not come until later)

Secondly. They would prepare generations of excellent recruits, properly brought up, who would enter the Army from choice and not through fear of starving.

Goodbye, my dear Bigge, and believe me

Sincerely yours,

Napoleon[15]

During this extended break in Italy he also started developing some of the ideas about a constitution for a Third French Empire — a subject he had been discussing for a long time with others such as Tristan Lambert. In a draft preamble he argued: 'A country of 36 million inhabitants cannot be governed on the basis of a democratic constitution by which every citizen participates in the running of public affairs...the prodigious inequality, intellectual and moral, which is found between the upper and lower classes of society (an inequality that science and the division of labour only serves to increase) demands that government be in the hands of the best qualified and that all public services should be careers. It is necessary therefore to secure respect for authority, stability and progress, the proper running of public services, to recreate a 'ruling' class which will be the actual aristocracy whose basis was originally laid down by Napoleon the First...The aristocracy in France should not be hereditary, it should be founded on merit...One will be obliged, without returning to the feudal system, without violating a man's legal equality, to create government officials' families, whose children's sole ambition will be to serve the country and to bear a name which will call memories of national glory...Access to the highest positions must be open to all, and those attaining them should be independent of the actual government so that favouritism disappears, and so that the elite of all political parties can serve the State, no matter what party happens to be in power.'[16]

In prolonged discussions with the writer Maxime du Camp at Camden Place the Prince opined that France was not really interested in political argument — that the mass of the people were only interested in a life of peace and quiet — in other words, the *status quo*. He told him that he envisaged a constitution which established some eighteen regional assemblies — all with powers to create their own budgets, like the United States and the Swiss Confederation. In this structure, the Central Legislative Authority would only deal with national matters such as military expenditure and foreign affairs. He also considered that war, as an instrument of policy, was almost an inevitability — for it prevented countries from sliding into mediocrity and it fostered a strong national morale.[17] From these and other writings, it becomes clear that, whereas he opposed a central parliamentary government he also rejected an absolute monarchy, on the sensible grounds that the

15   FILON, p. 237.
16   TURNBULL, p. 338.
17   FREREJEAN, p. 242.

inheritance of genius could not be guaranteed. Stability, in his view, could only be obtained by basing government on 'the principal social forces — religion, the army, the magistracy and property.'

Today there is only fragmentary evidence concerning the Prince's political philosophy and what little there is has always been subject to conflicting interpretations. Some, less favourably disposed towards the Bonapartes, have always argued that, basically, he would have instituted press censorship, an Estates-General to be held only every seven years, with assemblies for each province. Others maintain that, had he come to power, his administration would have been even more liberal than the last year of his father's. There is also evidence that he would have treated generously all those connected with his father's downfall although it is unlikely they would have been offered key posts. But subjective opinions about his supposed views are a poor substitute for hard facts, and the reality is that the young Prince was still clarifying and refining his own political beliefs, without committing very much to paper.

They did not leave Italy until March 1877. The Empress then travelled by sea to Spain to spend some time with her mother whose health continued to fail. The Prince returned alone to Camden Place, and during that spring and summer became deeply enmeshed in political activity. In the view of many Bonapartists the situation in France was now becoming propitious for a possible restoration and the time had finally come to directly involve the Prince.

In 1873 Marshal MacMahon had become the second President of the Third Republic. His term of office was six years. It was the supreme accolade for an ageing soldier who, ironically, owed everything to Napoleon the Third — for it was the Emperor who had patronised his entire career, finally creating him Duke of Magenta and Marshal of France. Not without reason, therefore, most people assumed he was really a Bonapartist at heart (it was said that the deceased Emperor had even earmarked him to become Minister of War in his restored Council), and many believed that he would deliberately see out his full term of office so as to enable the Prince Imperial to succeed him in 1879. However the Republicans had given notice that, if they gained more seats in the Chamber after the May elections in 1877, they would compel the old Marshal to stand down in favour of their own candidate. There was thus the prospect of further civil strife in France from which the Bonapartists might conceivably be able to take political advantage. But Eugéne Rouher and other party elders seemed to be at a loss over how best to exploit such an opportunity. Rouher, in particular, had never held strong policy views being just as opportunist as his former master, the late Emperor. Even now he could only suggest the usual tactics of forging temporary political alliances with the Conservatives and other anti-Republican groups, to be followed by disavowal of such groupings once power had been achieved. The Prince, on the other hand, was not in favour of patchy alliances, he wanted to clarify all the contentious issues and then, having identified them, make sure his party, and only his party, offered genuine solutions, ones which could command significant support. In short he wanted a manifesto with a range of detailed and well considered policies. During all these arguments, it became clear that the Prince did not share the prevailing view that the Marshal was at heart a Bonapartist and events were to prove him right.

In the summer of 1876 the son of the President met the Prince (they had in fact known each other as children) in the Officers Mess at Aldershot — a meeting which later became the subject of a pen and ink caricature by the cartoonist, Lionel Fawkes, in which he depicted the slender agile figure of the Pretender to the imperial throne, resplendent in the dress uniform of a British artillery officer, bowing gracefully to greet the hugely rotund figure of the overweight young MacMahon, sketched complete with frizzy hair and untidy frock coat. The implication of the cartoon was clear. But none of the MacMahons enjoyed a good reputation at Camden Place. The Empress, in particular, could not forgive the Marshal for conveniently being in hospital during the Battle of Sedan, and then subsequently keeping his distance from all the events which followed the Emperor's capitulation. She dismissed him as an ambitious egoist without an ounce of gratitude for all that her husband had done for him.

Although after the elections the Republicans succeeded in greatly increasing their majority in the Chamber and political uncertainty increased, the anticipated civil unrest did not occur and the Marshal managed somehow to continue in the office of President. Indeed, he was not to be forced into resigning until as late as January 1879, almost at the end of his official term of office. At the news of the elections the Empress delayed her departure from Spain, and on this occasion contemplated returning through France. In a letter, Louis responded to his mother's intention: 'For my own part, however ardent my longing to see my country once more, I shall never set foot in France save to command there. My pride could not endure a radically false position; I could not elbow my way among a crowd of careless people who once cried 'Vive l'Empereur!' when we passed. That would be your feeling too as soon as you entered the country where you reigned for twenty years! I say no more, so as not to influence your decision, but whatever it may be, I hope you will come back to me soon. For two months now I have been an orphan.'[18] In the event the Empress heeded his sensible advice and returned by sea.

During the turmoil of all these events in France the Prince, gaining in self-confidence, started to assert some authority as party leader, although he sensed that many leading Bonapartists would probably ignore his advice. He specifically warned Rouher: 'A dictatorship of the Marshal would be worse for us than his resignation...I have told our friends to be on their guard, and not to mistake his cause for the cause of the Empire. At bottom, he is ill-disposed to us, he is thinking of his own advantage and destroying France.'[19]

And Louis insisted that they must not be seen to be supporting the Marshal until they had first obtained his firm promise to back them. He wrote once more on this subject to his main supporters:

> If Marshal MacMahon intends to keep the balance even between all the
> Conservative parties, without regard to the strength of each, if he has no

18   FILON, p. 156.
19   JOHN, p. 393.

thought but to defend his own powers and to maintain the constitution of February 1875 as long as possible, we shall not enter into relations with his government. If, on the other hand, he means to beat the Radicals with any party he can, and whatever the results of his victory, we shall act in concert; for day by day it is clearer that no one can check the Radicals but ourselves... The Marshal will have to conquer or die, and he has no chance of success but under our banner; therefore, we must hold it steadily aloft. M. Rouher, to whom I have given precise instructions on this point, agrees with me absolutely. We shall do all that is possible to keep our friends quiet, and to prevent them from being swept away by the enthusiasm of a pretended victory.[20]

With rising expectations of a restoration the Prince had also given thought to the role of the French Army in the new Third Empire. He decided to write privately to the Duc d'Elchingen (now a retired general who, descended from Marshal Ney, had been one of his father's closest friends) a sort of manifesto which might eventually be released to senior army officers. In this draft statement (of which three rough copies were made but, in the event, none of them were actually despatched) the Prince explained how, in the expected political and social chaos: 'The son of the man who saved the nation from anarchy on the second of December, and the grand nephew of the man who saved it on the eighteenth of *Brumaire*, cannot without belying his name see his country ruin herself and remain inactive; and so he is determined, if power falls into the hands of the Republicans, to enter France, put an end to the reign of chicanery, and establish the reign of equity. He tells you so, General, without circumlocution; because, fortified by his own conscience, he feels he cannot be blamed by a man of duty and a man of the sword, and because he wishes to know if he will find a support, at such a time, in the old friends and servants of Napoleon the Third, who are now honoured chiefs in the French Army... (In the Third Empire) The Army will be the keystone of the social edifice, the great school of the nation...The Army must be respected in France as it is among our neighbours the Germans — and it will be, if ever I sit on the throne of France...That is what I have in my head, but if the general would know what is in my heart, tell him I love France, and am a soldier to my fingertips.'[21]

In a separate letter (which was eventually dispatched to the Duc d'Elchingen), he reiterated this view of the army's role in society: 'I love the French Army not merely because I am a soldier and a Frenchman to my very marrow, but because I consider that in it alone dwells the force that can first save French society and then restore its greatness.'[22]

But the Prince gradually became more and more disillusioned as the increased Republican majority did not lead to the sort of civil unrest in which he might legitimately intervene — with force if necessary. He was having to reluctantly accept that the majority of the nation was largely apathetic and indifferent to party politics

---

20 Ibid.
21 FILON, p. 157.
22 Ibid., p. 171.

and wanted only peace and prosperity. The Third Empire — if it ever came into being — could only emerge from the transparent failure of the Third Republic, bolstered by fear of widespread anarchy and possible civil war. At the moment there was no sign of either eventuality. In a letter to Raoul Duval, one of the unsuccessful Bonapartist candidates in the election, he described his own feelings; 'As events unfold themselves I perceive with distress how faulty are the political ethics of our country, and how hard will be the task of those who undertake the work of reformation. Ten years more of such a *régime* and France will be governed like the United States of America, by a clique of politicians, discredited in other careers, whose game is to exploit their popularity. In the eyes of every statesman and every honourable man truth and justice are on your side. The justification of your generous theory can be found in the words of Napoleon the First: "A nation more easily recovers lost money and lost men than lost honour".'[23]

The bizarre activities of 'Plon-Plon' did not help matters. For the second round of elections in October his second cousin had managed to persuade the Corsicans to elect him as their deputy for Ajaccio, exploiting the persisting attraction of his Bonaparte credentials. He now aimed to lead a break-away Bonapartist faction in the Chamber, people who were dedicated to his view that he, and he alone, was the only claimant to the imperial throne. Such open divisions within the party just further undermined its standing and credibility in the country. And the Prince's own calls for unity and restraint amongst Bonapartist candidates in these elections largely went unheeded; unjustified expectations were raised by many over-enthusiastic activists in France; some candidates even sought to be elected under the protective umbrella of the various Royalists factions so that, by the end, the whole party was left looking totally splintered, its morale seriously deflated.

In November Louis wrote in some anger to Rouher about these developments, 'Sincerity and rectitude are essential in politics as in everything else, and I am distressed to know that our conduct during this election can be charged with double-dealing.' When he learnt that a Bonapartist deputation had formally called on Marshal MacMahon to offer their support, he wrote again to Rouher: 'I confess I do not see what advantage the party can derive from this demonstration, and, if I had been told, I should certainly have advised against it. We have no interest in making common cause with the Government of 16th May. We were not with the Marshal on the eve of the battle, it is useless to range ourselves behind him on the morrow of the defeat.'[24]

In the same letter the Prince also stressed his absolute right, as leader, to veto and exclude from the party those Bonapartists who had been elected under the auspices of other groups: 'I am no longer willing that the policy of timid or false friends should always carry the day, and that the tail of the party should wag the head. It would be well, too, that none should imagine, as so many people do, that I do not occupy myself sufficiently with the affairs of my party, that is to say, with my business and my studies.'

---

23   Ibid., p. 159.
24   Ibid., p. 160.

Shortly after the Prince's death a *Daily Telegraph* correspondent, in a leader dated 23rd June 1879, recalled an official interview with Louis at Chislehurst about this time: 'His faith in the Napoleonic cause was robust and he spoke of the future as one who, though prepared to wait, believed that the hour would come when France would once more look to the Empire as the only form of government capable of securing order and prosperity...In drawing a parallel between the English and French character the Prince had recourse to an illustration which testifies as to a sound knowledge of both. "Let us suppose," he said, "that an Englishman and a Frenchman come across a piece of quicksand, the approach to which is surrounded at low water by a stone wall with the word DANGER visible in large letters written on it. The Englishman will carefully avoid it, and feel grateful to those who have warned him of the peril. The Frenchman, on the contrary, will climb over the wall, precisely because he is told not to do so, and as he sinks lower down on the other side, he will cry out against the Government, reproaching it with the consequences of his own egregious folly."

But privately he was now becoming thoroughly downcast. He had been quite mistaken in believing his hour had come. From recent events it was clear that the Bonapartist party, by itself, would achieve nothing through its warring factions and unseemly electoral practices. And he had also come to realise that Bonapartism, however disguised politically, was at heart a dynastic cause — and thus centred solely around him as a person. But he also sensed that the lure of his dynastic name was in itself no longer enough to attract the national interest his father had been able to achieve, almost without effort, in the mid 1800s. In the years immediately following the Franco-Prussian war the name Bonaparte, more often than not, merely invited derision. Louis was becoming distrustful of party politics, feeling that if he were eventually to be restored as a result of parliamentary intrigue, it would simply make him, as he described in a letter: 'the slave of certain men and of a whole party. I would never have accommodated myself to such a position and I dreaded rather than desired it.'[25]

Recent experiences confirmed his fears that, trying to win power through the aegis of one political party, overcoming the balances and checks carefully enshrined in the 1875 Constitution, was really becoming an unattainable objective, more especially now that same party largely ignored his wishes and thus appeared to undermine his standing as their putative leader. In seeking a return to a broad, nation-wide political consensus (the only sure springboard to power), he recognised that it was now entirely up to him — as an aspiring leader — to achieve such personal popularity and generate such enthusiasm within the nation as a whole, that he might, in time, be elected in his own right, over the heads of all political parties and factions. He declared his hand in a private letter to a friend dated 20th April 1879: 'The Imperial party has grown weaker and can effect nothing by its own strength. All hopes are centred on my person...I have had proof that people will only follow a man of known energy, and my care now is to find a way of making myself known.'[26]

---

25   Ibid., p. 188.
26   FILON, p. 188.

But despite all the disappointments the experience of recent months had been immensely beneficial. At only twenty-one he had shown a political maturity and grasp far in advance of his years. He now had a clearer understanding of the challenge he faced and how the real obstacles might be overcome. But all this would take time. He now resigned himself with the single remark, "I must be prepared to wait for ten years,"[27] consoled by the thought that there had been a thirty year interval between the reign of Napoleon the First and that of his father, and yet during that long interval, the name of Bonaparte had never been entirely forgotten.

In 1877 the Empress rented Lord Hardwicke's large house on the Isle of Wight overlooking the Solent. Here mother and son entertained everyone of note, including the young and beautiful Lillie Langtry who had just become the toast of the Prince of Wales's Marlborough set. Along with many other society beauties she warmed to the charm of the Prince Imperial, noting that he 'bubbled with youthful spirits and was a ready originator of practical jokes.' Indeed, it was common knowledge that: 'any prank or practical joke inspired by the 'P.I.' was applauded with delight by every host and hostess...married women were said to throw themselves at the head of the diabolic young Imperial character who treated them with exquisite indifference.'[28]

Lillie Langtry was herself to be a witness of one of his most famous pranks which took place during a spiritualistic seance at Cowes. The hostess, Mrs Crust, had arranged for the presence of a number of important people for, at this particular seance, besides the Empress (who had always been interested in the occult) and Louis, were the Prince and Princess of Wales as well as Mrs Langtry and several others. In an upstairs room the group arranged themselves around a large circular table and clasped hands. It was not long after the lights had been extinguished that strange things began to happen. When people heard the noise of furniture being pushed along the floor, and then articles striking the wall, they became so frightened that someone, almost in panic, nervously struck a match — and in the flickering light it became apparent that Louis had quietly left the table and was himself making all the weird sounds. 'Perhaps I was not as surprised as the rest', confessed Lillie Langtry, 'for I felt him let go of my hand and break the 'chain.' After this philistine interrupter had been respectfully put out of the room, the door carefully locked, and calm restored, we again waited in darkness and silence for something to happen, and in about ten minutes it did. Once more a 'manifestation' occurred, uncanny but tangible. Matches were struck again suddenly, revealing Louis yet again! He had climbed the side of the house with the aid of a wisteria and re-entered through the window. There he stood with several empty bags in his hand, while most of the 'investigators', and especially the Prince of Wales, were literally snowed over with flour.'[29]

The Prince of Wales clearly enjoyed the prank. Although fourteen years older than Louis, they frequently played the fool together. Lillie Langtry recalled how, during a weekend at one stately home, the two of them managed, at dead of night, to

27   JOHN, p. 400.
28   TURNBULL, p. 342.
29   TISDALL, p. 182.

hoist a live donkey up to the window of the owner's bedroom and somehow, dressing the beast in woman's clothing, tied its legs together to place it between the sheets to await the owner's arrival! The idea must have been Louis's — for had he not done precisely this with his own pony in the Tuileries years before?

But despite these constant high-jinks, and the frivolities of the Marlborough House set, the Prince of Wales was also aware that the young Frenchman had his deeply serious side. In many ways he felt considerable sympathy for him. Conscious of their respective birthrights both were at one in feeling frustrated and bored at their continuing exclusion from any meaningful role in their respective countries. But Bertie had long since discerned the real qualities of leadership in his exuberant and sometimes bumptious young companion, and recognised that these jollities so often provided a relief from sheer boredom.

During this particular holiday on the Isle of Wight the Empress and her son frequently went to Osborne House for meetings with Queen Victoria and her youngest daughter and constant companion, Princess Beatrice. Sir Henry Ponsonby, the Principal Private Secretary, always maintained that the only two people who were totally unafraid of Her Majesty were the famous Highland groom John Brown and the French Prince Imperial. At one particular dinner at Osborne House — usually a hushed affair, with over-awed people barely speaking above the level of a whisper — Louis sat next to the Queen and chatted to her animatedly in French throughout the meal. Afterwards a fellow guest asked him if the stern Queen did not terrify him. Louis looked at him in complete amazement. "Not in the least!" he replied, "the Queen's very fond of me."[30]

During the 1870s there was every conceivable rumour about Louis's alleged romances. In a sense he was the most eligible Prince in the whole of Europe. Whatever the queries and raised eyebrows over the pedigree of his parents, there were no such doubts about the imperial legitimacy of their only son — all he lacked was a throne. He may not have been particularly handsome, but he had youth, charm, an even disposition and a dashing manner. And there was nothing particularly shy about him; he mixed easily and sociably in any company, chatting away either in French or his always strongly-accented English. His manners were impeccable — gracious towards the many lovely and fashionable young ladies with whom he was now mixing, regularly attending balls, receptions, country house weekends.

One English aristocrat, in whose house the Prince had been a weekend guest, described him as unique, belonging neither to the country nor indeed to the age in which he had been born: '.In features, with his long oval face and black hair, attributes of neither of his parents, and his lean shapely head, he was a Spaniard of the Spaniards. One recognised in him no single characteristic of the Frenchman; he was a veritable hidalgo, with all the pride, the melancholy, the self-restraint yet ardour to shine, the courage trenching on ostentatious recklessness, and indeed the childishness in trifles, which marked out that now all but extinct type.'[31] This was a perceptive analysis.

---

30   JOHN, p. 417.
31   Ibid.

Gossip magazines such as *The World* were openly discussing the possibility of a match between Louis and Princess Beatrice. And in France the many Bonapartist newspapers constantly titillated their readers with the prospects of an imperial wedding. But French gossip did not particularly favour Princess Beatrice; their preferred choice was the beautiful Princess Thyra of Denmark, daughter of King Christian the Ninth and sister of Alexandra, Princess of Wales. Gossips could only savour the dynastic consequences of such a union. Apart from an elder brother who was to succeed to the Danish throne, Princess Thyra also had another brother who, in 1863, had been invited to become King George the First of the Hellenes. Furthermore, another sister had already ascended an imperial throne — for in 1866 Princess Dagmar had married the Tsarevitch of All the Russias. Were Louis now to marry the remaining daughter he would — at one stroke — have become the brother-in-law of the future King of Great Britain, the future Tsar, the future King of Denmark and the King of Greece. It is therefore not surprising that, when in the summer of 1878, he made a tour of Scandinavia his name was to be linked even more closely with the young Danish Princess. Indeed, it was even being claimed that he had undertaken that journey solely to press his suit further. Matters became so serious that, on 17th August 1878, shortly after the Scandinavian visit, the French Ambassador was to call on Disraeli, seeking confirmation of the 'approaching alliance between the Prince Imperial and the Princess Thyra.'[32]

However an earlier article in *Le Figaro,* dated 10th January 1878, purported to disclose the existence of Louis's mistress — a Miss Charlotte Watkins. It seems that she was a Chislehurst lady whom he had apparently met sometime on a train before joining Woolwich, and whom he had specially installed in a discreet house in London where she had given birth to a love child. But in a letter to Queen Victoria's secretary barely a month after the publication of the article, Captain Arthur Bigge expressed surprise: 'to hear the report of the Prince Imperial's liaison with a Chislehurst young lady and of its consequences — I don't believe it and especially after a lapse of years during which the story has never been mooted.'[33]

In her book on the Prince Imperial, published in 1949 and cast in the form of a 'fantasia' — part-fiction, part-fact — the authoress, Princess Marthe Bibesco, gave this mistress another name — Betzy Hunter — explaining that, although in love with Louis, she had finally declined to marry him on account of her humble background. And in his scurrilous play — *'Napoléon IV' (Drame en vers)* — first performed in Paris in 1928, Maurice Rostand inserted a scene to dramatise a putative meeting between the Empress and a pregnant young lady (again Charlotte Watkins) with whom the Prince (disguised under the name of Louis Walter) had fallen in love whilst in London! This same story — of a secret love affair with a young English redhead — appears in the recent 1997 French biography of the Prince by Alain Frerejean; yet this is specifically discounted in the parallel 1997 biography by Jean-Claude Lachnitt. Unfortunately the story, whilst attractive and romantic, is simply not sustained by convincing evidence. That is as true today as it was yesterday. Indeed, in 1928, Rostand's play caused a great deal of furore amongst

32   RA. B58/59
33   RA. Add. A34/29

those who still remembered the young Prince. Despite the passage of years, one of them, formerly Lieutenant Wodehouse of the Prince's Battery and now General Sir Josceline Wodehouse, wrote on 1st November 1928 to his old comrade in arms, Arthur Bigge, now Lord Stamfordham: '.I can truly say that of all the young men I have known none had a nobler nature and for none have I had such admiration, affection and esteem. I knew him, as you know, may I say intimately...I should say his mind was peculiarly free from sensual thoughts and that he was a pure-minded, unspoilt boy...Till this rotten play, one has never heard a breath of scandal about him.'[34]

In the small South African town of Utrecht there is today a house in which Prince Louis Napoleon is reputed to have secretly called on the daughter of the only significant Boer leader to fight alongside the British during the Anglo-Zulu war of 1879, Piet Lafras Uys. At the start of the war Uys was already a widower with nine children. In March 1879 the Boer farmer, with two of his sons, had been tragically killed whilst fighting alongside the British, and out of gratitude the High Commissioner had requested London to support the bereaved family by purchasing some farm land for them. It is thus far more likely that, far from being a romantic assignment as often implied, the visit (if it ever took place) was a simple courtesy call by the Prince in connection with Sir Bartle Frere's genuine concern over the Uys family. Indeed, the British government initially were not moved to provide the necessary funds and only did so after the personal intervention of Queen Victoria, discreetly prompted by General Sir Evelyn Wood.

Naturally the French and British public — then and now — revelled in such gossip, caring little whether it was based on fact or not. In any case most assumed that such a high-spirited young man would automatically be keeping a mistress — indeed, they would have only been baffled and disbelieving to be told otherwise. Yet, despite all these conflicting and competing rumours, there is still no firm evidence to indicate that the Prince had any significant emotional entanglement or sexual liaison with any of the many young ladies who featured in his life. But that is not intended to imply that this energetic young Frenchman was either sexually dormant or deviant. The numerous affairs between people in the Marlborough House set, encouraged by the scandalous private behaviour of the Prince of Wales himself, would have provided the Prince with plenty of opportunity for discreet private liaisons, had he so wished. Perhaps vigorous physical routines — riding, fencing, climbing and hunting — succeeded in keeping his natural desires at bay.

He frequently dined in London with his friend Arthur Bigge. After one such occasion at the Café Royale, they both had to rush to the station to catch the last train back to Chislehurst. As they hurried along through Leicester Square Bigge was a bit surprised to hear girlish voices from out of the darkness cheering them on with cries like "Vite, vite, mon Prince!" whilst others called out, "My, my, how he looks like his mother!" When they reached the platform, the Prince laughingly described his hidden admirers as: *"Les petites dames de Leicester Square!"*[35]

---

34   RA. Add. J/1561
35   KURTZ, p. 295.

There were always the high-class brothels of London in which many a rich aristocratic young man might be introduced to the pleasures of the flesh with total anonymity. But what little evidence there is suggests that the Prince deliberately declined to pursue such opportunities. Indeed, at a dinner party in Camden Place, one of the guests had expressed the view that it was quite impossible and impracticable to expect any man to lead a truly virtuous life. Whereupon another guest, the devout Tristan Lambert, had objected strongly, describing that as 'the view of an animal' — a reply with which the Prince was distinctly heard to heartily and vigorously concur.

It was in the hope of finally settling such rumours that, in 1878, Filon, in one of his regular letters, decided to raise the subject of marriage directly to the Prince. He received this robust reply:

> Marriage was not the object of my journey (to Scandinavia); in that case you would have been among the first to be told. It's possible that I may not wait to have a bald head like Corvisart, or a paunch like Rouher, before contracting a union, but at the moment I have no plan. Doubtless I can't aspire to marry for affection, but I have seen enough of life never to consent to marry against the grain. And I say that, not for selfish reasons, but as a man of honour.[36]

On a separate occasion he told Rouher in all frankness, "Marriage is a big question for a man who has made up his mind to fulfil all its duties."[37]

Given a choice, the Empress would probably have preferred Princess Beatrice. The Queen's youngest daughter was about the same age as her son and although not particularly beautiful, she had a shy, gentle and loving nature. But Eugénie also recognised the formidable difficulties which any marriage between them would arouse — the religious divide; the political objections from many quarters and the strongly expressed desire by Queen Victoria that, even after marriage, her youngest should always remain beside the mother who needed a permanent family presence through old age. It is not known how Princess Beatrice herself viewed the situation. She seems to have always avoided discussing the Prince, and long after her own marriage in 1885, declined to make any meaningful response to questions on this subject — even those from her own son. There is some evidence that at one period she may have been writing regularly to the Prince. After the death of the Empress in 1920 she appears to have privately requested that any such letters of hers which may have survived should be discreetly destroyed. Certainly nothing remains to indicate that any correspondence between them continued during the two months the Prince spent in South Africa. Yet there can be no doubt that her grief at his death was genuine and heartfelt — today at the foot of the Prince Imperial's tomb in the crypt of St Michael's Abbey in Farnborough there is only one wreath. The *immortelle* of white and purple porcelain flowers is marked simply — 'Princess Beatrice'.

---

36   JOHN, p. 415.
37   FILON, p. 175.

At the time of her own marriage Eugénie had been given a large emerald cross, set in diamonds, by the King of Spain. It had always been her intention to present this superb cross, cut in one piece, to the future bride of her son. Not long after the Prince's death she personally handed to Queen Victoria a sealed packet, with the request that it should not be opened until after the Empress's own death. But in subsequent years she clearly had second thoughts for she then asked for the packet to be returned. The puzzled Queen was both surprised and touched when Eugénie, now opening the packet in her presence, handed the emerald to her as a personal gift, explaining that it had always been intended for the Prince's bride.

The Paris Exhibition of 1878 was intended to signal the end of internal strife. With stability now guaranteed by an increasingly confident Third Republic, France wanted to renew her normal trade and commercial activities with the outside world. Many Bonapartists considered that the opening of the Exhibition, with its overseas visitors and global press coverage, would be an ideal setting in which to publicly announce the return of the Prince Imperial to France and a delegation came to Camden Place specially to persuade him. After a convivial luncheon for his guests, Louis, as always, listened very carefully to their representations, saying nothing. They pointed out to him that he had already become something of a cult figure — a symbol of youth and hope. That his picture was on public display in many of the nation's towns and villages. That thousands were simply waiting for his return. After listening to many similar exhortations he finally gave them their answer: "Gentlemen: let us look into the situation seriously and ask ourselves what would happen if I acceded to your wish. I go to a hotel: a demonstration is made under my windows. Some poor devils are taken to a police station for crying *'Vive l'Empereur'*. Next day, very early, a commissary of police accompanied by two plain clothes men, comes to take me to the frontier...No, *messieurs*, I shall return to France, you may be sure of that, when the hour comes; but it is I who will choose the hour."*38*

The delegation may have returned momentarily disappointed, but their renewed contact with the Prince's charisma had re-kindled all their old enthusiasm — the word spread quickly down to the lowliest supporter — 'Yes — we really do have a leader!'

Shortly after this meeting at Camden Place the Prince wrote to Rouher in France:

> *We* shall not overthrow the Republic; but it depends on us to profit by its eventual fall. If, strong in the justice and greatness of their cause, the friends of the Empire show themselves inaccessible alike to the discouragements and the fevers of party spirit: if they are always united, always prompt to defend our institutions, born with the century, and so much in harmony with its genius: if, imbued with the doctrines of imperialism, they never incline either towards the Royalists or towards the Jacobins — then France, disabused of the Republic, will not be long in finding its path, and then ten million voices will cry aloud: "These are the men who must govern us!" [39]

38   Ibid., p. 177.
39   JOHN, p. 403.

From time to time he rejoined G/24 Battery at Aldershot, but as he had no particular responsibilities of his own, he preferred to restrict such visits to the rigours of summer exercises and practice camps. With spare time at his disposal he now paid more attention to the finances of the Bonapartist party, studying a number of methods for future fund-raising. He also became more involved in various party newspapers, trying in vain to raise the intellectual level of the political argument.

He was soon writing to Rouher to specifically complain about one of the editors, 'When we placed M.Merruau at the head of *L'Ordre* I gave him strict instructions to allow nothing in bad taste, no polemics against our own people, and above all, that the policy of the party should not be lightly pledged. Today these three stipulations are a dead letter. There has been a return to sensational headlines, and the practice of excommunicating dissenting Bonapartists without reference to the responsible authorities is still in full swing.'[40]

It disappointed him to realise that so many of his suggestions, warmly received at the time, were soon allowed to lapse — until they were being pointedly ignored. To distract from the frustration he embarked on an intensive analysis of all the correspondence and campaigns of Napoleon the First. During these researches he was somewhat bemused to come across one of his great uncle's fundamental views: 'The English in general know nothing of the affairs of the Continent, particularly those of France.' But another dictum gave him much food for thought: ' The favourable opportunity must be seized, for fortune is female — if you balk her today, you must not expect to meet with her again tomorrow.'[41]

And to add to his disappointments he was now beginning to feel the absence and passing of so many people who had played such an influential part in his early life. His beloved 'Nana' had finally married a former Guards officer, M.Thierry, and returned to settle in France. Happily wedded himself, Augustin Filon continued to live in his home town Douai but was now seriously ill and almost blind. Nonetheless they continued to correspond regularly, at least once a month, but the Prince continued to miss the supportive presence of his former mentor. Then in 1878 old Dr Conneau, who had never really recovered from the death of his great friend the Emperor, himself passed away. The Prince was deeply upset for the wise old family doctor had always been like a second father. A few months later there had been the shock of the quite unexpected demise of the faithful ADC, Colonel Comte Clary. He had inexplicably succumbed to a recurring fever dating from the period of his service in the Mexican campaign.

Even Camden Place was becoming more and more gloomy. No longer was there the constant merriment and chatter of the two lively nieces — 'Marquinita' and 'Chiquita'. Encouraged by their father, the Duke of Alba, both girls had married abroad. 'Marquinita' was now entitled the Duchess de Medina Coeli, whilst 'Chiquita', the great favourite of both the Empress and Louis, married to the Duc de Tamames, had sadly died in 1876 during childbirth. Her unexpected death plunged the Empress once more into deep mourning, and the Prince felt the sudden loss of

40   FILON, p. 179.
41   DE CHAIR, *Napoleon on Napoleon*

his adored vivacious cousin very keenly. And whilst the former riding master, old Bachon, usually visited his star pupil at least once a year he was now beginning to find even that journey too much of a strain.

Fortunately, Louis Conneau and Espinasse would come over to Chislehurst whenever they could, and all three of them would often visit military establishments. After being shown around the home of the Royal Engineers at Chatham, the Prince wrote to his former Governor, Major-General Sir Lintorn Simmons:

> My dear General,
>
> Thanks to your kindness, my friends and I have spent a very pleasant and instructive afternoon at Chatham on Monday last. Colonel Cox was so amiable as to show us everything in detail; we were especially interested by that recently invented instrument called the telephone; I can't help thinking it will be soon be brought into use and found to be a great progress on the modern telegraph.
>
> What made me enjoy still more my visit to Chatham was that I met some few officers I had known at Woolwich as cadets.
>
> P.S. MM. Conneau and Espinasse wish me to express their deep gratitude for having been enabled to instruct themselves by visiting Chatham.[42]

By now the Prince was at the peak of his physical development. Despite adding about two inches over the last three years, he was still below average height and his legs always appeared stocky and shorter than most. Through constant riding and fencing he kept his figure trim and supple. His complexion had darkened a little, aided by a slight moustache, whilst the jet black hair maintained its distinctive parting. But, whenever he was bored or depressed, he would relapse into a sort of listlessness; at such times his face would become as deeply sad and melancholic as his mother's. At heart he simply could not bear to be inactive. Inactivity only made him restless and moody. But once his interest in something had been aroused, his being engaged in some vigorous physical activity or intellectual challenge, his manner would change completely. Then, by turns, he could variously display enthusiasm, energy, liveliness, even sympathy — as appropriate to the circumstances. And whenever his future was under discussion his manner would change yet again — for he could only talk about his birthright with the utmost seriousness and deliberation. On such occasions he would assume a noticeable air of authority and calmness — pointing out — 'I intend to do this' — 'I intend to do that'. Such authority undoubtedly sprang from his growing mastery of himself, and an awareness of the influence he was now beginning to exert on others. Filon was not exaggerating, nor was he being simply sycophantic when he once observed in his memoirs: ' His presence lit up and warmed the atmosphere around him. By a smile, a pressure of the hand, by every word and every gesture, he shed life, light and joy on those who approached him even for a moment.'[43]

---

42   JOHN, p. 408.
43   FILON, p. 164.

In the spring of 1878 the Prince was invited to be the guest of honour at two important banquets in London. The fact that, at the early age of twenty-two, a foreigner in this country with no recognised status, he should have been invited to speak before critical audiences of distinguished men was in itself a measure of his growing popularity and fame. At each banquet he delivered thoughtful addresses, composed entirely by himself, in excellent English. They made such an impact that both were widely reported in the press.

The first occasion was on 6th April when he spoke to the Institute of Civil Engineers in reply to the toast 'Our Guests'. After thanking the President for generous hospitality, and his 'tribute of respect' to the memory of the Emperor, his father 'who was always deeply interested in scientific questions,' the Prince went on to remark: "Our century has seen a great deal of conflict — many battles have been fought by man against man, though this is not the time or place to speak of them; and others have been fought by man against nature, and the victories which have been achieved in the latter will ever remain monuments to the honour of the generation in which they were achieved. Among the conquests which have taken place in our days none have been more profitable to mankind than the peaceful triumphs of industry. These victories are yours, gentlemen; it is therefore with a feeling of legitimate pride that I remember that my father belonged to your institution. I am glad to take this opportunity of expressing to the civil engineers my profound esteem and my heartfelt wishes for the continued prosperity of their most useful and admirable institution."[44]

Six weeks later, on 18th May, the Prince spoke at the Annual Press Dinner. In many respects this was the more important occasion of the two. Lord Houghton presided. This time Louis responded on behalf of the many distinguished foreigners who were also guests that evening. Another guest, Cardinal Manning, described the setting: 'It was a great assembly: statesmen, warriors, the chief administrators of the Empire of Great Britain in war and peace, learned men and men of letters were all there. He stood up in the midst of them, and his intelligent words, admirably chosen in our own language, and his powerful eloquence interested them to such a degree that they seemed to hang upon his lips.'[45]

As his speech progressed enthusiastic applause erupted at some of the key phrases. "The Press has become a necessity of our modern civilisation — a necessity of the commercial, scientific and political world" ... "The Press leads public opinion in the path of justice far better by stating facts than by defending the best causes with theoretical argument" ... "Amidst the European Presses the English is perhaps the only one which completely fulfils its mission"[46] This latter comment inevitably drew the loudest applause. Clearly, the Prince could not help but compare the frequent slanderous remarks about himself in various Republican newspapers and publications — to the apparent restraint with which the British royal family and other leading figures seemed to be treated in this country. To emphasise that point, and the need for the Press to disseminate reliable information rather than speculative

44   Ibid., p. 167.
45   Ibid., p. 168.
46   Ibid., p. 169.

theories, he subsequently had the whole speech reproduced in all the Bonapartist newspapers and journals in France. Afterwards, Cardinal Manning summarised his impressions: 'I said to myself as I listened — there is in this young man, whatever be his career, a power that will draw the masses after it and control them.'[47]

In July 1878 the Prince, accompanied by Comte Joachim Murat, a leading Bonapartist deputy and M. Franceschini Piétri, now his own private secretary, embarked — by invitation — for an official tour of Scandinavia. In fact the reigning house of Scandinavia had been French in origin and thus always politically sympathetic to the Second Empire. The Prince had long since wanted to meet his Bernadotte relatives, King Oscar the Second and particularly Queen Sophia who also happened to be his godmother. At that time the King (whose grandfather, Jean Bernadotte, had been one of the Great Napoleon's ablest Marshals) reigned over both Norway and Sweden. Besides these tenuous family ties, the Prince also wished to return the courtesy call paid to him at Camden Place by the Crown Prince of Denmark who had invited him to visit his father, King Christian the Ninth, in Copenhagen.

The whole journey around Scandanavia was a personal triumph. Everyone treated him as if his father was still on the throne. During his brief stay in Denmark, for example, the tricolour flew every day from his hotel; royal carriages were placed at his personal disposal; whilst sentries everywhere saluted him as if a member of their own royal family.

After settling into his hotel in Copenhagen the Prince was just finishing a letter to his mother, when he had suddenly to break off, scribbling: 'A knock at the door; it's the King!' In a subsequent letter he explained what had happened: 'As soon as I arrived in Copenhagen, I sent a telegram to the Grand Marshal of the Court, asking him to let me know the day and the hour when I could be received by their Majesties, then away from their royal residence, which is close to the capital. Returning next day to Bernsdorff, the King invited me at once to dine with him at 5 o'clock. I had just finished the letter I was writing to you and was getting ready to start when the King, who had come quietly into the hotel like any worthy citizen of his capital, without being recognised, made a sudden appearance in my room before I had time to hurry to meet him. That's the explanation of the "knock at the door; it's the King!" which I added to my letter, and which depicts pretty well my surprise at this unexpected visit, due to excessive politeness.'[48]

The Prince would have admired the comparative informality with which the Danish royal family mingled with their subjects. Such accessibility accorded with his own views on the relationship between rulers and their subjects. After a few days of generous royal Danish hospitality the Prince continued his journey north to Stockholm. But in subsequent letters about his stay in Copenhagen there is no mention of the twenty-five year old Princess Thyra, even though she was certainly present, together with the rest of her family, for much of the time. But few people (least of all the Prince) would have been aware of a tragic scandal concerning the King's beautiful youngest daughter. At the age of eighteen she had fallen deeply in

---

47 Ibid.
48 FILON, p. 172.

love with a Danish Army officer and in 1871 had secretly given birth to a baby girl. The affronted King persistently rejected the officer's pleas to be allowed to marry and two months later, in total despair, the young man had shot himself. Directly after the birth the baby girl had been adopted by an ordinary Danish family and seems to have disappeared from history. And whatever the press rumours about a possible romance with the Prince, the reality was that, shortly after his visit in the summer of 1878, she was quietly married off to Ernst August, Duke of Cumberland and Crown Prince of Hanover.

Staying at the royal summer holiday villa in the forests above the Christiana Fjord in Sweden, the Prince soon became great friends with Crown Prince Gustav who was twenty, and his two younger brothers, the seventeen year old Carl and twelve year old Eugene. Before long they were all involved in the Prince's spirited activities — clambering dangerously over crags and precipices, singing in chorus on their way back from fishing expeditions. Even the somewhat staid and stiff King Oscar was to become entranced by the vitality and freshness of his young guest. At dinner in the evenings, the Prince always managed to charm the Queen, his godmother, now a semi-invalid. The King gradually came to the conclusion that the Prince, in every respect, was indeed a superior person to his father and predicted a glowing future for him.

He wrote to the Empress at Chislehurst: 'Need I tell you how greatly I rejoice in your son's visit here? You have known for long my feelings towards you and yours, but what I should like to say now is that I am absolutely enchanted with him, and that this sentiment is shared by all who come near him. I have rarely, or never, met a young man who is so mature at twenty-two. He is interested in everything, enquires about everything, and his questions always show wide knowledge and excellent education. Already, he is extremely popular here and has been acclaimed all along his route with a warmth which is rare among us inhabitants of the North.'[49]

He found Louis's insatiable curiosity one of his most endearing traits and commented on this to a friend: "Why, he once asked me just now how long it took a vessel to get up steam! I hadn't any idea — I thought it might probably be ten minutes — I find it actually takes an hour and a quarter. But it's very improving, and one would certainly have to rub up one's knowledge if one were to be with him for long."[50]

As part of the visit programme the whole party made a steamer trip across the fjord to Christiana. It was an unusually hot day with little shade available on the exposed deck. Halfway across, the Prince suggested to the King that everyone ought to cool down with a quick swim in the fjord. The King demurred — apart from the indecorum of such activity, he would have to stop the ship and that, in turn, would needlessly delay the official reception at the other end as well as the departure of the royal train from Christiana. However the Prince did not appear to hear and, stripping off all his clothes on the spot, instantly dived straight off the poop into the water.

49   KURTZ, p. 293.
50   JOHN, p. 410.

The King immediately ordered the engines to be stopped and, turning to an ADC, instructed him to go over the side and bring the Prince back. With the ship now stationary and two men happily splashing around in the cool water, Crown Prince Gustav and two more ADCs likewise stripped off and proceeded to dive into the fjord. Soon there were five of them in the water, swimming around the ship, with the Prince springing from the back of one to the other as if riding dolphins. It took about thirty minutes to get everyone back on board again and for the journey to be resumed.

Such pranks likewise featured on the many train journeys the Prince made through Sweden and Norway. Out of sheer devilment he would often climb out of his carriage window and enter a station squatting on the roof. Yet everywhere he went the Prince was wildly feted and cheered. His carriage was invariably inundated with bouquets and flowers. During one short train journey he requested some refreshment. Discovering there was nothing to eat or drink on the train itself he decided to find some at the next station. Having disguised himself as best he could, the Prince: 'got out and we saw him speeding along the platform, a little dusty figure grey and dusty even to his eyebrows...Later on, we beheld him leaning out of a window of a second class carriage at the other end of the train, and watching in great amusement the crowds that gathered in front of the royal coach, and were engaged in staring at the equerry he had put there to fill his place. That was the last time we ever saw the Prince Imperial alive.'[51]

Thrilled by the warm reception at every stage of his trip through Scandinavia, the Prince travelled on to Arenenberg to join his mother on 10th August. He summarised his experiences: 'I have everywhere been the object of a regular ovation: the authorities, public bands, ladies, bouquets, everything. I was received as if my father were still on the throne.'[52] Much of the Prince's elation could probably be ascribed to the fact that, for the first time since 1870, he had actually stayed in a palace, surrounded by a court, once more the centre of attention. Before arriving at the family villa, the Empress had been to Vienna where, with her flair for the dramatic gesture, she had placed a crown in the name of her son on the narrow coffin, adorned with the heads of lions, which housed the remains of the young King of Rome — that other Prince Imperial who had died at the same age as Louis, likewise in exile.

Staying at Arenenberg there was, as always, a large house party and one particular guest, Madame Feuillet (the wife of the Empress's favourite author, Octave Feuillet) has left her own impressions of Louis whom she had last seen three years earlier:

> We hardly recognised the Prince, so tall had he grown, so animated and noble had his face become. He was a fine fellow of twenty three (he was, in fact, twenty two), with the grace of a perfect gentleman. Everyone who knew him at this time speaks feelingly of his charm, his kindness, his heart, the sincerity and rectitude of his sentiments. Everybody loved him. At dinner I

---

51   Ibid., p. 411.
52   FILON, p. 174.

was put beside him. He talked to me with animation and much intelligence of everything that concerned France, of our literature, of the works of Taine and Renan.[53]

She considered him to be very bright and well-informed, particularly about French politics. The young lady-in-waiting, Marie de Larminat, in attendance on the Empress at Arenenberg, despaired of ever describing the Prince properly. She could only recall somewhat inadequately, "I never saw anyone like him. The ardent vitality of his restraint seemed to mark him out as one of the elect. In those days I believed it with all my heart!"[54]

Although many of the descriptions of Louis's personality and presence at this time appear to be somewhat effusive, with those closest to him perhaps being more biased than most, there is nonetheless in these various intimate recollections a genuine sincerity and a common thread of admiration, which owe nothing to the social deference with which he was so often surrounded.

Whilst at Arenenberg he led parties on long expeditions across the Oberland, taking with him his cousin 'Chino' (Prince Murat), Espinasse and his close English friends, Bigge and Slade. Towards the end of the Nineteenth Century mountaineering was becoming increasingly popular and the Prince revelled in its challenges. Leadership on these expeditions came naturally to him, for he knew every crag, every hazard and he often deliberately tested the courage of his friends as much as his own. Away from politics and public duties, high in the mountains, breathing in pure air, in the company of dearest friends, the Prince could only revel in the sheer intoxication of it all — his whole being becoming so animated that he almost became another person — exuding vitality, energy and daring. And that person was also totally fearless.

But despite all these physical challenges he still experienced moments of gloom and despondency. In the aftermath of his wonderful reception in Scandinavia, where clearly ordinary people had delighted in his presence, he was still puzzled by the fact that everyone, everywhere seemed to want him — except his own people. In France, the persisting stigma of Sedan and the corrosive charge of personal cowardice in deserting the country at its lowest ebb, cast a permanent shadow over the Prince's standing in French society. His youth was passing — yet there seemed to be no prospect of returning home. He found it frustrating having to contemplate a long and tedious wait. His penchant for dramatic high jinks and mischievous practical jokes probably provided a safety valve for some of these pent-up feelings. Such pranks also helped to popularise his name, provided they did not degenerate into the simply idiotic. But Louis always knew the limits; he needed to safeguard his growing and justified reputation for strict personal morals and polite, gentlemanly behaviour. He believed profoundly that, unless his private life was truly free of scandal, there would be no chance whatever of withstanding the many scurrilous accusations which his enemies would always level against him. Even if most of that

53   Ibid., p. 167.
54   JOHN, p. 413.

hostility, he noted with sadness, now appeared to emanate exclusively from his own country.

In 1878 the Prince was frequently invited to hunt at various meets up and down the country. Everyone knew of his dash and daring during the chase, even if his audacity often irritated hunt masters and some of the more sedate riders. In November of that year he wrote a friend: 'On Tuesday last I hunted with the Queen's hounds for the first time. I enjoyed it greatly although it was more of a steeplechase than ordinary hunting. We covered thirty miles and jumped a considerable number of obstacles, and so my horse, though an excellent thoroughbred, was completely done up.'[55] Sometimes the beautiful Elizabeth, Empress of Austria, a renowned horsewoman in her own right, would appear as an honoured guest. On these occasions, spectators and riders alike were able to witness a dazzling display of incomparable horsemanship — as both deliberately rode hard — neck-and-neck — to jump and usually clear all the most difficult obstacles which the rest had carefully avoided.

And when not hunting, he was frequently to be seen at many of the popular Horse Shows. On one occasion, whilst a guest of the Duke of Westminster at Eaton Hall, the house party came out to watch a parade of huge Clydesdale stallions. One of them — difficult to control, rearing and snorting — was pointed out as 'an impossible ride'; indeed no-one had been able to remain on its broad back for very long. Despite top hat and cumbersome frock coat, the Prince immediately responded to the challenge; jumping over the rail he leapt straight on to the stallion's back. And no matter how the animal kicked and pounded it could not dislodge him. Yet, after very few minutes the huge stallion had become totally pacified, quietly ambling around the ring. Many of the house guests could only be embarrassed by such blatant exhibitionism, but most of the spectators could only cheer and applaud this dashing young French Prince who so obviously exulted in his formidable equestrian skills.

'When one belongs to a race of soldiers, it is only sword in hand that one gains recognition' the Prince had written shortly after arriving in South Africa. This was a plain statement of the course of action upon which he had now determined. With his unbounded self-confidence and recent military training he felt that, given the right circumstances, he could win glory on a field of battle, thus disarming all those critics and demonstrating to the French people his Bonaparte credentials for high office. Louis sensed that proven courage in battle, ideally authenticated by some citation or decoration, would be the surest and quickest way to attract favourable publicity. And he was not alone in that supposition. Twenty years later, a youthful Winston Churchill, likewise seeking political fame, was to take a similar route — campaigning for country, medals and publicity in a number of Great Britain's colonial wars.

After the political rebuffs of 1877 the Prince now deliberately sought opportunities for active soldiering. Initially he contemplated asking the French government for permission to join the colonial war then in progress in Indo-China but knew his application would be gleefully rejected. About the same time he also

---

55   FILON, p. 165.

expected that Great Britain would go to war with Russia, even if, as Filon had tried to argue, British forces would be too weak. The Prince disagreed, displaying a touching loyalty to his *alma mater*. 'The English troops,' he had written in a private letter, 'will march bravely to the unequal combat. And I shall seize the chances to show I am good for something. The latent condition of French affairs makes it possible.'[56] And he wrote at that time to Arthur Bigge, 'I am thirsting to smell powder.'[57]

But the Treaty of Berlin extinguished any prospect of a fresh war breaking out in the Near East. However, now that Austria had been accorded the right to occupy Bosnia and Herzegovina, it was conceivable that there might be some local resistance. In that event, Turkey would be most likely to intervene. The Prince wrote privately to the Emperor Franz Josef to offer his services as a volunteer officer in the Austrian Army now deploying to occupy the new territories. However Eugénie strongly opposed this move. She found utterly offensive the very idea of the son of the victor of Solferino wearing Austrian uniform, and shrewdly calculated that if there was no conflict, her son would probably spend all his time playing billiards and flirting with Italian singers! And should war break out he would probably end up fighting against the Turks, his father's old allies in the Crimean War or against the very Tsar of Russia who had been so kind to him during that visit to Woolwich. In earlier times the Empress's veto would have simply put an end to the matter. But nowadays she always tried to support him, even against her better judgement. Thus she eventually capitulated to his persistent pleadings and herself wrote a separate letter of supplication to the Emperor. The Prince was so convinced that his offer would be accepted that he could scarcely contain his disgust when, in his personal reply, the Emperor politely declined his services. But that irritation quickly evaporated once he learnt that the Austrian occupation had actually been completed without incident. So there was no military glory to be obtained there. He turned his attention to other opportunities.

---

56   JOHN, p. 413.
57   FILON, p. 176.

Chapter VIII

THE LONG VOYAGE

IN APRIL 1878 CAPTAIN BIGGE and Lieutenant Slade called at Camden Place to say goodbye to the Prince. Like many of the officers of G/24 Battery they had long since put their names forward as prospective volunteers for service in South Africa and both of them were now under orders to sail immediately. And they were to be both surprised and flattered when the Prince himself suddenly appeared, at dawn, on 25th April at the Southampton docks in order to bid them a personal final farewell. And as he sadly shook their hands, the Prince was only too aware of the circumstances which had prompted their sudden departure.

In the early months of 1878, due to rising tensions in South Africa, it had been decided to allow previously registered volunteers to join the small British forces already in Natal. There appeared to be a growing, but quite unwarranted fear amongst the British authorities in Cape Town that the formidable Zulu army was perhaps preparing to invade nearby Natal. By the end of the year King Cetshwayo had really been left with no alternative but to ignore an impossible ultimatum from the High Commissioner for South East Africa, Sir Bartle Frere, which required him, amongst other equally unacceptable conditions, to immediately disband the source of his power — the formidable *impis* — regiments of highly trained and disciplined warriors. The King was given thirty days to comply with the ultimatum. In the full knowledge that the Zulus would never accept such terms, existing plans for a pre-emptive strike into Zululand were put into effect.

And so Great Britain, at the personal whim of one of its High Commissioners and without any prior Cabinet approval, suddenly found itself at war with the formidable Zulu nation. Both Sir Bartle Frere and Lieutenant-General Lord Chelmsford, the General Officer Commanding Southern Africa, clearly expected the military campaign to be so brief and conclusive that, by the time the British Government had even become aware of the war being waged in its name, victory would have already been achieved and the putative threat to Natal removed. That this did not happen was largely due to an over-optimistic assessment of the logistical and terrain problems of mounting such a campaign, and a severe under-estimate of the military prowess of the Zulu forces.

On 11th January 1879, Cetshwayo's kingdom was brutally invaded by 17,000 mixed European and native troops, divided into three separate columns, all moving independently to converge on oNdini, the Royal kraal, where it was planned to employ all the modern firepower at Chelmsford's disposal to rout the Zulu army.

But, to everyone's surprise, on 22nd January the Zulus, in force, suddenly attacked one of these columns at a place called Isandlwana and in the ensuing carnage almost 900 European and more than 500 native troops perished. Only about 300 escaped. The Zulus took no prisoners.

This appalling news, when it reached England, was aggravated by clear evidence that the Zulus had disembowelled most of the bodies — in the traditional belief that if they had not slashed open the bellies of their fallen foes, their own stomachs would have swelled up like those of the dead. Rituals such as these — mutilating the dead, slaughtering the wounded, taking no prisoners — encouraged the widely-held view that Zulus were no more than savage barbarians, whereas they were a noble people in their own right, with a moral code and national discipline which commanded sincere respect from those who knew them well. The disaster at Isandlwana was received with some bewilderment in this country — for how could it have happened? The simple truth — that sheer military incompetence and not cowardice had been the root cause — did not filter into the public consciousness until much later. Even so, European newspapers could hardly help making gibes at the apparent incompetence of the British Army. The French, in particular, with their own experience of colonial wars successfully fought in Africa and elsewhere, greatly enjoyed adding to Britain's general discomfort.

The only response which could possibly assuage the national humiliation was to send out substantial reinforcements immediately. These included four major-generals, six infantry battalions, two regiments of cavalry, two composite batteries of artillery and a further batch of individual reinforcing officers, many of whom (like Bigge, Slade and Wodehouse) had previously registered their names as volunteers for service in South Africa. On 17th February Lieutenant Josceline Wodehouse had called at Camden Place to bid farewell. This was a defining moment.

After Wodehouse left, the Prince immediately went to his study and wrote a letter. After dinner that evening he could not sit still. Instead he paced up and down, whistling military tunes and teasing his mother. When she asked him the reason for his agitation, he could only reply, "You wouldn't sleep if I told you." She not unreasonably replied, "And do you think I shall sleep after that? I shall imagine all sorts of frightful things — for instance, that you are going to Africa."[1] He then admitted that she had guessed correctly; for that evening he had written to the Duke of Cambridge requesting permission to serve in Africa. At this the Empress burst into tears and withdrew to her room.

The following morning he pleaded for her understanding: "While even one of the officers of my battery stayed in England, I might have honourably remained here myself. But how can I show myself again at Aldershot when they will all be out there?"[2]

But the Empress argued back. "If anything happens to you, your supporters will not weep for you; they will have a grudge against you!"[3] But he persisted. What good could he possibly do at Camden Place? Confined to the house, how could he

1   JOHN, p. 422.
2   FILON, p. 185.
3   Ibid., p. 186.

ever show the public in France and elsewhere just what he was capable of doing? "Owing to the accident of my birth," he remonstrated, "I am not my own master. God has willed it so, and I cannot, even if I would, escape from the destiny which He has appointed for me...Whether I like it or not, I happen to be the nominal, and eventually effective head of a great party which believes itself to be — and which we believe to be — truly representative of France...Now what have I done hitherto to justify the hopes that people place in me?...Apart from a small number of my personal friends nobody knows me, and I can say that in France, although my name may be an emblem, my personality and my moral value, such as they are, are unknown...At the age of twenty-three I am still a child to them, and the majority of them treat me like one. This is so true, that whenever on any important occasion I have attempted to direct the Imperialist party, and to impress upon them a uniform policy in conformity with my opinion and personal wishes, I have not been listened to, and, as often as not, the party has acted in direct opposition to my advice...It is imperative, therefore, that I should take some step to assert myself, and to obtain the influence which is indispensable to my future. There is one thing a man can always do — that is, to show that he does not value his own life too highly, and is prepared to risk it without counting the cost."[4]

After all, he went on to argue, this was the ideal war in which to participate — the politics were entirely neutral; it was miles away in South Africa, fighting savages in a land where no conceivable European interest was at stake. He then changed tactics. In desperation he pleaded with her; "Do you want me to be *le petit Prince* all my life? Do you want me to pine away and expire out of boredom like the King of Rome?"[5] This time the Empress just listened. Recalling this conversation in later years she said, "I could not fail to realise the justice of many of my son's remarks, and this will explain why, although I still argued with him, I resigned myself at last to the inevitable."[6] She knew the strength of his determination, and privately it made her feel proud. In his persistence and idealism she could, after all, see something of herself.

Two days later she met him in the hall, downcast and miserable. He handed over a letter, saying, "I've been refused!" In his reply the Duke had explained: 'I regret to say that the Government are of the opinion that they cannot depart from the ordinary course adopted — that of declining permission to go on service excepting to such as are called upon to go as a matter of duty to the State.'[7] The Empress stared in disbelief as her son suddenly put his hands to his face, bursting into tears of anger and frustration. This was the first time she had seen him cry since that occasion, so many years ago, when he had been thrown into the sea at Biarritz. No longer could she continue to disregard his pleas for help. Bowing to the inevitable, she suggested a further letter to the Duke and that morning he submitted a second application:

4   FEATHERSTONE, p. 54.
5   JOHN, p. 423.
6   FEATHERSTONE, p. 55.
7   RA. Add. E1/8551

21st February 1879

Monseigneur,

I have just received the letter you wrote me. Before telling you how much it distressed me, I must thank Your Royal Highness for the flattering approval it gives to the motives that led me to this step. I should have been glad to share the fatigues and dangers of my comrades, who all have the happiness of being on active service. Though I am not so conceited as to think that my services can be useful to the cause I wished to serve, I nevertheless looked upon this war as an opportunity of showing my gratitude towards the Queen and the nation in a way that would be very much to my mind. When at Woolwich and, later, at Aldershot, I had the honour of wearing the English uniform, I hoped that it would be in the ranks of our allies, that I should first take up arms. Losing this hope, I lose one of the consolations of my exile. I remain none the less deeply devoted to the Queen and deeply grateful to Your Royal Highness for the interest you have always displayed in me. I beg you to believe in the feelings of sincere attachment of your very affectionate,

Napoléon[8]

The Duke was touched by this second request which, he noted, was devoid of any political aspirations. He passed it on to his cousin the Queen who likewise read it with compassion. In the brief covering note he added: 'I never saw a young man more intent upon going and the Empress his mother I hear quite takes his view of the case.'[9] In her reply the Queen noted the Prince's strong desire to repay her hospitality by fighting with her brave troops, but then pointed out: 'But I am glad that I am not his mother at this moment. Still I understand easily how in his peculiar position he must wish for active employment, but he *must* be careful not to expose himself unnecessarily, for we know he is very venturesome. I should like to see him before he starts.'[10] But it is not recorded that the Queen, as so often assumed, personally pressurised her cousin to allow the Prince to travel to South Africa.

At the same time Louis wrote a personal letter to his former Woolwich Governor, General Simmons, beseeching intervention on his behalf. But, unbeknown to the Prince, two days later his mother was to make a private call on the Duke of Cambridge at Horse Guards. Now quite determined that his second request should be accepted, she had only called to bargain over her son's conditions of service. One stipulation she insisted upon was that the Prince was never to serve with the irregular forces, nor with one of the native units. For his part, the Duke suggested that it would probably be best to attach him to Lord Chelmsford's staff in the role of unofficial 'spectator', but that the Prince should travel out in civilian clothes, paying his own costs, and only wear his artillery officer's uniform on arrival in South Africa.

Despite these favourable developments, the Prince had deliberately chosen not to personally approach the one person on whom the final decision, in fact, rested — the Prime Minister. But both Eugénie and her son were well aware of the intense

8   FILON, p. 186.
9   RA. R5/1c
10   RA. R5/12

dislike which Benjamin Disraeli maintained towards all members of the Bonaparte family and therefore neither sought nor expected his support. Indeed, when notified of the Prince's request, the Prime Minister opined that the whole idea, which could only cause offence to the French government, was most 'injudicious'. Furthermore he saw no particular reason why the Bonaparte heir should want to become involved in a British colonial war in South Africa (a war of which he personally disapproved) simply to show his gratitude to the people of this country. The Cabinet spent some time discussing the matter and finally decided to withhold their permission. But when the Duke of Cambridge informed Disraeli that both the Queen and the Empress Eugénie had insisted that the Prince be permitted to travel to Zululand solely as a civilian 'spectator', at his own expense, without any official sponsorship and that he was, in any case, planning to leave within days, the Prime Minister reluctantly gave way — afterwards telling an M.P., "Well! My conscience is clear. I did all that I could to stop his going. But what can you do when you have to deal with two obstinate women?"[11]

The Duke wrote a letter of introduction to Sir Bartle Frere, saying that the Prince was leaving for Zululand in the capacity of a 'spectator' He explained:

> He was anxious to serve in our army, having been a cadet at Woolwich, but the Government did not think that this could be sanctioned, but no objection is made to his going out on his own account, and I am permitted to introduce him to you and to Lord Chelmsford, in the hope, and with my personal request to you, that you will give him every help in your power to enable him to see what he can...He is a charming young man, full of spirit and energy, speaking English admirably, and the more you see of him the more you will like him. He has many young friends in the Artillery, so I doubt not with your and Chelmsford's kind assistance he will get on well enough.[12]

But this introductory letter made no mention of the fact that, although ostensibly a 'spectator', it had been agreed that the Prince might wear uniform on reaching South Africa nor had the Duke passed on to the High Commissioner (who also filled the appointment of Commander-in-Chief) the further stipulation that he should not be permitted to serve with irregulars or with native troops.

As expected, in France there was no official enthusiasm over the Prince's plans. Even staunch Republicans were dismayed at the prospect of a 'Son of France', albeit a Pretender to a disreputable throne, becoming involved in one of the Great Britain's interminable colonial wars. *Le Télégraphe* went as far as to point out that, under Article 21 of the Civil Code, any Frenchman who, without government authorisation, entered into the military service of a foreign power automatically forfeited his standing as a Frenchman. The newspaper had clearly disregarded the official notification from Great Britain that the Prince was travelling out at his own expense, not as a war correspondent, but in the role of civilian 'spectator'.

11   WEINTRAUB, p. 614.
12   RA. R5/1g

In truth, to most of his fellow-countrymen, it was quite inconceivable that Louis would participate solely in that capacity and most naturally assumed that he would be risking his life. Otherwise there seemed to be no point in him travelling out to South Africa at all. There was even the impertinent suggestion that the Prince would be 'advising' Lord Chelmsford how best to defeat the Zulus! The Bonapartists themselves not only feared that he might be killed but that, through prolonged absence in a far-away country, he would be unable to take immediate advantage of any favourable political opportunities which might suddenly arise in France. Some said that he was only going to South Africa to achieve glory in order to win outright the hand of Princess Beatrice. Many blamed his mother, asserting that she no longer cared about the future and really wanted him out of the way. Others considered that, on the contrary, she was so assertive that the Prince saw the war as the only means of escaping from her domination! The Prince tried to put many of these fears at rest in an open letter to Eugéne Rouher:

> My dear M.Rouher,
>   I am leaving Europe, and may be gone for some months. I have too many faithful friends in France to remain silent on the motives for my departure. For eight years I have been the guest of England. I completed my education at one of her military schools, and on several occasions I have strengthened the ties which unite me to the British Army by taking part in its manoeuvres. The war in which England is engaged at the Cape of Good Hope has assumed a gravity which it had not presented before. I wish to follow operations, and I shall embark in two days.
>   In France, where, thank God, party spirit has not killed *l'esprit militaire*, all will understand that I could not be satisfied to remain aloof from the fatigues and perils of that Army in which I have so many comrades. The time I devote to this contest between civilisation and barbarism will not be lost. Whether I am far or near, my thoughts will always be of France. I shall follow with interest and without uneasiness the gradual phases she may pass through, for I am sure that God will protect her. During my absence the partisans of the Imperial cause will remain united and confident, and will continue to give the country the spectacle of a party which, faithful to its doctrines, is always animated by feelings of the most ardent patriotism.
>   Receive, my dear Monsieur Rouher, the assurances of my sincere friendship.
>   Napoléon[13]

The Prince made no mention in this letter that he was, in fact, only authorised to observe the war. Nonetheless, a thoroughly alarmed Rouher immediately travelled to Chislehurst. But all his protestations were to no avail and the two finally parted in some rancour.

---

13   JOHN, p. 426.

The Prince subsequently wrote a separate letter to Comte Joachim Murat, inviting him to inform the other Bonapartist deputies of his personal conviction that nothing was going to happen in the next few months which would make his presence in Europe essential. He added: 'This war cannot draw me into a conflict which might compromise my political future. If God protects me, I shall speedily come back, strengthened by the tests of war and more worthy of the task I am to undertake.'[14]

On 24th February, three days before the Prince's departure, Eugénie wrote to her niece:

> My son is leaving with the English army for the Cape...Time alone can show whether he is right or wrong; if he returns in good health and there has been no important change in his absence, of course he will be stronger and will have gained in prestige. What I am most afraid of is that, out of ill-humour and so as to belittle his action, they will sneer at the enemy; we must not forget the efforts and sacrifices England is undertaking; therefore, the affair is serious.[15]

In a private letter to his friend d'Espeuilles, Louis attempted to clarify all the rumours about his precise status:

> I've had all the trouble in the world to get leave from the English Government. Today I've got it at last, but with all kinds of restrictions. I'm supposed to be sailing for the Cape as a traveller, and only when there am I to put on a uniform and attach myself to the General in command of artillery. So we must be careful to warn our newspapers not to say I start with my battery — it will be alright for them to say that I am hastening out to share the toils and perils of my comrades. They are too definite about my rank in the British Army, for it is quite unofficial.[16]

This letter reveals much about the Prince's true state of mind. By inviting Bonapartist newspapers to publicise that he was 'hastening out to share the toils and perils of my comrades' he clearly did not envisage himself living and working out in South Africa as a bystander, a mere 'spectator' of the real action. In fact, like his fellow-countrymen, he had not the faintest idea what was expected of him in the role 'spectator' (as referred to in such vague terms by the Duke of Cambridge) and as it transpired later, neither did anybody else. The muddle went further. Despite being dressed in the uniform of a British officer, he did not hold the Queen's Commission; therefore he had no executive authority over British troops and, as a non-participating 'spectator', could not legally be subject to military law and discipline. It was evident from the start that neither the Duke of Cambridge, as Commander-in-Chief, nor

---

14 FILON, p. 189.
15 JOHN, p. 421.
16 Ibid., p. 427.

the Prince himself had given much thought to the practicalities of being attached to, but not part of an army engaged on operations in the field.

But in another letter to Louis Conneau, written with the benefit of hindsight from South Africa on 20th April, the Prince, for the first time, touched on the putative political motives behind his decision, although the rhetoric may have been deliberately slanted for dissemination within party circles:

> Although my departure is already ancient history, I should like to go back with you to the causes that determined it. I asked no one's advice, and made up my mind in forty-eight hours; if my resolve was swift, it was because I had reflected at length on such a contingency and made my plans.
>
> Neither my mother's fears, nor the despair of the people about me, nor the exhortations of M.Rouher and my party, caused me to hesitate a minute or to lose a second of time; this will seem only natural to those who know me, but how many are they?
>
> The reasons that caused me to go are all political, and outside these, nothing influenced my decision.
>
> First. I might have hoped, before events that followed 16th May, that if my party increased its strength, the restoration of the Empire might take place without an upheaval, either through Parliament or through the Army. This restoration in the Spanish manner would have made me, like Alfonso XII, the slave of certain men and of a whole party. I would never have accommodated myself to such a position, and I dreaded rather than desired it.
>
> Secondly. Since October 14th, the scene is changed; the Imperial party has grown weaker, and can effect nothing by its own strength. All hopes are centred in my person; if that becomes great, the strength of the Imperial party becomes tenfold. I have had proof that no one will be followed but a man of known energy, and my care has been to find a way of making myself known.
>
> Thirdly. Writing letters of condolence, harbouring politicians, patting journalists on the back, hob-nobbing with them, and working with them to stir up social problems, that is what the headstrong call 'making myself conspicuous'.
>
> Others want me to travel throughout Europe with a great retinue, going, like the fairy tale princes, to view all the princesses and boast of my political elixir that will heal all social evils.
>
> This comedy, think the authors, must end like every good play, with a marriage.
>
> I have turned a deaf ear; I have not cared to let my wings be clipped by marriage, and my dignity refused to stoop to the part of princely commercial traveller.
>
> Fourthly. I have come to the conclusion that was not my part.
>
> When one belongs to a race of soldiers, it is only sword in hand that one gains recognition, and he who wants to learn by travel, must go far.

I had, then, long ago promised myself, first, to make a long voyage. Secondly, to lose no opportunity of seeing a campaign. The disasters of Isandlwana gave me the opportunity I wanted.

In France there was no crisis immediately to be feared to hold me back, as before the senatorial elections. The African war became suddenly popular in England, and was developing on a great scale without involving any European complications.

The scene of the war itself was worth the trouble of an uprooting, for the interest it offered a traveller.

Everything, therefore, urged me to go, and I went.[17]

There is no mention here of any 'debt' to England! But he freely acknowledges that unless he can make a name for himself the Bonapartist party is not going to prosper. He could hardly be expected to publicly admit what he knew full well to be the underlying motivation for all these recent events — that he had to seize the opportunity to demonstrate beyond doubt that he was neither a coward nor degenerate; that by now rejoining his closest English friends on active service he might yet win a glory in battle, a glory in which all his fellow-countrymen could share and take pride. This was a matter of personal honour which had to be satisfied, even if he had only been finally allowed to go to South Africa in the vague position of 'spectator'.

A number of the male staff in the imperial household at Camden Place, including M.Piétri, and almost twenty young party members from France, had all eagerly volunteered to accompany the Prince. Though touched by the gesture, he decided to reject all their offers. He rightly perceived that it would wholly inappropriate to join a British Army headquarters on active service, surrounded by a clique of his fellow-countrymen. Apart from the poor impression such an entourage would make, Louis did not wish to be advised or observed over his every action. He agreed only to take Xavier Uhlmann as his valet, but even then, intended to leave him behind in the base area and not take him up country. And he made clear to everyone his reluctance to take even a personal bodyguard into a British military camp. Fortunately General Simmons intervened. The military authorities had agreed to his personal representation that the Prince, just like any other officer on active service, must be accompanied by a British soldier orderly. But this sensible decision could only add to the ambiguity about Louis's precise status in South Africa.

At almost midnight on 26th February 1879, the eve of his departure, the Prince sat down to compose his final will and testament. That afternoon he had travelled to Windsor Castle, Kensington Palace and Marlborough House to make personal farewells to the Queen, the Prince of Wales, Princess Beatrice and other members of the royal family. There had been a final dinner at Camden Place when he had made a brief speech and shaken hands with everyone, including all the servants. Once his mother had retired for the night the Prince turned his mind to his dynastic duties — a last will and testament. There was nothing particularly morbid, prescient or

---

17   FILON, p. 188.

even unusual in this — most officers, of all ages, have felt moved to put their private affairs in order before going off to the uncertainty of war. And Louis knew full well that his driving urge to somehow achieve fame and glory in battle would inevitably place his life at risk. But in one respect the Prince's will does differ from the majority — it focuses almost exclusively on the act of dying.

THIS IS MY LAST WILL AND TESTAMENT

1. I die in the Catholic, Apostolic, and Roman religion in which I was born.

2. I desire that my body shall be laid beside my father's to wait until they are both transported where rests the founder of Our House, in the midst of that French people we, like him, deeply loved.

3. My last thought will be for my country; it is for her I would like to die.

4. I hope that my mother will keep for me when I am no more, the loving remembrance I shall preserve for her to my very last moment.

5. Let my private friends, my servants, the adherents of the cause I represent, be convinced that my gratitude towards them will only end with my life.

6. I shall die with a sentiment of the deepest gratitude to Her Majesty the Queen of England, to all the royal family, and to the country where for eight years I have received such cordial hospitality.

7. I appoint my dearly beloved mother my universal legatee, charging her with the following distribution:

I bequeath 200,000 francs to my cousin, Prince J.N.Murat.

I bequeath 100,000 francs to M.F.Piétri, in acknowledgement of his services.

I bequeath 100,000 francs to M.le Baron Corvisart, in acknowledgement of his devotion.

I bequeath 100,000 francs to Mlle de Larminat, who has shown such attachment to my Mother.

I bequeath 100,000 francs to M.A Filon, my former tutor.

I bequeath 100,000 francs to M.L.N.Conneau.

I bequeath 100,000 francs to M.N.Espinasse.

I desire my mother to constitute:

A life pension of 10,000 francs to Prince L.L.Bonaparte.

A life pension of 5,000 francs to M.Bachon, my former equerry.

A life pension of 2,500 francs to Xavier Uhlmann

I desire that all my other servants shall continue to receive their wages.

[The will then listed a number of personal mementoes to be chosen and given to Prince N.Charles Bonaparte, Duc de Bassano, M.Rouher, Major General Sir Lintorn Simmons, Mr. N.Strode, Father Goddard, M.Piétri, Baron Corvisant, and Mademoiselle de Larminat]

I bequeath to MM.Conneau, Espinasse, J.N.Murat, A.Fleury, P.de Bourgoing, S.Corvisart, my weapons and uniforms, all but the last I shall have worn, which I bequeath to my mother.

Codicil

I need not recommend my mother to omit nothing to defend the memory of my great uncle and my father. I beg her to remember that as long as there are Bonapartes, so long will there be representatives of the Imperial cause. The duties of our House are not extinct with my life; when I am dead, the task of continuing the work of Napoleon I, and of Napoleon III devolves upon the eldest son of Prince Napoleon, and I hope that my beloved mother, by seconding him with all her power, will give to those others of us who are no more, this last supreme proof of affection.

Napoleon

Chislehurst, February 27th, 1879

I appoint MM. Rouher and F. Piétri the executors of this will.[18]

In his will therefore the Prince had deliberately chosen to disinherit 'Plon-Plon', nominating in his place, Prince Victor, the eldest son. It is unlikely that the Empress had any foreknowledge of his intention in this respect which, inevitably, was to have severe repercussions for the Bonapartist cause after his death. Indeed the Prince by himself had no authority to change the lawful and legitimate succession merely to suit his personal wishes. But at least it gave him the satisfaction of repaying all the recent insults inflicted by his odious second cousin on both the Empress and himself.

At half-past six the following morning the Prince handed the document, which he had just signed and dated, to Franceschini Piétri It was then placed in a steel box which was locked and sealed.

Immediately afterwards, accompanied by the devout Tristan Lambert who had journeyed specially to Chislehurst earlier that morning, Louis went to St. Mary's Church where, after confession, he received Holy Communion. In conversation with Father Goddard the Prince told him of his fears that he might never see Chislehurst again and indicated to the priest exactly where he would like to be buried, beside his father. Subsequently he knelt for a long time in silent prayer at the Emperor's tomb. Indeed, he delayed so long that a reminder had to be sent, urging him to return to the house in time for departure. And whilst hurrying outside he suddenly recalled seeing the female verger hovering by the family pew. He had forgotten to say goodbye. In the sad days to come this old lady was to recall, with tears of pride and joy, how the young Prince turned and came back to shake her hand and apologise for his discourtesy — 'with his own lovely smile'.[19]

The Empress, with many of her staff, accompanied the Prince on his train journey to Southampton. Originally she had intended to sail with him as far as Madeira, but sensing the ridicule that might cause, Louis had finally managed to

18   Ibid., p. 190.
19   JOHN, p. 433.

dissuade her. On arrival at the station there was a huge crowd waiting to greet them. In a special departure editorial *The Morning Post* spoke for many when it pointed out: 'The anxieties which so constantly weigh upon the Empress Eugénie will of course be much aggravated by the absence of her son in that distant land amid the danger inseparable from war, but Her Majesty will be comforted by the feeling that he is following a noble profession, and that he is surrounded by attached comrades... He takes with him the good wishes of all Englishmen.'[20]

The officers of the garrison arranged a special farewell luncheon in a city hotel at which the Prince's health was drunk. General Simmons was also present, introducing the Prince to Rifleman Lomas, detailed to accompany him as an orderly. Aged 42, an experienced veteran, Lomas had previously served with the Rifles in the Crimea, India and Ashanti. At the docks a civilian ship -the S.S. *Danube* — was waiting with drafts for the 3rd/60th Rifles already on board. The Empress was first given a conducted tour of the ship after which she took leave of her son in the privacy of the Captain's cabin. Now dissolving into tears, she implored him to do nothing rash, and, above all, not to serve with any irregular forces. In the same way as she had blessed him before leaving for the Franco-Prussian war, Eugénie now made the sign of the cross with her thumb on the forehead of her kneeling son. Louis gave his word, promising also to write as often as possible and with a final public embrace at the head of the gangway, proudly watched his mother go down into the cheering crowds.

The ship sailed early that afternoon, 27th February, with the Prince standing on the bridge beside the Captain who, breaking with all precedent, had ordered the unfurling of a tricolour from the masthead. He had also placed his own cabin at Louis's disposal — an offer which had been politely declined until all the ship's officers collectively prevailed upon the Prince to reluctantly accept. From her hotel room window overlooking Southampton Water the Empress watched tearfully as the ship slowly passed from view and out to sea. And when she could see it no longer she simply collapsed once more into private weeping. But, before making the sad return journey to Chislehurst, Eugénie was handed a telegram. It was from Queen Victoria. 'I ask you, dear sister, to accept the expression of all my good wishes for your beloved son, who is departing accompanied by good wishes of the entire nation. May God bless and keep him.'[21]

Before crossing the Channel the ship had to make a final call at Plymouth. He decided there and then to make good his promise by writing his mother a short note — even though he had only been on board for seven hours. In it he explained: 'I can say to you in writing what I did not wish to tell you *viva voce*: how much the grief of leaving you is mingled in my heart with the delight of being on active service.'[22]

Writing to the Queen's Assistant Private Secretary the following day, General Simmons gave as his opinion: 'I feel quite sure that the fact of his being cast for the first time on his own resources with no friend near to counsel him will tend to

---

20   RA. R5/1k
21   RA. R5/1l. Translated from the French original
22   FILON p. 192.

complete his education as a man — he is so truthful, straightforward and free from vice that I feel confident he will gain credit and make friends wherever he goes.'[23]

A few days later, the Empress wrote to her niece: 'Would you believe that Princess Mathilde, to whom I wrote on my son's behalf, has not sent him a word of farewell, nor me a word of consolation! She might think he was wrong, but I don't believe the fear of his getting into danger will rob her of any sleep. Happily for my son, if he had to do without her good wishes, it was not the same here, in the Royal family...the Queen was *as tender as possible*; she sent a special train, so that he might take leave of her and embrace her... I've had a very affectionate note from Plymouth; in spite of his grief at parting from us, he is overflowing with joy at the thought of the campaign. May God protect him! Have prayers said for him that he may find an *opportunity* to distinguish himself, and may he return safe and sound.'[24]

The long voyage to the Cape was largely uneventful. During the early days he was soon performing gymnastic feats astride the rigging, playing with the many little children on board and generally making himself extremely popular. The *Danube* called at Madeira for two hours; here Louis made a number of pencil sketches which he used to illustrate his lengthy letters. They sailed on towards the Equator. Thereafter he described what happened:

> From the Equator the sea was extremely rough, and though the old ceremony of crossing the Line has fallen into disuse on board steamers, the Atlantic itself saw to it that we were baptised. The days are long between sky and sea: and so every means of diversion is sought after.
>
> Among the passengers are a great number of officers on leave or retired, militia captains, or simple adventurers who like myself are going to the Cape to make war or to seek their fortune. They call themselves 'volunteers' and each of them flourishes his sword a little. We thought it would be amusing to break the monotony of the voyage by having a grand parade on board to which each man should come in full dress and equipment.
>
> Chosen Commander-in-Chief I gave the order for a great review, and it was thoroughly diverting to see that line of Fradiavolesque uniforms rise and fall with the roll of the ship (*Another sketch*). This farce had its serious side, that of allowing us to improve our equipment and our uniforms by comparison.[25]

The Prince was very disappointed that the ship did not finally call, as expected, at the island of St Helena — for he had hoped to make a private pilgrimage to Longwood, the Great Napoleon's house, before reaching South Africa. And when his twenty-third birthday came round on 16th March he kept the occasion entirely to himself. Consequently there were no celebrations. Indeed, it was the first he had ever spent away from his family, and his mother wrote on that same day to his grandmother: 'I do not murmur against fate, for I would rather endure suspense on

23   RA. R5/2
24   JOHN, p. 435.
25   FILON p. 194.

his account than see him languid and declining. Exile is hard for him to bear and I cannot blame him for having acted according to the law of his blood, and sought afar and in dangers to make his name resound through his country. If God preserves him and gives him the opportunity to distinguish himself, the days we are now passing through, which are so dark and sad, will be the most brilliant of my life.'[26]

When the ship finally arrived at Cape Town on 26th March he was formally welcomed by Major Gossett from Lord Chelmsford's staff. There was an invitation to stay for a while at Government House. Louis described what subsequently happened to his mother:

> I went in a carriage, acclaimed by a many-coloured population, who had draped the windows with flags of many hues...Tonight Lady Frere is giving a grand dinner in my honour, and a reception afterwards...Tomorrow I leave for Durban, where I am eager to arrive, for a battle is expected.[27]

He omitted to mention that the Frere's own son, a young man the same age as himself, was serving as a lieutenant in Chelmsford's army.

It rained incessantly during the subsequent four day voyage to Durban where, a day after docking, he wrote again:

> Durban, April 2nd 1879
>
> Since my last letter, that is to say since I left Cape Town, I have lived in a state of anxiety and impatience comparable to that of an old troop horse yoked to a plough when he hears the trumpet sound the charge...My regret is not to be with those who are fighting; you know me well enough to judge how bitter it is. But all is not over and I shall have my revenge on my ill-luck. I was received on my arrival in Natal like a crowned head, although I wore a lieutenant's uniform. The ships were dressed with flags and the military authorities came to meet me. The country, which I have hardly had time to see, seems to me superb. Picture to yourself green hills undulating as far as the eye can see, and covered here and there with groups of trees of every kind. The trees are not lofty, but they keep their beautiful foliage always; the loveliest plants and the rarest flowers of our climates spring by the wayside. When one takes in the whole landscape, one cannot help comparing it with what England must have been (the country of the green hills) when the Saxons landed on it. Remember me to all those who are about you, and tell them not to imagine that I forget them.[28]

But on arrival he was downcast to learn that Lord Chelmsford was not actually in Durban but still up-country. He unburdened that disappointment to General Simmons:

26 JOHN, p. 438.
27 FILON p. 195.
28 Ibid.

However hard it is for a soldier to remain inactive when the others are fighting, I had to resign myself to my fate and wait here until the General comes back...Until then Major Butler has attached me to one of the batteries encamped around Durban, so that at all events I shall not follow the operations as a newspaper reporter...I am anxious to deserve as soon as possible the praise that people give me too early, for I am ashamed to be made such a fuss about before having done anything when so many who have nobly done their duty seem completely unknown.[29]

In a subsequent letter to the General the Prince also gave his first impressions of the people he expected to fight. He contrasted 'barbarism' and 'civilisation': 'too many people,' he wrote, 'make the latter consist of the material advantages they derive from it. For me civilisation exists in the moral ideas that gave birth to it. When these are forgotten, the civilised man falls below the level of the savage...I have already been struck in Africa by a fact that justifies that idea: it is the difference between the Cape natives and the natives of Natal. The latter are still half-warriors — living in kraals and following their ancient customs; the former have adopted European habits. The Kaffirs of Natal have kept some of the noble qualities that characterise man in a state of nature, while those of Cape Colony have lost all those qualities, and have learned nothing from the whites except to drink, to smoke, and to cover themselves with rags. As for the Zulus, they are certainly the finest black people in the world; among the soldiers there is no feeling of vengeance against them, nothing but admiration for such bold warriors.'[30] It is interesting to note that, at no time, did the Prince question the morality of the war in which he was so anxious to participate. Despite his acknowledgement of the sterling qualities of the Zulus, like most well-bred Europeans, like the majority of officers in the British Army, he also believed without question in the moral superiority of white peoples and in their right to intervene, by force if necessary, in order to rule over those they considered to be lesser breeds. Moral objections to the war, voiced at the time by such outspoken figures as John Colenso, the Anglican Bishop of Natal, were either derided or more usually, simply ignored.

As described in his letter to General Simmons, Major Butler, one of the Base Area staff officers, had arranged for the Prince to be attached to M Battery, 6th Brigade which was encamped at Cato's Manor about five miles out of Durban. Here everyone was very polite; he was addressed formally as 'Sir', but otherwise treated no differently to the other junior officers in the battery. Louis had already made up his mind to leave Uhlmann behind at Durban, taking only Lomas with him up-country. With a uniformed British soldier always beside him, it was understandable if most people simply looked upon the Prince as just another officer. He had already been fitted out with a set of officers' campaigning equipment — an 1872 Adams Mark II.45 inch service revolver (holstered on a shoulder strap), field glasses, linen map, a pocket Siphonia (a very light waterproof which could be carried in a pocket) and an officer's white 'foreign service' helmet. These stark white helmets were so

29   JOHN, p. 439.
30   FILON, p. 196.

conspicuous in the field that almost everyone deliberately toned them down, using improvised dyes. It is probable that the Prince's helmet — so pristine white in the photograph taken at Kisch's studio during his stay in Durban — would have likewise be dulled down by Lomas once they had moved up-country. For some reason the Prince's helmet had a unique distinguishing feature — a blue stopper in the top. He had already brought with him a number of swords, including the Great Napoleon's Austerlitz sword and a sabre which had belonged to Marshal Murat, and the choice of the day was carried suspended by two slings from a leather sword belt. Like all artillery officers he usually wore dark-blue trousers with matching patrol jacket. This fastened down the front with hooks, eyes and olivets, and was bordered all round with an inch of black mohair braid. Artillery officers in this dress did not wear any badges of rank; indeed, even in the infantry, only officers of the rank of Lieutenant-Colonel or above appear to have worn collar rank badges of any sort. To an outsider therefore it was almost impossible to readily identify the precise rank of any junior officer serving in the Anglo-Zulu war. Two unattributable sources refer to the Prince as being an 'honorary' captain, but any such rank does not appear in surviving documents or records of the time.[31]

Soon after arriving in Durban the Prince had to buy two replacement horses — the two he had brought out with him had not survived — one had been seriously injured, jumping his box during a storm and had to be put down; the other had been accidentally killed during disembarkation. On 3rd April Louis purchased a grey beast, described as 'calm, not at all disobedient'[32] (Louis tested him out with some pistol shots!) — a BaSotho pony called 'Percy'. He subsequently purchased a second horse called 'Fate'.

A number of officers likewise passing through the Durban base were formally presented to the Prince; one of them, Major Bindon Blood, later recorded: 'He had a charming manner, was very well informed and most promising as a soldier. He was also greatly interested in India, and I had several pleasant conversations with him about that country.'[33] Whilst waiting for Lord Chelmsford, Louis could not help wondering what his English friends might be doing and whether he would soon be able to catch up with them. In fact Lieutenant Wodehouse had accompanied Lord Chelmsford at the battle of Gingindlovu on 2nd April and at the relief of Eshowe the following day; whilst the other two, Captain Bigge and Lieutenant Slade, were much further north, with Colonel Henry Evelyn Wood, VC at Khambula, where some twenty-three thousand Zulu warriors had unsuccessfully assaulted the camp on 29th March. In a major battle the Zulus had suffered appalling losses; indeed, this defeat, after the successful defence of Rorke's Drift in January, had become the turning point of the whole war. Later Colonel Wood in his report on the battle was to make special mention of his supporting artillery: 'I have never known a battery so exceptionally fortunate in its subalterns...Bigge and Slade were unsurpassable.'[34]

---

31   WHITTON, p. 232.
32   LACHNITT, *Interrogatoire de Lomas par Louis Conneau et Jules Espinasse*, p. 288.
33   KNIGHT, *By Orders of the Great White Queen*, p. 209.
34   JOHN, p. 441.

To add to his frustrations the Prince now suddenly went down with Cape fever. Such illnesses were very common, usually afflicting most of the reinforcing troops shortly after arrival. But other sicknesses, such a dysentery and typhoid, were far more serious and were to significantly undermine the fitness of many units for prolonged campaigning. Surgeon-Major Scott arranged for the Prince to be temporarily isolated in a pleasant house in Durban along with Uhlmann. And he was only just getting back to his feet again when Lord Chelmsford returned from inspecting the troops now preparing for the second invasion of Zululand. On 9th April he formally called on the Prince and after introductory pleasantries, Louis handed over the letter he was carrying from the Duke of Cambridge. Lord Chelmsford read it carefully:

Feb 25/79

My dear Chelmsford,

This letter will be presented to you by the Prince Imperial, who is going out on his own account, to see as much as he can of the coming campaign in Zululand. He is extremely anxious to go out and wanted to be employed in our army, but the Government did not consider that this could be sanctioned, but have sanctioned my writing to you and to Sir Bartle Frere to say that if you can show him kindness and render him assistance to see as much as he can with the columns in the field. I hope you will do so.

He is a fine young fellow full of spirit and pluck, and having many old cadet friends in the artillery, he will doubtless find no difficulty in getting on, and if you can help him in any way pray do so — my only anxiety on his account would be that he is *too plucky* and *go ahead.*

I remain, my dear Chelmsford,
Yours most sincerely,
George[35]

The Prince then handed over a further letter — this one from General Simmons:

I am sure you will excuse me for writing to you to say that his object is to see service, and that he is quite prepared to rough it in any way which will enable him to see some work...He applied in the first instance to the Duke, who supported his application, for permission to join the Army, but the Government refused the request, and he has consequently not been posted.

When he thought his chance of seeing service was gone, and he saw so many of his old friends that he had made at the Academy and during the autumn manoeuvres were going, he was quite overwhelmed, and the Duke again interceded for him, when he was informed that the Government would not object to his going, and that every facility would be given him to enable him to witness the operations of the Army.

---

35   RA. R5/1f

He is very intelligent, thoroughly amenable to discipline; very zealous and active, a quick and accurate spectator and a good rider; can sketch ground tolerably and gives every promise of being a good officer. Having been attached to batteries during two series of manoeuvres, he has a fair knowledge of the movement of troops. His only fault is that which is common to youth, viz.:that he is rather impulsive, but of this I have little doubt he will soon get better.

I have thought you would excuse me for writing this concerning him, as it may be of use in disposing of him. He will be only too thankful if you can find some employment for him, and if there is no other way of accomplishing the object, he would, I believe, gladly accept a local commission.

The Empress would not, however, like him to be attached to a native corps.[36]

Lord Chelmsford looked at these two letters again. He was puzzled. Statements in them appeared to contradict one another and there was a distinct lack of clarity in the various sentiments being expressed. On the one hand, the Prince was to be assisted 'to see as much as he can with the columns in the field', but in what capacity? The eager young man standing in front of him was in the undress uniform of an officer of the Royal Artillery for which he had been trained, but both letters stressed that the Government had refused his request to join the army? And whilst he was expected to give the Prince gainful employment, even a local commission, he was not permitted to serve with native troops — the usual posting for any keen civilian who wanted to get involved in the war. Yet, at the same time, he was being warned that the Prince was '*too plucky* and *go ahead*' and that he was 'rather impulsive'!

Lord Chelmsford was tired and strained, still smarting from the disaster of Isandlwana for which he was now rightfully being held personally responsible. Many things had gone wrong and yet the subsequent local Court of Inquiry, convened by Chelmsford himself and reporting directly to him, had tactfully made no reference to the fact that by far the greatest errors lay in the General's own foolishness in needlessly dividing the force, his vague orders throughout, and the poor quality of the work produced by his small staff. But Lord Chelmsford was not unique in these shortcomings — a lack of experience and training in the higher direction of waging war, an ambiguity in defining military requirements — these were common characteristics of many senior officers of the period; many of whom, like the Duke of Cambridge himself, had served in the Crimean war where needless confusion and poor staff work had cost many lives.

Indeed, vagueness in expression, a general air of calm and *sang-froid*, coupled with a deep-rooted xenophobia, were attributes often deliberately cultivated by many officers during operations to secure the Empire throughout the Nineteenth Century. Such attributes were to derived, in part, from the whole notion of 'gentlemanliness' as sustained in the rigid class structures of most European societies of that time — from deep-rooted patriotic feelings; a yearning for respectability, coupled with

---

36   JOHN, p. 442.

financial and thus social independence. And the pursuit of respectability invariably required conformity to the values and views of the upper classes. In the British Army the purchase of commissions had only been finally abolished in the face of much opposition but eight years earlier, and consequently a large number of senior officers, regardless of their level of competence, continued to occupy important appointments, in careers which had been originally launched by such purchases and which had largely progressed through the customary financial increments. Indeed, in most fashionable regiments, it was almost impossible to be a commissioned officer of any rank without substantial private funds. Whilst this state of affairs may have saved the tax-payer much expense (since officers largely paid for their own upkeep) it inevitably fostered an amateurish attitude to soldiering, a somewhat cavalier outlook, a casualness towards competence, all of which were to persist well into the Twentieth Century. Unlike most Continental armies the British Army of 1879 had no centralised general staff and thus no body to professionally co-ordinate strategic planning at the highest level; in size it was comparatively small, a non-conscript army relying entirely on volunteers, officered mainly by members of the aristocracy and landed gentry. But had the Prince been commissioned instead into the huge conscript French Army of 1879 he would have found many similiarities. In fact, compared to many other professional civilian careers, the status and pay of young French Army officers were very low, with already poor promotion prospects further diminished by constant political interference and a discriminating patronage. Thus, few really able young Frenchmen joined or remained in an army where ability, hard study and accomplishment were, by themselves, no guarantee of advancement. Here, too, the cult of the amateur tended to prevail.

However, even by the time of the Anglo-Zulu war, the famous Cardwell reforms of 1873 were slowly beginning to bear fruit in the British Army. Flogging had finally been abolished, even though retained for certain offences committed on active service — there were even cases of such punishments in Lord Chelmsford's force and one, for drunkeness and insubordination, was actually witnessed by the Prince.[37] Yet in the French Army flogging had long been totally abolished. And the tactics of the British Army were also beginning to change — from the traditional stereotyped drills of European warfare towards a greater flexibility, as the army began to learn from bitter experience how best to defeat various opponents, each of whom had very different fighting traditions and systems, across terrain and in climates which were equally varied. But did the Prince realise that the greatest spur for change in the British Army had ironically sprung from France's own catastrophic defeat of 1870 — for Prussia's swift and decisive victory had shaken all the European powers into finally acknowledging the growing importance of military science — with its concomitant requirement for national strategic planning, equipment technology and improved military knowledge at all levels, particularly amongst senior officers?

The dominant military figure pressing for more reforms in the British Army was the highly-professional and competent General Sir Garnet Wolseley — one of the few intellectuals in post within the army at senior level. But, despite his best

---

37 FREREJEAN, p. 277.

efforts, it was still to be many years before the army itself created an effective general staff, formulating in the process operational procedures and systems — all designed to reduce the scope for ambiguity and vagueness in combat situations to an absolute minimum — and thus avoiding needless loss of life.

Lord Chelmsford had largely failed in his first attempt to invade Zululand because, despite expert advice to the contrary, he had underestimated the military effectiveness of the highly-trained and disciplined Zulu *impis*. He had also greatly underestimated the logistical problems — across terrain where an invading army had to transport its every single requirement; from tents to food, from boots to ammunition. Whilst advancing into Zululand in three separate columns may have baffled King Cetshwayo and inhibited him from counter-striking directly into Natal, it had also dissipated the strength of the invasion force which, with inept defensive arrangements, had resulted in the piecemeal destruction of the largest column at Isandlwana. Now regrouping his forces and preparing for another invasion Lord Chelmsford had a particular incentive to bring this whole war to a speedy conclusion. He was well aware of the Government's displeasure and the public's general disquiet over the disaster of Isandlwana, and the mounting costs of this opportunist unauthorised campaign. Chelmsford was also acutely aware that, unless he brought the whole business to a decisive conclusion very soon, steps would be taken to replace him as General Officer Commanding. Even now he was personally wrestling with some complex logistical problems, aggravated by the fact that many of the vital supply wagons he now needed for a renewed invasion had been abandoned, left stranded on the battlefield of Isandlwana.

So, as he now gazed at this alert young man standing before him, he felt keenly that the authorities should not have additionally burdened him with the responsibility of safeguarding the heir to the French imperial throne — a responsibility which had simply been imposed upon him without prior consultation. But he registered no formal complaint at the time. Lord Chelmsford was also somewhat perplexed that so important a personage had travelled out to South Africa entirely alone, without household staff or entourage. This would not have been the case had one of Queen Victoria's sons been sent out to join the invasion force. After the war a number of senior officers openly expressed disquiet that the Prince had joined the campaign unattended and unsupported. Unaware that it was the Prince himself who had insisted on travelling alone, most assumed that the Empress must have sanctioned this unusual state of affairs. Yet his decision to operate alone only added to the problems of deploying him satisfactorily where he would also be adequately protected. At the same time Lord Chelmsford also recognised that if he took the safe way out, and simply diverted the Prince to a secure base job down at Durban or in Pietermaritzburg, the likelihood would be that, either Louis would immediately return on the next ship in disgust or else get himself involved in some foolhardy adventure along the supply lines — and in either event, Chelmsford knew he would eventually have to shoulder the blame. After some reflection he sensibly avoided making the decision himself — he invited the Prince to decide how he could best 'observe' the invasion! To assist him he outlined the possible options — the Prince could either be attached to an artillery battery, but not as a combatant officer; or he could take command of a unit of irregulars, for which he would be granted a local commission; or, alternatively, he could be attached to the General's staff as his 'personal guest'.

For his part, Louis only requested that he should be treated like any other officer under the General's command.

In his reply to General Simmons's letter, Lord Chelmsford passed on the Prince's final choice:

> The Prince Imperial has consented to accompany me into the field, and without putting him in orders, I have arranged with him that he shall be considered as one of my personal staff. I hear that he is quite delighted at being so employed; and at all events his desire to serve under my command is a set-off to the criticism of those who consider I am quite unfit for my present command...I have already begged the Duke of Cambridge to assure the Empress that I will take every care of the Prince. He will have to rough it with us, but the climate is a healthy one and the out-of-door life we lead is one which seems to agree well with us all.[38]

Was Lord Chelmsford's self-esteem really so low that he felt obliged, in a letter to a fellow officer, to interpret the Prince's decision to join his staff as a reflection of that young man's confidence in his own capabilities as the Commanding General? If so, such an interpretation would inevitably colour their personal relationship in the weeks ahead and does much to explain the undue deference which Chelmsford always seemed to show towards the young Prince. Louis himself appears to have held no particular views about Lord Chelmsford's military capabilities; but he was to provide his own perception of the appointment in a letter to a friend:

> I am presently filling the post of a staff officer with the Commander-in-Chief; this is the best way of seeing, of learning, and of making war for me. I had the courage enough to refuse the command of a squadron of volunteers! Tempting as the offer was, I thought that the position I now hold would allow me to obtain more experience and to render more service.[39]

But Louis was exaggerating. He never filled any post as a staff officer, at this point, and his comment about the volunteers would appear to be at variance to his solemn undertaking to his mother never to serve with the irregulars, an undertaking about which, of course, Lord Chelmsford knew nothing when he made the offer.

But the General would have been more than content with the Prince's final choice. When he had first arrived in South Africa the previous year his staff had comprised of a mere assistant military secretary, Major (later Lieutenant-Colonel) John Crealock, and two personal aides. Most of the preparatory planning therefore for the first invasion had been undertaken by Chelmsford himself. Indeed, Major Crealock had openly complained: 'The general's headquarters staff is and has been all

---

38   JOHN, p. 444.
39   FILON, p. 198.

along (as I have so often said) miserably weak.'[40] Even now, planning for the second invasion, the staff was still small in size; at the most about ten officers, although others were to be attached for temporary duty. One way to reduce his own workload would have been to appoint a Chief of Staff but this Lord Chelmsford declined to do. Even more surprising was the fact that there was no separate Quartermaster-General's department and thus all movement planning and logistics had to be undertaken by the already hard-pressed Adjutant-General's staff. The burden on the few nominated officers forming the headquarters was therefore a very heavy one.

However before launching the second invasion in late May 1879, Lord Chelmsford did create a small but separate Quartermaster-General's staff, for which he sought specific approval from London. Additionally, amongst the recently arrived reinforcements, were over a hundred 'special service' officers who, being unattached to regiments, were at the disposal of the General for employment wherever required. Some of these were now to be temporarily attached to Lord Chelmsford's own headquarters. But, although the young Prince was not officially posted in field records as an extra *aide-de-camp* to the General Officer Commanding, his precise duties were never clarified. Lord Chelmsford had three *aides* already and social etiquette, in any case, would have inhibited the Prince from carrying out any functions of a personal nature. But, with the staff already overloaded, it was inevitable that Louis would actively volunteer for any worthwhile tasks — if only to justify his presence to the others and keep himself occupied. Compared to the enormous staff which had surrounded his father at the start of the Franco-Prussian war, the Prince must have been somewhat surprised at the small number supporting Lord Chelmsford. But, as far as the General was concerned, the principal advantage of having the Prince on his own staff was to enable him to keep a personal eye on his whereabouts — for, by nature, Chelmsford disliked delegation. Yet even in that assumption he was soon to be mistaken. With hindsight, it would have been more prudent to have followed General Simmons's hint and placed the Prince with his friends in an artillery battery where, at least, he would have been in the military environment with which he was most familiar and most appropriately trained. And in such an environment he would also have been more effectively protected and less exposed to danger.

Now that the decision had been made, Lord Chelmsford advised the Prince to stay behind in Durban for a few more days to complete his convalescence and then move up country to join the staff at Pietermaritzburg. The General, in his personal letters home, often expressed concern over the Prince's apparent poor state of health, wondering if campaigning in such conditions might not bring about a further deterioration. But his fears on that score appear to have been unwarranted.

Louis filled in much of the time by writing letters, and studying various documents sent out to him by Franceschini Piétri. On 20th April he is writing to his mother:

> Piétri has communicated to me extracts from papers and private letters which prove to me that our party have reconsidered their first impulse.

---

40   KNIGHT, Ian, *Zulu*. p. 19.

Public feeling in France has then been, as I supposed, favourable to my decision: but it is not enough to go, I must come back with honour! And for that I rely on God. The news I have from France shows me also that I was not wrong in denying the possibility of a speedy crisis. Without being a great doctor, it easy to see that the country is dying of a lingering illness and not of an acute disease.[41]

Whilst resting at Durban, Louis was delighted to meet a fellow-countryman, Paul Deléage. Aged twenty-nine the portly civilian hailed from the city of Toulouse. Ironically Deléage was only in South Africa in the first place because of the Prince Imperial. An ambitious journalist from *Le Figaro* (which was widely acclaimed for the quality of its political and literary reportage) he was also an anti-imperialist who, full of propaganda about the so-called Pretender to the imperial throne, had specifically requested his editor to allow him to witness and report on the Prince's expected 'antics' in South Africa! Brought up to believe that Louis was a stupid young man, thoroughly Anglicised, immature and backward, he was to be quite taken aback when they finally met. At first the reality was hard to accept but, in all honesty, Deléage could only transmit back to his surprised editor in Paris that he found: 'not a young man, but a Prince, with the simplicity and charm of an *esprit supérieur et distingué*...A Frenchman with all the qualities of our race.'[42] At their first meeting Deléage also noted that Louis had spoken French with so pure a Parisian accent, that it prompted him, on more than one occasion, to describe him as: 'a true child of Paris.' And the fact that Louis had lived in England for the last eight years seemed not to have Anglicised him in any discernible way. But — as with others — it particularly puzzled Deléage that the young Prince was entirely alone, without entourage. In time the journalist was to become an important insider reporting on the progress of the war and the fateful events which eventually engulfed the young Prince.

The journalist also came to recognise that, whilst Louis certainly did have an impulsive nature, he nonetheless made strenuous efforts to keep it under tight control and was willing to accept the discipline imposed by his military superiors. In more recent years the suggestion has grown that the Prince was, in fact, quite unruly and deliberately insurbordinate during these weeks in South Africa — but the evidence is not compelling. And once he had succumbed to the Prince's charm, Deléage began to report on his various activities in an open and unbiased manner — after all, the French journalist had no particular side to champion in this purely Anglo-Zulu conflict. But that did not lessen his deep distrust at the motives of the British in permitting Louis to participate in the campaign in the first place. He considered that it was an anxious state of affairs which could only have sinister political undertones. It was fears like these which greatly coloured Deléage's perception of the tragedy to come; and his subsequent reports to France were to profoundly influence the national reaction to that event.

---

41   FILON, p. 198.
42   JOHN, p. 445.

For his part the Prince was thrilled to find such an intelligent and lively fellow Frenchman in this distant place; they could exchange Gallic views about this very British colonial war; whilst he was quick to appreciate that Deléage's firsthand reports to Paris on his activities were going to be critical for the cause. He noted that not only did the journalist speak little English, but had not the slightest idea about military matters or the rigours of camp life. And he was also aware of the antipathy, sometimes bordering on downright hostility, which most senior British officers viewed the many civilian reporters accompanying the invasion force. As a foreign war correspondent, Deléage would probably have an even rougher time than his English counterparts, so Louis resolved to keep a brotherly eye on him whenever he could. Indeed he went further. Inviting the journalist to contact him over any difficulties, he was often able to act as a go-between, smoothing out many problems, earning Deléage's personal gratitude in the process.

On 19th April the Prince left Durban to join the staff at Pietermaritzburg although Lord Chelmsford himself had already left for Dundee up-country. Becoming impatient and bored, Louis tried to ride a frisky horse that had already thrown off a number of riders and, this time, was himself to be hurled on to a pile of stones and temporarily concussed. Clearly his illness had weakened him more than he realised.

During this time it is evident that he sought to improve his background knowledge by studying the little pamphlet entitled 'Zulu Army', which had been issued by the Intelligence department in November 1878. But in some respects this little booklet was already out of date. For example, it did not address such unwelcome developments as the massive further acquisition of rifles by the Zulu *impis*. At Isandlwana the warriors had been able to loot a large number (estimated at close to a thousand, doubling their previous holdings) together with many full boxes of ammunition. And whilst they were never able to employ these captured weapons *en masse* to their best effect, their opportunist even if wildly-aimed shots were nonetheless effective enough to cause many casualties during the second invasion. From studying the pamphlet Louis might have been able to deduce that, as the whole military culture of the Zulu nation inspired warriors to fight at very close quarters, they could always be defeated, even at long range, by sustained disciplined firepower provided it was directed from behind the security of fortified emplacements. Another important reference work, required reading for all staff and regimental officers, was *Regulations for Field Forces in South Africa 1878*, which detailed Lord Chelmsford's specific requirements for operations in the field — covering such matters as daily routines, ration scales, stand-to procedures, encampments, etc. The orders relating to staging camps had been specifically amended after Isandlwana to stress that, during the day, vedettes must always be posted to guard against surprise; that horses when grazing should have mounted guards; and that such camps, however temporary, should always be fortified by earthworks.

However the mild concussion did not prevent Louis from travelling with the staff when they moved up country, and he finally joined Lord Chelmsford at Dundee at the end of April.

From the headquarters camp, he found time to scribble a short note to the Empress, using his saddle as a desk:

Dundee, April 30th 1879

My dear Mother,

I am writing to you from Dundee where we arrived yesterday with the general staff. I don't know if the maps you have will indicate the exact situation of this strategic point which will be the base of our operations. I will tell you that our camp is about fifty-five miles north-east of Ladysmith, and only ten miles from Buffalo River *(the border with Zululand)*. In a week at the furthest we shall have reached the extreme line of our outposts near Conference Hill. All continues to go well here: though my comrades on the staff are all much older than I am, their society is very agreeable, and will help to make my life as pleasant as it can be in Zululand. My health is excellent and I should have nothing left to wish for if the distance that separates us allowed me to hear from you oftener. I hope you are well, that you have no worries, and that you are not too uneasy.

If you saw the extraordinary posture in which I am writing to you, crouching on my heels and using my saddle as a desk, you would, I am sure, excuse my bad writing.[43]

On 2nd May the Prince had travelled with Lord Chelmsford and his staff when they visited Colonel Henry Evelyn Wood, VC at Khambula. From the 90th (Perthshire Light Infantry) Evelyn Wood was a charming cultured officer, if somewhat vain, with a deserved reputation for military competence as well as outstanding personal bravery. In the view of many of the officers in South Africa it was really Evelyn Wood who had become the driving force behind the somewhat pedestrian Lord Chelmsford. Indeed, the purpose of this particular visit was to discuss the most suitable lines of advance for a second invasion. The General also introduced the Prince to Brevet Lieutenant-Colonel Redvers Henry Buller, VC, another officer of immense personal courage and charisma who was already making a significant contribution of his own in turning the tide of the war to Chelmsford's advantage. He also met Buller's principal staff aide, the loquacious and dashing Irish aristocrat Captain Lord William Beresford — himself to win the Victoria Cross later in the campaign. But his greatest pleasure was in linking up with his two English friends, Arthur Bigge and 'Keggie' Slade. Louis listened in some awe as they both explained how, having set out white stone range markers beforehand, they had fired their seven pounder guns — round after round, practically non-stop, for about four hours standing up in the open on the ridge, aiming straight into the massive Zulu onslaught with devastating results. The Prince already knew that both had now been officially 'mentioned in dispatches' for their conduct during the battle, and it filled him with envy. He wryly indicated to both of them just how the

---

43   FILON, p. 200.

gold medallions, presented to them personally by the Empress on their departure to South Africa, had brought them luck!

But not long after this visit, Arthur Bigge suddenly went down with a high fever and had to be evacuated to the base hospital in Utrecht where, later on, the Prince periodically called to see him. It was during the first visit that Bigge took the opportunity to carry out a promise he had long since made privately to the Empress; namely, to talk to Louis firmly about the dangers of foolhardiness. He subsequently wrote to his battery commander in England, Major Ward-Ashton: 'I must say I thought he had made a wise step in coming and at once imagined him returning home, at the end of the war, mentioned in dispatches, having gained some experience at all events of savage warfare, and silencing his enemies in France who represented him as weak and sickly...Knowing his temperament, [I] implored him not to do anything rash and to avoid running unnecessary risks. I reminded him of the Empress at home and his party in France. He said: "Oh, of course, yes, you are quite right, I shall take care."'[44]

But both Bigge and Slade, quite independently, had already seen the warning signs — that the Prince was in a heady mood, intoxicated by the fresh air, the vast open spaces, the excitement of riding on and on, deeper and deeper, ever closer to skirmish perhaps full battle with the Zulus. It was the thrill of the chase all over again — except this time the dangers were omnipresent. And as they had both already observed from those climbing expeditions around Arenenberg in Switzerland, these were just the circumstances to galvanise those natural qualities of leadership, but also invoke that streak of daring, bordering on recklessness, which could so easily become irresponsible. Although growing rapidly into manhood there was still an imbalance in Louis's personality. Arthur Bigge, in particular, had long since acknowledged the Prince's maturity in political matters yet he could not help noting that, when it came to the excitement of the chase, Louis could still behave quite recklessly.

Whilst at Khambula Louis had also been introduced to Archibald Forbes, now a veteran war correspondent but in former times the same newspaper journalist who had compiled that harsh sarcastic description of him as a boy in 1869. Nonetheless the Prince greeted him warmly with his usual good manners and charm, so that the gruff and uncompromising Forbes in due course felt compelled to update his earlier comments — this time writing: 'the boy of the Empire when the shackles of the Empire had fallen from his limbs...was no longer a buckram creature, but a lively natural lad.'[45]

From Khambula, Lord Chelmsford and his staff, including the Prince Imperial, rode on to Utrecht in the Transvaal where they established their main headquarters in a number of buildings on the outskirts of the town. The Prince occupied a small house. One of Lord Chelsmford's aides described their situation: 'The place itself is quite too horrid — a great swamp, lying in a big hole, surrounded by high hills, and a perfect nest of fever, as one would naturally imagine.'[46] But this

44   RA. R8/7
45   FORBES, Archibald, *Souvenirs of Some Continents*, London 1890
46   JOHN, p. 448.

did not bother the Prince. He listened with fascination as the staff discussed the details of the second invasion. In outline, as before, they would invade with three columns except this time each would be stronger than for the first invasion and two of them, once in Zululand, would converge and then march almost together for their mutual support, finally concentrating around the Royal kraal at oNdini. One of these — composed entirely of fresh reinforcing troops and designated the Second Division, under command of the recently-arrived Major-General Edward Newdigate — would come up from Dundee and cross the Blood River at Koppie Allein, where it runs almost due north to south. After crossing the river frontier the column would then head in an easterly direction. Lord Chelmsford's headquarters staff would also ride with this column. Another force (which even now was actually in Zululand, some eighteen miles north-east of Koppie Allein) would be called the Flying Column and placed under the leadership of Evelyn Wood (now promoted to the local rank of Brigadier-General). This column would move to the south-east so that, after a couple of marches, it would be able link up with the Second Division. A third column — the First Division — under Major-General Crealock (brother of Chelmsford's military secretary) was to march independently along the coastal strip, largely in a supportive and blocking role with a view to possibly establishing a sea-borne supply route.

At this stage it was impossible to fix a firm date for the invasion since it was still not clear how long the extensive build-up of reinforcements, logistic preparations and necessary route reconnaissance would take. As there were no roads, only a few rutted tracks used by traders' wagons, every yard of the planned routes had to be examined — and assessments made about overcoming such natural obstacles as rivers, marsh areas, hills and ravines. Existing maps would require up-dating and other areas of country, not yet mapped, would require careful surveys and field sketches. All this would take time. But Lord Chelmsford hoped to be on the move again towards the end of May — ideally before the onset of winter.

On 4th May the Prince sent a further letter to his mother:

> For two days we have been sleeping in our clothes, ready to leave our tents at the first alarm.
>
> Since we crossed the Buffalo River, we have been in the enemy's country and yesterday I thought we should meet some parties of Zulus, for we were following with a small escort the line of the Blood River which bounds the space occupied by the belligerent forces.
>
> I found to my great surprise several Frenchmen among the volunteer cavalry corps that cover the frontier. They are all old soldiers who don't know what to do in France since the profession of arms was abolished by the recruiting laws.
>
> They all came to find me and seem enchanted to see me.
>
> They are not, as you may well imagine, the *crème de la crème*, but that did not stop me from fraternising with them.

Passing by Utrecht, I shall see a man called Grandier and I will write you his wonderful history, when I have heard it from his own mouth. Up till now he is the only white man who has ever been at oNdini.

The French are sometimes quaint fellows. Lord Chelmsford's late cook was a Frenchman. He cooked very badly, but he wrote verses. This poor devil, named Laparet, who had followed the General 'for love of war' was killed at Isandlwana 'fighting like a lion'.

Goodbye, my dear mother, think of me and be assured that I think of you often.[47]

True to his promise he was to write again — a letter devoted entirely to the extraordinary adventures of Trooper Grandier, a Frenchman, serving with an irregular cavalry unit, Weatherley's Border Horse. He had been discovered alive by the Zulus immediately after the battle of Hlobane on 28th March. With their passion for killing temporarily spent the Zulus, most unusually, took him prisoner and brought him before King Cetshwayo at oNdini. Although closely questioned he was not treated harshly; subsequently, he claimed to have somehow escaped his captors and after many uncorroborated adventures, was finally found by a patrol in late April — wandering around almost naked not far from Khambula. This fact in itself raised many doubts about the escape part of his story, for it seemed more likely that the Zulus had brought him as close to the British camp as possible and then deliberately set him free. Despite these doubts, his unusual story did make him something of a hero in the British newspapers and the Prince was equally impressed. After talking with Trooper Grandier in Utrecht, he alerted Deléage, who in turn sent a special report back to *Le Figaro*. Whatever the precise truth of Grandier's tale there seemed little doubt that he had been captured — thus becoming the only white soldier to have been taken prisoner by the Zulus. In the same letter to his mother, the Prince added: 'I have perhaps spoken at too great a length of someone you do not know, but, at the moment, I have nothing very interesting to tell you that concerns myself...I am eager to do something worth doing.'[48]

Next day he wrote to Jules Espinasse:

Since the twenty-eighth of last month, Lord Chelmsford, one of whose aides-de-camp I am, is visiting the different cantonments of the troops moving towards the point of concentration of the Second Division which is to operate on the north-west frontier of Zululand. Every kind of difficulty prevents rapid movement, and now a month after the greater part of the troops disembarked, they have barely covered two hundred kilometres.

I have just seen Bigge and Slade, my two old comrades; I found them in the entrenched camp at Khambula, which was so boldly attacked by the enemy on the twenty-ninth of March.

The Zulus, they told me, manoeuvred with a unity that would have done credit to European troops.

47   FILON, p. 200.
48   Ibid., p. 201.

As soon as the artillery greeted them with its first discharge, the five columns that were advancing on the entrenchments spread out like skirmishers, and, taking advantage of the slightest shelter, the blacks dotted themselves all along the plateau up to within twenty paces from the shelter trenches. After five hour's fighting, the English drove them back and pursued them with their irregular horse.

For two days I have not had my boots off, but this life pleases me and is good for me.

Goodbye, my dear Espinasse, remember me to all my friends and be sure of my unchanging affection.

Your friend, and, one day, I hope, your comrade in arms.

Napoleon[49]

Deléage had likewise reached the new headquarters at Utrecht and on return from Khambula, the Prince gave him lunch and took him round the soldiers' wards in the military hospital. Louis sat beside each bed in turn, rolling cigarettes for the patients, chatting away to them in his excellent English, whilst managing to give the young journalist a running commentary in French to describe each man's case-history. Deléage noticed how the atmosphere in each ward became livelier whenever the Prince entered, since every soldier knew from past experience that he would spend time talking to each of them, looking carefully at the family photographs they often produced for his scrutiny.

That particular afternoon the Prince also used his influence to enable Deléage to have a brief interview with Lord Chelmsford. As always, the General was friendly and charming. Unlike many other senior officers Lord Chelmsford acknowledged the important role of press correspondents and always made himself accessible to them. A tall lean aristocrat, he treated all his officers and men, regardless of rank or position, with the same politeness and consideration. Graceful manners, derived from an inbred understanding of the myriad rules of social etiquette, were one of the hallmarks of a 'gentleman' and in this respect Lord Chelmsford and the Prince were always to be on an equal footing. And whatever views others may have held about the General's military capabilities (and many could be quite disparaging in their private letters home), there was general agreement that he was a most likeable and approachable man. But despite the gracious way in which he was received, the young French journalist, peering over his glasses, felt obliged to openly express his concerns about the Prince's safety. Chelmsford replied to the effect that he shared those concerns but the alternative was to surround Louis with a permanent escort — and that would be totally unacceptable to him and to everyone else. After all, hadn't the Empress permitted her son to come out to South Africa entirely on his own, accepting that some risks would have to be taken? Otherwise there was a real danger that the Prince might abruptly leave and return to England in disgust. He went on to explain, "Now that I am better acquainted with the Prince, and have learnt his worth, I accept my responsibility to the full...Indeed, I forget he is a Prince

---

49   Ibid., p. 239.

and think of him only as one of the most reliable officers on my Staff. He is entitled
to my full confidence. Every day I see more reason to congratulate myself on having
him with me."[50]

But the fact remained that the Prince had no specific duties to perform and
thus easily became bored and restless. He spent a lot of time pestering other staff
officers. What were these bales in the commissariat for? How much did each of
those packing cases hold? And how many men could be supplied from this pile of
rations, and for how long? How many wagons would be required to move that stack
of ammunition boxes? And for each question he would carefully enter the answers
in small notebooks. One of the staff officers, Brevet Lieutenant-Colonel Richard
Harrison, noted: 'At our bivouacs, and elsewhere, we frequently discussed military
and other matters, and I had to reply to his many questions about what was the
organisation of this and that in the English Army by telling him that the word with
us was hardly understood — the usual custom being for our generals to make such
arrangements, in the field, as they thought most likely to meet the circumstances of
the time.'[51]

The Prince would have been able to contrast that with the Prussian Army —
the superb organisation of which had been a significant factor in France's defeat.

On other occasions he would entertain the small headquarters with daring
feats of horsemanship, accompanied by equally thrilling displays in swordsmanship,
wielding a sabre over his head to neatly slice large potatoes thrown up specially into
the air. He also fashioned sticks of wood to look like Zulu *assegais* and persuaded
others to hurl them at him hard and fast. And the harder and faster they were
thrown the more vigorously he would duck and weave to avoid them. The agile
young Frenchman soon became a popular figure, with most people amused by his
Gallic bravado, tolerating his penchant for 'showing-off.' Above all they liked his
zest for life, his charm and concern for others. Many also derived special pleasure
at the recurring rumours that, on return from the war, he might even become the
Queen's son-in-law!

From Camden Place the Empress wrote a letter to her own mother in which she
showed a clear appreciation of the environment in which her son was campaigning:

> I'm hoping for important news because if the advance is not continued we
> will be obliged to wait till September, as the grass is burnt at the end of
> June, which means there is no fodder for cattle and, as a result, transport is a
> problem...I hope, too, for the sake of poor Lord Chelmsford who has had to
> fight against every obstacle, that he will not be deprived of his right to glory
> by someone else. If indeed he acts immediately then it is quite likely that the
> whole business can be ended quickly.[52]

But the Empress was not aware when she wrote that letter that the British
Government had already made a decision to supersede both Sir Bartle Frere and

---

50 JOHN, p. 451.
51 KNIGHT, *By Orders of the Great White Queen*, p. 225.
52 TURNBULL, p. 354.

Lord Chelmsford with a single supremo, General Sir Garnet Wolseley, who would assume complete civil and military powers in South Africa. But as Queen Victoria had been told that the Empress was so concerned about her son's safety that she was now toying with the idea of following him out to South Africa herself, she took the matter up with the Duke of Cambridge 'and General Wolseley, who was on the point of leaving England to replace Lord Chelmsford at the head of troops in Zululand, was entrusted, it was said, with orders for the Prince's return.'[53] But even if he had not been so entrusted, there can be little doubt that the imperious General Wolseley (who heartily disliked the Duke of Cambridge) would not have tolerated for one moment the presence of any 'spectator', even a Prince, loitering around his headquarters staff. It was the sort of casual unprofessionalism he so despised. The Prince would have been politely but firmly required either to return home, or divest himself of military uniform to remain, like a journalist, in a purely civilian capacity, fending entirely for himself.

On 9th May Lord Chelmsford appointed Brevet Lieutenant-Colonel Richard Harrison, Royal Engineers, to his staff as a full-time Assistant Quartermaster-General. This was an entirely new appointment with a wide range of responsibilities. An experienced officer, who had served with distinction during the Indian Mutiny and in China, Harrison was now to be placed in charge of collecting general information, surveying and reconnaissance, obtaining transport and supplies for the newly-formed Second Division. He was also made responsible for reconnoitring a passable route into Zululand for the Headquarters and Second Division, with secure overnight camp sites. To assist him in these tasks, he was allocated two junior officers in the full-time appointment of Deputy Assistant Quartermaster-General — Brevet Major Francis Grenfell of 60th Rifles (later Field Marshal Lord Grenfell) and Lieutenant Jahleel Brenton Carey of 98th ('Prince of Wales') Regiment of Foot, one of the 'special service' officers sent out with the reinforcements. With fourteen years of service and experience behind him, Carey had already shown himself to be good at patrolling and field sketching, updating and enlarging existing maps. Additionally, he was to be heavily involved in drawing entirely new maps of the many large tracts of Zululand which had never previously been surveyed.

By a strange irony, Carey had been educated in France and thus spoke the language fluently. It was therefore almost inevitable that, from the moment of joining the headquarters staff, he would establish a particular relationship with the young Prince. Within minutes of their first meeting Carey had produced photographs of his family — his mother, wife and three children. At that time the Prince could not have known that Carey was frequently to be seen fervently kissing these same photographs in public, much to the embarrassment of many of the officers. For despite the cloying sentimentality of the age, such emotional exhibitionism was considered to be entirely inappropriate from someone holding commissioned rank.

As soon as he realised that the Prince was going to be a sympathetic listener, Carey expanded into details about his family, his devout Protestant faith and lifelong admiration for all things French. Louis was soon to learn that he had been born in

---

53   FILON, Augustin. *Souvenirs sur l'Impératrice Eugénie*, p. 292.

Devon, the son of a vicar, and after attending a *lycée* in Paris had graduated from the Royal Military College, Sandhurst with a commission (which did not have to be purchased) in the 3rd West India Regiment. The Prince may not have realised that such a commission would be viewed as socially inferior to that of a good British regiment of the line and would therefore influence the attitude of many of his brother officers towards him. Carey had taken part in an expedition to Honduras in 1867, and then three years later, whilst on half-pay, had volunteered for duty with the humanitarian English Ambulance (the word at that time signifying a large but mobile field hospital) during the Franco-Prussian war. Although captured three times, he had been released on each occasion once it had been established that he was evenly helping the Prussian wounded as much as the French. On return to England that autumn he had succeeded in transferring to the 98th Regiment of Foot and had just completed the newly-established Army Staff Course at Camberley before arriving with the reinforcements Carey was to earn much praise for his work with Colonel Harrison: 'He was an officer of outstanding promise and a glutton for duty...no more zealous or useful officer in South Africa...he had got together an impressive amount of invaluable information and he toiled night and day.'[54]

But this commendable report inevitably focused on the performance of his military duties; it revealed little about his true character. Although intelligent and resourceful, many also considered that he was highly-strung and for all his outward religious piety, both unstable and unreliable. His nervousness would become most apparent whenever he was mounted, as though riding horses in general never really agreed with him. He was certainly a glutton for work, but this was perhaps less for its own sake than to obtain the approval of others, an essential requirement in sustaining Carey's morale. In the pursuit of patronage from his military and social superiors, he could often be both sycophantic and deferential. On the other hand he had only recently earned an official commendation and favourable press reporting for his conduct and enterprise when, on 3rd April, the troopship *Clyde* on which he was travelling out from England with many troops had finally been shipwrecked on its way from Cape Town to Durban. But even so he was not particularly popular nor did he have any close friends amongst his brother officers. One of them, Captain Lane of the Rifle Brigade, recalled Carey as 'no good as a soldier except for military surveying and field sketching.'[55] Most people looked upon him as a somewhat isolated figure. In many ways Louis's presence in the headquarters was to give the insecure Carey a psychological boost, for now he could ingratiate himself with a Prince of France, safe in the knowledge that he was the only officer on the staff able to converse fluently with him in his own tongue.

---

54   FEATHERSTONE, p. 68.
55   RA. Add.J 1556 Letter to Lord Stamforham, dated 28th October 1928.

Chapter IX

A Chilling Prediction

ABOUT THE MIDDLE OF MAY, Brigadier-General Wood instructed Colonel Redvers Buller to find a route for his Flying Column, south from Khambula into Zululand. And as Colonel Harrison also wanted to establish a route for the Headquarters and Second Division eastwards from Koppie Allein he asked if he might join Buller's patrol for this purpose.

When he heard the news the Prince Imperial begged Harrison to allow him to accompany the patrol. The Assistant Quartermaster-General sensibly referred the request to Lord Chelmsford. Since the party would consist of two hundred troopers from the Frontier Light Horse (an all-volunteer force raised and commanded by Colonel Buller himself) together with a small detachment of Bettington's Horse (another irregular mounted unit), Chelmsford judged the Prince would be well protected and gave his permission. Accordingly, on 13th May, Colonel Harrison, accompanied by the Hon.W.Drummond (chief of the Intelligence Department) and the Prince, set off for the main forward base at Conference Hill in order to collect rations for both men and horses. Each of the officers was accompanied by a soldier servant and three horses, with all their essential requirements carried in the saddle-bags.

They spent that night at Conference Hill. Louis refused the customary officer's patrol tent; he also declined the use of a soldier's bivouac, choosing instead the same rough sheet of canvas as used by the irregulars. He was quite determined to live up to the standards, set by himself in that essay at Woolwich on the duties of an officer towards his men: 'sharing their hardships, their privations.' And so, under this inadequate and coarse covering, he lay awake all night — shivering with cold. However the following morning, before they set off, the Prince was delighted to learn that the base, with its elaborate entrenchments, was now going to be re-designated *Fort Napoleon* in his honour — he felt it particularly appropriate since he had passed the night there in rougher conditions than anyone else! He was still trying to become acclimatised to Zululand, with its extremes of baking hot days, interspersed with sudden chilling downpours of rain and nights which, particularly during the winter months of June, July and August, could be bitterly cold.

Colonel Buller's party of some two hundred irregulars, together with native BaSotho troopers, arrived shortly afterwards and later that morning the whole patrol, now including the detachment of Bettington's Horse, started to move off towards Koppie Allein, about fifteen miles to the south west.

It was the first time the Prince had been in close proximity to all these volunteers who formed such an important element of Lord Chelmsford's army. Most of them were tough, hard-bitten mercenaries. They had come from all over Europe as well as from within South Africa, volunteers fighting for the attractive pay of five shillings a day compared to the single shilling being paid to the regular British soldiers. In their ranks were disgraced 'gentlemen', fugitives from justice, deserters from ships, escaped criminals, drifters from the towns of South Africa, even Boer farmers driven from their homes by repeated Zulu attacks. 'There were Frenchmen who could not speak a word of English, and Channel Islanders whose *patois* neither Englishmen nor Frenchmen could fully understand.'[1] Yet, through the sheer force of his robust personality, and by the example of his personal bravery and skill in battle, Colonel Redvers Buller had somehow managed to bind this strange assortment of social outcasts together and weld them into an effective fighting force. And unusually for an officer of his rank (he was officially a substantive Captain, who had been promoted early to Brevet Lieutenant Colonel), he also insisted on sharing all his soldiers' hardships when out on patrol, sleeping rough and eating the same food. Nonetheless he tolerated no nonsense from anyone. When one of his troopers once turned up late and drunk on parade, hurling personal abuse at him, Buller made no response, other than to instruct everyone to set off. But after they had gone several miles into enemy territory Buller suddenly halted the patrol, and brusquely told the trooper to dismount and clear off.

That night — 14th May — before entering Zululand itself the whole party bivouacked in a deserted farm near Koppie Allein. The horses were knee-haltered and permitted to graze overnight in a nearby mealie field. The Prince was offered a private room in the farmhouse but declined, preferring to sleep on the mud floor with all the others, including Colonel Buller, wrapped up in greatcoats and blankets trying to keep warm.

At daylight the following morning they crossed the Blood River into Zululand, turning towards the south, entering into country dominated by jagged hills and plains which were deeply scored by dried-up water beds — for there was not much water to be seen this time of the year. Whilst the large patches of tall Kaffir grass might possibly conceal groups of Zulu warriors, they certainly obscured many deep white ant holes into which horses could so easily stumble and slither, jettisoning their riders. By day it was burning hot, with flies constantly flitting from horse to rider, irritating both in equal measure. Riding proudly in the lead beside the legendary Colonel Buller the Prince felt a renewed sense of elation — after all, this was the experience he had come to savour, moving ever deeper into hostile territory, closer to danger. All that really remained to complete the morning's exhilaration was for a band of Zulus to suddenly spring up in front of them. But as they entered the valley of the river Ityotyozi they suddenly encountered Lieutenant Carey out on a separate reconnaissance with a large escort of eighty dragoons. To come across such a heavy force of regular cavalry, resplendent in their smart uniforms, trotting in disciplined formation, all to protect one solitary junior staff officer aroused

---

1   FORBES, Archibald. *Barracks, Bivouacs and Battles*, p. 137.

much ribald comment from amongst Colonel Buller's volunteers. This did not go unnoticed by Carey.

At about half past ten they stopped to rest the horses and boil water for tea and coffee. They also took the opportunity to have a quick meal. Throughout the whole campaign such meals, whilst on patrol, invariably consisted of a little tinned meat, some ration bread or biscuit, perhaps a little jam, with a soothing cup of coffee or tea. For greater security even these sparse meals would be taken only during the hours of daylight.

It was not long before they resumed the patrol. Around midday, just as the Prince was beginning to imagine that perhaps Zulus did not really exist, a group of about fifty suddenly appeared on a feature marked Sihayo's Hill, a few hundred yards away. Most were on foot with about eight on horseback. For a moment there was the prospect of a sharp skirmish, but once they had assessed the size of Buller's force the scouting Zulus soon began to melt away. This was not unusual. Throughout the campaign the Zulus rarely stood and fought defensive actions; they always preferred to take the offensive, to engage in close-quarter fighting, and whilst their tactical training was largely based around envelopment attacks, they were also very adept at enticing their enemies into well-planned ambushes. Despite this danger some of the troopers automatically set off in hot pursuit, with Colonel Buller bellowing at them to return at once — but the Prince was already out of earshot, far ahead of the others, his sword drawn, trying to close on a solitary Zulu who had lingered behind. But the warrior did not delay — he soon turned and fled. Nonetheless the Prince continued his lone pursuit until he was almost out of sight, oblivious to the dangers of galloping straight into an ambush. Colonel Buller, red-faced and furious, immediately ordered a small detachment to bring him back. During the wait he turned to Colonel Harrison, telling him in no uncertain terms that never again would he take this young hothead out on patrol. And when Louis, flushed with excitement, finally returned, Colonel Buller could only look at him askance. Yet nothing was said. This was quite uncharacteristic since Buller was renowned for his outspokenness, particularly to senior officers and social superiors (later on in his career he was to have a damaging public row with the Prince of Wales). He would not have made any exception, even for a Prince, but on this occasion, for reasons known only to himself, he chose to curb his violent temper. And yet the Prince would not have taken any offence had the error of his solitary pursuit been explained to him — there and then. From Buller's point of view, as he seethed inwardly in anger, it was almost beyond belief that, by personal recklessness, this excitable young man might well have endangered the whole force. Indeed the patrol could have been needlessly diverted from its planned axis of reconnaissance simply to retrieve the Prince. Louis seems not to have appreciated that the sole purpose of this particular incursion was detailed route-planning — not Zulu hunting. But, whilst the Colonel may have said nothing directly to the Prince at the time, he nonetheless resolved to make a strong complaint to Lord Chelmsford later.

The patrol continued along a route to the north until darkness fell. For protection that night they formed a large ring with all the horses, heads facing inwards, saddles and bridles on, with each rider lying down beside his mount on the grass. There could be no fires and no hot drink. Louis, totally unaware of Colonel Buller's annoyance at his bravado, was too excited at the day's events to sleep properly. And his exhilaration was only to be intensified when he learnt that, in his honour, officers of the patrol now proposed renaming Sihayo's Hill — *Napoleon Koppie*. And yet, to the great irritation of many of the others, the proud Prince, shivering through a second cold night, spent part of the time pacing up and down to keep warm, humming quietly to himself some French martial airs.

By 16th May they were safely back at a new camp, near Wolf Hill, which had been established for Brigadier-General Wood's column.

Blissfully content over his recent experiences, the Prince slept that night in the comfort of an officer's tent — a sleep of utter exhaustion. It was well beyond dawn, and the time for the camp stand-to, before Lomas finally managed to arouse the Prince, only to hear him sleepily decline breakfast. Evelyn Wood considered this to be unsoldierly and shortly after the Prince had fallen back to sleep, he threw open both flaps of the tent and shouted: "Here come the Zulus!" In a flash, the Prince had leapt out of the tent, sword in hand. The General politely bowed his head, and with a smile said, "And now, sir, I hope you'll consent to have breakfast with me?"[2]

And a few days later, the Hon. W. Drummond wrote to his father: "Uncommonly cold work — the Prince Imperial...was out with us — he thought it manly not to take a blanket, and the result was that for two nights he had to walk about the whole time trying to warm himself. He is very nice and very intelligent."[3]

Later that day, 17th May, after the party had returned to Conference Hill, Colonel Buller took the opportunity to formally complain to Lord Chelmsford about the Prince's recklessness. He bluntly told Chelmsford that he would no longer accept any further responsibility for his safety. Indeed, he went so far as to argue that, from now on, Louis should only be employed on internal staff duties within the perimeter of secure camps. Whilst Lord Chelmsford felt that he could not simply confine the Prince to tasks within a camp, he nonetheless gave a written instruction to Colonel Harrison stating that, under no circumstances, was Louis ever to be allowed to go on patrol into enemy-held territory without his personal approval, and that whenever the Prince was doing survey work close to any camp he must at all times be accompanied by an officer and escort. He also formally assigned the Prince to Colonel Harrison's staff as one of his 'unofficial' assistants, thus regularising an arrangement which had existed for some time. It was all a far cry from his nominal position as a non-combatant 'spectator'.

In his recollections, published in 1908, Colonel Harrison understood that the Prince was being loaned in order to collect and compile information concerning the distribution of troops and supply depots. But as the Prince had no status in the army, he could not be appointed a Deputy Assistant Quartermaster-General in the same way as Major Grenfell and Lieutenant Carey. Nonetheless, Harrison was given to understand that Louis was not to be treated as a Royal personage but like any other officer on his staff. When Lord Chelmsford personally informed the Prince about his new duties, he also took the opportunity to stress that it would be much

---

2   JOHN, p. 454.
3   RA. R5/11

appreciated if he always sought permission before leaving camp. The Prince was somewhat nonplussed by this particular requirement since he had always previously asked permission and had never left camp without it. At the time, it would have made much more sense had the General spoken to the Prince with less deference and a great deal more realism about the possible consequences of his past ill-judged actions which might have endangered others as well as himself. Louis would have readily accepted such plain speaking from Lord Chelmsford, or indeed from any other senior officer. But, as far as the Prince was concerned, no-one in authority had made any comment to him about his dashing behaviour — which to him was no more than the traditional *élan* expected of any junior French officer — and thus was not even remotely aware of the upset it had caused.

Paul Deléage was most surprised to learn by chance from *The Times* correspondent in Dundee that the Prince had actually been on a scouting party operating in hostile territory. He failed to see how that news equated with Lord Chelmsford's earlier undertaking to him regarding the safety of the Prince. This disquieting discovery resurrected all his earlier fears about the sincerity of British intentions towards Louis, who demonstrably was now becoming more and more drawn into a war in which British military competence had already been found wanting.

Whilst Colonel Buller's patrol had established a route southwards for Brigadier-General Wood's Flying Column, a detailed route for the Headquarters and Second Division east from Koppie Allein still had to be reconnoitred and finalised.

Colonel Harrison therefore decided to organise a further patrol to go out again immediately on 17th May, this time taking only five mounted European irregulars (who would also lead spare ponies) under Captain Rowland Bettington, and twenty native BaSothos, also under command of their own officer. With the addition of Lieutenant Carey, the whole patrol would number twenty-nine. They planned to take with them only three days provisions, allowing for the horses to be fed exclusively on the veld. Arrangements were also made to meet up with Colonel Buller and some four hundred of his mounted force at a point eastward of the Ingutu Mountains.

Once more the Prince immediately asked to join the patrol but Colonel Harrison, recalling Colonel Buller's earlier comments to him about the Prince's recklessness, politely rejected his request. On this occasion he did not even refer the matter to Lord Chelmsford. Instead, he sent the Prince back to Utrecht to join other members of the headquarters staff. Louis thereupon eagerly asked Colonel Harrison if he would change his mind were Lord Chelmsford personally to give his consent, and Harrison nodded his agreement. Having now determined to appeal direct to the Commanding General, Louis galloped off at high speed for Utrecht but on the way he caught up with Brigadier-General Wood, who kindly agreed to intercede with Lord Chelmsford on his behalf. The General gave his verbal consent, which was relayed back to the Prince. In this manner therefore he obtained the necessary permission to go on his second patrol into enemy territory — only one day after the first.

By the morning of 17th May Colonel Harrison had already started and was now two miles across the Blood River on the Zulu side before the Prince, accompanied only by Lomas, finally caught up with the patrol. This time they would be probing much deeper into hostile territory. Although Colonel Harrison was nominally in overall charge the escort was directly under the command of Captain Bettington. Everyone knew that the elderly New Zealander was, by far, the most experienced officer in the patrol and that he had personally raised the volunteer unit which was named after him. In fact, Bettington had gained previous experience fighting in the 9th Cape Frontier War; above all, he was familiar with the country and he probably knew better than any regular military officer just how to deploy the irregular troopers to the best advantage.

Whilst the Prince grew to admire Captain Bettington, he continued to regard the volunteers of his mounted unit with some amazement. They never seemed to parade formally, they mounted their horses individually and when they happened to be ready, would start off in straggling files. To his eyes they appeared to be a slovenly and ill-disciplined group of people whose reliability was probably questionable. The only item of dress they appeared to have in common was a distinguishing red puggaree around their slouch hats, whilst the majority were armed with Swinburne-Henry carbines. These were single-shot weapons without safety catches. Not surprisingly therefore it had proved safer to load the carbines only when absolutely necessary. It was, in any case, awkward to feed the weapon with ammunition whilst on horseback, particularly when riders were trying to steady their mounts. And from horseback the weapon had to be fired with one hand, like some top heavy pistol, making it only effective at point-blank range. Dismounted, however, the troopers could always produce a steady rate of fairly accurate fire. Unlike most of the regular British officers Captain Bettington declined to carry a sword, considering it to be nothing but an encumbrance whilst on horseback. For preference he carried a revolver, long knife and a riding crop. But more than any single weapon, the irregulars always relied on the dash and speed of their fit horses to either scatter the enemy or extricate themselves out of tight corners.

By the evening of 17th May, at the end of their first day, the patrol had already ridden without mishap almost forty miles deep into Zululand. They had been moving south of *Napoleon Koppie* towards the pre-arranged meeting point with Colonel Buller and his detachment. This was to be a map co-ordinate within a mile of a Zulu kraal known to be on the upper Bashee, east of the Ingutu Mountains. But once the sun had gone down on that first day, Captain Bettington became convinced that their overnight camp was under observation. It was a favoured Zulu tactic — to keep an enemy under surveillance during the night in order to launch a surprise attack at first light. Everyone therefore was instructed to start walking, leading their horses as quietly as possible, for about another mile until they reached the better security of a dried-up ravine or 'donga'. Here for the rest of the night the horses were kept saddled, tied together in a circle, whilst every man lay down beside his own mount to sleep. BaSotho sentries were posted with orders to keep circulating around the donga until daylight. Even so, they remained vulnerable to a surprise Zulu attack and few managed to sleep.

Captain Bettington later described the tenseness of that particular night: 'Even to strike a match or say a word, except in a whisper, was strictly forbidden. In front, in the rear, on the right or left, BaSothos were stationed as sentinels with orders to walk towards each other. Then the men could take some rest; the Prince was stretched upon the ground like the others, sharing his scanty covering with Lomas, his orderly…so the night passed, troubled only by false alarms given by one of the officers, Lieutenant Carey.'[4]

Carey's nervousness was not unique. Many of the reinforcing officers and units had become the cause of innumerable false alarms in this way, particularly at night. It would appear that, during their long voyage to South Africa, they had all heard so much about the military prowess of the Zulus that many arrived in Natal completely unnerved. Consequently there were to be many false alerts during the second invasion, when on more than one occasion friendly piquets were unfortunately mistaken for the enemy and shot dead. And yet the Zulus rarely attacked during the hours of darkness; apart from the sheer impracticalities of command and control, these were also the hours for evil spirits to take control. One of the few exceptions had been at Rorke's Drift, four months earlier, but here the battle lust from fighting fiercely all afternoon and evening had simply been extended into the hours of darkness in the hope of achieving a rapid victory.

After a further morning's ride there was still no sign of Buller's party. Colonel Harrison began to ponder the wisdom of pressing on alone. Bettington, knowing that part of the country particularly well, finally persuaded him that their security lay, not so much in the size of the escort but in the protective measures they must now take. On this basis Harrison decided to continue, moving east along the ridge of the Ingutu Mountains, trying to find a route leading into the Nonwendi River valley and thence on to the Ibabanango Mountain. And on the way, they would be passing north of the huge ravine in which the Zulu *impis* had crouched just before pouring down on Isandlwana.

And, as far as Isandlwana was concerned, Lord Chelmsford had already decided to re-visit the battlefield. In two days time a large force, of about brigade size, led by the new cavalry commander Major-General Frederick Marshall, would be setting out for the site which was now only a few miles to the south of Harrison's own patrol route. The troopers would also be leading enough pairs of horses to bring back about forty of the abandoned wagons. Whilst the opportunity would also be taken to cover some of the rotting bodies with stones, many more visits would have to be made over the next few weeks before that gruesome task would finally be completed.

Along the Ingutu ridge Captain Bettington rode out in front, his troopers covering the way ahead and the flanks; the Prince Imperial and Colonel Harrison followed directly behind. Lieutenant Carey rode with the native BaSothos. Every now and then the patrol would stop to allow both the Prince and Carey to dismount and take compass bearings. Sometimes both of them would quickly sketch the outlines of the ground spread out below them to the north — across which the Second Division was expected to march towards oNdini.

---

4   FILON, p. 203.

But as the patrol, moving in a south easterly direction towards the top of the Ingutu Ridge, entered a gully leading up to a kraal, there was a sudden outburst of firing, with wildly-aimed bullets ricocheting off the boulders all around them. Immediately Captain Bettington, armed only with a riding crop, led his troopers in a charge straight up the steep path towards the sound of the firing. There was no alternative. The patrol could not continue as long as the enemy occupied the commanding heights. The Prince was seen to deliberately dismount in order to draw his sabre; then springing back into the saddle, swiftly caught up with the others along the narrow track, made treacherous by innumerable loose rocks, with the horses inevitably stumbling and slithering as they climbed. Waving his sabre excitedly the Prince kept close behind Captain Bettington. Colonel Harrison now removed his helmet and signalled the BaSothos to move forward. But in the event only two of them galloped up to join him; the remainder did not arrive until the top had been reached. And on the top about sixty Zulus began their usual tactics of trying to surround individuals as they began to appear — but the continuing momentum of the charge took them by surprise, their centre rapidly began to give way and after letting off a few more badly-aimed shots, they all suddenly turned and fled away from the kraal they had been occupying. Captain Bettington immediately halted his troopers; this time the Prince did not dash forward in solitary pursuit.

After they had searched the huts and recovered some of the equipment looted from Isandlwana, including saddles, they set fire to the whole kraal. Afterwards they took the opportunity to have a hasty meal before darkness fell. As they sipped their coffee, Captain Bettington proposed that, to commemorate the Prince's first encounter with the enemy, the burning homestead should now be designated on their maps as *Napoleon Kraal*, with the rise itself called 'Harrison Kop'. The Prince was delighted. It seemed as if his name was now being generously used to denote a number of reference points in many of the areas adjoining Natal and Zululand. There was nothing particularly unusual in this — many of the new European townships and unmapped topographical landmarks were being named after prominent individuals. But the frequency with which his own name was being used was somewhat unusual. Unbeknown to him, the First Division advancing on the coast route, would also name one of their entrenchments on the Umlalazi as *Fort Napoleon*. These frequent spontaneous gestures to the Prince, usually made on the spur of the moment by individual officers, reflected the genuine regard and affection with which he was widely held.

During the meal Captain Bettington also took the opportunity to try and persuade Louis to dispense with a sword altogether and rely instead on a pistol. He reminded the Prince how he had been compelled to dismount in order to draw the long sabre, but Louis replied in words which Bettington was never to forget; "I make a point of always having mine, not so much to attack, as to defend myself if I were surrounded. I should die fighting and then death would have no pangs."[5]

As the patrol resumed, they captured a few stray horses, and on one occasion came across three men in red coats, armed with *assegais*, walking casually straight

---

5   Ibid., p. 204.

towards them, perhaps returning to the kraal oblivious of the earlier skirmish. As he was not certain whether they were Natal natives in British service or just friendly Zulus, Colonel Harrison trotted forward to observe them more closely. As he did so Captain Bettington, rightly sensing that their intent was hostile, suddenly galloped at speed past him, shooting one dead with his pistol and scaring the other two away.

The patrol continued moving in an easterly direction, deeper into Zululand, penetrating as far as the valley of the Nondweni, (which confusingly, on some maps, was also referred to as the Upoko River) reconnoitring up the slopes of Alarm Hill, near which ran the old wagon track from Rorke's Drift to oNdini. Colonel Harrison reckoned that he had now established a passable invasion route for the Headquarters and Second Division — the 'going' on the top of the Ingutu Hills was reasonable, the only possible difficulty being the descent into the valley at the eastern end. Although there was still no sign of Colonel Buller's party Harrison felt that they had now probably gone far enough and later that afternoon decided to return to base.

Towards evening they camped beside a deserted kraal to cook a meal and then, leaving the fires alight, moved off on foot as soon as darkness began to envelope them. Walking away, they could just make out small groups of Zulus collecting behind them, with some actually dancing around one of the fires, shouting blood-curdling war cries. Bettington now strongly urged Colonel Harrison to ride on non-stop through the night, navigating by stars and compass, so as to cross the Blood River and reach the safety of Conference Hill by dawn. But even as they wearily approached the base camp perimeter, during the routine first light stand-to, there was further tension. Colonel Harrison recalled hearing an officer instructing his men: "Now, boys, be ready — when I give the word to fire, fire low — I see them coming — look out, boys — remember to fire low."[6] Although constantly shouting their own identification, they nonetheless had to advance very cautiously before the jittery troops finally lowered their rifles and allowed them to pass.

When the Prince, accompanied by Colonel Harrison, arrived at the main headquarters at Utrecht later that afternoon Brigadier-General Wood personally welcomed him: "Well, sir, you've not been *assegaied* yet?" "No — not yet", Louis replied, laughing despite his fatigue. But then he looked the General firmly in the eye, adding more seriously, "But while I've no desire to be killed, if I had to fall I should prefer an *assegai* to a bullet. It would show we'd been at close quarters."[7]

Colonel Harrison recalled in his memoirs that, over the six days covered by both patrols, they had ridden almost two hundred miles, and that of the last thirty-six hours, twenty-five had been spent in the saddle. He referred to the fact that the Prince had enjoyed it all immensely and personally compiled a most excellent report with their route recommendations. This report, in the Prince's thick handwriting, including many compass bearings and a large field sketch, eventually covered both sides of four sheets of official blue notepaper. Whilst the Prince made scant mention of their skirmish with the Zulus, towards the end of the report he did pen some observations about the BaSothos — offering a clue towards explaining later events:

6   KNIGHT, *By Orders of the Great White Queen*, p. 224.
7   JOHN, p. 457.

'I must however mention what struck me in the BaSothos' conduct. As long as they have white men by their side they feel confident and are as scouts of the greatest use, but left alone they cannot be relied upon.'[8] The report was eventually passed on to Lord Chelmsford. At the same time Colonel Harrison also recalled the impression that the Prince had written: 'a long account to the Empress of the French in England of all he had seen and done.'[9]

In fact the Prince did not write directly to his mother. His letter of 21st May was brief and addressed to Piétri. Clearly, he did not wish to alarm the Empress. 'I have just returned from reconnaissance we were away six days. A few shots were exchanged but nothing happened to speak of. We were in the saddle for twenty hours out of twenty-four. Please send the enclosed letter on to M.Rouher.'[10] The enclosed letter dealt with the quality of a proposed Bonapartist candidate (a certain M.Godelle) for one of the wards of Paris — for, despite all the excitement of recent days, the Prince continued to attend to his political duties.

But the happenings of this second patrol were soon to reach a much wider audience. The Empress, writing to her mother, quoted directly from an exaggerated report which had appeared in *The Times* on 21st May: 'The Prince Imperial, while riding out from the camp with several officers was surrounded by the enemy. Three of our local levies were killed. The Prince put his horse at a *krantz* (i.e. rocky descent) and had a narrow escape. All are well.'[11]

In a subsequent letter the Empress gave her mother a more accurate résumé: 'The French papers say that my son stormed a kraal and that to commemorate this feat it has been given the name of *Kraal Napoléon*. I do admit that I am a bit wary of the exuberance of the Latin races and so I prefer to put more faith in the *Daily News* which merely says that he has distinguished himself without giving the details as to where and how.'[12]

But it was Major Grenfell who made the most chilling and accurate prediction in this letter to his family in England dated 24th May:

> The Prince Imperial is with us and was in great danger last Tuesday. He and Colonel Harrison joined a reconnaissance of Buller's, missed their escort and went on with only five men. The Zulus caught them at the top of a hill where they came under fire. The Prince drew his sword and charged up the hill, shouting. His ferocious yells (and, I conclude, his likeness to his great uncle) alarmed the Zulus who fled, but they had to pistol a Zulu before they got out, which they did all right, but slept two nights in the open, very cold and miserable...He is a plucky little chap and will, I think, get himself shot before this campaign is over.[13]

8   RA. R5/13
9   KNIGHT, p. 225.
10   FILON, p. 201.
11   KURTZ, p. 302.
12   FILON, p. 355.
13   GRENFELL, p. 47.

At Utrecht the Prince recounted all his recent adventures to Paul Deléage, explaining, "I enjoy these little outings, they suit me perfectly — but if I had to be killed, I should be in despair at the thought of falling in one. In a great battle, very well, it's for Providence to decide; but in an obscure skirmish — ah, no, that would never do!"[14]

It was after returning with the Prince from this patrol that Lieutenant Carey was formally introduced to Paul Deléage. But the rotund French journalist had recently experienced hair-raising adventures of his own. Intending to link up with Brigadier-General Wood's headquarters, he had foolishly set out alone one afternoon from Conference Hill but so lost his way that he was compelled to spend a terrifying, lonely night wandering about in the hills. The episode had quite shaken him. Consequently he was now full of remorse, acknowledging the Prince's gentle chiding at his own rashness. "Really," said the Prince with a grin, "you'll get yourself killed before I do."[15] But at least, Deléage reasoned, the Prince did actually care about what happened to him, which was more than could be said for all the Englishmen around him.

Indeed, since that first meeting in Durban he had grown to admire Louis so much that he now felt impelled to berate many of the British officers over what he considered to be their indifference to his fellow countryman. Did they not appreciate what a wonderful fellow he really was? Why did they all take such little notice of him? To his surprise, when specifically asked for their opinions, they nearly all agreed that Louis was indeed a splendid fellow; it was just that they did not choose to express such views in the open and demonstrative manner to which French people were accustomed. Why, otherwise, would they have named so many places on their maps in his honour? There were, of course, a small number who would always view the Prince as a complete outsider, a foreigner, a Napoleonic upstart, who ought not to be wearing a British officer's uniform and getting involved in this tiresome, minor war. And one spoke for many when he observed to Deléage: 'After all, what's the Prince supposed to be doing in this row? He'll get no credit from us, and I can't see what good it's to do him in your own country, unless he goes back a cripple — and even then!.'[16] Unfortunately, throughout the war, Deléage never did understand the attitudes of these Englishmen, who seemed to him to be so insensitive and indifferent.

Not surprisingly, therefore, the French journalist immediately took to Lieutenant Carey — a friendly and unassuming officer, who spoke his language so fluently and who, in his manner, appeared to be so un-English. Deléage certainly found him much easier to get on with than most of the other officers in the camp. Carey told the journalist about his admiration at the Prince's conduct during the patrol, how they had even snuggled together for warmth during that cold night in the donga and the courageous way in which the Prince had charged up the hill in front of others to engage the enemy. Although Carey inevitably glossed over his own part in causing false alarms at night, Deléage nonetheless quickly appreciated

14   FEATHERSTONE, p. 74.
15   DELEAGE, p. 34.
16   JOHN, p. 458.

that the Prince, in all modesty, had probably told him only half the story of his own exploits during the patrol.

When, later on, he learnt that the journalist's baggage had gone astray on its journey to Utrecht, Carey immediately offered to share his own tent. And thus Deléage was able to observe at first hand how Carey would often work into the early hours of the morning, sitting at the folding table, finishing off a field sketch or completing some particular map survey report. The journalist likewise noted Carey's devotion to his family; on the table where he worked stood a framed photograph of his wife and children, and he more than once told Deléage that his family was more important to him than life itself.

Back at Utrecht, supported by the Prince's report and field sketches on a recommended route for the Headquarters and Second Division, Colonel Harrison discussed the options with Lord Chelmsford. However Colonel Buller, having genuinely mistaken the location of the exact *rendezvous* with Harrison, had already reconnoitred a suitable route for the division — about ten miles further north. Relying on Buller's greater experience, Lord Chelmsford finally opted for the latter. Amongst other attractions, this northern route would keep everyone well clear of the gruesome battlefield of Isandlwana. It was decided that force would enter Zululand from Koppie Allein, link up with Brigadier-General Wood's Flying Column by the river Ityotyozi and thereafter follow, in general terms, the same route, with each column forming its own defensive laager for overnight stops. But even with the general lines of advance now resolved there was still a requirement for detailed route sketches and precise locations for those overnight camps. For these on-going tasks, Colonel Harrison intended to employ Lieutenant Carey, operating from Conference Hill and the Prince Imperial, who in principle would remain in the headquarters. Colonel Harrison also recalled in his memoirs handing the Prince written instructions that he was never to leave the camp without a proper escort. His task would be to sketch the camps occupied by the headquarters, and the roads they would use when on the march.[17]

That the safety of the Prince at this time was also uppermost in Lord Chelmsford's mind is evidenced by a personal letter he wrote to his wife the following day:

> The Prince Imperial went out on reconnaissance a few days ago and nearly came to grief. I shall not let him out of my sight again if I can help it.[18]

But, as so often with Lord Chelmsford, his best intentions turned out to be impracticable. Once the second invasion had been launched he was far too pre-occupied to keep a personal eye on the constant whereabouts of his imperial guest, but there would have been nothing to prevent him issuing even stricter orders to Colonel Harrison and perhaps taking a few moments to personally and politely admonish the Prince for his past recklessness. After all, from the day of the Prince's arrival, he had been receiving sequential reports about Louis's impulsiveness — a trait

17   KNIGHT, p. 226.
18   FEATHERSTONE, p. 74.

about which he had first been warned in writing by General Simmons, and about which he had now received two separate verbal reports, one from the outspoken but influential Colonel Buller, and yet still he had taken no direct action.

Once the excitement of his second patrol into Zululand had died down the Prince began to feel bored and restless for more action. With time to spare, he reverted to drawing caricatures of the people around him including Colonel Reilly, the staff colonel responsible for the Royal Artillery, and Paul Deléage. To absorb some of his energies he was tasked by Lord Chelmsford personally, in the presence of Brigadier-General Wood, to draw up plans for the construction of additional fortifications for the encampment on Conference Hill which Chelmsford intended to become the principal advance supply depot for both columns. "The fort," explained Lord Chelmsford to the Prince, "must be capable of being defended by a very small number of men, and containing a great quantity of provisions and munitions of war, with the necessary transport wagons."[19] The Prince immediately started work, setting out the more detailed requirements at the head of his written report: 'to construct a redoubt for 100 metres affording protection to storehouses capable of holding one month's provisions for 5,000 men and 1,000 horses.'[20] He took all the appropriate measurements, making copious notes, illuminated by a variety of pencilled sketches. He worked on this project enthusiastically, making full use of his Woolwich training, whilst at that same time producing a plan which showed by its original innovations that he had firmly grasped the differences between the European and African environments. His proposals and drawings caused so much favourable comment that he actually toyed with the idea of completing a wider analysis, under the title: *South African compared to European Warfare.* He even drafted the first five pages of such a study, dividing it into an appreciation of the South African terrain and climate, followed by a review of the organisation of the Zulu Army, demonstrating why its particular culture, training and equipment made it best suited for purely offensive operations.[21] But the study remained unfinished. And in the event his plan for Conference Hill was never really implemented, for Lord Chelmsford suddenly decided to switch priorities. On 24th May he ordered the advance supply depot to be transferred from Conference Hill, further south west to Koppie Allein.

Two days later the Prince wrote at length to his mother:

> Since my last letter, my life has been most sedentary, especially in relation to the nomad habits one gets into out here. A week spent in my tent affects me like a week spent in a feather bed, for the canvas ceiling has its charms in comparison with the vault of the sky. But, as I have already many times written to you, the life I am leading here pleases me and does me good. Never have I felt so strong and energetic.
>
> Lord Chelmsford, acceding to my desire to be employed on something, has attached me to the Quartermaster-General, Colonel Harrison of the

---

19   FILON, p. 204.
20   RA. 5/13. The original is held in the archives of the National Army Museum.
21   RA. R7/60 — a copy of the original.

Royal Engineers, and I compose his whole staff, which is and will remain a
very slender one, though I am growing fat.

General Simmons will tell you better than I could explain to you the
nature of my duties, which are those of Deputy Assistant Quartermaster-
General.

Tomorrow, the Second Division and the general staff leave Landman's
Drift to make for Koppie Allein. That is our first step towards oNdini, and
if the proverb 'only the first step costs' were always true, we should have a
cheap victory, for our first march will cost us nothing.[22]

It was, of course, disingenuous of the Prince to imply that he was the sole
officer on Colonel Harrison's staff, but clearly he wanted to impress upon her the
importance of his new position, so far removed from that of passive 'spectator'.
He was also mindful of the fact that Rouher and other party officials were almost
entirely relying on his regular letters to the Empress for up-to-date news of his
various activities, which, in turn, would be relayed to all the Bonapartist newspapers
and journals in France. Recently Deléage had shown him newspaper reports of a
number of speeches which his supporters in France had made on the occasion of
his twenty-third birthday earlier that March. The Prince asked the journalist as to
whether he considered the contents of these speeches to be exaggerated. "Well, they
might have had that effect on people who don't know your Highness. I read them
with great pleasure, and I liked particularly the brilliant paradoxes of M. Mitchell."
When asked what those were, Deléage replied, "that on the most democratic and
republican grounds, your return was both necessary and imminent." "Indeed!" was
the Prince's only comment, as he turned his horse and galloped off to join the
others.[23]

On 27th May both Lord Chelmsford's Headquarters and the Second Division
began their move to Koppie Allein, prior to crossing the Blood River for the
second invasion. During the short journey the Prince rode for a time alongside the
Commanding General, but later on peeled away to join Paul Deléage towards the
back of the column. As they trotted along the stony trackway the Prince raised an
issue which, for the first time, revealed his awareness of the xenophobic attitudes
of many of the officers with whom he shared a mess tent. He startled Deléage
by asking him point-blank: "Do you know that 'saying', that an Englishman is
worth five Frenchmen?" In response Deléage tried to shrug it off as a just another
peculiarly English joke but the Prince persisted; "But *do* you know it? The other day
I was in my tent, and heard it just outside. I was very angry — and I've been anxious
to speak to you about it."[24] So the young journalist opined that English courage was
made up of *sang-froid* and sheer obstinacy — whereas Frenchmen were fiery and
impetuous. Deléage elaborated; "The Englishman, with his *caractère pratique*, dies by
order or by necessity; he dies, in short, when there's nothing else he can do. As for
us — we know how to die without a formal command; we find in our temperament

22   FILON, p. 205.
23   DELEAGE, p. 36.
24   JOHN, p. 464.

the irresistible force that hurls us on danger."[25] The Prince liked that explanation — it raised his spirits. He now abruptly changed the subject altogether. Whilst comparing this English war against the Zulus with the civil war then being waged in Spain between the Carlists and the government of King Alphonso the Twelfth (who had formerly studied at the Royal Military College at Sandhurst and whom the Prince knew well) he let slip a remark which the journalist later recalled as being so typical: "I cannot understand anyone seeking to gain a throne by means of civil war."[26] That evening, at Koppie Allein, Deléage passed on some information he had just obtained from Paris — that M.Godelle had won the seat for the Bonapartists. The Prince was delighted at the news; he teased the journalist with the quip that the party, at long last, was beginning to re-conquer Paris!

During the morning of 31st May Louis was sitting in his tent studying the map and sketches, checking the route along which the division would be traversing to reach the camp site already selected for 1st June, just north of the Itelezi Hill. He felt both excited and frustrated — excited at the prospect of a major show-down with the Zulus, but frustrated by the realisation that confined to the camp he would probably not be allowed to witness it. Already orders had been issued to General Newdigate's column, detailing the order of march for the main body of infantry and cavalry on Sunday, 1st June, to a camping ground on Itelezei Hill, some six miles forward. During the advance cavalry patrols would be scouting some miles ahead and then fall back on the new camp. Even now wagons were being loaded, with some tents being struck in anticipation. Indeed, the whole camp was teeming with activity as Colonel Glyn's 1st Brigade prepared to lead the Second Division's invasion of Zululand. They would be spending the rest of the day getting across the Blood River to a new staging camp on the far bank from where, on 1st June, they would begin their march towards Itelezi.

And as the Prince studied the details of the division's proposed route he recalled crossing over this same ground with Colonel Buller on 15th May, and the memory of it simply strengthened his resolve. As far as he knew a reconnaissance was still required of the route to be taken from the Itelezei overnight camp to the camp area for the subsequent night of 2nd June. But he had to wait until Colonel Harrison returned that evening before asking permission to go out with a proper escort the following morning — 1st June — to explore beyond the first night's site along the selected route to the second. Like most of the staff Colonel Harrison was tired, feeling the strain of inadequate sleep and many tense hours spent in the saddle. Up until now there had been no opportunity to closely survey the area chosen for the second night's camp — although it had been provisionally earmarked to be on the Ityotyozi River. Now that the invasion was underway, with columns having already left their supply bases to cross the Blood River, Lord Chelmsford's earlier instructions about confining the Prince to the immediate area of static camps could no longer be realistically applied.

As he glanced at the map Colonel Harrison recalled that the area under review was the same previously reconnoitred two days earlier, on 29th May, by Lieutenant

25   Ibid.
26   FILON, p. 205.

Carey, escorted by yet another large force of dragoons (about which he had once again been ridiculed) and that no Zulus had been reported then, nor since. Indeed in a subsequent letter to his wife, Carey had described how: 'The whole of Zululand that I have traversed is quite deserted now, there being but a few old women left in the kraals...We expect to be attacked in 3 or 4 days as we get on.'[27] On that same day, 29th May, Lord Chelmsford himself, together some of his staff, had patrolled almost 22 miles deep into Zululand across much the same ground. And only the day before a group of four officers, led by Major Herbert Stewart, had made a reconnaissance through that same section of country, finding all the kraals deserted.

In fact there had been no significant skirmishes with the enemy for quite some time; the Zulus appeared to be offering no resistance whatsoever to probing reconnaissance patrols; indeed, a feeling was growing that most of them had probably withdrawn by now from innumerable kraals dotted over the countryside, having been summoned to the Royal kraal oNdini to concentrate for the final battle. And now that both invasion columns would be starting their advance fairly close together, one coming down from the north, the other from the north west, they would each be regularly sending out cavalry flank patrols to keep in contact, and these would be criss-crossing at frequent intervals over that same area. It would appear therefore that there could be little danger and so the Colonel gave the Prince permission, provided he was accompanied by the usual escort. It is probable that Harrison envisaged this being commanded, as before, by Captain Bettington. Inexplicably, he did not clear this decision personally with Lord Chelmsford, as stipulated in earlier instructions. At the subsequent court-martial Harrison disclosed that the Prince had, in fact, been given orders to survey a camp site by the Ityotyozi River. With hindsight it may seem surprising that a young man, with only the training of Woolwich behind him, should have been entrusted with the onerous responsibility of surveying an overnight bivouac for a whole division, with its attendant requirements for defensive security, fuel and water. It can only be assumed that Colonel Harrison, knowing of Lord Chelmsford's high regard for Louis's skills, genuinely considered that it was within his capabilities and thus acceptable. But it is far from clear that this particular task had actually been delegated to the Prince. Despite that unambiguous statement at Carey's court-martial in 1879, in his 1908 memoirs, Harrison recalled only that he had agreed to the Prince's request to extend his sketch beyond the first night's camp and make a reconnaissance of the road to the next camp site. He made no mention of instructing the Prince to undertake any additional task.

It is conceiveable that, during their private discussion, Harrison also agreed that Louis should also check the pre-selected site and, in the event of unforeseen impediments to its use, examine possible alternatives. Whatever the confusion over his precise instructions — it is clear beyond doubt that it was Louis himself took the initiative in wanting to go out on a reconnaissance for which he officially obtained Colonel Harrison's sanction. It is therefore not surprising if, from that moment on, the Prince himself was to assume supreme responsibility for carrying out whatever tasks had been agreed between them.

---

27   RA. R5/15

Shortly after Louis departed Carey came into the tent to discuss a number of problems. He asked if he might be permitted to join the patrol in order to complete some of his earlier field sketches of the route towards the Ityotyozi Valley and take more compass bearings. Colonel Harrison agreed. In his memoirs he recalled: 'I said "Yes", and added that he could look after the Prince, and see that he did not get into any trouble.'[28] Clearly he did not expressly nominate appoint Lieutenant Carey to command the escort, nor did he subsequently inform the Prince that Carey would be in overall charge. He presumed that Carey, being the senior combatant and the only commissioned officer in the party, would automatically assume command and that the Prince would recognise that circumstance. But he overlooked the fact, or does not appear to have been aware, that most people, including Carey himself, thought the Prince enjoyed the status of an officer.

This misconception was almost inevitable. Indeed, from the moment Louis had been placed with Colonel Harrison's staff, Lord Chelmsford had given instructions that he should be treated — not as a royal personage — but in the same way as any other officer. This was no more than the Prince himself had requested at their first meeting. But the idea of Louis being a mere 'spectator' had long since been buried under the weight of recent events. And the confusion as to his status and rank was aggravated by the fact that throughout the war Royal Artillery officers, in the blue patrol dress they habitually wore, did not announce their particular rank by means of collar badges. This practice however was to be changed only a year later, in 1880, when all badges of rank were returned to shoulder lapels and thus permanently displayed. Even Captain Molyneux, one of Lord Chelmsford's three official aides-de-camp, later testified on oath at Carey's court martial that whilst the Prince was not an *official* aide-de-camp he was always genuinely puzzled as to his exact status. And Lieutenant Carey consistently maintained that he considered himself to be inferior to the Prince in military rank, even though he, Carey, almost nine years older, had already served for fourteen years as an officer. Inexplicably, he himself was never called upon to explain why he had come to that conclusion, even though the Prince's status formed a critical part of his subsequent defence. Perhaps he considered that, because Louis was a foreign Prince he may have, like others of foreign blood, been accorded some honorary rank in the British Army which was senior to his own. But, as if to confirm the reality of the rank situation, on 6th June (only five days after the Prince's death) Carey was promoted to Captain in the London Gazette — an automatic promotion based solely on satisfactory years of service.

After arranging to join the patrol, Carey returned to find the Prince trying to sort out some field sketches which had been put together rather hastily. Carey immediately offered to correct them for him — and he was now to sit up late into the night, re-drafting the whole document by the light of a lantern. Thus for much of the last evening of his life, instead of working on the sketches, Louis was able to chat with a number of colleagues. No doubt he would briefed many of them about his new responsibilities for checking that camp site, for he was always anxious to demonstrate his usefulness and acceptance as a member of the staff. He had a

---

28 KNIGHT, p. 226.

long discussion in the open air with his former detractor, Archibald Forbes of the
Daily News. The seasoned war reporter confessed that he had learnt his trade, on the
side of Prussia, during the Franco-Prussian war of 1870 and that he had actually
witnessed the Emperor and the fourteen year old Prince riding hurriedly away from
Longueville the morning the artillery shells had landed in the garden. He also told
Louis all about his experiences in the later Russo-Turkish conflict. Afterwards the
Prince went over to one of the other tents to pay a call on Lieutenant Horace Smith-
Dorrien, with whom he had also become particularly friendly. Smith-Dorrien (one
of the few officers to survive Isandlwana and who was to rise to general rank in the
First World War) wrote later of their encounter that night: 'The Prince Imperial,
wearing the undress uniform of the Royal Artillery...endeared himself to all...he was
especially friendly to myself. He took a deep interest in the organisation of every
branch of our force...he was in my tent until 11 p.m. on the night before going out
on his last patrol...extracting from me a promise to write him a treatise on bullock
transport.'[29]

Shortly after dawn on the morning of 1ˢᵗ June it became apparent to both the
Prince and Carey that no escort had actually been detailed for that morning. Louis
went to raise the matter personally with Colonel Harrison in view of the written
instruction he had been given earlier about not leaving camps without an escort.
There had been some rain in the last few days and even now there was still a slight but
persistent drizzle. Consequently the Prince was wearing a light waterproof over his
patrol jacket. Colonel Harrison left his tent to find Major-General Marshall in order
to inquire about the provision of a cavalry escort. It is not clear whether the cavalry
general was made aware that the escort was intended for the Prince; he certainly
made no mention of any such awareness in the private report he subsequently
submitted direct to Queen Victoria. There is the view that he had already instructed
his brigade-major, Herbert Stewart, not to permit another sizeable regular cavalry
patrol to accompany Carey again. Clearly the General must have told Colonel
Harrison that all his own squadrons were fully committed that morning; for shortly
afterwards Colonel Harrison completed the necessary requisition warrant for an
escort of six irregular European troopers and six BaSothos, handing it over to Carey
to process with Major Stewart, the cavalry staff officer responsible for allocating
mounted escorts. The Colonel had deliberately included BaSothos because they had
proved invaluable for scouting — they would invariably detect any Zulu activity
long before any European. At the same time he also arranged for the Intelligence
Department to provide a friendly native guide to help with the identification of
geographical features and the names of the Zulu kraals.

Archibald Forbes also happened to be present with Major Stewart when Carey
came into his tent at about half past seven that morning to deliver the warrant.
Forbes subsequently recalled that no mention was made, at that time, that the escort
was intended for the Prince Imperial. Nor was that task spelt out in the warrant
itself. Major Stewart accepted the order for the six troopers of Bettington's Horse,
but handed Carey a separate requisition form for the BaSotho scouts, suggesting

---

29   SMITH-DORRIEN, p. 32.

that time could be saved if Carey himself were to take it over to the native lines. Carey agreed, saluted and left. Outside he unexpectedly met Deléage and invited him to come along with the patrol. The journalist was tempted. But it was the Prince who finally talked him out of it, explaining, "I'm afraid it won't be much fun. We're not going further than the next camping-ground."[30]

---

30   JOHN, p. 469.

The Empress Eugénie and the Prince Imperial, Franz Winterhalter, 1857

Napoleon III, by Franz Winterhalter

The Empress Eugénie and the Prince Imperial, 1860

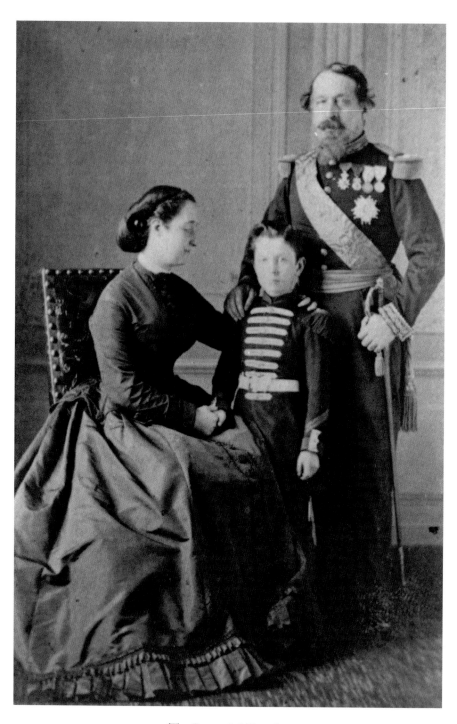

The Imperial Family

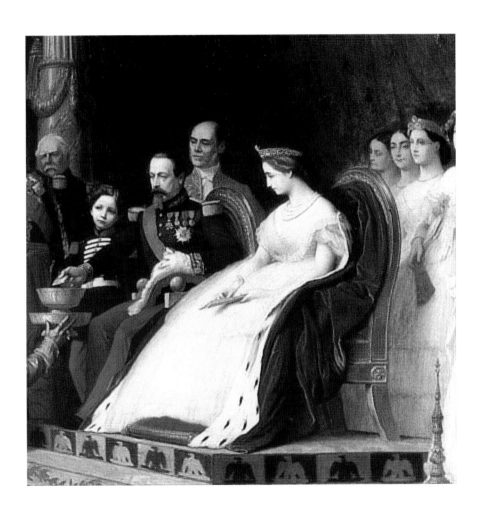

The Prince Imperial with his parents, Jean-Léon Gérôme, 1871

The Prince Imperial at the age of 14, 1870

The Prince Imperial, by Charles Porion

The Prince Imperial during the Zulu War, 1879

Death of the Prince Imperial, by Paul Jamin

Transfer of the bodies of Napoleon III and the Prince Imperial
to Farnborough Abbey, by Robert Taylor Pritchett

The funeral procession of the Prince Imperial on the road to St Mary's Church, Chislehurst

St Michael's Abbey Church, Farnborough

Tomb of the Prince Imperial in the crypt of St Michael's Abbey

Chapter x

His Face to the Foe

O N THE WHOLE the terrible events of Sunday, 1st June 1879 are all well documented. Apart from the formal transcripts of the official inquiry, and the subsequent court martial, there are innumerable unofficial recollections by many others, who although not eye-witnesses to all that occurred nonetheless subsequently expressed their opinions in private letters and other accounts. The circumstances of the sudden death of the Prince had a traumatic effect on many people, giving rise to strong feelings of disquiet, even disgust, which inevitably coloured their first opinions. And about a year later, a few months after the end of the war, the Zulus most directly involved were traced and eventually persuaded to provide their own testimonies. Whilst the main events of the tragedy are beyond dispute, there are nonetheless many discrepancies and even contradictions in the details. The Zulu account is particularly confusing. And all the English and French versions of the tragedy continue — even to this day — to be at variance. Unfortunately, modern biographers and commentators have an unusually large menu of distortions, inconsistencies and even inaccuracies from which to construct a viable version to support their own particular theories and prejudices. But even allowing for imperfect memories and fleeting impressions — and the inevitable stress under which everyone was working at the time — it is difficult to escape the conclusion that many of these differences stem from the anxieties of some people, either to shield themselves from blame or deflect the responsibility on to others — for, as with so many major human tragedies, there was no one single cause but rather the cumulation of a number of errors and misunderstandings which set in train the tragic events of that day.

It was approaching nine o'clock when Lieutenant Carey rode over to the cavalry lines to collect the six troopers of Bettington's Natal Horse. These had been personally selected by Captain Bettington. It must be the greatest misfortune that, owing to other duties that day, he himself was unable to command the escort — for had he done so the tragedy would most probably have been averted. Nonetheless, he did not nominate another officer to replace him, but selected instead two NCOs (Non-commissioned officers) — Sergeant Robert Willis and Corporal Grubb — to supervise the men. Grubb spoke fluent Zulu and had previously served sixteen years with the Royal Artillery before becoming a farmer in Natal. The four troopers were Le Tocq, Abel, Cochrane and Rogers. Le Tocq happened to be a French-speaking Channel Islander, an old sailor from Guernsey.

The BaSotho scouts had been instructed separately to report to the Quartermaster-General's tent at nine. The Prince now came up alone leading his two horses having decided, on this occasion, not to take his orderly Lomas with him — earlier, he had told him not to bother, explaining the trip was only going to be a short one. As they waited for Carey and the others the Prince offered his second horse to the native guide to enable him to keep up with the party without having to run the whole way alongside. Louis also took the opportunity to scribble some last lines to his mother, using a page torn from his personal note-book:

> Koppie Allein
> June 1st 1879
>
> My dear Mother,
>   I am writing hurriedly on a leaf of my note-book; in a few minutes I am off to select a camping-ground for the Second Division on the left bank of the Blood River. The enemy is concentrating in force, and an engagement is expected in a week's time. I do not know when I shall be able to send you any news, for the postal facilities leave much to be desired. I did not want to let slip this opportunity for embracing you with all my heart.
>   Your devoted and dutiful son,
>   Napoleon
>   P.S. I hear of M.Godelle's splendid election. Pray tell him from me how delighted I was at this good news.[1]

And the Prince handed this final letter to Archibald Forbes, requesting him to ensure its onward dispatch to England. It was now to be carried in one of the postal sacks by Kaffir runners, travelling in relays from camp to camp, day and night, down to the coast.

The letter also confirms just how, in the space of a few weeks, the Prince had moved from the role of 'spectator', with no definable status, to the position of a junior staff officer who, relying on his own words, had now been entrusted with the heavy responsibility of locating a secure overnight site for the whole of the Second Division — a force which totalled more than 5,000 men and 600 wagons, plus oxen teams. No doubt this news would make a significant impact on his mother, his friends and political supporters. But in his telegraphed report to London describing the death of the Prince, Lord Chelmsford concluded by lamenting the fact that he himself had no prior knowledge that Louis had been given this particular task. Yet at no time during the later correspondence and press briefings, does Lord Chelmsford seem to have questioned the suitability of the young inexperienced Prince to undertake such a demanding operational responsibility; he concentrated instead on the fact that the BaSotho scouts had not been present on that day and that the escort, as a consequence, was inadequate.

For they still had not appeared. As so often during this war there had been yet another misunderstanding. Far from reporting to the Quartermaster-General's tent,

---

1   FILON, p. 209.

they had collected instead by the cavalry lines, where Major Stewart, amidst all the confusion of striking camp and moving out, assumed the patrol had already left. He therefore instructed them to ride off at once to catch the others up on their way to the Ityotyosi Valley. They subsequently took no further part in the day's events.

It was now half past nine. Impatient at the continuing delay the Prince took charge, insisting that they should make a start, leaving instructions for the BaSothos to follow on. Carey raised no objections and the patrol mounted to move out of Koppie Allein. Despite the drizzle of the early hours, the sun was now shining brightly and another warm day was in prospect. Before reaching the Blood River, Carey sent a messenger to Captain Shepstone, the officer in charge of the BaSotho scouts, querying their whereabouts and the trooper returned with the information that they now planned to meet up with the patrol on the ridge between the Icenzi and Itelezei hills.

As they crossed the Blood River and closed up to Itelezi about seven miles away, they came across Colonel Harrison and Major Grenfell reviewing the site for the first night's halt, an area just to the north of the Itelezi Hill. In his recollections, Colonel Harrison stated that he noted that only the European troopers were with the patrol, and inquiring about the BaSothos, added: 'I enjoined them not go forward without them'.[2] In his own memoirs Major Grenfell noted that it was the Prince who had refused to wait for the BaSothos. No doubt influenced by his earlier criticism about the reliability of these native troops Louis had simply responded by arguing, "Oh — no, we're quite strong enough."[3] Indeed, in his impatience, Louis now started to move off but even as Carey made a motion to call him back, Colonel Harrison indicated he should now follow, adding, "Don't interfere with the Prince."[4]

Such remarks merely added to the confusion as to who exactly was in command. On this occasion the Prince appears to have behaved as if this was just another Arenenberg expedition in which he was naturally the leader; after all, as he had explained that morning in the note to his mother, had he not been specifically tasked to choose that overnight camp location? Consequently this was not just another patrol in which he was coming along for the ride, to gain experience, learning from others. Nor were experienced officers such as Colonel Buller and Captain Bettington going to be present to make the decisions and issue the orders. The task of route reconnaissance and site surveys were demanding responsibilities over which he expected to exercise full control. And Carey seems to have been quite content to accept the Prince's authority — after all, he had his own sketches to complete, a technical task which was incompatible with full time command of an escort. This was precisely the reason which had prompted his own request to join the patrol in the first place. But whatever thoughts were crossing Carey's mind at this time, the fact remained that the Prince, throughout the whole period of his service with the British Army, had always loyally followed the instructions of his superiors; on no single occasion had he ever deliberately disobeyed military orders. Nonetheless, he probably viewed Carey rather differently — not as his military superior (which

2   KNIGHT, p. 227.
3   RA. R5/18
4   FEATHERSTONE, p. 78.

he technically was) but rather as a congenial mess companion, conversant with his country and language, with whom he had a relaxed relationship. In any case Carey was always to be somewhat deferential in his various dealings with the Prince who, with his Gallic charm and commanding ways, was almost everything that Carey was not.

At the court of inquiry, Carey insisted that Colonel Harrison had told him at the start not to interfere in any way with the Prince, for the Colonel wished him to have the entire credit for the patrol. Carey constantly re-emphasised this point — during interviews with the press, in his written reports to Colonel Harrison, during his evidence at the inquiry — and it was never refuted. On this basis therefore Carey assumed the Prince was in overall command. Yet this particular matter was not discussed in the proceedings of the subsequent court martial — even though the question of command was to be the mainstay of Carey's defence. On the other hand, during the court martial, the survivors did state that, in their opinion, the Prince had conducted himself like a commander, issuing out all the orders. When specifically pressed by Carey to state who they thought was actually in command, Trooper Le Tocq answered emphatically, "The Prince." Corporal Grubb and Trooper Cochrane replied that they did not know, but they thought that only the Prince had given out any commands. Sergeant Willis said, "I do not know who was in command, but I think it was the Prince." But he did point out, however, to the Court that they had all been instructed to report in the first place to Lieutenant Carey, and not the Prince, before starting out that morning.[5] It is also worth noting that in all the French accounts of the tragedy, including the most recent, Carey is always described as being in sole command of the escort, himself issuing the orders to mount when the Zulus attacked. In fact, the recorded evidence shows that all the formal words of command on that day were given out by the Prince.

But this confusion over command was further aggravated by the unexpected decision of Major Grenfell to now accompany the patrol for the first section of their journey. It is not clear why he took this step other than that he simply had a couple of hours to spare. With no BaSotho scouts immediately in sight, Grenfell assumed that they were already operating well ahead and thus carrying out their scouting duties. And in Carey's mind both Colonel Harrison and now Major Grenfell had, by their lack of insistence, appeared to condone the Prince's declared wish to set off without ensuring the presence of the native troopers. For Carey, in particular, the size of the patrol would inevitably be a sensitive subject. He had already experienced many wounding comments about the comparatively large escorts which had accompanied his previous patrols; thus he now felt thoroughly inhibited from making a fuss over the size of this one.

The Prince, accompanied by Major Grenfell, was riding out in front. Familiar with the area Louis confidently pointed out to Grenfell the most obvious landmarks on either side of the ridge along which they were now moving. And when they

---

5   *Proceedings of a general court martial of Lieutenant J.B. Carey, 98th Regiment.* Tried at Camp Upoko River, Zululand, 12 June 1879. War Office Papers 91/48 held at the Public Record Office (PRO), Kew. These proceedings are also to be found in NORRIS-NEWMAN — *In Zululand With The British*, Appendix H, p. 301-312 and in FEATHERSTONE — *Captain Carey's Blunder*, p. 129-142.

finally reached the end, where it finally sloped down to a valley, Grenfell noted that: 'the landscape was bare of trees or cover and therefore, as the Zulus had no horses, with even the smallest escort perfectly safe.'[6] They had now descended towards the axis of the planned route for the division and were heading towards to a suitable spot for the second night's camp which, in theory, ought to be about ten miles further on — the average distance which could be covered daily by the heavy ox-drawn wagons. Here was the confluence of the Ityotyosi and Tombokala Rivers, an area which, on the map, had already been earmarked as a suitable locality.

Lord Chelmsford and his staff meanwhile were preparing to leave Koppie Allein, the forward supply base, for Itelezei. Mounting his horse, he looked round and asked, "Where is the Prince?" One of the staff replied, "Sir, he's with Colonel Harrison." Acknowledging the reassurance with a nod of the head, Lord Chelmsford now turned his mind to many other pressing concerns.[7] In fact, Colonel Harrison, at that time, was checking the water supply for the first night's halt and making arrangements for the arriving units to be guided to their allocated areas north of Itelezi Hill. When Lord Chelmsford himself arrived with his staff, Colonel Harrison briefed him on the layout of the proposed laager without making any reference to the task he had earlier entrusted to the Prince. Everyone assumed therefore that Louis must be occupied elsewhere in the camp area. Afterwards Colonel Harrison withdrew altogether to his tent in order to draft the orders for the subsequent advance on 2nd June.

The patrol crossed open grass country for several miles. The Prince and Major Grenfell continued in the lead, with Carey and the troopers all behind. In appearance there could not have been a greater contrast. The three officers were themselves dressed quite differently — the Prince in his customary dark-blue patrol dress, Major Grenfell of 60th Rifles in dark 'rifle-green', and Carey of 98th Regiment in the usual bright scarlet infantry frock — uniforms now well soiled by the dirt and dust of campaigning but nonetheless distinctive enough. They all wore the dulled white foreign service helmets, with black polished boots and spurs, gleaming swords and scabbards, pistol holsters on shoulder straps. The Prince was riding his BaSotho pony 'Percy' whilst the native guide was mounted on 'Fate'. The only other grey in the patrol was ridden by Trooper Rogers. The troopers looked like the irregulars they were, heavily bearded, dressed in an assortment of dark, scruffy jackets, with bandoliers and carbines slung over the shoulder, all wearing slouch hats with red puggarees, some even sucking on clay pipes.

As they reached the crest of a small hill overlooking the Ityotyosi Valley, Major Grenfell turned back so as to attend to the bivouac problems at Itelezei. As he rode away, he inclined his head towards the Prince and called back: "Take care of yourself...and don't get shot!" The Prince pointed at Carey: "Oh no! He'll take very good care that nothing happens to me!"[8]

---

6   GRENFELL, p. 37.
7   FILON, p. 209.
8   FEATHERSTONE, p. 80.

About seven miles south east from Itelezei the patrol reached the end of the ridge. Here, at half past twelve, on the Prince's orders, they halted astride a flat-topped hill above the river.

Had Captain Bettington been in command of the escort this halt would surely have never been sanctioned, for now the whole party was needlessly exposed to view from miles around. From the hill, looking behind them, the camp site at Itelezei was now totally out of sight and as they scanned the ground all round with their telescopes, the bare almost treeless landscape appeared to be quite empty but, of course, they could not peer into the many gullies criss-crossing the whole area. But there was no sign of any Zulus nor were they expecting to see any. Whilst they rested, the Prince looked at his watch and then made this last entry in his pocket notebook — '1.20. Extremity of ridge between the Tombokole & Ityotyozi...Good camping ground on slope south of donga.'[9] and underneath the entry he sketched a view of the country, including the distant hills. It is not clear which particular donga Louis was referring to, but wherever that camping-ground was, the patrol did not subsequently survey the area properly in the detail that an overnight laager would require. Instead, the Prince pointed out to Carey the location of *Napoleon Koppie* to the south west beyond the Ityotyozi River. And below them, barely a mile away, they could just pick out a small kraal which their native guide named as Etuki. It seemed to be nestled in a sea of tall yellow Kaffir-corn, with a small stream close by. Carey now busied himself completing the map route for the Second Division's line of march. When they had been on the top of this flat-topped hill for about thirty minutes Carey suggested off-saddling, but even as the troopers turned to their straps, the Prince intervened and told them instead to merely loosen the girths, saying to Carey, "It's hardly worthwhile to off-saddle for a quarter of an hour...we'll go down to the huts by the river, where the men can get wood and water, and cook something."[10]

Carey gently demurred at this proposal. He felt it best to remain where they were — on a secure hill with good all round observation. But the Prince simply shrugged off his concerns and effectively overruled him by now calling upon the troopers to re-tighten their girths and re-mount. He then led them down from the hill into a valley, with the large Ityotyosi River curving away on the southern side. Unbeknown to them, even as they descended from the hill, they had now come under observation.

They finally reached the kraal at about forty minutes past two o'clock. It was quite small, consisting of six huts surrounding a large circular stone cattle-pen. Kaffir-corn and tambookie grass, about six foot high, surrounded the east, west and south sides of the huts, and thus provided perfect cover for a concealed approach.. The only exposed area was to the north. Here the ground was comparatively open for about two hundred yards, before gently descending into a dry donga which gradually deepened to about six to eight feet. During the rainy season this would feed a torrent of water into the Ityotyosi River.

---

9   RA. R7/16
10 FEATHERSTONE, p. 80.

On that peaceful, warm Sunday afternoon, this whole kraal area, with its concealed approaches from three sides, was an extremely exposed place in which to halt for any length of time. Captain Bettington, had he been present, would have never permitted such a halt and Carey should have determined likewise. He was fully aware of their vulnerability, but continued to allow himself to be overruled by the Prince. There can be little doubt that he too had been lulled into a false sense of security. After all he had been twice previously in this particular area without seeing any Zulus; and during his most recent trip, had ascertained from a solitary native woman in a nearby kraal that all the menfolk in the area had left to join the King's forces gathering at oNdini. As for the Prince, he had sufficient basic military knowledge, as well as recent experience of patrolling with such experienced Zulu fighters as Colonel Buller and Captain Bettington, to have noted the common sense security precautions which they took at all times, regardless of the threat and regardless of the size of the escort, to protect the soldiers for whom they were responsible. Had he therefore learnt nothing? Or was it his lifelong romanticised view of war — allied to all the excitement of leading a patrol of his own — were these the factors now clouding his own military judgement? For, in essence, they were about to repeat the same mistakes which, although on a totally different scale, had already occurred at Isandlwana — where, because of similar illusory sense of security, no proper defensive arrangements likewise had been made. And whilst Carey may have been somewhat mesmerised by the Prince's presence, this would not have applied to the hard-bitten irregulars, who would have had little idea as to who he really was and probably cared even less. But they were not like regular soldiers — unquestioningly obedient. They were not even subject to the same rigid disciplinary code. Yet, like soldiers the world over, their prime concern was with survival. It is therefore all the more baffling that none of them, not even the two NCOs, saw fit to make any comment to either officer about their continuing exposure. Perhaps they reckoned that their stay in the kraal would be brief; perhaps they, too, had been lulled into a false sense of security by the apparent absence of Zulus in this particular area. And since the last major battle had been almost two months ago — on 2nd April at Gingindlovu down by the coast — there had been a discernible lowering of alertness amongst many of the veterans and seasoned volunteers, in contrast to the new arrivals. May they have felt inhibited by the fact that, on this occasion, they were not being commanded by one of their own officers? And yet they themselves had noted that all the huts had been occupied recently; indeed, at the entrance to one of them was a pile of freshly-chewed sugar cane. Trooper Cochrane had even drawn the attention of Sergeant Willis and Corporal Grubb to the three mangy native dogs still sniffing around. It therefore must have been quite evident to any alert observer that the kraal had only recently been vacated, either by the normal inhabitants or by temporary residents, and that the continuing presence of the dogs, in particular, was a sure indication that Zulus could not be far away.

Despite their obvious vulnerability the Prince now gave out instructions for the horses to be unsaddled. When in enemy country commonsense required that only a half of the patrol's horses should be off-saddled at any one time. They were then allowed to wander off individually into the grass to graze at will. No-one was tasked to supervise them. The native guide was sent down to the river to obtain water with which to make coffee. The two NCOs looked towards the Prince and Lieutenant Carey. Louis, being tired, had now settled down with his back against the stone cattle enclosure wall. And after looking around the kraal for a while Carey then came back and joined him. The irregulars must have continued to wonder why no sentries had been posted and why no precautionary orders had been given to load carbines? Had one of their own officers been present on the patrol they might have complained loudly about their exposure, but in the end, they simply shrugged their shoulders and went on sipping coffee, puffing from time to time on their clay pipes.

Yet it was a well-understood operational rule that the horses on patrol in daylight must always be kept saddled, and that the bridles of only one third to a half, at most, might be removed at any one time to allow feeding and watering, and then only under constant supervision. And everyone knew that, during any halt, regardless of length, sentries must always be posted. Why? Because it was a well-evidenced fact that the Zulus were able to run very long distances at high speed and then, appearing seemingly from out of nowhere, finally stalk their prey, making the best use of all the available cover. These were some of elementary rules for local protection, spelt out clearly in operational manuals and learnt by bitter experience in the early months of the war, which were to be totally disregarded that afternoon. The only possible explanation for this lamentable lack of prudence must be the lax feeling, which seems to have infected all of them, that they were not actually in enemy-held territory at all, but in country which everyone considered to be clear and thus safe.

The reality was to be somewhat different. From the moment the second invasion had got under way, many of the advancing troops were to be subjected to sporadic skirmishing — for the Zulus continued to harass patrols and the leading elements with sniping and sudden ambushes, all the way to oNdini.

That afternoon at the kraal Louis and Carey amended their maps and completed their sketches. There appears to have been no discussion about that camping ground referred to earlier in the Prince's notes. Indeed, with time apparently on their hands, the two of them had started an animated conversation, in voluble French, about Napoleon Bonaparte's campaign in Italy during 1796! Although the native guide tried to intervene in order to draw their attention to a pile of warm ashes which he just had detected at the front of one of the huts, their discussion continued unabated. It was as though everyone was participating, without a care in the world, in some pleasant day's picnic during a routine summer military exercise.

Meanwhile a scouting party of about thirty five to forty Zulus, warriors from the iNgobamaksi, uMbonambi and uNokhenke regiments (*amabutho*), led by a chief called Sabhuza, were moving closer to the kraal, under the cover of another deep donga which led to the edge of the river. Before long they were to divide into two groups.

It had just gone half past three. Looking at his watch, Carey politely suggested to the Prince that they should perhaps now collect up the loose horses, re-saddle and prepare to move on. It would soon be getting dark, and they had many miles of return journey to make. But the Prince, enjoying their pleasant rest, saw no reason to hurry and said they should wait another ten minutes. But even as he was speaking, the native guide came up from behind the huts, calmly pointing out that he had just seen a solitary Zulu moving over a nearby rise close to the river. As Carey could not understand what the man was saying he called for Corporal Grubb to give them a translation. As he did so, the Prince got to his feet, giving out the order, which Carey then repeated, for everyone to collect up their horses. As many of these, without proper supervision, had inevitably wandered off deep into the grass, it took a further ten minutes to get them all together, properly saddled. Even at this point no defensive measures were taken. No orders were given to load carbines before mounting — a common sense routine precaution given their particular situation. As Carey appears to have been the first to saddle his horse — he simply mounted quite independently. Whilst he may have given out few instructions of his own that day he clearly decided not to await for the Prince to issue any formal order for everyone to mount. Trooper Rogers took longer than the others to collect his horse and was now having difficulty in tightening the girth. But he was the only one not ready. The remainder, standing roughly in line at their horses' heads, facing the Prince, heard him call out in a clear voice the customary command: "Prepare to mount!"

Each man gathered in the reins, placed his left foot in the near stirrup and grasped the pommel of the saddle in anticipation of the next command: "Mount!" But that order, if it was ever given, was to be drowned by the sudden spluttering of multiple rifle shots, followed immediately by cries of "*Usuthu!*" and "*Nanga amagwala amangsi*" (Here are the English cowards) as Zulus burst from out of the long grass into the kraal area. About ten or so were armed with rifles, firing wildly. There was utter pandemonium. The shots, all of which were wide of the mark and caused no immediate casualties, inevitably startled the horses, who now began to buck and rear. One after the other, with terrified eyes, nostrils quivering, they turned away from the noise, starting to bolt in the direction of the donga, so that those riders who had not yet fully mounted could only cling on in the hope of regaining the saddle. Trooper Rogers lost complete control of his horse; it now cantered away with stirrups flying, leaving him behind, alone. Somehow managing to load his carbine, he ran towards the shelter of the huts but a warrior soon caught up with him, driving an assegai deep into his back. Despite this blow, Rogers managed to turn round and loose off a round, but it missed the Zulu who then swiftly killed him.

Trooper Le Tocq had mounted but, as his horse shied again, he carelessly dropped his carbine. Immediately slithering off to retrieve it, he managed somehow to get his left foot back into the stirrup. But as he heaved himself upwards, he could only fall on his belly over the saddle, and in this precarious posture was rapidly borne away by his fleeing horse. Corporal Grubb had managed to mount, but was far from secure on the saddle, hanging on desperately as his horse likewise bounded across the donga. The native guide ran into the area of the huts and was never seen alive again. Some of the Zulus kept up a hail of erratic fire at the fleeing horses and one of these wild bullets caught Trooper Abel in the back, just below the bandolier. As it struck, he threw up his arms, and sliding sideways from the saddle quickly crumbled to the ground. It is not known whether the shot itself killed him or the stabs of Zulu *assegais*.

It would seem that only Lieutenant Carey was properly astride his horse at the moment of the Zulu attack. Even now, more and more of them were pouring into the area. There was no time for any concerted action — at this moment of pandemonium, command, discipline, cohesion really counted for nothing. There could be only one response. *Sauve qui peut!* Every man for himself! He reined in his startled horse, swung it round and then set off at full gallop towards the safety of the donga, with the others seemingly pounding hard behind him. As he went in deeper and deeper, he half-turned, shouting for everyone to wheel to the left from out of the donga and rally on the far side.

By now Trooper Le Tocq had managed to swing himself upright in the saddle, and as he galloped past Corporal Grubb, called out: "Stick firm to your horse, boy, and put in the spurs! The Prince is down!"[11] Grubb quickly glanced behind him.

The Prince was indeed in difficulties. Startled by the sudden noise, his horse 'Percy' had shied violently, and then immediately started off in the same direction as the others. It was only Louis's grip on the holster strap which prevented him from falling forwards on to the ground there and then. He desperately tried to curb the mare but she was now moving so fast that he simply could not get his foot into the violently swinging stirrup. On other occasions he would have risked vaulting straight into the saddle, but the horse was now moving too erratically, slipping out of his control. As he sprinted alongside over the next hundred or so yards, he managed to continue holding on to the strap. Suddenly, Trooper Le Tocq, at that time still lying across the saddle and quite unable to assist, galloped past, shouting out, "*Dépêchez-vous de monter sur votre cheval, Monsieur!* (Hurry to get on your horse, sir)."[12] He said later that Louis did not answer. Thus, by a strange irony, the last words the Prince ever heard were those in his own language.

But the situation was still recoverable. After all he had, on many previous occasions, been able to vault directly on to a galloping horse. All that was needed was a firm grip, then with one mighty heave, he could perhaps leap forward on to the saddle, but his grasp on the holster strap was far from firm and he dared not risk trying to change it. But without a firmer grip he knew he could not gain the necessary leverage for that leap. He continued to run at speed alongside the horse, but even as Le Tocq was thundering past and calling out to him, 'Percy' was quickening the pace and Louis felt the terrified horse gradually pulling away from him, putting his tenuous grip on the holster strap under even greater strain. Finally it slipped out of his grasp altogether. As he stumbled forward towards the ground one of the hooves gave his right wrist a very sharp blow. The momentum of his sprint alongside meant that he could not now recover his balance; hitting the ground, he rolled over a couple of times in the dust. And when he was finally able to sit up, out of breath, somewhat dazed, he could see the horse had gone on well beyond recall — now over fifty yards away, 'Percy' was rapidly closing up on the others.

Rising groggily to his feet, he instinctively fumbled for Napoleon's sword. But it was no longer in the scabbard. In fact, the sword had slipped out many yards behind during his efforts to mount. But his right hand was now so painful that he

---

11   PRO, Kew
12   Ibid.

had to use the left to awkwardly draw the revolver from his belt. The other pistol, still in its holster, was strapped to the disappearing horse.

His eyes flickered for a second over the approaching Zulus — there seemed to be about seven of them. They all were bunched close together, and moving towards him somewhat warily. He abruptly turned away and started running once more, avoiding any *assegais* by deliberately weaving to and fro down the slope some two hundred yards deeper into the donga where, by a little mound, he abruptly stopped and turned around to face his foes. By now he must have realised that the situation was hopeless. For whilst running into the donga he would have been able to see all the other horses, with or without riders, galloping away out of sight. There seemed little hope of them now being able to rally in time to gallop back and rescue him. But he would have reasoned that if he simply continued running away, deeper into the donga, one of his pursuers would eventually spear him in the back — and thus he might fall and be seen to have died like a coward — fleeing his foes.

Annoyed by his failure to mount 'Percy', vexed at the unexpected loss of his sword, with the adrenalin strongly pumping all round his body, he probably experienced little fear. As he confronted the huge black warriors now slowly closing in on him, naked except for loin-coverings, their fierce faces sweating with blood lust, their powerful physiques taut and braced for combat, clutching small cowhide shields (*umbumbuluzo*) and *assegais*, there was a weird momentary pause. The Zulus had expected their victim to continue running away. They were thus somewhat taken aback to see him suddenly stop, and then deliberately turn to face them at the mound. Were his last thoughts about France? His dear mother? Or did he try and concentrate his racing hyperactive mind on dying courageously — with honour?

To their further surprise he now started walking slowly towards them. A warrior called Langalabalele drew back his right arm and flung the first *assegai*. The Prince fired wildly at him with his left hand, but missed. He had never before fired a pistol with that hand. The *assegai* thudded into the flesh of his thigh, but the Prince immediately yanked it out, and gripping the handle in his damaged right hand, prepared to use it as a weapon himself. From walking, he now suddenly rushed at the warrior, firing yet again but still the bullet went wide. A further shot likewise went awry. Langalabalele dodged behind another called Xabanga, who quickly brought the Prince's rush to a halt by piercing his chest with one of the two *assegais* he had thrown in his direction.

At this point Louis seems to have stumbled, his foot perhaps caught in a hole. Seizing their opportunity the others began to close in on him. He tried in vain to switch the pistol to his right hand Still he managed to hold them back, fighting desperately with the *assegai*, using his good left arm to ward off a flurry of stabs and thrusts. The Zulu tactic, unless one of these happened to kill an opponent outright, was to simply continue striking, however wildly, until the enemy finally collapsed.

The warriors attacking the Prince were to comment later that he constantly manoeuvred to prevent any of them striking him from behind. More Zulus were now pouring into the donga. As they continued to beat at him with their shields, jabbing with their *assegais*, the Prince, becoming weaker from the mounting loss of blood, gradually sank down into a sitting position, whereupon the Zulus, now towering over him, quickly began to hack him to pieces. A warrior called Klabanatunga, stabbing crudely against his forehead, felt the point of his *assegai* slip deep into the right eye, penetrating the brain. This blow alone would have brought him a swift death. The Prince's bleeding body gradually slumped backwards to lie spread-eagled on the ground.

It had all taken less than a minute.

Thereafter, in accordance with their custom of *hlomula*, whereby other warriors might share in the glory of a courageous death, more Zulus 'washed their spears' with quick jabs into the lifeless body. They then roughly stripped off all his clothes, leaving only the collar of gold medallions around his neck. Again, in keeping with Zulu ritual, warriors now dressed themselves in items of the Prince's uniform in readiness for the subsequent cleansing ceremonies. The corpse was not disembowelled deeply enough to spill out all the intestines, although a deep bloody gash was nonetheless inflicted right across the stomach in accordance with a dread of *umnyama*; a fear that, unless the spirit of the slain was allowed to escape in this way, then the killers' own stomachs would bloat and swell, causing death. Some paces away the Austerlitz sword of Napoleon was picked up from the dust and handed to Sabhuza. All the dogs still in the kraal were also killed. Now that darkness was falling they began to collect up the loose horses and prepared to move off. The Prince was left lying naked in the blood-soaked grass, and as the full moon rose that night, it lightly bathed his lacerated figure with the white pallor of death. He was the only Bonaparte to ever fall in combat — ironically, in the uniform of a British officer.

Almost a year later General Sir Evelyn Wood personally questioned ten out of the twenty Zulus who had been directly involved in the ambush. His wife took written records of their various and often conflicting accounts. He asked them why they had not mutilated the Prince. "Because of the gold chain hanging round his neck...we feared his ghost." And they added, "He fought like a lion at bay." "Why like a lion?" "The lion is the bravest beast we have seen."

One of them pointed out that he had fought so tenaciously that, "We did not dare close in on him until he sank down facing us, when we rushed on him."[13] Many of them noted how the other soldiers had all immediately galloped off, even though, as they did so, more than one had turned to see the Prince trying to mount his own horse.

Captain Arthur Bigge, who accompanied the General, concluded from their various accounts that, whilst the scouting party had originally numbered about thirty, because it had divided into two groups on approaching the kraal, only about ten warriors had actually been involved in leading the initial attack. In his view, therefore, it would have been comparatively easy for the survivors to have effected the rescue of the Prince. But that was not the opinion of the fugitives.

From various directions, the fleeing riders had now emerged from out of the donga. Corporal Grubb, desperately trying to load his carbine in the saddle, had accidentally dropped it; Troopers Le Tocq and Cochrane had crossed the donga directly after Lieutenant Carey, whilst Sergeant Willis and Corporal Grubb had

---

13   RA. R10/20

crossed separately lower down. As the horses bolted into the donga, Carey had shouted out for everyone 'to bear left' with the intention of trying to rally, believing that the whole patrol, like him, had succeeded in fleeing from the kraal area. In the event when he finally pulled his horse up he realised that only two troopers had reined their horses behind him. He was horrified to see that the Prince's distinctive grey mare had also been galloping along behind them, riderless. When he asked the troopers if they knew what had happened to the Prince, Cochrane said simply, "I fear he is dead." At that, Le Tocq nodded his agreement.

As Sergeant Willlis and Corporal Grubb caught up with the others, Grubb informed Carey, "I looked back and saw the Prince clinging to the stirrup-leather and saddle underneath his horse for a few lengths…then he fell…I think his horse trampled on him."[14]

Amidst the confusion and fear, Carey now had to make some crucial decisions. Although in some mental turmoil, he struggled hard to think clearly and logically. Four of the patrol appeared to be missing. The whole purpose of the escort had been to protect the Prince but it seemed to have failed him The broken ground behind them hid the kraal area from view, but presumably the donga must by now be alive with Zulus. The chances therefore were that the Prince had fallen, perhaps from a stray bullet, but whatever the reason, he must by now be presumed dead. As that realisation began to seep through his mind, Carey experienced wave after wave of sickening nausea. Yet it never occurred to him to turn back far enough to see with his own eyes what had actually happened.

And judging from the first reports by the others, both Troopers Abel and Rogers, being dismounted, must also be presumed dead. The native guide had disappeared altogether. Already, to his left, he could see more Zulus moving at speed through the high grass, whilst others were already crossing the donga further down. Since Zulu warriors were quite capable of keeping up with a galloping horse there was a very real possibility they might soon be surrounded. The choices were limited but stark. They could either beat a hasty retreat at once, or else return to look for the Prince.

Clearly, in that event, there would be a fight — but Carey was the only one armed with both a pistol and sword, and of the four surviving troopers, only three had single-shot carbines which, on horseback, would only be effective at extreme close range. But once that first shot had been fired it would have been almost suicidal to attempt to re-load from horseback, surrounded by Zulus. But to mount an attack dismounted would be even worse — Corporal Grubb had no weapon at all, and at least one of them, suitably armed, would have to stay behind to guard their six horses with which to make their escape. Consequently, any attack on foot would have to be launched with only two armed men — against an obviously larger force of Zulus.

It was also beginning to dawn on Carey that, if he did decide to order everyone back, they would have somehow to fight their way as far as the kraal if they ever hoped to rescue or recover Troopers Rogers and Abel, as well as the native guide. And he also appreciated that there was a real possibility that, even if he ordered

---

14   FEATHERSTONE, p. 85.

a return, the irregulars might refuse point blank to do so. Indeed, three of them subsequently stated quite openly that it would have been quite futile going back to try and rescue the others. They would have all been killed. On balance, Lieutenant Carey concluded that he should not risk any more lives; that they should now withdraw rapidly to the north west, and hope to meet up quickly with Brigadier-General Wood's Flying Column which could not be that far away.

The light was now fading. With more Zulu bullets now whizzing uncomfortably close to their position, Carey called for everyone to follow him — away from the donga area. Corporal Grubb now mounted the Prince's horse, being the finest and strongest in the patrol, whilst leading his own. So all the survivors, headed by Lieutenant Carey, cantered away towards the approaching Flying Column.

In later years, Mademoiselle Thérèse Gaubert, one of the Empress Eugénie's secretaries, disclosed that she was in the company of the Empress on 1ˢᵗ June — at the very hour when the Prince was killed. Suddenly, Eugénie seemed to smell violets — the favourite flower of the Bonapartes — and she had an intuitive feeling that her son was thinking of her at that very moment.

As they cantered, Carey sensed that, after all this, his life was going to be irrevocably changed. Already the die was cast. He could see himself carrying all the blame — for everything — the smallness of the escort; the halt in the vulnerable kraal area; the failure to post sentries, to load the carbines, to secure the horses — their total failure to protect the Prince. But, as he constantly tried to re-assure himself, was there really any alternative to *sauve qui peut* in the face of such a sudden and overwhelming attack — and on that, surely, there would be unanimous support from all his comrades?

That evening it was to be Carey's further misfortune, at about four miles from the site of the ambush, to now meet up with a small reconnaissance group which included the two most distinguished and decorated officers of the Zulu war — Brigadier-General Evelyn Wood and Colonel Redvers Buller — riding ahead of the Flying Column. There are conflicting accounts about what happened next. The controversy is not helped by the fact that neither officer, in their subsequent written recollections nor in any recorded conversation, made any reference as to what was actually said and so this speculative resumé is based entirely on hearsay comments by others who simply happened to be present.

Colonel Buller saw Lieutenant Carey first from afar, and commented to others, "Why, the man rides as if the Zulus are after him!" and, as they got closer, he called out, "Whatever is the matter with you?"

A white-faced Carey replied, "The Prince Imperial is killed!"

"Where is his body?" Carey turned to point at the valley behind, and Colonel Buller, after searching around with his telescope in the fading light, finally spotted some Zulus leading horses away about three miles off.

"Where are your men, sir?" he asked fiercely. "How many did you lose?"

"They're behind me. I don't know."

"You ought to be shot, and I hope you will be. I could shoot you myself."

At this point Brigadier-General Wood came within earshot. Realising at once that all was not well, he asked sharply:

"Where is the Prince, Lieutenant Carey? Speak, sir, what has happened?"

"The Prince, I fear, is killed, sir."

The General stared for a moment in silence, barely able to comprehend what he was hearing.

"Is that the case, Lieutenant Carey? Tell me instantly, sir."

"I fear 'tis so, General."

He continued to stare at Carey for a while, and then added bitterly,

"Then, sir, what are *you* doing here?"[15]

After that final pointed question from Brigadier-General Wood — a question which was to be asked by many others in the months ahead — Lieutenant Carey was brusquely told to return his party to the Itelezei camp. As darkness was now falling, even the totally fearless Colonel Buller considered that it would be imprudent to re-enter the donga before daybreak.

About seven thirty Carey, having reached Itelezei, staggered into the mess tent. Major Grenfell happened to be dining alone. "Why, Carey," he called out, "you're very late for dinner. We thought you had been shot." Greatly agitated, the other replied, "I am alright, but the Prince is killed."[16] Major Grenfell immediately took Carey across to Lord Chelmsford's tent. Colonel Harrison recalled that Carey had likewise reported to him that evening, informing him briefly about the circumstances which had resulted in the Prince's death. I said, "You don't mean to say you left the Prince?" He replied, "It was no use stopping; he was shot by the first volley." And I said, "You ought to have tried, at all events, to bring away his body."[17] When Harrison received no response, he instructed Carey to write out a full report immediately.

The Colonel then went to Lord Chelmsford's tent to ask permission to ride out immediately to look for the Prince. Severely shaken, the General declined his request, adding, "I don't want to lose you too." Lord Chelmsford was completely overwhelmed by the news, coming, as it did, on the very first day of the second invasion which was intended to atone for Isandlwana. Already he could anticipate the political furore and the personal consequences of this latest disaster.

The news, meantime, soon spread throughout the camp. The four surviving troopers were freely describing their experiences to anyone who cared to ask, including the many war correspondents. Archibald Forbes, in particular, lost no time in making an immediate report to the *Daily News*, in which he promptly castigated Carey for leading the flight to safety. He also personally checked the holster strap on the Prince's saddle and concluded that it had not been made of leather at all, but merely paper-faced. The correspondent of the *Natal Mercury* noted that, attached to the saddle, were two saddle-bags and two holsters. One of the latter was intact, whereas the other, on the left hand side, had clearly been clutched and squeezed in the vice-like grip of someone holding on to it for dear life. The connecting band had been torn almost, but not quite, in two.[18]

---

15   Ibid., p. 88.
16   WHITTON, p. 244.
17   KNIGHT p. 227.
18   MOODIE, p. 171.

Paul Deléage had only just arrived in the camp that evening when he learnt, in casual conversation with an artillery officer, that the Prince Imperial had been killed. In total disbelief, he insisted that he be given immediate confirmation in French. Horrified, he then ran directly to Lord Chelmsford's tent. The tall General was standing outside, his face drawn and haggard. In a quiet subdued voice, he told the Frenchman that the Prince was indeed missing, probably killed; that his horse had come back riderless; but that only Lieutenant Carey could really explain what had happened.

Deléage now burst in on Colonel Harrison, who was having his evening meal with Carey and another staff officer. The journalist launched into a barrage of questions, in rapid French to Carey and in halting English to Harrison. But he obtained little clarification. Carey, exhausted and overwrought, now treated his former close colleague for the journalist he was, confining himself to a few general remarks, whilst claiming ignorance over what precisely had happened. No, he had not seen the Prince after the sudden ambush. Yes, he had lost two irregular troopers and a native guide, but he had no idea as to what had happened to any of them. The journalist felt mounting anger at Carey's deliberate vagueness — he instinctively knew he was not being told the whole truth.

Deléage left the dining tent without a further word, looking for the search party which he expected to be leaving for the donga and which he intended to join. But as he wandered round the tents he was appalled to learn that no search was even planned for that night. Officers explained to him that it was far too late to achieve anything in the darkness. The intention was to mount a full search party at first light, and in order to join it, the Frenchman was invited to report himself to the cavalry lines at five o'clock. In vain did Deléage plead that, with the full moon, there was surely enough light; that only a few miles away the Prince might still be alive, wounded, waiting for rescue; and even if he was truly dead, what about the animals and birds of prey scavenging his remains? He began remonstrating with everyone he saw, regardless of whether they stopped to listen to him or not. Finally a senior cavalry officer took him to one side and spelt out the reality. Despite the moon, it would still be very difficult to find the Prince during the night; and experience had shown that horses were particularly prone to breaking their legs in unforeseen ant holes whilst traversing open country in the hours of darkness. A very large expedition had already been arranged for early the following morning and the journalist must be content with that.

So there was nothing that Deléage could now do but roundly curse the English in his voluble French, and abruptly remove his personal belongings from Carey's tent. He believed in all sincerity that none of the officers around him cared in the slightest. Many of them suffered his taunts and accusations in stoic silence, and in the mess tent he was finally offered a stiff drink to calm his nerves. But in his subsequent reports to *Le Figaro*, Deléage gave an appalling picture of general English indifference, thus strengthening later rumours in France that '*la perfide Albion*' had deliberately engineered the Prince's death. With his judgement that evening gravely distorted by genuine distress, the young Frenchman had, in fact, totally misread the situation. The English may not have openly expressed their shock in an emotional and hysterical manner, but the fact remained that there was not a single officer or soldier in the camp that night who was not deeply disturbed by the news. The 'PI' had been an immensely popular figure with all ranks. It seemed inconceivable that his dashing figure, his infectious enthusiasm and Gallic charm would no longer enliven their daily round. 'There was little sleep in the camp that night, and long after the bugles had sounded "lights out", the soldiers lingered in groups and talked with bated breath of this new disaster'.[19]

Carey had no companion to share his tent that night. Sleep was impossible. After completing his formal report to Colonel Harrison, the only thing he could do was to unburden himself to his wife:

> Itelezi Ridge Camp
> 12 Midnight 1st June

My own one, you know the dreadful news ere you receive this by telegram. I am a ruined man I fear, though from my letter which will be in the papers you will see I could do nothing else. Still the loss of a Prince is a fearful thing. To me, the whole thing is a dream; It is but 8 hours since it happened.

Our camp *was* bad, but then I have been so laughed at for taking a squadron with me that I have grown reckless and would have gone with two men.

Tomorrow we go with the 17th Lancers to find his body. Poor fellow! But it might have been my fate! The bullets tore around us, and with only my revolver what could I do? The men all bolted and I now fear the Prince was shot on the spot as his saddle is torn as if he tried to get up. No doubt they will say I should have remained by him, but I had no idea he was wounded, and thought he was after me.

My horse was nearly done but carried me beautifully. My own darling! I prayed as I rode away that I should not be hit and my prayer was heard. Annie! what will you think of me! I was such a fool to stop in that camp! I feel it now though at the time I did not see it. As regards leaving the Prince I am innocent, as I did not know he was wounded, and thought our best plan was to make an offing.

Everyone is very kind about it all here, but I feel a broken-down man. Never can I forget this nights adventure.

My own, own sweet darling, my own little darling child, my own little Eddie and Pelham! Mama darling, do write and cheer me up! What will the Empress say! Only a few minutes before our surprise, he was discussing politics with me and the campaigns of 1800 and 1796, criticising Napoleon's strategy and then talked of Republics and Monarchies! Poor boy! I liked him so very much! He was always so warm and good natured. Still I have been surprised, but not that I am not careful, but only because they laughed at all my care and foresight, I should have done very differently a week ago but now had ceased to care. Oh! Annie! How near I have been to death. I

---

19   JOHN, p. 475.

have looked it in the face, and have been spared. I have been a very, very wicked man, and may God forgive me! I frequently have to go out without saying my prayers and have had to be out on duty every Sunday. Oh! for some Christian sympathy. I do feel so miserable and dejected! I know not what to do; of course all sorts of yarns will get into the papers and without hearing my tale I shall be blamed; but honestly Pet between you and I, I can only be blamed for the camp. I tried to rally the men, in the retreat, and had no idea the poor Prince was behind. Even now I don't know it but fear so from the evidence of the men. The fire on us was very hot, perfect volleys; I believe thirty men or more were on us. Both my poor despised horses have now been under fire. The one I rode today could scarcely carry me, but did very well coming back. Oh! I do feel so ill and tired! I long for rest of any kind. This daily work on the saddle all day is very trying and this excitement has broken me down. If the body is found at any distance from the Kraal tomorrow, my statement will appear correct. If he is in the Kraal why then he must have been shot dead, as I heard no cry. *Enfin! nous verrons.* Time alone will solve the mystery.

Poor Lord Chelmsford is awfully cut up about it, as he will be blamed for letting him go with so small an escort.

The Times and Standard correspondents have been at me for news, also the Figaro, but the Daily News will give a garbled version as he is away from here at present.

Pet! My own treasure, I cannot write more! Good night my own one, I will try & let you know a few words tomorrow. I now try to sleep till réveille at 5 A.M. and it is now nearly one and so very cold. God bless you, my own one! J.B.[20]

This letter was not produced in evidence at the court martial. However, through strange circumstances, it did eventually come to the personal notice of both the Empress Eugénie and Queen Victoria, and was deliberately used by the latter as part of her personal campaign to discredit Carey. It was thus seen by a large number of people. The majority of those who read it considered it to be a full admission of guilt on Carey's part. But others viewed it less harshly; noting that it was a very private and emotional letter, composed in the immediate aftermath of a deeply traumatic experience, by someone, who wearied through lack of sleep and nervous exhaustion, was writing intimately to the person closest to him and thus making disclosures in a rather loose and uninhibited way, points which could easily be twisted into an admission of guilt. It offers the only insight into Carey's true feelings directly after the disaster. By way of contrast the formal account of the incident, addressed to Colonel Harrison, and written earlier that same evening, is a model of clarity and factual, restrained reporting.

Unlike the letter, this account was produced as evidence at the court martial. Even so it is particularly noteworthy that, in neither document, both written on the day of the disaster, does Carey make any reference to the question of command. The most damning admission in the letter is to blame himself for not asserting his authority more over the site of the camp, thus acknowledging by implication that he did have some executive responsibility for the patrol. But in that same letter to his wife he also reveals his sensitivities, based on previous experiences, about the actual size of the escort. And his expression of thankfulness at the way his own tired horse had carried him 'beautifully' to safety, and the recurring gratitude over his own narrow escape from sudden and violent death, grated on the feelings of those who read the letter, creating a most unfavourable impression. So what Carey under great strain had written privately to his wife that night could be described as publicly undermining his own precarious position.

At five in the morning, Paul Deléage reported promptly to General Marshall's tent. But he was very taken aback to learn from one of his staff that the search party was going to comprise of detachments from practically every available regiment and mounted unit in the two advancing columns — a full squadron of Lancers, another squadron of heavy Dragoons, mounted irregulars from Brigadier-General Wood's Flying Column, a complete regiment from the Natal Native Contingent, with a troop of BaSotho scouts on horseback. There was also to be an ambulance unit. To assemble such a large force inevitably took time, and Deléage became increasingly agitated at the inevitable delays. But, in truth, everyone was longing to make a start: 'for the suspense and anxiety since Lieutenant Carey's arrival last night could hardly have been exceeded had he brought news of a second Isandlwana.'[21]

The force finally totalled over one thousand men. It had been deliberately so constituted in order to show proper respect to the dead Prince. Inevitably the advance of the Second Division had been cancelled for that day. But in Deléage's eyes the whole business — the size and the delay, the cancelled advance — simply smacked of further hypocrisy from people who, yesterday, when the Prince was alive, had been quite content to see him wander off into hostile territory with an escort which could only total six. His shock at the sudden loss of the Prince was now being corroded by a gnawing bitterness.

Taking almost two hours to assemble the search party did not finally leave until seven. As it set off, Lord Chelmsford stood on a nearby knoll and watched the long column slowly pass by. Lieutenant Carey, in front, acted as guide. Following directly behind him were an ADC to Lord Chelmsford, Captain Molyneux of 22nd Regiment, Major Grenfell, Lomas and Surgeon-Major Scott, who had attended the Prince during his illness in Durban. Lieutenant Bartle Frere, son of the High Commissioner, was further down the column.

In due course they approached the fatal donga. A horse lay dead and another, still alive but severely wounded, was immediately dispatched on the spot. The body of a speared dog lay beside one of the huts. Trooper Rogers was found first, not in the actual kraal area where he had last been seen, but to one side in the long grass. He had been deliberately moved by the Zulus who, in accordance with their custom, never allowed dead bodies to remain in their homesteads. Naked, disembowelled, hideously mutilated, he had been the first to be killed. About a hundred yards from the kraal, in the direction of the donga, they found Trooper Abel — stripped naked, his belly likewise ripped open, with his horribly disfigured face wrapped up in a bloodstained piece of flannel. The Prince was found last of all, further down the donga. His body was about 250 yards from the kraal.

He, too, was totally naked, with the exception of one sock. The other, with its embroidered 'N', had been discarded a few feet away. There was no sign of his uniform, sabre, revolver or helmet. He lay on his back, with arms slightly crossed, head turned to the right side so that the cheek rested on the ground. His left arm was deeply lacerated. It had obviously been used to ward off blows and was almost cut to pieces. The left eye was half-closed, and the right had been completely crushed by the jab of an assegai, but his face otherwise looked peaceful. The body appeared to be mass of wounds. Whilst there was a deep gash across the stomach, it was not considered sufficiently deep to constitute the normal Zulu disembowelment. Indeed it appeared as if the ritual might have been started only to be mysteriously terminated. Nor, unlike the others, had any part of his face and body been deliberately mutilated. Indeed, the body was not particularly bloodied since most of the bleeding had been internal.

Surgeon-Major Scott and Deléage gently turned the Prince over to look at his back. Had he been shot from behind earlier during the flight — as Carey had believed possible and now desperately hoped would prove to be the case? But there were no no bullet wounds; there were no entry marks of any sort. His back was practically unblemished except for two slight lacerations, which were clearly the points of exit from deep thrusts to the front. It looked as if the Prince had truly died as he would always have wanted — face to face with the enemy. There appeared to be seventeen or possibly eighteen assegai wounds, all to the front of the body. But many of them looked to be so slight that they were probably inflicted after death. Only two of the many thrusts were probably fatal; the one which had been deflected from the brow and which had penetrated the brain through the right eye, or possibly the deep wound inflicted over the heart. Either of these would have killed the Prince instantly. Surgeon-Major Robinson, the regimental medical officer of the 17th Lancers, agreed with Scott's analysis. It was also obvious to everyone present that there had been a very fierce struggle — the grass in the vicinity of the body had been trampled over a large area, and was now deeply stained with blood. Lying amongst the battered blades of grass were three spent revolver cartridges and a single assegai, its blade broken in two. His spurs, twisted out of shape and covered with blood and mud, were picked up from close by. Still tightly clutched in his damaged right hand was a tuft of Zulu hair.

Major Grenfell later recorded: 'It was a sad sight, as we, his English brother-officers, stood round the dead body of the hope of the Imperialists of France, the Prince's servant weeping bitterly, and we all felt the great disaster and the deep disgrace which had fallen on the British Army.'[22]

---

22   GRENFELL, p. 39.

Paul Deléage leaned forward, kissed the stiff hands and moving to one side burst into uncontrollable weeping, clutching his head in his hands. He was to bitterly recall that impudent boast: 'One Englishman is worth five Frenchmen', and how, on this occasion, it was exactly five Englishmen who had survived. Lomas knelt down sobbing. Lieutenant Carey looked on, trying to remain in control, his feelings totally numbed by the appalling sight before him. Leaning forward, Captain Molyneux gently unclasped the collar of gold medallions from around the Prince's neck. They included a miniature of his mother; the Pope's medal sent at his baptism; a medal of the Virgin Mary; one of Saint Michael (the protector of France) given to him by the Abbé Deguerry and lastly, the seal of his great uncle, Napoleon the First. The collar was placed in an envelope, together with some locks of his short, jet black hair. A horse blanket was then wrapped round the body, another blanket was attached to four lances to make a bier on which the Prince was reverently laid. The senior officers then gathered behind and the procession slowly made its way through an impromptu guard of honour formed by the 17th Lancers and King's Dragoon Guards. The party then passed to one side of the kraal (which was soon to be set on fire) towards the waiting ambulance. The large force finally reached the Itelezei camp about two o'clock that afternoon where a funeral service was being planned.

Captain Molyneux submitted an immediate report to Lord Chelmsford:

2nd June 1879

My Lord,

In accordance with your instructions, I this morning accompanied the cavalry commanded by Major-General Marshall to find the body of His Highness the Prince Imperial. Surgeon-Major Scott, Lieutenant Bartle Frere, and the servant of his Imperial Highness were with me.

He was found about two hundred yards north-east of the kraal...The body was stripped bare except for a gold chain with medallions, which was about his neck. His sabre, his revolver, his helmet, and his other clothes had disappeared, but we found in the grass his spurs with their straps, and a sock marked N...The body had seventeen wounds, all in front, and the marks on the ground as on the spurs indicated a desperate resistance.[23]

Carey, in a follow-up letter to his wife, dated 3rd June, described the scene: 'He was in the donga on his back quite naked covered with assegai wounds, disembowelled but not otherwise mutilated...I remained to bury the other poor men. Our friendly Zulu was only found and buried today.'[24] In fact, the body of the native guide had been found some considerable distance from the kraal and judging by his appearance, he, too, had put up a fierce fight.

Lord Chelmsford meanwhile had telegraphed the news direct to the Duke of Cambridge. The message, in Chelmsford's own hand, took over two weeks to reach Madeira on board the *Balmoral Castle*, from whence the Eastern Telegraph Company telegraphed it to London, via Falmouth, where it arrived on 19th June.

23   FILON, p. 214.
24   RA. R5/15

After explaining how the Prince had been sent out on patrol along the route to the camp site for 2nd June, he added that Louis had just given the order to mount when the ambush took place. Lord Chelmsford completed the telegram with the words: 'I myself was not aware that the Prince had been detailed for this duty'.[25]

On the afternoon of 2nd June, the Commanding General communicated with the High Commissioner, Sir Bartle Frere:

> The body has been recovered...I shall bury it here with such military honours as are possible. I suppose my enemies in the English Press will make a raid upon me again and endeavour to throw the whole blame upon my shoulders. I have always felt that it was somewhat unfair to saddle me with the responsibility which naturally would be attached to such a charge, but I had to accept it with all the rest.[26]

This somewhat pathetic outburst was the only formal complaint Lord Chelmsford ever made about the whole affair. But, by unilaterally deciding that the Prince should be buried in South Africa, he was yet again exceeding his authority and showing a lack of political judgement — for such a final resting place for the heir to the French throne was plainly out of the question. Perhaps he felt a speedy local burial would dampen public concern over what had happened. However a number of his senior staff officers soon impressed upon him that the remains should, at least, be returned to England and not surprisingly, Paul Deléage argued likewise. Lord Chelmsford changed his mind.

Lieutenant Wodehouse was one of those in the camp who helped carry the Prince's body in a blanket to the hospital tent, recalling nearly fifty years later that: 'my hands were stained with his blood.'[27] In the hospital tent Lomas tenderly washed the body and then re-clothed it with the Prince's own linen. At four o'clock that same afternoon the first of a series of funeral services took place. At Itelezi camp many units from the halted Second Division paraded in a hollow-square, presenting arms, whilst Father Ballard, the Roman Catholic chaplain, led a short procession with prayers for the dead. The body had been wrapped in a tricolour and secured to a gun carriage. Lord Chelmsford, as chief mourner, walked directly behind the carriage, grim and drawn, leaning heavily on his cane. Directly behind him came members of his staff, Paul Deléage and pipers of the 21st Fusiliers playing a solemn lament. The French journalist: 'For myself, who alone in that sad procession had the civilian's privilege of walking bareheaded, seeing as we passed the flag of England droop slowly to the ground, a *Royal Salute*, before this corpse wrapped in a tricolour.' He then added another paragraph which revealed just how perceptively he had come to appreciate the real problems which had vexed his young friend; 'I thought how deeply shall they repent whose insults drove this unfortunate Prince to prove his manhood even to the cost of his life, when history shall relate how, in this far-off

---

25   PRO, Kew
26   RA. R5/20a
27   RA. Add.J/1561 — Letter from Sir Josceline Wodehouse to Lord Stamfordham dated 1st November 1928.

land, the last of the Napoleons brought honour by his very death to the banner of France.'[28]

After the service was over, the body, escorted by a squadron of Lancers, was returned to the supply base at Koppie Allein where, through the night, army surgeons endeavoured to embalm the corpse as best they could, finally placing it in a rough deal casket, filled with sand and straw, to steady the body through the long, bumpy journey by ambulance down to Durban. At the start of the Prince's solemn return journey — ironically along the same route which he had taken to join Lord Chelmsford two months earlier — the staff issued a special Order of the Day:

> The mortal remains of Prince Louis Napoleon will be transported tomorrow at half-past nine to the Roman Catholic church at Durban, to be afterwards embarked on Her Majesty's ship the *Orontes* for England.
>
> In following the coffin which contains the corpse of the Prince Imperial of France, and in rendering to his ashes the last tribute of respect and honour, all troops in Natal will remember:
>
> 1. That he was the inheritor of a powerful name, and one of great military renown.
>
> 2. That he was the son of England's strongest Ally in times of danger.
>
> 3. That he was the only child of a widowed Empress, who now remains without a throne, an exile and childless, on the shore of England.
>
> To enhance the sorrow and respect which they owe to his memory, the troops will bear in mind that the Prince Imperial fell in fighting under the English flag.[29]

There were further religious ceremonies at various stages during the long journey to England. From Pietermaritzburg, the officer in charge, Major-General Clifford, who was responsible for safeguarding all the garrisons and lines of communications in Natal, and himself a Roman Catholic, dispatched the following memorandum to Sir Bartle Frere in Cape Town:

> Sunday evening, 8th June
>
> Great pressure of work prevents my sending your Excellency such report on the sad end of the late Prince Imperial Louis Napoleon as I could wish. The papers I send you will, I trust, give you an idea of our endeavours to show our respect and heart-felt sorrow for the sad end of the poor young Prince. His body arrived here at 2 p.m., and with the Lieut-Governor and all the military and civilian inhabitants of Pietermaritzburg, we received him at the entrance to the town, and escorted him to the Catholic school room, where in the presence of properly constituted legal authorities, M Uhlmann, the Prince's confidential servant, M Deléage, correspondent of *Le Figaro*, Colonel Mitchell, Colonial Secretary and myself, we verified his identity

28 FILON, p. 215.
29 JOHN, p. 483.

and placed our signatures to the necessary legal documents, one copy of which I placed in his coffin, one I sent home for the Secretary of State for War, and one to him also for the Prince's mother. I took the responsibility for the transfer of the body to better coffins (wood and lead) on myself, and am thankful I did so. Nothing could be better than the medical arrangements made. The body is now resting in the little Roman Catholic chapel here, and we are doing all we can to show our deep sorrow and sympathy in this great national calamity. After service tomorrow at 8.30, the body will be moved under escort to Durban, where all will again be done that circumstances will admit of to show our sorrow and respect. I hope to get to Durban on Tuesday; though I am very anxious at leaving my post here at such a moment, still I think showing respect of our late charge is now my first duty.
    (Signed) H.H.Clifford
    Major-General[30]

    In the procession through Pietermaritzburg the gun carriage bearing the casket had been wrapped in a tricolour, with the Prince's horse 'Percy' following directly behind — the stirrups being booted reversed in time-honoured fashion. Over the saddle a pall had been thrown, edged in white satin and figured with the Napoleonic emblem, and with the Prince's initials. On the casket itself lay one of the Prince's swords, a white helmet, and wreaths and crosses of violets, roses and camellias. When the body had been transferred to a fresh casket, all those present agreed that his remains had not decomposed at all and that the face of the Prince was just as calm and at peace as when he had been found. For the service, the small chapel was crowded with civic dignitaries as well as many notable Protestants, including Bishop Colenso, who had steadfastly opposed the war against the Zulu nation.

    The grief-stricken, Xavier Uhlmann, the Prince's valet, had travelled up from Durban specially to undertake the identification, but had been so overcome by the experience that he was quite unable to accompany the coffin the rest of the way down to Durban. He did however ask for a number of mementoes to be placed beside the body before its departure from Pietermaritzburg — a rosary blessed by Pope Pious the Ninth, and photographs of the Emperor, the Empress and the Prince's much loved cousin, Louis d'Albe. On arrival at Durban, it was estimated that about seven to eight thousand people turned out in the streets to watch in silence as the solemn procession made its way to the quayside. On 11th June the tug *Adonis* conveyed the casket in fairly rough seas across the bar to H.M.S. *Boadicea*. That journey took about an hour. The casket was raised up from the tug by tackle from one of the yard arms and placed in the Commodore's cabin. The ship sailed at nine on the evening of 12th June. Colonel Pemberton of the 3rd/60th Rifles, due to return home on sick leave, had been nominated as the army's representative to accompany the coffin and now Paul Deléage, Xavier Uhlmann and Lomas, were all given permission to travel on the same ship.

---

30 FEATHERSTONE, p. 104.

At Cape Town, on Sunday 15th June, the casket was further transferred to H.M.S.*Orontes*. Once on board there were more religious ceremonies led by the Roman Catholic Bishop of Cape Town, Dr John Leonard. Other ships in the harbour fired solemn minute guns. Sir Bartle Frere personally led the mourning, in the presence of his family (including his officer son who had assisted in the recovery of the Prince's body) and all the members of the Cabinet. Many who were present commented later on the obvious sincerity of the Frere family's grief. Indeed, when the casket was finally placed in the ship's chapel, Lady Frere personally laid upon it a handsome cross of palm-leaves and immortelles whilst her daughter covered the steps with beautiful floral wreaths. H.M.S. *Boadicea* concluded the ceremony by firing twenty-three minute guns and the *Orontes* then set sail for England that same evening, expecting to arrive at Portsmouth about 8th July.

Shortly afterwards the Bishop wrote to Lady Frere about a private visit the Prince had paid to the Cathedral on his arrival. In the letter he explained that a painting of the Crucifixion had been presented earlier by his father: 'When the Prince Imperial was passing here in March last I mentioned to him that the Emperor was a benefactor of this mission and that the picture...was the gift of his father. He seemed somewhat surprised and promised to come and see it on his return...as I remember..., during our conversation, he stated, "if I do return".'[31]

As soon as the first funeral service had been completed at the camp at Itelezi, Captain Bettington took the opportunity to take purely factual statements from each of the survivors. It is not clear what use was finally made of these particular statements. No doubt, Bettington wanted to satisfy himself as to the conduct of his own troopers, particularly as he had been personally responsible for their selection. In his own account Carey explained that he, not the Prince, had given the final order to 'Mount!'. He had made this same point earlier whilst briefing the correspondent of *Home News*, who had specifically included it in his dispatch.[32] Likewise, in the written report he had compiled for Colonel Harrison on the night of 1st June, he stated that he, not the Prince, had given the order to 'Saddle Up'.[33] In talking to Captain Bettington and earlier to inquiring newspaper correspondents, he also disclosed that, knowing that the men's carbines were unloaded, he had judged it better to clear the long grass before rallying and making a stand.[34] None of these important points, clearly indicating that Carey considered himself to have been in charge, were ever produced as evidence by the prosecution during the subsequent Court Martial. Had this been the case much of Carey's defence argument would have been undermined.

It is not known if the details of Captain Bettington's investigations were ever passed to Lord Chelmsford's staff or indeed whether they formed the basis for the General's subsequent actions. It is conceivable that the immediate taking of these statements gave rise to some local press reports that an official inquiry had, in fact, been undertaken. Speed in taking this evidence was undoubtedly essential since the

---

31   RA. R5/23
32   MOODIE, p. 148.
33   PRO, Kew
34   MOODIE, p. 149.

Second Division intended to resume its delayed advance by abandoning the Itelezei camp early on the morning of 3rd June. By nightfall they hoped to reach the second overnight bivouac area which, ironically, was not far from the site of the ambush and which had been previously occupied the night of 2nd June by the Flying Column.

Over the next seven days Lieutenant Carey continued with his usual staff duties under Colonel Harrison. The atmosphere in the headquarters was abnormally strained. Quite apart from the inevitable nervous tension at the prospect of battles yet to come and tiredness amongst staff officers trying to co-ordinate this fresh invasion of Zululand, there were the persisting recriminations surrounding the distressing death of the Prince Imperial. One of the correspondents — Charles Norris Newman — described the atmosphere: 'The whole circumstances of the affair...became the subject of a good deal of discussion and no little animadversion, even amounting to strong condemnation for pusillanimity in many quarters.'[35] Nonetheless most of the irregulars considered that flight, in all the circumstances, had been the only practical and sensible course. Yet others took the view that an immediate return, charging aggressively back into the kraal, might have been enough to scatter the Zulus. They pointed out that Zulu scouting parties were usually expected to avoid unnecessary fighting whilst obtaining information and that consequently, if vigorously attacked, might well have broken off the engagement. Staff officers, such as Major Grenfell, wondered if Colonel Harrison had properly fulfilled his own particular responsibilities with regard to the Prince's safety. Had the whereabouts of the patrol been cleared beforehand with Lord Chelmsford? And why had the escort been so small?

The General's military secretary, the outspoken and unpopular Lieutenant Colonel Crealock, wrote to his brother, Major-General Henry Crealock, on 2nd June: 'It has been a great blow to us this sad death of the poor Prince Imperial. He had been attached to the quartermaster-general's department for work, though he messed with us, and he was delighted with duties, but rashness or overboldness, fearlessness or whatever you call it, was a very marked feature of his character. He (The Prince) mentioned...casually about 7 or 8 a.m. he was going out with Colonel Harrison to the next camping ground 10 miles from this place and 17 from the last, to chose the camp...and as I had spoken to Harrison — and the general also — a few days previously about not permitting the prince ever to be unaccompanied by an officer and escort, I thought nothing more of it...no-one but the prince is to blame for the rashness of off-saddling at such a place and at such a distance...had I known he was going with no-one but Carey and 6 men I should have certainly spoken to Lord Chelmsford about it...We are all very grieved, sorely so, for everyone loved the lad, so frank and kind-hearted and plucky — too much so. His ambition and industry and love of soldiering were such as to have ensured him success hereafter.'[36]

But the majority of the regulars also felt very keenly that in blindly following a *sauve qui peut* Carey had somehow stained the unwritten honour code — a code that expected British officers to show steadfastness under fire and a willingness to go to the aid of stricken comrades, even at the risk of death.

35   NORRIS-NEWMAN, p. 195.
36   RA. R5/20

Lieutenant 'Keggie' Slade, who was with the Flying Column, wrote to his mother on 2nd June: 'Neither Carey nor his men made the slightest attempt to stand, and in plain words *they ran away* and left the poor dear little prince to die fighting on foot, single-handed. I cannot tell you what we all think of Carey's behaviour, but will tell you what Buller told him to his face yesterday when they met — "You ought to be shot." I think I may safely say that this is the opinion of every man in the column. To think that a British officer should leave any man, much more the Prince Imperial of France, to fall into the hands of the Zulus without making the slightest attempt to save him is too disgraceful...I hope he will be tried by court martial and kicked out.'[37]

It would seem that the Zulus had begun to appreciate that the brave young man they had so recently killed was someone special. Captain McLeod Nairne, 94th Regiment, wrote home on the same day the Prince's body was recovered, 2nd June; 'There were several kraals at Jambokala where the prince was killed, and in one of them was found an old woman who informed Marshall's interpreter that she knew all about it and that the men who did it were her sons and families, 30 in number and that they had made off at day-break as they got wind of Marshall's visit. She also said that they heard that they had killed a great (*Enkos*) king. This shows you what wonderful scouts the Zulus are.'[38]

Carey still felt very miserable and isolated, but the earlier self-pity was slowly giving way to a conviction that he had genuinely tried to act in good faith. By now he was regaining sufficient self-confidence to want to argue his case officially and thus clear his name. It seems strange that Lord Chelmsford appears to have taken no steps whatsoever to formally inquire into the whole affair, and it was Carey himself who had to take that initiative. On 10th June, nine days after the incident, he formally requested a Court of Inquiry and that same day wrote again to his wife in a more assertive manner:

> I now find that there were thirty men against us or thereabouts — some say sixty. It was a complete surprise...I am afraid I shall get into a row about it, but my conscience is clear. No efforts of mine could have saved the Prince, though perhaps I ought to have attempted it, but my horse was nearly done and could scarcely carry me. The Zulus were turning our flanks and the horses of two men appeared fagged, and a river full of quicksands was in our rear, therefore in the circumstances I considered it necessary to find the drift over it to secure our retreat.
>
> I have asked for a Court of Inquiry, and it sits tomorrow, General Marshall as president. I shall get wigged for the positions I took up, but trust nothing more. I may be tried by Court Martial, but I trust in my cause as it is good. I certainly told the Prince I considered the kraal safe, and I did so. I had twice been near there, once with a small escort of 3 other officers and saw nobody. Captain Stewart had ridden out with 4 officers only one day [before] to the same spot...This is a fearful business, but I do not fret, though at times I get

37   National Army Museum
38   *Royal United Service Institute Journal* 79, 1934, p. 749-751

very miserable. I do so long for the whole thing to be over. I get so done up with hard work that I can only throw myself on the ground and sleep sometimes.[39]

This letter indicates that Carey now appreciated that his failure to lead a return charge would become the principal criticism of his conduct. Once again, he makes no mention about who was in command but now admits that he told the Prince that the kraal was safe. He justifies this by explaining that the area had previously been visited and found free of the enemy. By implication therefore he was implying the lack of any defensive precautions had been due to that advice. But the fact that Captain Carey himself felt moved to request a Court of Inquiry is an interesting reflection on the state of confusion within Lord Chelmsford's busy headquarters during this critical time. There must be a supposition that, if he had not so acted, the whole matter might have lain dormant perhaps until the conclusion of the war later that same year. And yet to have continued delaying an inquiry until that time could have resulted in formidable judicial problems. Regardless of Carey's personal position, the matter simply could not be left as it was — the press was already starting to stir public opinion in both France and Great Britain. In fact there was no legal impediment to Lord Chelmsford deciding, there and then, to suspend Carey temporarily from his staff duties whilst a proper inquiry was undertaken. Perhaps he feared that any inquiry, although convened by him, might implicate him personally and thus further damage his already fragile reputation. He had to some extent been shielded during the proceedings of the Inquiry into Isandlwana but there was no guarantee that he would be exonerated in this one.

But there was another perhaps more pressing factor to distract the General. As the second invasion was getting underway, rumours were reaching him that a dissatisfied British government had already nominated a successor to replace him, and his overriding concern therefore was to now bring the war to a speedy conclusion before any such replacement arrived in South Africa. In fact, as far back as 26th May, the government had formally announced that General Sir Garnet Wolseley had been appointed, with supreme civil and military powers, to replace Sir Bartle Frere and, by implication, Lord Chelmsford. On 15th June Lord Chelmsford officially learnt for the first time that Wolseley was already at sea, on his way to assume military control. His whole mind therefore was now concentrated on reaching oNdini and bringing the war to a close as quickly as possible.

Yet Carey's request for an official inquiry to clear his name appears to have suddenly galvanised the Adjutant-General's department. Perhaps there had also been separate promptings from London although, on the basis of time alone, this would appear unlikely. From early June the home correspondent of the *South Australian Register* had been reporting a press release in South Africa that Lord Chelmsford had ordered an inquiry into all the circumstances of the Prince's death, having been directed to do so by the Secretary of State for War. The reporter also indicated that the sole purpose of the inquiry would be to establish who had been

---

39   RA. R5/15

responsible for sending the Prince into hostile territory with such a small escort — the predominant concern at the time. This report had probably been triggered off by Bettington's own inquiry. Perhaps that is why Carey's request for an official inquiry met with such a prompt response — for the court was convened immediately and began its hearings the following day — 11ᵗʰ June.

Earlier that morning, somewhat to his surprise, Carey was informed that, as promulgated in General Staff Order Number 113, he was now being removed altogether from his appointment as Deputy Assistant Quartermaster-General, to be 'attached to the 24ᵗʰ Regiment'. He later interpreted this sudden dismissal as implying that, in the eyes of the staff, he was already guilty of an offence and that he was therefore being punished before his case had even been heard. Although this particular argument was reviewed and later firmly rejected by the court martial, Carey persisted with it on his return to England. Legally, however, Lord Chelmsford had full authority to act in this way, independent of any other disciplinary action which might be taken.

The president of the inquiry was Major-General Marshall, the cavalry commander, and the two members were Lieutenant-Colonel Malthus 94ᵗʰ Regiment and Major Le Grice, Royal Artillery. It is not known precisely what its terms of reference were other than 'to inquire into the circumstances of the Prince's death.' It certainly did not restrict its deliberations, as suggested in the press, as to: 'who had been responsible for sending the Prince into hostile territory with such a small escort'. Nor did the inquiry fully consider the wider issues, such as the Prince's status and Lord Chelmsford's specific instructions to Colonel Harrison about Louis's movements away from camp, with the requirement to obtain his personal approval for individual patrols beforehand. But at the start of the proceedings, Carey, for the first time, produced the argument that he had not actually been in command of the escort and repeated an earlier assertion that Colonel Harrison had specifically instructed him not to interfere with the Prince in his duties. By implication therefore the Prince should be held responsible for the lack of any protective measures during the halt in the kraal. For his part, Harrison admitted failing to give Carey a direct order to command the escort but argued that, taking all the circumstances into account, only Carey could have assumed that responsibility. If Carey had not volunteered, he would have nominated another staff officer to accompany the Prince. The Colonel also acknowledged finally permitting the patrol to continue despite the fact that the BaSotho troopers were not present.

After listening to other related points, and having visited the site of the ambush, where an official sketch was made, the inquiry assessed all the evidence and submitted their conclusions to Lord Chelmsford that same evening:

> The Court is of opinion that Lieutenant Carey did not understand the position in which he stood towards the Prince, and as a consequence failed to estimate aright the responsibility which fell his lot.
>
> Colonel Harrison states that the senior combatant officer, Lieutenant Carey, Deputy Assistant Quartermaster-General, was, as a matter of course, in charge of the party; whilst on the other hand Carey says, when alluding to

the escort, "I did not consider I had any authority over, after the precise and careful instructions of Lord Chelmsford as to the position the Prince held."

The Court is of opinion that Carey is much to blame for having proceeded on the duty in question with a portion only of the escort detailed by Colonel Harrison. The Court cannot admit the irresponsibility for this on the part of Carey, inasmuch as he took steps to obtain the escort and failed in so doing; moreover, the fact that Harrison was present upon the Itelezi range gave him the opportunity of consulting him on the matter, of which he failed to avail himself.

The Court, having examined the ground, is of opinion that the selection of the kraal where the halt was made and the horses off-saddled, surrounded as it was by cover for an enemy, and adjacent to difficult ground, showed a lamentable want of military prudence.

The Court deeply regrets that no effort was made, after the attack, to rally the escort, and to show a front to the enemy, whereby the possibility of aiding those who had failed to make good their retreat might have been ascertained.[40]

This last comment already reflected the views of many officers and a trial by court martial was therefore inevitable. And it is evident that these conclusions had been anticipated by the staff for a Field General Court Martial was convened to meet without delay, the following day, 12th June, in the camp which had now been established on the Upoko River. The charge against Carey had been hurriedly drawn up on the advice of the Judge Advocate's representative in Zululand, Major Anstruther of 94th Regiment. It read;

For having misbehaved before the enemy on June 1st, when in command of an escort in attendance on His Imperial Highness Prince Napoleon, who was making a reconnaissance in Zululand; in having, when the said Prince and escort were attacked by the enemy, galloped away, and in not having attempted to rally the said escort or in others ways defend the said Prince.'

This court was presided over by Colonel Glyn, CB. He was in command of the 1st Brigade in the Second Division column. The members were Lieutenant-Colonel Whitehead, 58th Regiment; Lieutenant-Colonel Harness, Royal Artillery; Captain Courtney, Royal Engineers and Captain Pleydell-Bouverie, 17th Lancers. Major Anstruther, 94th Regiment, was the officiating Judge-Advocate. The prosecutor was Captain Brander of 1/24th Regiment and Captain Crookenden, Royal Artillery, was appointed defence counsel. None of these officers, including Major Anstruther, were particularly experienced in legal matters; at that time, all of them were primarily engaged in fighting a war. As Colonel Harness wrote on 14th June, 'My time for the last four days has been entirely spent on a most unfortunate business — the trial of

---

40   FEATHERSTONE, p. 110.

Carey, 98th Regiment.'[41] It is therefore not surprising that some aspects of the case were ineptly handled.

Indeed Major Anstruther himself, in a letter home, recalled some of the difficulties: 'The nuisance besides is that I can't get a book of reference anywhere; there is not one in the camp, so I have to do the best I can, in fact bring commonsense to bear on technicalities...I feel very sorry for Carey.'[42]

Carey pleaded Not Guilty and chose to conduct his own defence throughout. He based the whole of his case on two key points — that he was not in command of the escort and that, faced with a sudden ambush by a large enemy force, there was no viable alternative to *sauve qui peut*. All the four survivors, although prosecution witnesses, were closely cross-examined by Carey. They all agreed that the Prince Imperial had given the impression that he was in command. Three of the troopers further confirmed that, had they been in the Prince's situation, they would not have expected the others to hazard their lives trying to rescue them. Only Trooper Le Tocq, the last to speak to the Prince, considered that he would have expected one or more of the others to come to his rescue.

But, in his summing-up, the prosecuting officer effectively highlighted the charge against Carey:

> Think of the distance he (the Prince) was able to run after the vanishing horsemen — 250 yards according to Le Tocq, and about 225 yards by the map in a direct line — yet the Prince is left to his death by a party of mounted men, armed with breech-loading rifles, who had gained the comparative safety of the donga, in full view of which this brave young man was simply hunted down without a hand being raised in his defence.[43]

The court sat for five days altogether, working long hours each day. There was some pressure to complete the proceedings as quickly as possible. Already skirmishing operations against the Zulus were gathering momentum and the Upoko River camp itself was in a state of flux, liable to be vacated at any time. Furthermore, the more senior officers had pressing operational commands which required their presence. This situation may have accounted for the fact that, surprisingly, the court itself did not examine the site of the ambush (unlike the inquiry) and relied entirely on verbal descriptions and the previous inquiry sketch map, to envisage the scene. Yet — like the inquiry — the court martial did not address the wider issues relating to the circumstances of the Prince's death — it concentrated almost exclusively on the detailed events of 1st June, as required in the indictment. Yet despite the widespread shock and disgust at the Prince's appalling death, the court clearly went to considerable lengths to hear impartially all aspects of the case in which Carey was given ample opportunity to defend himself. However, although referred to in the proceedings, the actual text of the Judge Advocate's summing-up was not included amongst the papers and is not known to this day.

41   CLARKE, *Invasion of Zululand*, p. 143.
42   National Army Museum
43   PRO, Kew

On the last day, in closed session, the court voted a verdict of Guilty, and sentenced Captain Carey to be cashiered. At this stage, however, they were not required to formally notify the prisoner. But as the court had been re-opened in order to take evidence as to character and record of service it must have been evident to Carey that he had most likely been found guilty. Not surprisingly, the court's findings followed much the same pattern and content as those of the inquiry — indeed, some of the sentences were to be repeated, word for word. But even so the severe punishment of cashiering was to be tempered by an equally strong recommendation from Colonel Glyn, the president, to Lord Chelmsford for leniency on the grounds that: 'the prisoner was out for the second time only with the Prince Imperial and for the first time as the senior officer and did not appear to realize that he was in that position — the prisoner was employed on duty independent of that of taking charge of the Prince — the weakness of the escort in that it was composed of men not under the same discipline as soldiers and that they were not under one of their own officers — the prisoner was evidently under the impression that the Prince Imperial held some military status and was the senior officer — the prisoner's length of service and the high character he bears as testified by several superior officers.'[44] Lord Chelmsford then wrote a personal statement about Carey, which was attached to the proceedings prior to their dispatch to London, in which he made his own strong recommendation for leniency. He expressed the opinion that Carey was not a coward but that, startled by the suddenness of the attack, he had probably lost his head and forgotten that it was his duty to try and rally the men.

Afterwards Carey felt that he had handled his own defence well and was hopeful that he might, in the end, secure some sort of acquittal. However since the court's findings and sentence were subject to review by the Judge Advocate-General, and then confirmation by the Queen and the Duke of Cambridge before they could be made public, officially Carey had no idea of the outcome when he was returned to England, under military custody, aboard the Indian troopship, *Jumna*.

---

44   Ibid.

Chapter XI

A Crown of Thorns

WHEN THE NEWS OF THE PRINCE'S DEATH reached London late on 19th June 1879 the Duke of Cambridge was with a private party at the theatre. When an aide tip-toed into the box during the final act and began whispering in his ear, the Duke started, leapt out of his chair and hurried to a nearby anteroom to read the telegram from Lord Chelmsford. He then left the theatre in order to consult with his staff.

Queen Victoria was likewise informed that same evening by a separate telegram, sent by Lady Frere to her principal secretary, Sir Henry Ponsonby. About to retire for the night, she gave full vent to her feelings in her private journal:

> Just before 11 a telegram was given to me, with the message, that it contained bad news. When I, in alarm, asked what, I was told it was that the Prince Imperial had been killed. I feel a thrill of horror in even writing about it. I kept on saying, "No, no, it can't be!"...To die in such an awful way is too shocking! Poor dear Empress! her only child — her *all* gone! I am really in despair. He was such an amiable good young man who would have made such a good Emperor for France one day. It is a real misfortune. The more one thinks of it, the worse it becomes. Got to bed very late, it was just dawning! and little sleep did I get.
>
> Had a bad, restless night haunted with this awful event and seeing ever before me those horrid Zulus, thinking of the poor Empress, who did not yet know the awful news. Was up in good time. My accession day, 42 years ago; but no one thought of it in the presence of this frightful event. Had written many telegrams last night. Got one from Lord Sydney, saying he was going down this morning to Chislehurst to break the dreadful news to the poor Empress.[1]

Besides being the Queen's Lord High Chamberlain, Lord Sydney also happened to be the Lord Lieutenant of Kent, living at Frognal not far from Chislehurst, and as a distinguished neighbour, he had frequently paid social calls on the Empress and knew her well. Having already received news of the Prince's death by telegraph direct from Lady Frere, who specifically requested him to ensure that the Empress was notified before the press reports reached her, he set off at once

---

for Camden Place. On arrival at about nine-thirty, Lord Sydney encountered Lady Simmons, who had just reached the house herself, accompanied by a friend, Lady van Straubenzee.

Once in the house they were surprised to discover that, although many of her household already knew, the Empress herself still had not been told. In fact, the newspapers had all been deliberately removed from that morning's mailbag by a considerate Post Office official and although puzzled by their absence, the Empress had already started opening the morning's mail, beginning with a private letter from Captain Arthur Bigge — in which he assured her that all was well, and that despite the rough conditions in which they were living, everyone was enjoying life. As she finished reading Bigge's brief note, she spotted an official envelope in the pile from London formally addressed to M. Piétri. It was, in fact, a communication from the Duke of Cambridge. Whenever the secretary was absent (on that occasion he was in Corsica) she herself usually opened all official letters and this one included a phrase ' the distressing news from Zululand'. Thoroughly alarmed, Eugénie sent for the Duc de Bassano. In earlier discussion with Lord Sydney the ailing Duc had already acknowledged that it was going to be his responsibility, as Chamberlain to the imperial household, to inform the Empress But in the event his nerve failed him; and in her presence he could only stammer out that the Prince had been wounded. She rose from her chair in some alarm, saying that she would leave at once for South Africa, but when the old courtier began shaking his head, mumbling that it might be too late to make the journey, she started to become really agitated. Fortunately, at this moment, Lord Sydney and Baron Dr Corvisart entered the room together. As the Empress customarily only received visitors singly, she now feared the worst. Lord Sydney gently broke the news. She did not faint, nor break into hysterics, nor even cry — but simply fell back into the chair and sat there, as motionless as a statue, staring vacantly into space.

Lady Simmons and her friend, having decided not to personally intrude on the Empress, had already begun to make their way out of Camden Place, trying to avoid the many reporters in the grounds who were constantly pestering any available household staff with questions. But just as they were approaching the gates, a policeman finally caught up with them with a message that the Empress wished to see Lady Simmons. In the room, which had now been darkened, the Empress continued sitting quietly alone, but when she saw her friend enter she finally broke into tears. As Lady Simmons held her in her arms, she could only exclaim, "Oh! Madame"[2] — kissing her fervently on the forehead, trying to murmur appropriate words of condolence. Between the sobs, she told Lady Simmons that, only two days ago, she had received a letter from her son in which he said that he had met with his great English friends, Bigge, Slade and Wodehouse — that he was so happy, and all that remained to complete that happiness was for him to hear from her more frequently.

The Prince's death was a devastating blow which Eugénie, for the rest of her life, was never to really comprehend. Indeed it was often said that it took another

---

2   KURTZ, p. 309.

twenty years before she seemed to finally emerge from her sorrow and desolation. During the immediate days to come she would sit alone in a darkened room, eating very little; spending most nights in private prayer in the little chapel. She seemed to be beyond consolation. Father Goddard remained at her side for many hours, saying nothing but prayers for the Prince's soul.

From Balmoral Queen Victoria sent her a private telegram: 'My daughter and I have shed bitter tears for the dear young Prince who was so promising and the loss of whom is a misfortune for the future, and who died doing his duty in my service'[3] — then immediately left for London, arriving at Camden Place on 23rd June. It is clear from her journal entries that she genuinely expected to be greeted with reproaches and bitterness. After all, both the Empress and her son were the guests of this country and the young Prince had been in the particular care of her army. Eugénie had already lost her throne, her husband, and now her only son and heir. And with his death, the Napoleonic cause in France had likewise suffered a devastating blow. Queen Victoria's heart truly went out to her. She felt particularly ashamed, indeed angry, that the whole of her army in South Africa had proved quite incapable of protecting the young man who had been entrusted to them.

On arrival at Camden Place the Queen was received in the hall by Lord Sydney, the Duc de Bassano, the Duchesse de Bouchy, Prince Joachim Murat and several other French gentlemen. She was shown directly to the Empress's room. But when they met there were no reproaches. Victoria gently held Eugénie in her arms. Between the copious tears, the Empress recalled that: 'he had never caused her a moment's sorrow,'[4] but that he had been utterly determined to go out to South Africa. If there had been no other way, she believed that he would have even considered enlisting as an ordinary soldier. She felt deeply that he might have suffered dreadfully in those last moments; she also mentioned some rumours that two Zulus might have deliberately led them all into an ambush. But she also took the opportunity to ask the Queen if his uniform might be recovered, for clearly she was, by now, aware of that last request in his will and determined to fulfil it to the letter. The Queen, shocked at Eugénie's deathly appearance and by the discovery that she had not eaten at all in the last two days, begged her to take more nourishment and insisted that her personal physician should attend at once. Sir Willliam Jenner subsequently reported back to the Queen, "Your [own] visit has comforted her and after you left she ate something because she said you had told her she ought and she knew you would tell her only what was right, and Her Majesty added, 'I will always try to do what the Queen wishes and tells me.'"[5] But, despite Queen Victoria's encouragement, the Empress soon descended into black despondency, wishing only her own speedy death even as she prayed for her son's soul. Now a total recluse, she did not leave Camden Place for almost a month and then only for a brief walk in the garden.

On 21st June the Secretary of State for War, Colonel Stanley, interrupted the proceedings of the House of Commons to read out Lord Chelmsford's telegram. The

---

3   Ibid., p. 310.
4   RA. QVJ: 23 Jun 1879
5   Ibid.

news was received in sombre silence. At the same time he stressed that the Prince had no commission in the army and that the government bore no responsibility whatsoever for his journey to South Africa — which had been made entirely in a private capacity. Three days later the Duke of Cambridge read out to the House of Lords copies of the letters of introduction which he had sent to both Sir Bartle Frere and Lord Chelmsford, and which effectively confirmed the government's position. Subsequently, the Prime Minister expressed the deep regret of the whole nation at the loss of the Prince, 'whose life had been so cruelly and — he could not help expressing his own opinion — so needlessly sacrificed.'[6]

But in private conversation Disraeli could only cynically observe: 'A wonderful people, the Zulus. They beat our Generals, they convert our Bishops, and they write *finis* to a French dynasty!'[7]

In a personal note to the Queen the Duke of Cambridge confessed: 'I am really in utter despair and I feel as deeply as if I had lost a very dear and near relation.'[8]

On 21st June, anxious to learn for herself exactly what had happened so that, in turn, the Empress might be protected from irresponsible rumours, the Queen, with the approval of her cousin, personally telegraphed Major-General Marshall, the cavalry commander in South Africa, instructing him, as the president of the inquiry, to submit as soon as possible, directly to her, a comprehensive account of the Prince's death.

On 22nd June, the Lord Chamberlain ordered Court Mourning for ten days until 2nd July. Four days later Colonel Stanley, in response to a number of questions tabled by several members, informed the House of Commons that Lord Chelmsford had attached the Prince to his personal staff, and by reading extracts from his letters to Lady Chelmsford, confirmed that the General Officer Commanding: 'had done everything possible for the safety, comfort and well-being of his illustrious guest.'

As the news of the Prince's death spread throughout Europe there was a spontaneous and impassioned reaction. Many sympathetic European courts immediately announced their own periods of official mourning. In Britain there was a deep national sigh of genuine sorrow. In fact this particular tragedy was to cause far more press comment and public discussion than the earlier disaster of Isandlwana. Eventually it was to become the most talked about event of 1879. For days it almost dominated newspaper headlines and leaders. The Prince had already won considerable popularity in this country before setting out for South Africa, and his lonely but heroic death at the hands of the Zulus moved a great many people to tears. It was not until later that the furore about Captain Carey's conduct, and the news of his subsequent court martial, began to overtake the circumstances of the Prince's death as the top news story. And then it was not long before many sections of the press began to argue that, in truth, Carey had simply been made the scapegoat for the inadequacies of others, more senior, who were collectively and equally responsible for setting the stage for the loss of the Prince. Within weeks a wave of public sympathy for the disgraced Carey started to gather momentum.

---

6   MOODIE, p. 155.
7   *Cambridge History of the British Empire*, Vol 8, p. 478.
8   RA. R5/76B

In France, the news caused an immediate storm of protest and recriminations. There was a surge of Anglophobia. As long as he lived the Prince would always be a threat to the stability of the Third Republic, but now that he was dead and that threat removed, even the most ardent Republican could rage over Britain's evident treachery. There was an unexpected resurgence of national sentiment about '*le petit Prince*' — the true Child of France.

And in the eyes of many Bonapartists and others, England could now legitimately be blamed for all their past and present misfortunes. To them the logic seemed irrefutable. For had not Napoleon the Third, with his lifelong obsession for close ties with Great Britain, allowed himself to be seduced from his paramount duty of protecting France's true interests? Furthermore, had he not died at the hands of English surgeons? And now the Prince too had been needlessly killed, ostensibly in the care of the British Army whilst fighting in one of Britain's petty colonial conflicts.

But if the Prince had proved unable to unite the French people in life he certainly succeeded in death. Paul Deléage had already reported the circumstances back to *Le Figaro* and practically the whole of the French press now took up his theme — that the Prince had been betrayed by the British Army and by one of its officers, Captain Carey, and that both were entirely responsible for the tragedy. As more detail became available concerning the actions of Captain Carey the cry went up, 'Oh! To see it printed in their journals and to think the nation is not wiped out, that it's impossible to sink their accursed island *et ce peuple froid, barbare, perfide, infâme!*'[9] It seemed that, alone, out of the whole patrol, only the courageous young Frenchman had seen fit to stand his ground and fight the Zulus whilst his English comrades, led by Carey, had deliberately abandoned him to his terrible death.

The *vice-empereur* Eugéne Rouher was so stunned by the news that he remained speechless for about an hour, with his half-demented wife shrieking that it would be best for them both to die. The Bonapartist party started in its slide into bitter despair. 'In the presence of death,' wrote the *Moniteur*, 'universal political divisions should be silent. As for ourselves we do hesitate to incline before the mourning of a woman thrice sanctified by misfortune, who has borne the title of Empress of the French. There is not a mother in France — and, we may add, there is not a man of heart — whom her sorrow does not strike and her grief does not touch.' *Le Journal des Débats* added: 'In the presence of so tragic an end we can only remember one thing — that the Prince was a Frenchman, and that he has died a soldier's death.'

The first Requiem Mass for the fallen Prince was celebrated at Saint Augustin church in Paris on 26th June. This solemn service was attended by hundreds of people; the church was filled to overflowing and many people had to stand outside. In the front rows were 'Plon-Plon' accompanied by his children, Marshal MacMahon and family, and the Queen Mother of Spain. The Papal Nuncio headed the large diplomatic contingent in full dress uniform. The government, on this occasion, made no attempt to interfere — nor, over the next few weeks, did it oppose the very many memorial services for the Prince being held up and down the country in every city,

9 JOHN, p. 486.

town and village. And whilst many extreme Republicans publicly saluted the Zulus, the general mood throughout the country was sadness, tinged with anger, at the loss of such a prominent young Frenchman in such bizarre circumstances.

Thus, over the next few weeks English travellers to France found it prudent to keep out of public view, and even English firms in Paris and elsewhere felt obliged to close their shops and shutter their windows until passions had cooled. No-one in France could accept that the Prince had been killed, accidentally, like any other soldier on the field of battle — he could only have been murdered, perhaps assassinated, and therefore somebody must be held to blame. The less responsible elements of the French press inflamed public hysteria further by stating, as a fact, that the Prince had been deliberately led to his death by the British — in connivance with others. The conspiracies had variously involved either Queen Victoria, or Leon Gambetta, or the Communists, even the Freemasons! The Freemason conspiracy theory, with its suggestion of secrecy and mystery, was finally developed into a full length book — *La Mort du Prince Impérial (Les crimes maconniques)* — which was published in 1891, with a special foreword by the Prince's great Catholic friend, Baron Tristan Lambert!

But one of the more telling jibes was the widespread feeling that the British Army would have taken a great deal more care had one of Queen Victoria's own sons been out in South Africa. This theme was also developed by some of the British press. On 21st June *The Morning Post* commented: 'Had an English Royal Highness been attached to the staff of Lord Chelmsford what blame would not have been imputed had he been allowed not once, but repeatedly, to proceed upon small and dangerous reconnaissances?.'

In its leader on that same day, *The Daily Telegraph* attempted to smooth French feelings: 'At least his death on duty with the valiant British Army should be accepted by the French people as an expiation — if expiation were needed — for the disaster and humiliation of Sedan...The young Prince was neither coddled nor spoilt; and the Emperor Napoleon the Third knew how to rule and, upon occasion, to rebuke his son.'

In its edition of 28th June the *Illustrated London News* spoke for many when it observed: 'The Republic has been strengthened by an event which most Republicans, as well as others, will personally deplore...but it is not in a political so much as in a personal sense that the untimely end of the Prince Imperial will be viewed by the world at large. So much promise nipped in the bud! Such manliness, modesty, gentleness and highly-trained intelligence snatched from this life by the hands of a few barbarians! Such a cruel contrast of what is — with what might have been.'

There was even the suggestion in some newspapers that, had the Zulus at the time realised the importance of the brave young white officer they had so viciously hacked to death, they might have chosen to remove the body — and dictate subsequent peace terms to Lord Chelmsford and thus inflict an even greater humiliation against Great Britain than the disaster of Isandlwana. On 28th June *The Army and Navy Gazette* published a lengthy article which offered strong support to Lord Chelmsford, explaining: 'The cares of the Commander of an Army in the field are too absorbing to admit the functions of Governor of a Royal visitor being added.

The Prince was simply a private individual acting as a volunteer, and had to take his chance with other private individuals present, such as newspaper correspondents.' But this approach conveniently ignored the fact that, unlike them, Louis had been wearing a combatant British officer's uniform and had undertaken military tasks as agreed by senior officers.

But, out of all the many questions and comments, three viewpoints in particular stood out — effectively answering most of the others. On 24th June *The Times* shrewdly pointed out that the Prince had only gone out to South Africa in the first place in order to win a military reputation for himself, and to achieve that, he would inevitably want to be exposed to danger. He had to be seen as brave, daring and courageous. He could not be seen as shielded and cosseted everywhere he went, for this would only play into the hands of his political opponents. Elsewhere, in a minor provincial newspaper, one reporter had echoed the Prime Minister's own perceptive comment by adding: 'The excitement is too great to reason calmly on this subject: but the reflection is forced upon us, that here has been solved one of the most difficult problems of French history.' To that *La Liberté* added 'Perhaps the Prince's premature end spares him the hazards and trials of an existence which politics would have ruined as was the case with his father.'

Augustin Filon lay ill and almost blind in his Paris apartment in the Rue de Ponthieu. He could hear newspaper boys outside, crying out about the death of a Prince, but when he asked for the details was told it was the Prince of Orange. This deception was kept up for almost two months, with neighbours collaborating to keep the paper boys away from the street, until one day, when his sight suddenly improved, he perceived his wife was dressed in black. Then he realised the truth. But it was not until 1881 that he was well enough to travel to England and meet once more with the Empress.

At Camden Place the party faithful and supporters gathered to offer their condolences. But Eugénie saw practically no-one. Indeed she rarely spoke at all, communicating only her essential needs by brief notes. As the Vicomtesse Aguado wrote to a friend: 'The Empress has been sitting for three hours in her armchair without speaking or moving, her hands in mine. I only knew she was living by the slight pressure of her poor, thin hands when my weeping became too violent and she wished to stop my tears.'[10]

Despite her bitterness over what had happened, Eugénie harboured no vindictive feelings towards Captain Carey. Indeed, when Queen Victoria next visited Camden Place, the Empress specifically asked the Queen that no action should be taken against him, as 'he may have a mother'[11]. Naturally, this would hardly have been her attitude if she had been a reigning Empress — but, shorn of all power and in lonely exile, there was no real alternative to magnanimity. The Queen, of course, appreciated that Eugénie would have had little understanding of her constitutional position, which effectively precluded her from interfering with the course of justice, but nonetheless Victoria promised to see what could be done. At that stage, Victoria felt that Carey himself had probably just panicked but, unlike

10   JOHN, p. 488.
11   RA. O35/60 — Letter from Queen Victoria to Lady Frere dated 23rd July 1879

the defenders of Rorke's Drift when so many of her brave soldiers had won Victoria Crosses, this escort, in terms of personal courage, had simply been found wanting. But her attitude was to harden in the weeks ahead.

It has often been said that both the Queen and the Empress constantly argued for leniency and their pleas greatly influenced the Duke of Cambridge's final judgement on the Carey case. But, in fact, the Empress was meticulous in not lobbying the Duke personally with her views (although she did make public a statement calling for no recriminations) and the Queen had never taken the view that Carey must be treated leniently. In any case, whatever their private opinions, they made absolutely no difference. The constitutional position throughout was clear. Even though the Queen had strong personal feelings about the whole business, she was quite powerless to intervene in the administration of justice.

The proceedings of the court martial, as was customary, were first perused by the Judge Advocate-General, Mr Cavendish Bentinck, and his deputy, Mr James Cornelius O'Dowd. They quickly concluded that Carey's conviction could not be upheld. In the first place there was no record on the first page of the proceedings to indicate that the president, and the individual members of the court, had actually been sworn-in — as required under military law. It is not clear how this fatal omission occurred. The Judge Advocate-General accepted that the swearing-in might conceivably have taken place, but deplored the absence of any written record to that effect. This omission alone was enough to raise serious legal difficulties about validity of the trial itself. Should it be considered advisable, for example, to reassemble the same court, the omission, if established, could conceivably render the whole proceedings null and void. Furthermore, the Judge Advocate-General could not understand how Carey could have been charged with failing to 'defend' the Prince, when he had never been specifically ordered by a superior officer to do so, any more than he could have been charged with failing to 'defend' the two troopers and native guide who had likewise perished on that day. And what, in these contentious circumstances, constituted 'misbehaviour'? Mr Cavendish Bentinck could not help but conclude that the focus, in both the indictment and in the evidence, had been almost entirely on 'defending' one particular person, who also happened to be a Prince, but the legal issues applied equally to all those involved. There were other concerns. In the charge against him Carey was described as 'being in command of the escort' and thus primarily responsible for what had occurred. But the evidence did not sustain this statement — indeed, quite the contrary. Looking at the transcript it appeared that right up until the last moment actual command had been exercised by the Prince. Furthermore, the court, in its final recommendation for mercy, had also specifically supported the contention that Carey was under the impression that he was not in command; that he was junior in rank to the Prince.

The customary procedure in these matters was for the Judge Advocate-General to forward his recommendation direct to the Queen who would then automatically give her confirmation. The documents would then be returned for him to forward on to the Adjutant-General who, in turn, would submit the whole proceedings to the Duke of Cambridge for his final ruling as Commander-in-Chief. However, in the case of Captain Carey, the Judge Advocate-General's office chose to act quite differently. Alert to all the political ramifications which might possibly arise from Carey's acquittal and aware of the Queen's deep personal interest in the case, he decided to discuss the matter with her beforehand at a special audience in Windsor Castle. At first the Queen was keen to have the same court re-assembled. But, regardless of the legal problems, she was to learn that this course had already been rejected outright by the Cabinet, who, most unusually, had also been given copies of the proceedings to enable them to consider the wider political aspects. Yet, at the end of the day, all these departures from the norm made absolutely no difference to the final outcome of the Carey case. The Judge Advocate-General's concerns about the validity in law of the court martial were supported by the highest legal authority in the land, the Lord Chancellor, Lord Cairns. Carey's conviction, therefore, could not be upheld, regardless of the political or military consequences, or the personal views of any particular individual. In a letter to the Duke of Cambridge, dated 16th August, the Deputy Judge Advocate-General notified the Commander-in-Chief that the Queen had been advised not to confirm the proceedings.

But Victoria only accepted this advice with the greatest reluctance. She recognised that she could not 'confirm' a sentence which was dubious in law, but nonetheless considered that Carey should not be permitted to continue serving in her army:

'I daresay,' she wrote in a terse note to the Duke of Cambridge, 'that *legally* Lieut. Carey has *not* committed a fault *capable* of being punished *as an act of cowardice*, but I *do* think that *no* Prince, or far less than a Prince, that no friend, no Superior — no fellow-creature should be left in great danger, without those with him or one of them being prepared to lay down his *life for him*. I am sure *thousands* would do it.'[12]

The Empress was quite unaware of all the controversy surrounding the court martial proceedings. It had been her hope that perhaps the Queen would exercise her royal prerogative to grant Carey a full pardon which, whilst not absolving him from blame, would release him from formal retribution. But, in confiding this hope, she clearly did not understand the legal position nor indeed the depth of the Queen's own feelings about Carey.

On 8th August, at the height of all the clamour, the Empress issued her only public statement about the death of her son, sentiments which were widely published in both France and England and which were read everywhere with considerable sympathy and respect. Her tolerance and magnanimity in the face of so much personal provocation and distress struck a deep chord, and had some influence in calming the situation.

> My only source of earthly consolation I derive from the thought that my beloved son fell like a soldier, obeying orders in a duty assigned to him, and that those who gave him these orders did so because they believed him competent and useful.

---

12   RA. R7/82

Enough of recrimination: may the remembrance of his death join in a common regret all who loved him, and may no one suffer either in reputation or in material interests — I, who can desire nothing more in this world, make this as a last request.

Speak in this sense to all, English or French.

Eugénie[13]

The Duke of Cambridge was in a difficult situation for which he was not particularly well equipped intellectually to resolve. Despite the legal advice, there was great pressure from within the army that Carey must be punished and seen to be punished, if the honour of the officer corps was to be upheld. The Adjutant-General strongly recommended that, whilst the sentence of the court martial might legally be quashed, Carey must still be blamed publicly for abandoning the Prince. No junior commander of soldiers, it was argued by a number of senior officers apart from General Ellice, should ever get the impression that it was considered acceptable to abandon those soldiers to a danger from which he had taken steps to personally remove himself. But the Duke also felt obliged to take into account the Empress's well known views for leniency, as expressed in her recent public statement, and the strong feeling in the country that Carey had simply become a scapegoat for others who had made their own contribution to the tragedy. With more and more information now becoming public, people could judge that feeling for themselves — in turn, the Government had officially disclaimed all responsibility for the Prince's presence in South Africa; the Duke of Cambridge's guidance to Lord Chelmsford, now published in full, had been ambiguous; Colonel Harrison had demonstrably failed to carry out Lord Chelmsford's written instructions regarding the Prince's safety; and the smallness of the escort had finally placed Carey in an impossible situation, not of his making.

As these issues were being vigorously debated privately within Horse Guards and publicly in the newspapers, the Zulu war was finally brought to an end. On 4th July 1879, barely six months since the first invasion, the Zulu *impis* were ruthlessly broken by the concentrated firepower of modern weapons and their Royal kraal, oNdini, razed to the ground. It burned for four days. All that remained was the capture of King Cetshwayo and the political dismemberment of his former kingdom. Eleven days later, on 15th July, Lord Chelmsford formally handed over command to General Sir Garnet Wolseley, and accompanied by Brigadier-General Wood and Colonel Buller, all in need of a complete rest, he returned to England.

On 16th July the Queen received the private report from Major-General Marshall. In it he described all the known circumstances of the Prince's death, but in the preamble he also observed: 'Everyone was much struck by the fund of knowledge he possessed regarding the affairs of South Africa. Not only had he grasped the political situation but his acquaintance with the habits and customs of the Zulus and with the geography of their country was a result that could but have been due to careful and accurate study.' Over the page he disclosed that: 'Upon 29

---

13   FILON, p. 228.

May a forward reconnaissance was made by Lord Chelmsford and his staff for some 22 miles in advance including the neighbourhood of the kraal where the Prince was attacked.' In the final paragraph he summarised everyone's feelings: 'The Army had received a stunning blow. From all ranks the cry was heard — could they have only been with the Prince.'[14]

Captain Carey himself finally arrived under close arrest at Plymouth on 20th August. He had little idea of what to expect, and was totally taken aback at the warmth of his welcome at the dockside.

A city dignitary offered a petition, signed by nearly three thousand citizens, expressing their complete confidence in his valour as a British officer. And it was not long before Carey realised that a large section of the British press was actually championing his cause. Journalists considered that many others besides senior officers were just as much to blame for the circumstances which had cumulatively led to the disaster — a finger might well be pointed at the Queen herself who, after all, together with the Empress, had personally lobbied for the Prince to be allowed to go to South Africa against the expressed wishes of the Prime Minister and of the Cabinet.

In due course Carey was to receive the formal congratulations of the Leicester Liberal Club, and from many other comparable organisations who, in a typically British way, had now begun to feel some sympathy for the underdog. He now started giving interviews to journalists, consistently emphasising that the Prince himself had been in command of the patrol and that it was his decision, not Carey's, to off-saddle in the vulnerable kraal area. He also hinted that Louis was often boastful about his position, and tended towards insubordination. But during all these interviews he took particular care not to implicate any of his superiors. But the more he spoke, the more favourable was the publicity he received and the more confident he became. Whilst Carey undoubtedly had a case in his favour — at least on the scapegoat issue — and enjoyed much sympathy in certain quarters, he now foolishly proceeded to gradually undermine that support by persistent exaggeration, even blatant lies. The Empress could only express her disgust at the growing public sympathy for Carey in a letter to her mother: 'If I wanted him pardoned I was far from thinking that they would *glorify* a man whose only claim to posthumous fame is that he saved himself as fast as his horse could carry him, leaving behind him a comrade and two men.'[15]

But few members of the public — least of all the Queen and Empress — could really acknowledge the reality of what had happened on that fateful Sunday afternoon. How many people knew that it was the Prince himself who had sought permission to mount the patrol in the first place? And many conveniently overlooked the fact that the Prince himself had insisted on leaving without the BaSotho escort — troopers who would have protectively screened the kraal throughout that halt. And there could hardly be public recognition that the Prince himself was as equally engaged as the others in fleeing out of the ambush; that he had taken no steps of his own to assist those — such as Trooper Rogers or the native guide — who were

14   RA. R7/33
15   RIDLEY, p. 605.

in the greatest danger of losing their lives before his was even threatened. There was also the uncomfortable fact that, despite his known prowess with the pistol, even after three shots, the Prince had been unable to wound, let alone kill a single one of his attackers. It was being said that in final desperation Louis had hurled the pistol at the nearest assailant — but subsequent testimonies by the participating Zulus made no mention of any such dramatic flourish.[16] Furthermore, even if he had not actually ordered the patrol to halt in such a vulnerable locality, he must nonetheless share some of the blame for that unwise decision — making a further contribution to the disaster by also delaying their subsequent departure. Louis was renowned for his superb horsemanship yet he had apparently failed to mount his horse without stirrups, a feat he had accomplished many times elsewhere. And even if he had successfully mounted and escaped, would he then have rallied the patrol, charging back in order to rescue the others? Or would he have agreed with Carey that to return immediately would have probably resulted in the needless loss of all their lives? And, in those circumstances, would Carey have been court martialled for failing to defend the two troopers and Zulu guide, with the Prince a key witness? But such unpalatable observations and queries could hardly be expressed, let alone discussed. In any case they have been totally inadmissible to either Queen Victoria or the Empress, as well as to many others, both within the army and outside. The Prince had died the death of a hero — and nothing, nothing whatsoever, must ever be allowed to tarnish that fact.

Many people who knew the Prince well were particularly puzzled at the apparent inability of the Prince to vault on to his horse — an equestrian skill for which he was particularly renowned. Captain Lord William Beresford, 9th Lancers, when being decorated with the Victoria Cross after the war, privately told the Queen that he had been out with Louis but two days before, and held the same horse he had ridden on 1st June — but he noticed that the Prince, for all his great agility, seemed to have some difficulty in mounting. Lord William said to him, "He's too high for you, sir." — to which he observed: "No!" The problem appeared to be his artillery patrol trousers — they were too tight — interfering with his ability to mount. 'Lord William maintained it was *that* which had prevented him from mounting — and *not* the breaking of the saddle strap.'[17] And Lieutenant Wodehouse support this view. Almost fifty years later he recorded in a letter: 'As far as his failure to mount I am sure there was no question of any part of his saddling giving way, it was naturally all good and new. There was a *sauve qui peut* and his horse probably plunged and broke away.'[18]

Accurate or not, this evidence is certainly consistent with the condition of the saddle today — as displayed in the *Musée National du Chateau de Compiégne*, north of Paris — where neither the holster, nor saddle straps, appear to have been ripped in two.

---

16   RA. R 10/20. After the war General Sir Evelyn Wood personally questioned ten of the Zulus involved, his wife making written record of their individual testimonies.
17   RA. R8/56
18   RA. Add.J/1561. Letter from General Sir Josceline Wodehouse to Lord Stamford ham dated 1st November 1928

It is a reflection of the social attitudes of the period that, during all the public debate and controversies, little consideration was given to the fate of the two irregular troopers or the loyal Zulu guide, even though a query on their fate and burial was, on one occasion, raised in the House of Commons. On 11th August Mrs Harriet Carey wrote a letter to *The Echo* in which she stressed that her son, ever the soldier's friend, had personally taken steps at the time to see they were all decently buried. At the site today, whilst there are individual crosses for Troopers Abel and Rogers, and a small central plaque showing their names and the circumstances of their deaths, there is no reference to their Christian names, nor even to their initials. And inexplicably, even today, there is still nothing to properly commemorate the loyal native guide who had not immediately abandoned the patrol when the danger had first become apparent, and whose mutilated body had finally been found about a mile away from the kraal. In many ways his conduct had been the most courageous of all.

On 20th August Carey — the day of his disembarkation — had been officially informed about the findings and sentence of the court martial by Prince Edward of Saxe-Weimar, the general commanding the Southern District. But directly after learning that he had been found guilty and sentenced to be cashiered, he was also handed a copy of a despatch from the Horse Guards to General Sir Garnet Wolseley in Zululand, dated 16th August.[19] Signed by the Adjutant-General on behalf of the Duke of Cambridge, it formally notified the fact that Her Majesty had not confirmed the proceedings of the court martial since the charge had not been sustained by the evidence, and that therefore the prisoner could now be released. Whilst the despatch completely exonerated Lord Chelmsford himself, it did include sharp criticism of Colonel Harrison's inadequate arrangements over the command of the patrol. It also strongly deplored the manner in which Captain Carey had finally withdrawn from the ambush scene, without first ensuring that nothing could be done to save their comrades. But the Duke did not specifically address the *sauve qui peut* controversy, and, by implication therefore, was presumed to endorse immediate flight in the face of sudden danger.

The following day Carey issued a statement of his own, welcoming the acquittal, considering that his honour as an officer and English gentleman had now been fully vindicated.

But the Duke of Cambridge's despatch, once in the public domain, simply raised far more issues than it settled, and throughout August and September a vigorous debate continued to rage within the popular press and in many military journals both in Britain and abroad, about its implications. Some considered that, although acquitted, Carey should have been publicly and unequivocally admonished for abandoning everyone, not just the Prince. But one of the most contentious issues was the Duke's apparent endorsement of the *sauve qui peut* philosophy, which was quite unacceptable to many officers. Whereas a newspaper such as *The Morning Post* considered immediate withdrawal: 'To be the legitimate and customary word of command when a reconnaissance party is suddenly attacked', General Simmons

---

19   RA. R8/34 — See Appendix A for full text.

promptly intervened with this indignant reply: 'There had been *no* word of command after the word "mount". If Carey believed the Prince to be in charge, how had he dared to go off and leave him without an order?' But, in any case, he went on, 'what was military duty at such a time?' No written law was needed, any more that it was needed by a climbing party in Switzerland; men held together and helped each other out, 'by the laws of comradeship'. There were no cases in which the party had deserted a comrade, so long as there was the slightest chance of saving him. And then he cited the well-attested deeds of Buller, Beresford and others, 'who, at imminent risk of their own lives have given glorious proof during this unfortunate war that they did not recognise the *sauve qui peut* principle when on reconnaissance.'[20]

And yet the same Colonel Buller, who had so castigated Carey immediately after the ambush, later began to excuse him, arguing that it was the officer's first time under fire (which in Carey's case was not true) and that, 'to the end of his career, (he) refused to condemn a man for one mistake'.[21] But Colonel Buller was well known for frequently contradicting himself. Colonel Harrison, still serving in Zululand, took strong exception to the Duke's particular criticism of his competence — and subsequently submitted further written evidence in refutation which has never been made public. In any case the criticism had absolutely no effect on his career. He clearly had many champions of his own. Colonel Buller personally told Queen Victoria that, "Colonel Harrison...could not be blamed...for he had most nervous and responsible duties to perform".[22] After the battle of oNdini, to the surprise of many, General Wolseley gave the comparatively junior engineer colonel command of Brigadier-General Wood's former Flying Column; subsequently he was appointed a Companion of the Order of the Bath for his services during the war. Indeed, by the end of his military career, Harrison had risen to general rank and secured a knighthood.

Queen Victoria, having granted Carey her commission in the first place was irritated to discover that she did not have the power to order its removal.

Many in the army were utterly disgusted at Carey's release. Captain Bettington expressed his own feelings in a private letter to the Duc de Bassano, 'I trust Her Majesty knows that had it been fated that I should have been in Carey's place, I should have taken the same care of His Highness as I did on previous occasions, and that if I could not have saved him I would have remained with him.'[23] Captain Arthur Bigge lamented, 'Whenever I think of the last moments of his life, when I think of the desperate struggle he must have endured while the helping power was disappearing further and further in the distance, I sorrow for his cruel death and think how different it all *might* have been, indeed *ought* to have been...His enemies in France will now at all events learn what a formidable foe he might have been had he lived...I shall never forget him.'[24]

---

20   FEATHERSTONE, p. 162.
21   POWELL, *Geoffrey. Buller: A Scapegoat?* Leo Cooper, London 1994
22   RA. R8/82
23   KURTZ, p 315
24   Ibid., 314.

Another officer in Lord Chelmsford's army probably spoke for many when he opined; 'Everyone here believes that if Lieutenant Carey had kept his men together, and faced about too, opening fire as they came on the Zulus, if they had been cool enough to do it, the Prince would have been saved. It was the stampede that encouraged the enemy to leave the hiding-place from which they had fired.'[25]

Even Rifleman Lomas told Queen Victoria during a special audience at Windsor Castle: "I would have died a hundred times to save him."[26]

The majority view within the army recognised that, in the first horrifying moments of the ambush, an immediate *sauve qui peut* flight may have been unavoidable but the abrupt withdrawal from immediate danger also afforded an opportunity for a calmer consideration — and if it was not possible to have rescued the Prince there and then, the most honourable and courageous action would have been to have returned and died — fighting alongside him.

In France the unexpected news of Carey's release from arrest and punishment simply intensified public condemnation. It resulted in the most disparaging comments about the British Army, its code of conduct, and the alleged collusion between the various factions in English society, from the Queen downwards, to pervert the course of justice. For the French the acquittal was but confirmation of a perfidy which had long since been suspected, and which no amount of English explanation would ever dispel.

On his return from South Africa at the end of September the journalist Archibald Forbes gave a lecture on the war at Shoreditch. When he described finding the Prince's body, he emphasised, "I wish to speak tonight only of brave men, and therefore I will ask to be excused from making any reference to Lieutenant Carey." This remark caused an immediate uproar, with someone calling out above the din: "Three cheers for Carey!" — whereupon these were enthusiastically given by many in the audience. Forbes was at a loss to know why anyone would want to cheer a man 'who had run away', leaving his comrades to their fate. He could only put it down to the peculiarly English penchant for always championing the underdog. In his book *Memories of War and Peace* he wrote of the Prince he had once ridiculed: 'To be slain by savages in an obscure corner of a remote continent was a miserable end, truly, for him who was once the Sun of France.'

There was a further aspect to the Carey story which is still a mystery. About a week after the Prince Imperial's funeral in England, a certain Miss Octavia Scotchburn visited his wife and persuaded her to hand over the emotional letter which Carey had written from his tent during the night of 1st June. Miss Scotchburn considered that if the Empress could only see the letter for herself she would be moved to sympathy for the Careys. On 23rd July she duly posted the letter to the Empress, adding that Mrs Carey had given her approval, requesting Eugénie to read the contents and then return it. In fact, Marie de Larminat, the Empress's lady-in-waiting, replied that, because Eugénie was still very distressed, a copy of the letter would be taken with a view to showing it to her later. Although, in time, the Empress did look at the letter and had it translated into French for a number of

25 FEATHERSTONE, p. 176.
26 RA. R7/2

friends, she still took no further action during the period when the public controversy over Carey was at its height. In this she showed remarkable restraint considering the potential damage the letter could do to Carey's case. But she had no wish to further embarrass or humiliate the Queen, or her army. The letter remained with her until 31st August, by which time the controversy over the Duke of Cambridge's dispatch had begun to abate, when she sent a copy to Queen Victoria, describing the background circumstances, but also explaining that she had refrained from taking any action earlier for fear of influencing the final outcome of the Carey case.

In vain did Queen Victoria try to establish exactly who Miss Scotchburn was — some reports indicated that she was a teacher, living in Dartmouth, who had been in Paris during the Second Empire and who, after Sedan, may have been arrested as a Bonapartist spy. But the mystery remains. Whoever she was, she clearly missjudged the situation for publicising what Carey had written that night could only aggravate the situation.

Indeed, armed with the letter, Queen Victoria now took steps of her own to try and force Carey to resign from the army. She arranged for copies to be sent most senior officers, as well as to a number of leading political figures, inviting their personal comments. And when the officers who had distinguished themselves in the Zulu War were specially presented to her at Balmoral she ensured that each person likewise received their own copy. Nobody had any excuses to make for Carey; everyone considered the letter a full admission of guilt. But Queen Victoria was mistaken in thinking that social pressures alone would finally drive Carey into resigning his commission. On the contrary, now that he had been released and thus exonerated, Carey had misguidedly concluded that only one further act was needed to totally clear his name — a personal audience with the Empress. To that end he started communicating with the Duc de Bassano at Camden Place, letters in which he sought the Empress's agreement to officially receive him. For a while the Duc responded to the letters, pointedly disregarding the request for an audience whilst politely inviting Carey to publicly withdraw some of his earlier statements which placed the blame wholly on the Prince. Eventually Carey's letters became so clumsy and insensitive that the Empress herself finally instructed her lady-in-waiting to bring the whole correspondence to an immediate end. He thus received a short, terse note from Marie de Larminat: *'L'Impératrice juge inutile de poursuivre cette correspondence.'*

But that did not deter Carey. Despite the lack of response, he continued writing to Camden Place. But from now on all his letters were simply forwarded, unopened, to the Queen. She, in turn, arranged for them to be translated and further copied for distribution, without comment, to people of influence. Handing one of the letters to Disraeli, she told him that, in her view, it was quite scandalous that Carey should have been released. In his reply the Prime Minister said that whilst he agreed in principle it was, taking all the circumstances into account, probably the best course. But to forestall her inevitable wrath, he took the precaution of confirming to her in writing: 'He is a caitiff, and yet the Court Martial had so mismanaged the case...

that it is highly probable that if their verdict had been sanctioned, this mean wretch might have been transfigured into a hero or a martyr."[27]

But Captain Carey persisted in continuing his military career. He finally rejoined his regiment in Malta and went on to serve with them in India. It has always been said that his brother-officers simply turned their backs on him whenever he appeared, and that all refused to speak to him. But such a situation, if true, would surely have become quite intolerable for so highly a strung individual who constantly craved the approval of others. It would seem reasonable to assume that he could not have been shunned by every single person, and that he did have at least a degree of sympathy, if not support, from even within his own regiment. He died only four years later from peritonitis whilst serving in Karachi.

HM Troopship *Orontes*, carrying the remains of the Prince Imperial, arrived off Portsmouth on 9th July. The country of his exile had now prepared to receive him like one of its own national heroes. On the personal instructions of Queen Victoria a naval warship had been sent to escort the vessel the remainder of the journey from Madeira. At Portsmouth the Admiralty yacht *Enchantress* ploughed out through heavy seas, coming alongside the ship in the early hours of 10th July to receive the heavy box casket and convey it to Woolwich. On board were a large number of senior army officers, French officials, as well as personal friends, including Prince Joachim Murat (representing the Bonaparte family), Vicomte Aguado, the Marquis de Bassano (son of the Duc), Comte de Turenne, M.Rouher, M. Piétri, Baron Dr Corvisart, Louis Conneau, Bizot and Espinasse. But, because of the rough sea conditions, the elaborate arrangements for receiving the casket had to be scaled down and consequently it was finally transferred to the yacht without the planned religious service or gun salutes. Placed in a cabin on the after-deck which had been turned into a chapel, the casket was now to be directly attended by Captain Bigge, Uhlmann, Deléage and Lomas. General Simmons also transferred to the vessel for its voyage to Woolwich.

But the *Enchantress* had a very difficult passage along the south coast and did not arrive until four o'clock that afternoon. The riverside was lined with silent spectators. The whole garrison, soldiers and civilians, had turned out in force. There was also a contingent of about three hundred French mourners. A huge canopy had been erected on the quayside. The imperial casket was lifted ashore by sailors in the presence of a special guard of honour formed from the Company of Gentlemen Cadets and to a salute from the band of the Royal Artillery. It was then borne to a small building at the western end of the wharf. Formerly an armoury, the interior had now been totally draped in black, the entrance decorated with Napoleonic emblems. Shortly after the casket had been settled, the Prince of Wales and the Dukes of Connaught, Edinburgh and Cambridge entered, all wearing ribbons of the honorary *Légion d'honneur* and the French military medal. They formally paid their respects, after which all the English representatives quietly withdrew. Outside the Prince of Wales summoned Colonel Pemberton and asked for a personal briefing about the tragedy. Meanwhile, Eugéne Rouher had insisted that French law must be

---

27   RA. R8/74

applied and the remains now officially identified, despite last minute representations to the contrary by Eugénie's private secretary, M Piétri. The Empress had repeatedly urged a dispensation so that her son's remains might be left in peace but, as so often in the past, the Bonapartist faction continued to ignore her wishes, suspecting a possible trick.

Beside Rouher and Piétri, the French group included Prince Joachim Murat, Baron Dr Corvisart, Dr Evans, Louis Conneau and Xavier Uhlmann. When the casket was finally prised open and the Frenchmen peered in, they saw with horror that the hasty embalming at Koppie Allein had totally failed and that decomposition had long since begun. The ravaged face was totally unrecognisable. Uhlmann slowly crumbled to the floor in a faint. Although deeply distressed himself, Baron Dr Corvisart started examining the remains, looking for evidence of that earlier operation on the hip, whilst the American dentist, Dr Evans checked the dental debris against his records. It was the number of gold fillings which settled the identification. After a while Rouher, choking with emotion, declared himself 'satisfied' that this hideous figure was indeed Prince Louis Napoleon. But his declaration alone was quite inadequate to dispel the later rumours that the remains were, in fact, those of a complete stranger; and that the Prince alive, or his body dead, had simply vanished for ever into the myths of history.

With the formal identification completed, the remains were now transferred to an inner leaden shell and then placed into a splendid coffin of mahogany, covered with dark violet velvet and decorated with gilt handles. This was lifted on to a Royal Artillery gun-carriage, to be drawn by six black horses, and covered with both the Union Jack and French tricolour. At about seven the procession set off for Chislehurst. Throughout the short journey the coffin was escorted by three batteries of Royal Horse Artillery and a squadron from the 5th Lancers. Twenty-three guns fired in salute from Chislehurst Common. At Camden Place, in the large picture gallery, the coffin finally lay in state on a catafalque which had been covered with a violet velvet pall, embroidered with golden bees — the Napoleonic emblem. On it rested the same ribbon of the *Légion d'honneur* which had graced the Prince's cradle, and countless wreaths, one of which, inscribed in the Queen's own hand, bore the words: *To him who lived the purest of lives, and died the death of a soldier, fighting for our country in Zululand.* The walls were adorned, not totally in black but in white with black drapes to honour the Prince's blameless youth. The ceiling was covered with imperial emblems. Marie de Larminat, always something of an Anglophobe, could only express her disgust as she now gazed in tears at the coffin: "We gave them a young man at the height of his charm and beauty, and now they return us a corpse."[28]

That night the Empress maintained a sleepless vigil in prayer beside the bier. But at the end of the gallery the Prince's closest French friends — Louis Conneau, Bizot and Espinasse — all kept a discreet watch, maintaining their own personal vigil. At five in the morning Father Goddard said Mass before the catafalque, after

---

28   KURTZ, p. 332.

which she was finally helped to her room to remain in seclusion for the rest of the day. In accordance with custom she did not attend the funeral.

In her feelings of guilt and shame at the Prince's needless death, Queen Victoria strongly argued that his funeral was the one opportunity to publicly make amends to France and to the Bonaparte family, and she therefore intended to be present herself, together with her immediate family. She also expected the attendance of all her Ministers. Furthermore, she proposed at some point during the ceremony to personally place the Order of the Bath on the top of his coffin. But these proposals were to prove totally unacceptable to the Prime Minister and the Cabinet. Disraeli pointed out that the government of the French Republic would interpret any royal funeral for the Prince as a political insult. The Cabinet also strongly advised her not to bestow the Order posthumously in this manner — which was against all precedence. But the Queen did not give in easily; she continued to harangue her exasperated Prime Minister. She was well aware of Disraeli's deep distaste for all the Bonaparte family, and the special dislike he had always shown towards Louis himself, but the Prime Minister could have been under no illusions as to the depth of her feelings. In the end she achieved a partial success. The Prince did have a truly royal funeral (although she did not attend the service herself), but her wishes about the Order of the Bath and attendance by the whole Cabinet had to be quietly abandoned. But the Queen's palpable anger at the Cabinet's refusal to attend persuaded two of her Ministers, that of War and the Colonies, to have a last minute change of heart. Both subsequently felt it prudent to be present.

The Prince Imperial was buried on 12th July 1879. As the Queen intended the funeral was an occasion to be remembered — conducted with all the splendid panoply of deep mourning which so characterised the ceremony of death, and particularly high-ranking death, in the late Nineteenth Century. Starting from an early hour, thirty-two special trains set out from London, carrying over eleven thousand passengers to Chislehurst. Almost a thousand policemen were on duty to direct the traffic and control the huge crowds, thought to exceed forty thousand, now assembling on the Common. The Queen, accompanied by the Princess of Wales, Princess Alice and Princess Beatrice, together with a large suite, drove into the grounds of Camden Place just before eleven o'clock that morning. After being received in the hall by the Duc de Bassano, the royal ladies entered the picture gallery to kneel in private prayer at the catafalque.

Subsequently, in the room which had formerly been the Prince's study, various members of the Bonaparte family, led by 'Plon-Plon', were presented to the Queen. Victoria thought him looking older, plumper and balder — in fact, now more like his uncle, the Great Napoleon, than any other member of the family. On this occasion he was very subdued and studiously polite to the Queen. When she offered her condolences, he could only mumble, *'C'est bien triste. Votre Majesté a été si bonne'.*[29] His sister, Princess Mathilde, was however more assertive. She simply could not understand how the Empress had ever allowed a Napoleon to go and fight for the British in the first place, and in response to the Queen's condolences, she replied

---

29   RA QVJ: 12 Jul 1879

rather tartly that Louis must have been quite 'mad' to have risk his life in this way. The Queen gently parried that unworthy remark by observing that she considered it to be only natural that the young Prince should want to distinguish himself — '*de faire quelque chose*' — with his life. The Queen was also introduced to 'Plon-Plon's eldest son, Victor who, at seventeen, had been nominated by the Prince Imperial as his successor, and to his younger son, Prince Louis Bonaparte, then thirteen.

The Empress had been shown her son's will shortly after his death. At an emergency meeting on 15th June party supporters had declared 'Plon-Plon' to be their new leader. But as the details of the will leaked out a second meeting was held on 30th June in Eugéne Rouher's house in Paris. The Empress, despite her overwhelming grief, still had the presence of mind to try and prevent them from publishing the will — rightly anticipating that the controversy over the succession would bring about a terminal split within the Bonapartist party. But, as usual, Rouher and his colleagues disregarded her cabled wishes and published the details. Rouher, in particular, had no wish to continue serving the imperial cause under Prince Jerome Napoleon or either of his sons, and therefore chose to make this his final act before quitting politics altogether. Not surprisingly, 'Plon-Plon' was outraged at being further disinherited and challenged its legality. He immediately blamed the Empress. Yet he never sought to discuss the matter with her; indeed, during his presence that day at Chiselhurst as chief family mourner he chose not to meet her. He pointedly declined an invitation to take tea privately afterwards. Although Princess Mathilde accepted Eugénie's goodwill gesture, her brother abruptly left the house immediately after the funeral.

At eleven o'clock, the coffin was carried out of the house on the shoulders of ten officers of the Royal Artillery and placed on a special gun carriage, drawn by six horses. As before the coffin was draped with the flags of France and Great Britain. At the front of the carriage stood two soldiers carrying a huge wreath. With arms reversed, some two hundred Gentlemen Cadets from the Royal Military Academy led the procession to the little church of St Mary's, barely half a mile away, followed by the mounted Royal Artillery band with muffled drums, playing the solemn Dead March from *Saul*, and then the gun carriage itself. The coffin was covered with wreaths of flowers, including one from Queen Victoria placed there at her personal request. Two artillerymen sat in front holding the Empress's own wreath of white flowers. On either side, in dress uniform, walked the Prince of Wales, the Dukes of Edinburgh, Connaught and Cambridge, the Crown Prince of Sweden and Norway, the Prince of Monaco, the Duc de Bassano, and Eugéne Rouher. The gun carriage was followed by the Prince's horse, led by a groom, not 'Percy' from Zululand but his favourite horse in England, 'Stag', caparisoned in black and gold. Xavier Uhlmann and Lomas walked on either side. 'Plon-Plon' together with his two sons, then led the long procession of mourners which included other members of the Bonaparte family; many leading figures and generals of the Second Empire (but not the former President, Marshal MacMahon, who had been specifically forbidden to attend); almost ninety deputies from the French Chamber of Deputies; the Turkish, Austrian, Italian (but not French) ambassadors; representatives of the Army and Royal Navy, and many personal friends.

The Queen and her suite were shown to a specially erected black-draped dais from where they could watch the whole procession as it made its way to the church. It began to rain, but despite the light drizzle thousands, many dressed in black, turned out to watch in silence as the Prince made his last journey, the route lined by the 5th Lancers and other regiments. Gentlemen raised their hats in salute, whilst many stood with heads bowed as the cortege slowly moved past. Three batteries of the Royal Artillery on Chislehurst Common solemnly fired minute-guns until the procession had arrived outside the church. Here a further detachment of Gentlemen Cadets formed a lane through which the coffin was borne towards the entrance. As it passed, the detachment fired three volleys from their rifles.

Once inside the church all the English officers filed away, giving pride of place to the Prince's former military tutors and aides, who now stepped forward to take their positions at each corner of the coffin — the former Commander Duperré (now an admiral), General the Marquis d'Espeuilles, Commandant Comte de Ligniville and the old riding groom Bachon. During the Requiem Mass 'Plon-Plon' remained standing throughout, staring directly ahead, pointedly refusing to participate in the ceremonies. Unsure of Catholic ritual, the Princess of Wales felt it prudent to remain on her knees throughout, until one of the priests gently motioned her to rise.

Sitting alone in a darkened room in Camden Place the Empress could hear the solemn minute guns telling her that her son was being laid to rest beside his father — in the private memorial wing which she had specially built on to the church in 1873. Thereafter, from twelve o'clock, almost ten thousand French supporters alone filed through the little church to pay their last respects. At the same time, Masses were being specially offered for the Prince throughout Great Britain, in the Dominions and Colonies, in America and in many of the cities of Europe. And one of the Prince's distant cousins, Cardinal Lucien Louis Bonaparte, offered the first Mass in his titular church in Rome to the Prince, a service which was attended by senior Italian figures as well as by many foreign residents.

As Queen Victoria and Princess Beatrice were preparing to leave the Empress sent a message, inviting Her Majesty to call and see her. The room was in almost total darkness, but after the two sovereigns had embraced each other, they both burst into tears. The meeting only lasted a few minutes; little was said. The Empress then asked specially for Princess Beatrice, and when the Queen's youngest daughter came into the darkened room and knelt before her, the Empress reached out, raised her up, and embraced her tenderly.

It was only a day after the funeral that Eugénie, venturing into Louis's room, was horrified to see that the saddle had suddenly arrived from Zululand. She fainted at the sight. Already there was a steady stream of Louis's last letters and each one was tearfully read time and time again. Over the next few weeks, she became obsessed by a desire to know every single detail about the events of 1st June, asking to see every relevant newspaper report and magazine article. Constantly seeking assurance that Louis had not cruelly suffered in his last minutes, Baron Dr Corvisart and Louis Conneau between them soothed her by explaining that, in the heat of the moment, with all the fever pitch excitement and the adrenalin pumping through his body, the Prince would have probably felt little pain. Understandably, most people did their utmost to shield the Empress from any distressing fact, supporting her burning desire to visualise her son's last struggles in the most heroic terms. Inevitably, she was soon to commission an artist — Protais — to produce oil paintings of his gallant charge at *Napoleon Kraal* and later, of his body in death, sword in hand. These remained amongst her possessions for the rest of her life.

Amongst the personal belongings which also now began arriving from South Africa she discovered, rolled up in a truncheon, a page cut out from a radical French newspaper which repeated all the former insults about Saarbrucken and which described the Prince's illness during those early days in Durban as 'the hereditary disease of the Bonapartes'. Over the years, Louis had rarely complained to her about these taunts — but she was beginning to realise that they had, in fact, been upsetting him for a long time. She had also found other equally derogatory newspaper cuttings referring to the Saarbrucken bullet incident, his putative cowardice in fleeing France and the Prince's alleged incompetence at Woolwich tucked away in a locked drawer in his study. The Empress could only complain bitterly to her friends, "You see! It wasn't the Zulus that killed him. It was the French papers."[30] General Simmons could feel equally aggrieved. As a former Governor of the Woolwich Academy, he continued to receive abusive letters from France, vilifying the Second Empire, and seeking a public statement from him that the Prince Imperial had really been a nincompoop Gentleman Cadet. To add to the insulting accusations, many of the envelopes were left deliberately unstamped, boldly annotated — *Payez la poste.*

Eugénie tried to draw consolation from all this — she told Queen Victoria of her growing certainty that her son's death: *'was to be*, and that he may have been spared much anxiety and sorrow.'[31]

She would spend hours talking to Xavier Uhlmann, who was still grieving so deeply that he had hardly been able to walk in the funeral cortège. She quizzed Lomas as well. He told her of his sorrow at not participating in the patrol of 1st June, since it would have been his duty, as always, to hold the Prince's horse to enable him to mount. He also reassured her that, in death, her son's face looked peaceful and content. The Empress felt drawn to this straightforward old soldier who was so clearly devoted to Louis; she subsequently invited him to stay on at Camden Place in her personal service which he did, in the position of senior groom, for many years.

Towards the end of August Lord Chelmsford and Colonel Redvers Buller both called to pay their personal respects. The former Commanding General brought with him the Prince's sword and riding boots which the Zulus had returned a few weeks after his death. During various abortive peace negotiations prior to the final battle of oNdini, Lord Chelmsford had insisted on their return. They were eventually found in Sabhuza's kraal, and emissaries from the King had brought Napoleon's sword, together with his riding boots, to the British headquarters on 30th June. Lieutenant Lysons, an aide to Brigadier-General Wood, and a great admirer of the Prince, personally retrieved the sword and duly handed it over ceremoniously to Lord Chelmsford in front of the Flying Column.

---

30   JOHN, p. 497.
31   RA. 035/60 Letter from Queen Victoria to Lady Frere dated 23rd July 1879

During the visit to Camden Place Lord Chelmsford also told the Empress, "how much he was beloved by everyone that knew him and how well prepared to be suddenly called upon to give an account of his stewardship...I am certain that a fairer-minded, more straightforward, right judging gentleman could not be found."[32]

Shortly afterwards Captain Molyneux, Lord Chelmsford's aide-de-camp, was granted a special audience. He told her in detail how they found her son's body, and she was particularly gratified to have confirmatory reassurance that his features showed no sign of any pain and that his face, in death, had seemed to be entirely at peace. The young officer also handed over the envelope with the medallions and locks of hair. Directly after his visit she wrote in some anguish to her mother in Spain:

> He told me that my beloved child, finding himself pursued, turned to fight till the end. He looked death in the face like the hero he was. What a drama, what grief! He thinks the struggle went on for a long time, as my son was an expert with his weapons and the ground around showed that his resistance had been desperate! And we must say that God in His mercy gave him such a death!
>
> My head spins at this thought and the crown of France must indeed be accompanied by many struggles and sorrows for there to be any consolation from the letters I still keep receiving! Death is preferable to that crown of thorns people call the crown of France.[33]

Major-General Marshall, the cavalry commander, also called at Camden Place and described her son in glowing terms: "The boy had the noblest, finest character in the world, pure and brave as any hero in history."[34] But she drew particular comfort from a public speech given at dinner by General Sir Evelyn Wood — when he referred to all those who had given their lives whilst under his command:

> In remembering those brave spirits, and that gallant youth — the son of England's Ally — whose mother is our honoured guest, I am reminded of the question and answer in Shakespeare, for humanity is the same in all ages:
>
> *Your son, my Lord, has paid a soldier's debt.*
> *He only lived but till he was a man,*
> *The which no sooner had his prowess confirmed*
> *In the unshrinking station where he fought,*
> *But like a man he died*
> *Had he his wounds before?*
> *Ay — on the front.*
> *Why then — God's soldier he be!*

32 RA. O35/123 Letter from Lord Chelmsford to Ponsonby dated 30th August 1879
33 TURNBULL, p. 368.
34 JOHN, p. 507.

Had I as many sons as I have hairs,
I would not wish them a fairer death.

Of the gallant Prince Imperial we may say: 'Ay — all eighteen wounds in front'[35]

The Army and Navy Gazette devoted a complete leader to the death of the Prince which aptly summed up the feelings of most officers: 'The grief of the British nation...and its sympathy with the heart-broken mother seem to increase rather than diminish. It is almost as if we had lost one of our own Princes and were sharing the sorrow of our Queen. Everything known...was to his advantage. He possessed... every quality which constitutes the true hero. Amiable, unselfish, upright, single-minded, clever, clear-headed, of noble sentiments, pure in morals, high-spirited, and endowed with rare personal courage, he was a noble example to his age.'

General Simmons had been profoundly upset at the Prince's death — apart from his frequent public interventions during the furore in the press over the circumstances, he also disclosed his personal feelings in a letter to a brother officer, pointing out that he had seen a great deal of the Prince Imperial: 'since he was first placed under my charge by his father in 1872, and from his peculiar position was so often consulted by him as to his studies and pursuits and he had become so free and open with me that I had long since learnt to appreciate his many good and high qualities, his perfect truth and honesty of purpose, his self denying perseverance in his endeavours to fit himself for the high position to which he believed that some day France, by the Will of God, would call him, and his thorough determination that no act of his should ever cast a reproach upon his name or country, or upon this country and its institutions which from his education amongst us he regarded with gratitude and affection...He was also quite a young philosopher, very quick and generally accurate in observation and fond of generalising.'[36]

And recalling the Prince's personal qualities many years later, Lieutenant Wodehouse described: 'one occasion, when there was some skylarking going on, one of the Prince's young French friends made some slight offensive remark or gesture, the Prince was very angry. '*Mais c'est ignoble*' and I only mention this to show how scrupulously high minded he really was.'[37]

Queen Victoria now took steps of her own to assist the Empress on the long road to recovery. She invited Eugénie to travel north to Scotland and take a complete rest in her private residence at Abergeldie, close to Balmoral, and after much persuasion the Empress agreed. About the middle of September, accompanied only by Marie de Larminat, she occupied the isolated and unpretentious castle-house for a few weeks. Here, in all weathers, she would go for long walks across the moors sometimes alone, sometimes with her lady-in-waiting. On other days the Queen would often call in for a chat, accompanied by her Highland groom John Brown;

---

35   Ibid., p. 508.
36   RA. R7/59 Letter from General Simmons to Lt Colonel Pickard 22nd July 1879
37   RA. Add.J 1561 Letter from Sir Josceline Wodehouse to Lord Stamfordham dated 1st November 1928

on more than one occasion, she would take Eugénie to a local beauty spot where the two of them would sit together entirely alone, sipping tea and reminiscing about former days. The Queen, knowing of Eugénie's particular pleasure in the company of Arthur Bigge, also arranged for the young officer to be on hand, temporarily attached to her staff at Balmoral.

She herself also grew to like the young artillery officer, thus starting a personal relationship which was to blossom into permanent royal service, with Bigge eventually resigning his commission to serve as Assistant Royal Secretary under Sir Henry Ponsonby. In her journal entry for 27th October 1879, the Queen noted: 'After tea saw Captain Bigge with whom I had a long talk. His grief for the poor Prince's untimely death is very great, and he would do anything for the dear afflicted Empress. After Khambula Bigge became very ill indeed, and the Prince Imperial came to see him in hospital when he said he hoped they would meet again soon! This was only a week before the Prince was killed and, humanly speaking, it seemed more likely that Lieutenant Bigge would die than that the other should happen. He cautioned and begged the Prince to be very careful which he promised he would. The great misfortune seems to have been that the Prince was attached to the staff instead of with his old battery, where such a catastrophe could never have happened, and secondly, that he had not one of the French gentlemen with him. Captain Bigge said that the Prince was so good, so excellent, and that, the older he grew the more this would have showed itself.'[38]

By November, under the supervision of Lieutenant Colonel Villiers, President of the Boundary Commission, the Prince's lacerated and bloodstained uniform had finally been recovered from various Zulu kraals. All these items, together with the residue of his personal belongings, arrived in England the following January. The original intention had been to have the clothes thoroughly cleaned before return to the Empress, but she directed otherwise. After positive identification by Uhlmann and Lomas in London, Colonel Villiers finally brought them with him to Camden Place. The items included Louis's pith helmet (with its distinctive blue stopper), his waterproof coat, the slashed artillery patrol jacket (which the Zulus had clumsily sewn together), the breeches, a woollen shirt and bloodstained chamois leather hunting waistcoat. Additionally, there was his leather pouch still filled with 22 cartridges and a purse containing some money.

Despite her distress at seeing the tattered, bloodstained garments, Colonel Villiers was at least able to give Eugénie some comfort. In a small ticket pocket of the lightweight waterproof coat (the pocket siphonia), which the Prince had worn earlier that fatal morning to keep off some light drizzle, he had found a crumbled piece of paper which could have been torn from his notebook. In what appeared to be the Prince's very faded handwriting the following words had been scribbled: '1.30 June 1st — Started from Itelezei to find camping ground for 2nd Division; escort under Captain Carey'. Describing these words as 'a voice from the grave'[39] the Colonel produced the note as irrefutable proof that Carey had been in charge of the patrol on that day. Startled by the discovery Eugénie showed the scrap of

38   BUCKLE, *Letters of Queen Victoria*, Vol 3, p. 45.
39   FILON, p. 208.

paper to General Sir Evelyn Wood, who in turn used it to confirm that not only had Carey been officially in command of the escort, but that the Prince had also been aware of that fact. Indeed General Wood referred to the scribbled note in his own autobiography *From Midshipman to Field Marshal*, where he repeated the same interpretation; that the scrap of paper proved that the Prince could not be held responsible for the disaster. Others likewise concluded that the discovery of the note neatly solved the vexed problem of who precisely was in command that day.

But had the General inquired more carefully into all the circumstances he would have quickly concluded that the scrap of paper must be a forgery. The Prince's notebook had already been recovered intact and the last entry, timed at 1.20, referred to their activities on the flat-topped hill before descending down to the kraal. But apart from the time error, the patrol had not, in fact, started from Itelezei — it had formed up and then set off from the old camp at Koppie Allein, on the left bank of the Blood River. At Koppie Allein the Prince had left his personal belongings; here he had scribbled that last letter to his mother, describing the patrol and its purpose. It was only after the ambush that the fugitives had returned to the new camp — at Itelezi. And why had the scrap of paper been torn out of the notebook and tucked away separately in the ticket pocket of the lightweight waterproof (which the Prince had only briefly worn earlier that morning) when the notebook itself had been recovered intact? But the most compelling evidence of all lay in the reference to Carey's rank. On 1st June he was still a Lieutenant — indeed, he was not officially promoted to Captain until five days later. In South Africa Carey was only ever known as 'Lieutenant Carey'; but by the time he had come to public notice in England and France he was then always correctly referred to as 'Captain Carey'. The faked note was clearly an attempt to apportion blame and must have therefore been deliberately fabricated, either by a devotee of the Prince or by a detractor of Carey's. Perhaps Colonel Villiers himself — who did not conceal his own private distress at witnessing the Empress's anguish — felt driven to provide some calming evidence of his own. For, intentionally or otherwise, despite its cruel deception, this scrappy note had succeeded in giving much needed comfort to a distraught mother.

She also derived solace from a number of public speeches about her son. At a dinner of the Trinity House Corporation, the Duke of Cambridge, for the first time, disclosed that the Prince Imperial had wanted to go out to South Africa to show his gratitude to the Queen and to the country which had not only offered him refuge, but had treated him so generously. The Duke also disclosed more detail about their various communications: 'As to his courage, singly enough I had observed on several occasions the intense dash in his character, and in a letter I have from him he thanks me for having given him a hint on that very subject. I had said to him that he should not run unnecessary risks or expose himself unnecessarily; I gave him that hint; but so strong was his desire to see service, and to show the noble spirit which dwelt within him, that he could not restrain his feelings in any way, and if the opportunity occurred he would only be anxious to go to the front. The result is deplorable; but there can be no question the feelings were noble and generous, and I am only grieved that a life so valuable should have been so unhappily cut off.' In the same speech, he had described the Prince as 'a thoroughly good, high-minded, high-principled young man.'[40] The Prince of Wales — the future King Edward the Seventh — was to publicly lament: 'If it had been the will of Providence that he should have been called to succeed his father as Sovereign of that great country our neighbour, I believe he would have proved an admirable Sovereign and that he, like his father, would have been a true and great ally to this country.'[41]

Within the British Army there was a feeling that a suitable memorial to the Prince should be erected. This proposal was endorsed by the Duke of Cambridge and a special committee, under his chairmanship with the Prince of Wales and the Duke of Connaught as members, was established to oversee the arrangements. It was decided to limit any one individual contribution to one pound. *The Times* commented: 'There cannot be any doubt that the Army will eagerly seize this opportunity of testifying to the intense feeling of sorrow and pain which pervades its ranks...Few events in our time have aroused among all classes such overpowering sympathy, and it is well that this sentiment should be expressed by some memorial which will be a permanent and public record of it.' With the considerable sum subsequently raised, the committee commissioned Baron Gleichen to sculpt a bronze statue of the Prince, standing alone, with binoculars and sword, wearing the undress uniform of an officer of the Royal Artillery. There was considerable discussion over the statue's proposed location.

The Prime Minister was notified of the Monarch's views in a letter of 20th June 1880, 'The Queen agrees in thinking that Woolwich would be the fittest place for the Army's memorial...to the dear young Prince Imperial...He studied there with great distinction and served with the Artillery — and it will be an example to *all* to follow him in his pure and unselfish and very studious life! But it will *also, alas!* be a perpetual reminder that he was deserted by an English officer — who (from some extraordinary mis-management) still wears the Queen's uniform.'[42]

The statue, positioned at the apex of the lawn facing the front of the Royal Military Academy at Woolwich, was unveiled by the Prince of Wales on 13th January 1883.

Arthur Bigge thought the statue, 'good as to likeness of attitude though the figure is of a rather stouter built man than the Prince.'[43] That November General Simmons took the Empress to see the statue and show her round the Prince's rooms in the Academy.

Many years later — in 1947 — when the Woolwich Academy was finally closed down a detachment of Royal Engineers transported the statue to the Royal Military Academy at Sandhurst where, facing the New College square, it continues to provide a permanent remembrance of the special 'Queen's Cadet'.

Eugénie was fifty-three when the Prince Imperial was killed. At the time she herself did not expect, nor indeed wish, to survive much longer; she certainly did not expect to live on for another forty one years. Early in 1880 therefore she decided to

---

40   FEATHERSTONE, p. 143.
41   ARONSON, p. 163.
42   RA. A52/35 Letter from Ponsonby to Gladstone dated 20th June 1880
43   RA. J87/17 Letter from Captain Bigge to Queen Victoria dated 13th January 1883

make a pilgrimage to Zululand — in time to be able to spend the first anniversary of Louis's death in the donga where he had died. She wrote to Piétri on 3rd January:

> I feel myself drawn towards this pilgrimage as strongly as the disciples of Christ must have felt drawn towards the holy places. The thought of seeing, of going over the last stages in the life of my beloved son, of finding myself among the places on which his eyes looked their last, in the same time of year, to spend the night of the first of June, watching and praying over his memory! — this has become a need for my soul and an aim for my life. Since the end of the war has allowed me to think of this possibility with more chance of its fulfilment, it has been my ruling thought. This idea sustains me, and revives my courage; without it I should have no power to re-act and I should let myself go, waiting for sorrow to wear me out...I am under no illusions, I know the griefs that await me over there, the long and painful journey, the fatigues of so rapid a voyage, but all disappears before the thought of Itelezei.[44]

Queen Victoria immediately offered the Empress every assistance, recommending General Sir Evelyn Wood as the best person to organise and lead the expedition. Eugénie greatly admired General Wood and was content to place herself in his care — in return, the General only requested that the Empress, for her own safety, must agree to abide by all his instructions! As a serving officer, General Wood was compelled to go on half-pay for the four month trip; however Queen Victoria made arrangements to provide him with £5,000 to meet all the expenses and, on return, the General was still able to hand back £3,600! The British government likewise offered every facility for her journey in which she was to be accompanied by Lady Wood, the Marquis de Bassano, Surgeon-Major (now Colonel) Scott who had found the Prince's body, Captains Bigge and Slade, and by a number of other officers as well as Rifleman Lomas. Also included in the party was the Hon. Mrs Campbell, the wife of General Wood's principal staff officer, Captain The Hon. Campbell, who had also been killed during the war. The Empress took an instant liking to Mrs Campbell, the daughter of an Anglican bishop, and found her constant presence a great comfort. Captain Bigge had been privately instructed by Queen Victoria to keep her properly informed by letter about their progress, and this he did at regular intervals.

They embarked at Southampton on 25th March, a few weeks before her fifty-fourth birthday, sailing the following day, and after an uneventful voyage arrived at Cape Town on 16th April. Although the Empress had quite enjoyed the sea trip she started becoming very depressed in Cape Town, weeping frequently, and as a consequence, found herself quite unable to speak with Sir Bartle Frere, still the Governor-General of the colony. Whilst in the city the Marquis de Bassano went to the castle in which King Cetshwayo was now being held captive. The King took the opportunity to express his nation's regret at the death of the great *induna*, whilst

---

44   FILON, p. 230.

reminding his visitor that he had responded promptly to Lord Chelmsford's demand for the return of his sword — this being the first news he had received about the unfortunate event. But the King appeared to have no particular knowledge about the events of 1ˢᵗ June; he could only say that he believed that only about ten of his warriors had been involved in the ambush..

From Cape Town, the Empress wrote to the Queen: 'What cruel emotions I felt when I saw the places from where my poor child started full of hope and believing that he had found the opportunity for showing he was worthy of his name — that heritage which is so hard to bear...What misfortune that the Emperor should have married a Spaniard, and I a Napoleon! Our son naturally had to be the victim. Through my race I gave him the gift of Quixotism, the readiness always to sacrifice all to an ideal: the Emperor gave him the obligations of his name. And all in the middle of the Nineteenth Century when materialism closes in on us like weeds from all sides.'[45]

The ship arrived at Durban a few days later. By the end of April the party, which with mounted police escorts and guides now totalled about eighty people, had started their long journey into the interior. They covered the three hundred miles from Pietermaritzburg to the river Ityotyosi in about four weeks. For most of the way the Empress travelled in a spider carriage accompanied either by Lady Wood or Mrs Campbell. During the overnight halts, Eugénie would sometimes sit sadly in her tent reading yet again the Prince's letters; on other occasions she would set off for brisk walks before darkness fell. After visiting many of the sites known to the Prince — *Fort Napoleon* (Conference Hill), Khambula, Wolf Hill, Koppie Allein and *Napoleon Kop* — they finally reached the Ityotyosi on 25ᵗʰ May, in good time to become thoroughly orientated before the date of the actual anniversary. As soon as they arrived at the scene of the ambush that evening the main party held back so as to allow the Empress to walk alone, accompanied only by Lomas, down the donga to the place of her son's death. She seemed to know exactly where to go. But then she experienced a terrible pang of disappointment. In front of her was a scene quite different from the one she had always imagined.

Two months earlier a working party, commanded by Major Stabb, 32ⁿᵈ Regiment, had transported to the site a memorial cross which had been specially carved in Pietermaritzburg. This had been commissioned by Sir Bartle Frere, and Major Stabb had erected it on the personal orders of General Sir Garnet Wolseley. Although officially commissioned, the cross had in fact been ordered privately and discreetly by Queen Victoria, who wished it to be emplaced in good time for the Empress's visit. Later on, the Government of Natal was to formally protest at the lack of prior consultation.

On the front the following letters had been engraved:

THIS CROSS IS ERECTED BY QUEEN VICTORIA IN AFFECTIONATE REMEMBRANCE OF NAPOLEON EUGÉNE LOUIS JEAN JOSEPH THE PRINCE IMPERIAL TO MARK THE SPOT WHERE WHILE ASSISTING IN A

---

45   KURTZ, p. 316.

RECONNAISSANCE WITH THE BRITISH TROOPS ON 1ST JUNE 1879 HE WAS
ATTACKED BY A PARTY OF ZULUS AND FELL WITH HIS FACE TO THE FOE.

Directly after the Prince's body had been recovered, a detachment of the
King's Dragoon Guards had left a small commemorative pile of stones to mark
the precise spot. Major Stabb therefore arranged for the cross to be erected on a
solid foundation of concrete directly behind this small cairn. He was assisted by
local Zulus — some of whom may have taken part in the ambush. The party had
also dynamited part of the donga walls in order to ensure that, during the rainy
season, any water flowing down to the Ityotyosi would be deflected well away from
the memorial site. In addition, they had planted some hardy trees which had been
brought specially from the Pietermartizburg botanical gardens. Finally, using the
stones from the kraal cattle enclosure, they had built a small wall to delineate and
surround the whole complex.

But Eugénie was unhappy and distressed at the scene now in front of her. In a
letter the Marquis de Bassano described the site, and her feelings:

> Near the cairn raised by the soldiers on the morning on June 2nd, 1879,
> a cross had been erected by order of Queen Victoria. All vestige of the
> grass trodden by her son and watered with his blood in his last fight had
> disappeared beneath a layer of white cement, surrounded by an iron railing.
> The soil of the donga had been carefully raked as far as the top of the banks
> which bordered it. The two soldiers who were killed in the skirmish of June
> 1st at the same time as the Prince were buried a few paces away, with the result
> that the spot represented the peaceful and orderly appearance of an English
> cemetery instead of that of a wild ravine which had witnessed a scene of
> death and carnage. The Empress experienced a bitter disappointment, if one
> can rightly apply this commonplace word to this particular instance.[46]

Everyone could sympathise with the Empress in her dismay, and Captain Slade
immediately arranged for the offending layer of cement to be removed first thing
the following morning. During these drawn out days at the Ityotyosi, waiting for the
anniversary, the Empress slept badly and ate very little. She spent much of the time
praying at the site and with her own hands, planting little shrubs brought specially
from the garden of Camden Place. She also planted a willow and an ivy shoot by
the cairn marker where he had actually fallen. But, despite her own depressed state,
she continued to show great kindness and consideration for others. One evening,
Captains Slade and Bigge together with Mrs Campbell, had set out for a long walk
and become hopelessly lost. Fortunately, whilst stumbling around in the darkness,
they managed to perceive a light in the distance — it was a lamp being carried
personally by the Empress who had ventured out, alone, beyond the camp site in the
hope of guiding them safely back.

The Marquis wrote again on 29th May:

---

46   FEATHERSTONE, p. 190.

The Empress can see from her tent the road taken by the Prince from the kraal to the donga; and as it is exactly the same season, the maize and the grasses are the same height as they were this time last year. As she goes from her tent to the donga she can picture the poor Prince, running by the side of his horse, vainly trying to mount him, and prevented from so doing by the tall grass (taller than myself by 30 or 40 centimetres), crossing a first branch of the donga, climbing a bank, and then stopping to meet his foes in a small hollow before one reaches the main donga — which was crossed by Carey at a point eighty paces away from the Prince with great ease as we have all been able to verify for ourselves. The Empress is continually going over this tragic road, and passes most of her time in what we may now call the cemetery.[47]

On the day of the anniversary, 1st June, he wrote again:

We had arranged to be collected here as many as possible of the Zulus who took part in the attack of June 1st. Eighteen men have come, about the same number are still missing. As the Empress wished that the inquiry should be conducted by General Sir Evelyn Wood, he began to question the Zulus the day after our arrival. I am the only other person present at these examinations which have now lasted three days. Nothing is more painful than to find one's self face to face with these savages, and listen to them explaining how they pursued and killed our poor dear Prince, accompanying their recital with what they consider appropriate gestures, and which are horribly significant! Up to now we cannot draw any very certain conclusions from their confused and often contradictory accounts; but they all agree that the Prince turned and fought like a lion, and fired three revolver shots, and that they left the medals on his corpse, as their custom is not to despoil of their neck ornaments brave men who die fighting. They all confirm the flight of Captain Carey, and they showed us the place where he crossed the donga, eighty paces above the point where the Prince stopped. We have crossed the donga on horseback, with the Empress exactly at the same place, and we have verified that it is impossible not to have seen it from it the whole of the hollow now occupied by the cairn and the cross; one of the Zulus even told us that, if the fugitives had but turned round, they would have stopped the pursuit.[48]

They were also able to establish that the warriors had been sent out by King Cetshwayo to identify the routes being taken by the invading columns. They had first spotted the patrol at the point when they were making their way down from the flat-topped hill towards the kraal. Totalling about forty, the Zulus had then split into two groups, one to attack the party resting in the kraal and the other to cut off any possible retreat through the donga. They also revealed that King Cetshwayo's

47 Ibid.
48 Ibid., p. 191.

orders were that, in battle, they were to kill everything that moved — hence the spearing of the kraal dogs. Another puzzle which General Wood was able to resolve concerned the sword. The Empress had a vivid picture of Louis falling, Napoleon's sword in hand; the Protais painting she had commissioned showed his prone dead body, right hand still clasped round the hilt. She was therefore dismayed to learn from the General that, during the skirmish, he had somehow dropped the sword and had fought only with his pistol and an assegai. As Captain Slade wrote later: 'I tried to persuade the Empress that it was much braver even to turn and defend oneself with one of the enemy's arms than with one's sword.'[49]

Eugénie expressed her own feelings in a letter to her private secretary:

> My dear Monsieur Piétri,
>
> You are doubtless aware that I am only a few steps from the place where my beloved son rested before he was surprised by the Zulus. Here also I take my rest, but I do not sleep, my soul is full of bitterness, regrets and sorrow; it is a curious thing, but I can only find peace near these stones which mark the spot where he fell, fighting, with his last breath, "like a lion", as the Zulus say.
>
> If you were to see this spot, you would understand the surprise attack and the events which followed it, but what one cannot understand is how this man left a brother officer and two soldiers to their fate without giving them the least support. I have retraced for myself the road which he took, and he must have seen the Prince and heard the revolver shots, because we have experimented with one, and the man who was sent in Carey's tracks heard the shots quite plainly...It fills my heart with bitterness to think that this precious life has been so wantonly sacrificed, and that this child, left alone, fell fighting like a brave soldier with no witnesses of his courage except a handful of savages one degree removed from brute![50]

Thus the Empress was able to confirm for herself the most damaging point levied against Carey by the prosecuting officer at his Court Martial.

She spent the night of 1st June, alone, in silent prayer beside the cross at the foot of which a number of candles had been lit. Afterwards, she made a record of her sensations:

> More than once I saw black heads appear on the top of the slope; they moved into the openings in the long grass so as to watch me. Those eyes were curious but in no way hostile. I prefer to think that they expressed sympathy and pity... And these without doubt were the men who had killed my son on that very spot.
>
> Towards morning a strange thing happened. Although there was not a breath of wind, the flames of the tapers sank down as though someone had tried to extinguish them. And I said to *him*: "Is it you, are you there? Do you mean me to go away?"[51]

---

49   RIDLEY, p. 612.
50   FEATHERSTONE, p. 192.
51   JOHN, p. 514.

Once the anniversary had passed, Eugénie was only too anxious to get back to Chislehurst. On their return journey however they diverted from their route to cross the battlefield of Isandlwana. Although, by March 1880, confirmation had been made that all the dead had now been decently interred, they were still unpleasantly surprised to see so many relics of the defenders lying strewn around. On reaching the coast, they sailed direct to England from Durban, with the ship calling at Saint Helena. The Empress visited Longwood, making the sad comment, "I am the only person named Bonaparte who will have visited the place where the founder of our race died."[52]

But, on her return, there was no respite from controversy concerning the Prince Imperial. A special committee had been established under the chairmanship of Lord Sydney to arrange for the erection of a suitable national monument to the Prince, to be paid for by public subscription. The Dean of Westminster agreed that it should be placed inside the Abbey. He then took steps to publicly justify his decision: 'The tragic associations connected with the fall of a great Prince, bearing a historic name, fighting under the English flag, and giving his life for the country which had received him and his parents as guests, and which had learned to honour him personally for his blandness and engaging character, were such as to give him claim to be ranked among those Princes to whom Westminster Abbey has at various times given shelter or erected memorials under its roof.' The sculptor Johannes Boehm immediately started work fashioning a white marble representation of the Prince, depicted like a mediaeval knight, lying on a tomb in an artillery officer's uniform, sword in hand, helmet at his feet. But after Dean Stanley's public statement there were strong protests from radicals and others in Britain, and from the French government which had already succumbed to a popular but totally unfounded rumour that the title — Napoleon IV — was going to be carved at the foot of the monument.

Frederic Harrison, the radical freethinker, declared, "The Abbey is the resting place of great Englishmen, not of foreign conspirators. To carve on it a name which stands for treachery and bloodshed, and so to make it serve the plot against a friendly people, is an outrage."[53] Respected journals such as *The Graphic,* in its edition of 26th July, queried what exactly the young Prince, aged only twenty-three, had achieved in his short life to merit such an honour. It could not even be claimed that he had died like a hero fighting England's battles and such a monument could only give offence to France, already 'scandalised by our absurd Bonaparte-mania.'

Despite the protests the Dean declined to change his mind — and in this he was now to be openly supported by the Queen. Almost £50,000 had been collected towards the Prince Imperial Memorial Fund when a surprise resolution in the House of Commons, opposing the planned monument, was carried by a majority of 15 votes. The Queen was angered. She wrote to the Prime Minister, 'The Queen has been greatly shocked and disgusted at the success of Mr Brigg's motion and at the language used to Britain's most faithful ally, as well as the want of feeling and

---

52   RIDLEY, p. 612.
53   Ibid.

chivalry towards the memory of a young Prince, who *fell* because of the *cowardly desertion* of a British officer, and whose spotless character and high sense of honour and noble qualities would have rendered a monument to him a proud and worthy addition to Westminster Abbey, which contains many of questionable merit. But where is chivalry and delicacy of feeling to be found these days amongst many of the Members of Parliament?'[54]

Thoroughly annoyed at this rebuff by the House of Commons, the Queen announced that the monument would be erected instead in the royal chapel of Saint George, Windsor. This did not lessen the controversy. Further protests and petitions opposing this plan were now directed to the aged Dean of Windsor, a nephew of the 1st Duke of Wellington. But the Queen stood her ground — responding to all objections with the irrefutable argument that this royal chapel came under her personal jurisdiction.

On 27th July, after an absence of four months, the Empress landed at Southampton, to be greeted personally by Princess Beatrice. The Queen, in particular, just hoped that she would not become aware of the furore over the Prince's monument but letters of protest from indignant Frenchwomen were already waiting for her at Camden Place. Eugénie thereupon insisted on seeing the full transcript of the House of Commons debate and subsequently wrote to Queen Victoria, imploring her to drop the whole proposal of erecting any monument, even at Windsor, fearing it might undermine Victoria's authority and position as Monarch. At the same time she made up her mind to leave England altogether to spend the rest of her life in the family villa at Arenenberg. It took the combined efforts of Queen Victoria; Lord Sydney; Generals Wood and Simmons; and many others, to finally persuade her to remain in this country.

On the subject of the monument in Saint George's Chapel, the Queen wrote to Eugénie: 'it is the resting place of my grandparents and my father and many of my ancestors, and where I have raised monuments to my Uncle Leopold, King of the Belgians, and to the King of Hanover — where it will be safer and quite as much in sight as at the Abbey. Windsor already has a chapel dedicated to the memory of my dear husband. And how could there be a better place for the monument to your beloved son — 'who wore the lily of a blameless life', as Tennyson said of my husband — than that beautiful chapel where his father's banner floated until his death, and which contains the plaque with his arms?'[55]

General Wood added his voice to those who wished to see the Prince honoured in this way, writing to the Empress: 'I fear your refusal must pain your English friends more than it can please your countrymen. I entreat Your Majesty to pardon my frankness.'[56]

However when the memorial was unveiled in the autumn of 1880, the Empress capitulated, writing to Captain Bigge, 'I have been glad to see the beautiful monument and the place where it stands. The Queen, who feels with those who suffer and, what is rare, has the courage to show her feelings, has completed the work

54   BUCKLE, *Letters of Queen Victoria*, Vol 3, p. 119.
55   JOHN, p. 512.
56   RA. R10/119

of those that by affection for my dearest child wished for a durable monument to him.'[57] As equally poignant, perhaps, was the private presentation to the Empress some weeks later of her son's campaign medal — the silver South African War Medal with its special clasp '1879'.

In September 1880 Lady Ely, one of Queen Victoria's ladies in waiting, received a private letter from an Englishwoman, married to a Frenchman and now living at Joigny in France. The writing and spelling left much to be desired, but the sentiments were clear enough. The writer thanked the Queen of England, adding: 'I am over poured with grief and joy to receive the portrait of my dear beloved Prince Imperial...I know my dear beloved Prince is in heaven and he sees all, and he is pleased that Her Majesty has sent his portrait to his poor Nana...it is a great comfort to me to know that his Highness is in heaven for he is better off there than in this wicked world that would have been all pain to him, it was for that God called him out, to be killed in the Zululand for God wished the world to regret him, and so it did...I remain your obedient servant,...Jane Thierry'[58]

Whilst Eugénie may have been finally persuaded not to leave England she was still determined to move away from Camden Place despite the fact that the people of Chislehurst had specially honoured her by erecting, in 1880, their own twenty-seven foot high memorial to the Prince — a Runic Cross of gray granite — a monumental tribute which still dominates the common today. There were many reasons to move, but overriding them all was the Empress's longfelt desire to build a fitting mausoleum for Napoleon the Third, which would now need to include their son, along the lines of the mausoleum to Prince Albert at Frogmore.

Advised and supported at every stage by General Simmons, she finally bought Farnborough Hill, a large house in Hampshire, together with 257 acres of land on which to build a chapel and mausoleum. In her new home she established, in the style of the age, a special room which was called the *Cabinet du Prince.* In the hall outside stood the Carpeaux statue in marble of the young Prince with his dog Nero, now surrounded by tall African grass and flowers which the Empress had brought back from the donga. In the room itself the bookcases were filled with all his favourite books, on the walls were some veiled paintings depicting the moment of the Prince's heroic death, and two glass cases contained personal mementoes of his childhood, his father, and the last years. In one of the cases she placed his lacerated shirt, still stained with blood, and the collar of medallions from around his neck which Captain Molyneux had brought back. Inside was an inscription: 'Thy will be done.' In a corner of the room stood the golden boat-shaped cradle which had been presented by the people of Paris on the occasion of his birth. The key to the room was held personally by Xavier Uhlmann and only a few were permitted to enter.

She always kept in contact with her son's lifelong friend, Louis Conneau. He was the youngest Captain in the French cavalry, with a brilliant career in front of him. But now that he had unexpectedly been enriched by the handsome legacy from his closest friend, he started to live beyond his means, despite the fact that

57   KURTZ, p. 323.
58   RA. R10/149

the Empress additionally provided him with a regular personal allowance. When in 1886 he fell deeply into debt Eugénie intervened, paid off all his bills, whilst at the same time taking draconian measures with his various creditors, solicitors and bankers to ensure there could be no repetition. Conneau responded to the Empress's generosity — and to her strict counter-measures; he continued with his military career, giving valuable service into the First World War. In 1887 she wrote to him from Farnborough, where she was supervising the last stages in the construction of the mausoleum:

> My dear Conneau,
>   I feel like you that the steady march of the years cannot diminish the memory of him who felt for you so strong and constant an affection. It seems incredible that eight years have passed. The void which he has left has not been filled for any of us. Here, I find that work has made little progress, because the winter has been grim, but I hope that the year will not end without my having the two coffins brought to me here.
>   Do your work well for the sake of his memory, and believe in my affection,
>   Eugénie[59]

The following January the remains of her husband and son were moved, as desired by the Government, without fuss or undue publicity, to the newly-completed mausoleum beneath the abbey.

The Empress spent many of her remaining years travelling. But she never returned to Arenenberg — the memories were too painful. In 1906 she generously presented the family villa as an outright gift to the canton of Thurgau and today it is a museum. But she travelled as far as Egypt and Ceylon, obtaining permission to cross France on the way.

With the Prince's death she totally lost all interest in politics. Nonetheless, when 'Plon-Plon' was arrested for threatening, as a solitary individual without the backing of the party, to hold a plebiscite for the restoration of Empire in January 1883, she journeyed at some risk to Paris in order to intercede specially on his behalf. In a hotel she met with all the party leaders and urged them to rally round him — 'I have forgiven him, surely you can forgive him too?'[60] But the party continued to ignore her pleas not to publicly disown him. When the Republican authorities finally punished him by expulsion from the country, she made him particularly welcome at Farnborough on a number of occasions. He even attended the first anniversary Mass for the Prince. But he never really warmed in his attitude towards her.

As the years passed, she aged with grace, whilst finding a renewed zest for life. At the age of seventy she even learned to ride a bicycle. She visited the cinema, rode in cars and looked forward to a flight in an aeroplane. She died in Spain on Sunday, 11th July 1920 — in her ninety-fourth year — muttering quite simply, 'it's time to go.' She had always considered Sunday to be her unlucky day — for on that day the

59   KURTZ, p. 324.
60   JOHN, p. 515.

Prince Imperial had been both born and killed. It had also been the day on which she had fled from the Tuileries in 1870. But before she died she did, at least, have the satisfaction of knowing that the humiliation of Sedan had finally been avenged through the defeat of Germany in the First World War.

Her body was returned to Farnborough, and her funeral in St Michael's Abbey was attended by King George the Fifth and Queen Mary, Princess Beatrice, and the Kings and Queens of Spain and Portugal.

The abbey and crypt mausoleum of Saint Michael (the patron saint of France) had been built astride the hill facing the Empress's Farnborough house between 1883 — 1888. She personally paid for all the building and furnishing costs, employing a French architect, Gabriel Destailleur. It was said that the dome of the church was added and designed, at the express wish of the Empress, to resemble the famous dome of Les Invalides where Napoleon the First is buried. After the tombs of father and son had been transferred from Chislehurst in 1888, she invited Premonstratensian canons to leave France and take up permanent residence in the adjoining monastery. Amongst their duties they were required to say Requiem Masses three times a year — on 9th January for Napoleon the Third, on 5th May for Napoleon the First, and finally on 1st June, for the Prince Imperial. In 1895 these religious were replaced by Benedictine monks from the Abbey of Solesmes in France. This began the daily round of Benedictine work and prayer which continues to this day.

Today the imperial family lie beside each other, finally at peace, in the crypt of the abbey. Outside, at the foot of the steps leading from the abbey building down to the crypt, is the door which was always used by the Empress when attending divine service. The tombstone nearby is that of Franceschini Piétri, the devoted secretary. On the far side, beside the abbey wall, lies another loyal servant — Xavier Uhlmann.

In the crypt itself Napoleon the Third's granite tomb, which had been donated by Queen Victoria, stands in the north transept. Above hangs his Garter banner, and on the walls surrounding the tomb are two bronze tablets recalling the belated gratitude of the Italian people towards their former champion.

The Empress rests in a separate niche, higher up in the wall directly behind the altar — her tomb fittingly dominates the whole crypt, with her husband and son lying to either side below.

The Prince's tomb is in the south transept. At the foot is Princess Beatrice's cluster of white and purple porcelain flowers; to one side are his own small *prie-dieu* and special chair rescued from the chapel of the Tuileries. A memorial plaque from the Bonapartist party of France hangs above.

Nearby hang three photographs, in a single frame, oldcrowned by the imperial eagle. They portray Napoleon III, the Empress Eugenie, and between them Louis, Napoleon IV, le '*petit Prince.*'

* * *

The scene in the crypt is both majestic and intimate — majestic in projecting an imperial grandeur and intimate in portraying a family at rest. The tragic death of any young man at the threshold of life must always be a source of sadness and regret, but the early demise of the Prince Imperial is particularly poignant. Born a Prince of the Blood he automatically enjoyed privileges and status in a society which would always show him deference. But unlike many others he sought to earn that deference by his own character and conduct. Despite his youth he was to display a charisma and courage which finally succeeded in arousing the admiration of a whole nation; of people who were not his kinsmen and who had formerly been his country's bitterest foes. Of his personal magnetism there can be little doubt. Indeed, those who came into the closest contact with him, from Queen Victoria down to the humblest British soldier, could not help but be drawn to this charming, amiable but supremely self-confident young Frenchman, who always took his responsibilities seriously and who defended his birthright in the noblest of terms. As a result of determined application and hard work at Woolwich, against the twin handicaps of age and language, he had shown considerable powers of intellect as well as military aptitude. And in his embryonic dealings with the Bonapartist party he had begun to show a political maturity and judgement ahead of his years.

But there was more to this public image than mere charm, determination and youthful achievement; he also possessed all the qualities which constitute a national hero. Despite being heir to the name and calling of the Great Napoleon Bonaparte, he was quite willing to wear a British military uniform and participate in its wars in order to face the challenges and dangers of active service. And his personal bravery and courage must be beyond dispute, despite recent attempts to present a contrary view.[61] This obsession with achieving worthiness lay behind much of the impulsiveness and reckless daring which marred his conduct. For he never really recovered from the shame of being compelled to abandon France in its moment of deepest humiliation, and the subsequent taunts of cowardice from many of his fellow-countrymen wounded him deeply. Indeed, these damaging accusations had driven him to an obsessive belief that his personal honour had somehow to be redeemed. Thus, he went out to South Africa to gain a reputation for courage and heroism in battle, without which he could never hope to attract the attention of the French people and add lustre to the family name. And in the tragedy of his early death he had, ironically, succeeded in achieving that reputation.

Otherwise, it can only be speculative to consider what might have been. Had the Prince returned from the Anglo-Zulu war with honour, his personal courage established and unchallengeable, he would have done much to discredit the insidious propaganda of his political opponents and gain a standing in French society in his own right. In his political views he would undoubtedly have further matured to produce an attractive manifesto to put before the electorate. And he would have certainly given a divided and dispirited Bonapartist party the strong leadership it sorely needed, whilst sharpening its political focus and discarding its more dubious practices. But Bonapartism as a political force would continue its decline, and perhaps the Prince would have finally discarded the party as the springboard to power. It is possible therefore that the subsequent Panama scandal, the Dreyfus affair, and all

---

61   See Appendix B — copy of pamphlet by Stanley G. Hutchins, dated April 1973 — *Chislehurst's Monumental Myth.*

the other financial and social upheavals which so rocked the foundations of the Third Republic towards the end of the Nineteenth Century, might have enabled the Prince to attract a significant personal following from amongst the disenchanted middle classes and aggrieved social groups. And when the charismatic General Boulanger, supported by many officers and political factions, including Royalists and Bonapartists, postured to seize power by *coup d'etat* in 1889, Louis might well have been able to take advantage of that unstable situation, perhaps securing enough popular votes to finally attain power — although not necessarily with the title of Emperor, perhaps as Prince-President like his father before him.

In that event his deep and sincere gratitude to Great Britain would have resulted in an even closer *'Entente Cordiale'* than was achieved by his great friend, King Edward the Seventh. Thereafter, the uncertainties increase. But any assumption of power would not have spared France the trauma of the First World War, for it enabled her to avenge the defeat of Sedan and regain the lost territories of Alsace-Lorraine. And within European politics there would have been little change to that vision — *'Pour la Patrie'* — which has always animated the rulers of France.

There seems to have been a widespread agreement that the young Louis showed real promise. Perhaps there was within him the genetic spark of his great uncle which, in time, might have flared up to inspire a life of great achievement. But he did not live long enough to either fulfil his personal destiny or influence the fortunes of his countrymen. Nor did his death profoundly change the course of French or European history. Indeed, there were many who sincerely came to believe, like his mother, that his early death was perhaps a blessing in disguise, for his life otherwise could only have been fraught with insuperable difficulties and frustrations, with no guarantee that his birthright would ever be achieved. But hindsight does not enable us to draw any firm conclusions either way. Perhaps his claim to fame must rest on the fact that he was the last of the Bonapartes to display real political and military potential, with enough personal qualities of heroism and idealism to make him one of most appealing and also one of the most poignant Princes of all time.

Appendix A

OFFICIAL DESPATCH FROM THE HORSE GUARDS ON THE COURT MARTIAL OF CAPTAIN J.B.CAREY, 98TH REGIMENT OF FOOT

(RA.R 8/34)

Horse Guards, War Office
August 16th, 1879

Sir,

    The proceedings of the general court-martial assembled at Camp, Upoko River, Zululand, on 12th June, 1879, for the trial of Lieutenant.J.B.Carey, 98th Regiment, on a charge of misbehaviour before the enemy, having been submitted to the Queen, Her Majesty has been advised that the charge is not sustained by the evidence, and has accordingly been graciously pleased not to confirm the proceedings, and to direct that the prisoner be relieved from all consequences of his trial. Captain Carey is released from arrest and will rejoin his regiment for duty.

    The trial having been set aside, the Field Marshal Commander-in-Chief offers no remark on the proceedings, but His Royal Highness has received Her Majesty's commands to make known his observations on the occurrences of 1st June last, as they have come under his notice in official reports.

    His Imperial Highness Prince Napoleon was, at his own request, permitted to proceed to South Africa, in order to witness the operations in Zululand. He was provided with private letters to Lord Chelmsford, describing his position, and stating that it had not been thought right, even if it had been possible, to comply with his earnest desire to be commissioned as an officer of the British Army. The Commander of the forces in South Africa made such arrangements as seemed to him desirable under the condition of the Prince's non-official position, and attached him at first to his own personal Staff, and afterwards, with a view to provide him with some occupation, to the department of the Quartermaster-General.

    The Prince was treated in all respects as if he had been a junior officer of the General Staff, with this exception, that Lord Chelmsford gave the most stringent instructions that His Imperial Highness was not to be permitted to proceed on any distant reconnaissance without his special permission, and that, when employed in surveying operations in close proximity to the camp, his party was always to be provided with a sufficient escort and to be accompanied by an officer.

    His Royal Highness desires it to be known that he entirely approves of Lord Chelmsford's arrangements for the reception and occupation of the Prince; and that he considers the orders issued for his protection were marked with judgement and adapted to the occasion.

The reconnaissance which the Prince was allowed by Lieut-Colonel Harrison, the Assistant Quartermaster-General, to make on the 1st June extended to a considerable distance from the camp. Lord Chelmsford's permission had not been sought or obtained; all the arrangements were made under Lieutenant-Colonel Harrison's orders; and the Lieutenant-General commanding had reason to believe that throughout the day the Prince was in the company of Lieutenant-Colonel Harrison, who was occupied in guiding a column in its change of camp.

Lieutenant-Colonel Harrison doubtless believed that in his arrangements for the expedition he had sufficiently complied with Lord Chelmsford's instructions to himself. In the opinion of the Field Marshal Commander-in-Chief he was mistaken. His orders to Lieutenant Carey were not sufficiently explicit, and he failed to impress upon the Prince the duty of deferring to the military orders of the officer who accompanied him, and the necessity of guiding himself by his advice and experience.

If Lieutenant-Colonel Harrison had displayed more firmness and forethought in his instructions to Lieutenant Carey and to the Prince, His Royal Highness cannot but think that the train of events would have been averted, which resulted in bringing a handful of men, in the middle of the enemy's country, into a position so well calculated to invite surprise and to court disaster.

Lieutenant Carey from the first formed a wrong conception of his position. He was sent, not only to perform the duties of his staff office, but to provide that military experience which his younger companion had not yet acquired. If his instructions were defective his professional knowledge might have prompted him as to his duty.

He imagined, but without the slightest foundation for the mistake, that the Prince held a military rank superior to his own, and acting throughout on this strange misconception, he omitted to take for the safety of the party those measures of precaution which his experience had taught him to be essential.

At the moment of attack defence was impossible, and retreat imperative. What might have been done, and what ought to have been done when the moment of surprise had passed, can only be judged by an eye-witness; but His Royal Highness will say, and he feels that he speaks with the voice of the army, it will ever remain to him a source of regret that, whether or not an attempt at rescue was possible, the survivors of this fatal expedition withdrew from the scene of the disaster without the full assurance that all efforts on their part were not abandoned until the fate of their comrades had been sealed.

> I have the honour to be,
> Sir,
> Your obedient servant,
> G.H.Ellice
> Adjutant-General

Appendix B

Chislehurst's Monumental Myth

or

The Bunk of a Bonaparte

Louis E. N. Bonaparte, known as the Prince Imperial, was the only legitimate child of Napoleon the Third, who declared himself Emperor of the French in December 1852. The latter fathered quite a few others! The Spanish born Eugenie, Empress, gave birth to the P.I. in 1856.

Destined for imperial glory by his parents, he was dressed in the costume of a grenadier at nine months, attended reviews dressed in Imperial Guard uniform at the age of two years, promoted at six years to the rank of corporal and on his eleventh birthday was given his military establishment of one general, three colonels and a naval captain!

At fourteen years dressed up in the trappings of an imperial officer, he had hovered near the battlefield of Sedan and when defeat was imminent shed his uniform, donned civilian clothes, and fled over the Belgian border to safety. A drummer boy of the same age would have been classified as a deserter.

With his mother he found refuge in England. In spite of his knowledge of the terrible disasters of war he, at the age of twenty-three, was permitted to go to Zululand as an observer attached to the British Army. At Itelezi, the mapping party of which he was a member was surprised by the Zulus. Like all the others he attempted to bolt but, although an expert horseman, trained from childhood, he could not vault onto his horse when the girth leather broke.

Evidence was given by surviving soldier witnesses that the Prince Imperial was last seen running into a donga (ditch) pursued by Zulus.

The fact that he was found face upwards does not establish his bravery. The medical evidence was that he died from the first thrown assegai which penetrated an eye. Subsequent stabs can be attributed to the Zulu warriors' custom of ensuring death. Certainly there were no Zulu casualties, although the P.I. was armed.

The story by Chislehurst pro-Bonapartes that he was deserted by his companions is untenable. Two soldiers, Abel and Roberts, had been killed (plus a native collaborator) before the death of the P.I.

Indeed there is evidence that the P.I. could be held to have contributed to the disaster. On it being reported that a Zulu had been sighted Lieut Carey had suggested that the party depart. The P.I. wanted another ten minutes rest, but after five minutes agreed to a departure. This evidence, by more than one soldier witness, poses the question as to what extent this delay put the party to hazard — and worse.

The image, fostered in Chislehurst and elsewhere, of this Bonparte dying heroically is at variance with facts established from modern research.

Stanley G. Hutchins

April 1973

BIBLIOGRAPHY

ARONSON, Theo. Queen Victoria and the Bonapartes (Cassell 1972)

BARLEE ELLEN,Life of the Prince Imperial of France (Griffith and Farran 1880)

BARRY, St John Nevill. Life at the Court of Queen Victoria. 1861-1906 (Webb & Bower 1984)

BIBESCO, Marthe Princess. Prince Imperial (The Grey Walls Press Ltd 1949)

CHRISTIANSEN, Rupert. Tales of the New Babylon — Paris 1869-1875 (Sinclair-Stevenson 1994)

CLARKE, Sonia. Invasion of Zululand 1879. (Johannesburg 1979)

CLARKE, Sonia. Zululand at War (Johannesburg 1984)

COUPLAND, Sir Reginald. Zulu Battle Piece (Tom Donovan 1948)

DE CHAIR, Somerset. Napoleon on Napoleon. An Autobiography of the Emperor(Cassell 1992)

DELÉAGE, Paul. Trois mois chez les Zoulous et les derniers jours du Prince Impérial (E. Dentu Paris 1879)

DES GARETS, Marie Comtesse (de Larminat) de Garnier. Souvenirs d'une Demoiselle d'Honneur: L'Impératrice Eugénie en exile (Calmann-Levy Paris 1929)

ELLIOT-WRIGHT, Philipp. End of the Second Empire (Osprey Publishing Ltd 1993)

EMERY, Frank. The Red Soldier (letters from the Zulu War 1879) (Jonathan Ball Paperbacks 1977)

EVANS, T.W. The Memoirs of Dr Thomas Evans 2 vols (ed. E.A. Crane London 1905)

FEATHERSTONE, Donald. Captain Carey's Blunder (Leo Cooper Ltd 1973)

FILON, Augustin. Memoirs of the Prince Imperial (Heinemann 1913)

-Souvenirs sur l'Impératrice Eugénie (Calmann-Levy Paris 1920.)

FORBES, Archibald. Barracks, Bivouacs and Battles (London 1891)

FORBES, Archibald. Life of Napoleon the Third (London 1899)

FORBES, Archibald. Souvenirs of Some Continents (London 1890)

FREREJEAN, Alain. Napoléon IV — Un Destin Brisé (Albin Michel Paris 1997)

GIRARD, Louis. Napoléon III. (Fayard Paris 1986)

GRENFELL, Field Marshal Lord. Memoirs (London 1925)

GUEST, Ivor. Napoleon the Third in England (British Technical and General Press 1952)

HARRISON, General Sir R. Recollections of a Life in the British Army During the Latter Half of the 19th Century (London 1908)

HORNE, Alistair. The Fall of Paris (Macmillan & Co. Ltd 1965)

JOHN, Katherine. The Prince Imperial (Putnam London 1939)

KNIGHT, Ian. Brave Men's Blood (Greenhill Books 1990)

KNIGHT, Ian. Zulu — Isandlwana and Rorke's Drift (Windrow & Greene London 1992)

KNIGHT, Ian. "By Orders of the Great White Queen" (Greenhill Books 1992)

KNIGHT, Ian & CASTLE Ian. The Zulu War — Then and Now (Plaistow Press London 1993)

KNIGHT, Ian The Anatomy of the Zulu Army (Greenhill Books, 1995)

KURTZ, Harold. The Empress Eugénie (Hamish Hamilton 1964)

LACHNITT, Jean-Claude. Le Prince Impérial 'Napoléon IV' (Perrin Paris 1997)

LANO, Pierre de. The Empress Eugénie. (Osgood, McIlvaine & Company London 1895)

LEGGE, Edward. The Empress Eugénie and Her Son (Grant Richards London 1916)

LONGFORD, Elizabeth. Victoria R.I. (Weidenfeld & Nicholson London 1964)

MARTIN, Theodore. Life of the Prince Consort. Vol 3

J.P.MACKINNON & S.H.SHADBOLT, The South African Campaign of 1879 (Sampson Low, Marston, Searle, and Rivington London 1880) (Republished Greenhill Books 1995)

METTERNICH, Princess Pauline de. Souvenirs 1859-1871 (Plon Nouritt Paris 1922)

METTERNICH, Princess Pauline de. The Days That Are No More: Some Reminiscences (ed. E Legge London 1921)

MITFORD, Bertram, Through the Zulu Country: Its Battlefields and its People. (London 1883)

MOODIE, Duncan Campbell Francis. The History of the Battles and Adventures of the British , the Boers, and the Zulus, in Southern Africa, from 1495 to 1879, including every Particular of the Zulu War of 1879 (Adelaide, 1879) (Republished North & South Press 1988)

MORRIS, Donald R. The Washing of the Spears (Jonathan Cape Ltd 1966)

NORRIS-NEWMAN, Charles L. In Zululand with the British throughout the War of 1879 (London. 1880) (Republished Greenhill Book 1988)

PHILLIPS, William Peter. Death of the Prince Imperial in Zululand 1879. Hampshire County Council Museums Service Publication 1997)

RIDLEY, Jasper. Napoleon III and Eugénie (Constable London 1979)

ROTHWELL, John Sutton (Compiler), Narrative of the Field Operations Connected with the Zulu War of 1879 (HMSO, London, 1881)

SHEPPARD: HRH George, Duke of Cambridge. Volume 2 (London 1907)

SMITH-DORRIEN, Horace. Memories of Forty-Eight Years' Service (London 1925)

TAYLOR, Stephen. Shaka's Children. A History of the Zulu People (Harper Collins 1994)

TISDALL, E.E.P. The Prince Imperial: A Study of his Life amongst the British (Jarrolds 1959)

TOMASSON, W.H. With the Irregulars in the Transvaal and Zululand (London 1881)

TURNBULL, Patrick. Eugénie of the French (Michael Joseph 1974)

THE LETTERS OF QUEEN VICTORIA: Edited By A.C.Benson and Viscount Esher. Volumes II and III. (John Murray London 1908)

LETTERS OF QUEEN VICTORIA: Edited by George Earle Buckle, Volumes 2 and 3 (John Murray London 1926)

WEINTRAUB, Stanley. Disraeli — A Biography (Hamish Hamilton London 1993)

WHITTON, F.E. Service Trials and Tragedies. (London 1930)

WOOD, Sir Evelyn. From Midshipman to Field Marshal (London 1906)

YOUNG, John. They Fell like Stones. Battles and Casualties of the Zulu War, 1879 (Greenhill Books 1991)

ZELDIN, Theodore. France 1848 — 1945, Volume 1 Ambition, Love and Politics (Clarendon Press 1973)

Albert, prince, 8, 14, 20, 22, 100, 279

Aldershot, 60, 131–33, 137, 141, 151, 162, 164

Alsace, 46–47, 55, 80, 97

Arenenberg, 113, 124, 132, 156–57, 186, 278, 280

Austerlitz, 6–7, 10, 31

Austria, 17, 19–21, 24, 39, 43, 46, 49, 56, 72–73, 158–59, 264

BaSothos, 199–201, 210, 214–16, 231

Bazaine, François Achille, 55–58, 62–63, 80–81, 83–84

Beatrice, princess of the United Kingdom, 18, 99, 146–47, 149, 166, 169, 263, 265, 278, 281

Belgium, 22, 70–71, 74–75, 81, 93, 116, 120, 278

Berlin, 43–44, 46–47, 49, 62, 159

Bettington, Claude 193, 198–201, 208, 210, 213, 215, 218–19, 237, 241, 258

Biarritz, 17, 19, 29–30, 83, 163

Bigge, Arthur, 131–32, 137, 148, 157, 159, 161–62, 176, 185–86, 188, 246, 261, 269, 271–72, 274, 278

Blood River, 187, 194, 197, 201, 206–7, 214–15, 270

Bonaparte, Jerome Napoleon ('Plon-Plon'), 4, 9–10, 19, 23, 30, 44, 48, 58, 61–63, 81, 92, 98–99, 117, 143, 171, 249, 263–65, 280

Bonaparte, Mathilde, 10, 40, 48, 173, 263–64

Bonaparte, Napoleon I, 2, 5–7, 9, 11, 13, 19–20, 22–24, 31, 34, 37, 40, 47, 60, 68, 91, 94, 98, 113, 135, 139, 143, 145, 151, 154, 173, 176, 233, 263, 281–82

Bonapartism, 13, 15–16, 85, 87, 92–93, 100, 113, 119–20, 122, 140–41, 143–44, 150, 166, 207, 249, 282–83

Boulogne, 5, 8, 36, 52, 129

Britain,   22, 162, 248–49, 257,
                        277
Buller, Redvers,   185, 193–98, 202,
                        204–5, 207, 226, 239,
                        254, 258

Cambridge,   10, 94, 115, 122,
                        125–27, 131, 162,
                        164–65, 167, 177–78,
                        181, 191, 233,
                        244–46, 248, 252–54,
                        257, 260–61, 264,
                        270–71
Camden Place,   78–79, 81–82, 84,
                        86–87, 90–91, 93–94,
                        96–97, 99–100, 105,
                        108, 112–13, 116–17,
                        123, 127, 132–36,
                        139–41, 149–51, 154,
                        161–62, 169, 190,
                        246–47, 251, 260,
                        262–63, 265–67, 269,
                        274, 278–79
Cape Town,   161, 166–67, 173–74,
                        192, 235, 237,
                        272–73
Carey, Jahleel Brenton,
                        191–92, 194–97,
                        199, 203–4, 208–11,
                        213–22, 224–33,
                        237–44, 248–49,
                        251–61, 269–70,
                        275–76
Cetshwayo, king,   161, 188, 254, 272,
                        275
Châlons-sur-Marne,
                        36, 55, 57–62
Chelmsford, Frederic,
                        164–65, 174, 176–82,
                        184–89, 191, 193–97,
                        199, 202, 204–5,
                        207–9, 214, 217,
                        227–28, 231, 233–35,

                        237–42, 244–45,
                        247–48, 250, 254–55,
                        259, 266–67, 273
Chislehurst,   78–80, 83, 85–86,
                        89–90, 93, 113,
                        116, 120, 129, 144,
                        147–48, 152, 155,
                        166, 171–72, 245,
                        262–63, 277, 279,
                        281
Conneau, Louis,   28, 36–37, 47–48,
                        84, 87–90, 93–96,
                        103–9, 117, 123, 129,
                        131–33, 135, 151–52,
                        168, 176, 261–62,
                        265, 279–80
Corvisart, Lucien,
                        37, 93, 96, 149, 246,
                        261–62, 265
Cowes,   89, 94–95, 145
Crimea,   4, 8–10, 14, 56, 172

De Larminat, Marie,
                        82, 114, 135, 157,
                        170, 259–60, 262,
                        268
Deléage, Paul,   183–84, 189, 197,
                        203–7, 211, 228,
                        231–36, 249, 261
Denmark,   42–43, 46, 147, 154
Dover,   77–78, 85, 124
Dundee,   184–85, 187, 197
Duperré, Charles,
                        68–71, 75, 77, 79,
                        265
Durban,   174–77, 180, 182–83,
                        192, 203, 231,
                        235–36, 266, 273,
                        277

England,3, 5–6, 8–9, 18,
22, 34, 37, 71–72,
74–75, 77–78, 81,
83, 85, 88, 91–92, 95,
97, 109, 111, 116,
122, 125, 127, 134,
137–38, 144, 162,
166, 169–70, 172,
174, 183, 186, 189,
191–92, 194, 202–3,
206, 214, 233–35,
237, 241, 244, 249,
251, 253–54, 259,
264, 269–70, 277–79

Espinasse, Jean,37, 113, 135, 152,
157, 170–71, 176,
188–89, 261–62

Evans, Thomas,74, 77–78, 262

Farnborough,34, 149, 280–81

Filon, Augustin,2, 16, 18, 22–23, 26,
28–30, 33, 35–36,
38–40, 47, 49, 52, 60,
63, 70–73, 75, 78, 80,
83–84, 88–89, 91,
94–98, 103–5, 107–9,
112, 114–15, 117,
119–24, 126, 128,
133, 136–37, 139,
141–42, 144, 149,
151–52, 154, 156,
158–59, 162, 164,
167, 169–70, 172–75,
181, 183, 185, 188,
191, 199, 202, 205–7,
214, 217, 233, 235,
251, 254, 269, 272

First World War,19, 210, 280–81, 283

Florence,135–37

Flying Column,187, 193, 226,
238–39, 258, 266

Fontainebleau,29, 76

Forbes, Archibald,
40–41, 186, 210, 214,
227

Franco-Prussian war,
15, 20, 34, 36, 38, 42,
58, 128, 144, 172,
182, 192, 210

Frossard, Charles Auguste,
35, 38–39, 50–51,
57, 63, 84, 123

Germany,45–46, 49, 52, 67, 72,
74–75, 80, 124, 138,
281

Gladstone,89, 271

Glyn, Richard,207, 242, 244

Goddard, Isaac,91, 96, 98, 113,
170–71, 247

Grenfell, Francis,191, 196, 202,
215–17, 227, 231–32,
238

Grubb, Jim,213, 219, 221–22,
224–26

Gull, William,93, 95–96

Harrison, Richard,
191–93, 195–202,
204–10, 215–17,
227–30, 237–38,
241–42, 254, 257–58

Isandlwana,162, 180, 184, 188,
199–200, 204, 210,
219, 227, 240

Isle of Wight,74, 89, 97, 145–46

Italy,5, 14, 19–23, 43–44,
49, 56, 60, 63,
135–37, 139–40, 220

Itelezei,217–18, 227, 269–70,
272

Khambula, 176, 185–86, 188–89, 193, 273

Koppie Allein, 187, 193–94, 197, 204–7, 214–15, 217, 235, 262, 270, 273

Lebreton, Madame, 73–74, 79, 87, 90

Le Figaro, 147, 183, 188, 228, 230, 235, 249

Le Tocq, Nicholas, 213, 216, 221–22, 224–25, 243

Lomas, 172, 175–76, 196, 198–99, 231, 236, 261, 264, 269, 273

London, 6, 9, 79–81, 84, 91–92, 116, 127, 147–49, 153, 182, 186, 214, 233, 240, 244–47, 258, 263, 269

Lorraine, 80, 85, 97

Louis Philippe, 5–6, 10, 13, 28

Lourdes, 19

Lyons, 14, 41, 92

Madeira, 171, 173, 233, 261

Magenta, 20, 118, 135, 137, 140

Marseilles, 14, 41, 46

Metternich, Pauline, 19, 73, 77–78, 84

Metz, 49–51, 53, 55–58, 60, 62–63, 65, 80–81, 84

Mexico, 15, 24–25, 41–44, 56

Molyneux, William, 209, 231, 233, 267, 279

Murat, Joachim, 90, 170, 247, 261–62

Natal, 161, 174–75, 180, 199, 213, 235, 273

oNdini, 161, 187–88, 199, 201, 206, 219–20, 240, 254, 258, 266

Paris, 2–4, 8–9, 12, 14–15, 17, 22, 28–29, 33–34, 36, 38, 40–41, 44–46, 48–49, 52, 55–63, 66–67, 69–73, 75, 78, 80–83, 86–88, 90, 92–94, 113–14, 119–20, 124, 130–31, 147, 183–84, 192, 202, 207, 249–50, 256, 260, 264, 279–80

Pietermaritzburg, 180, 182, 184, 235–36, 273

Piétri, Franceschini, 97, 154, 171, 182, 202, 246, 261–62, 272, 281

Plymouth, 172–73, 255

Portsmouth, 37, 237, 261

Prussia, 2, 15, 19, 39, 42–45, 48–53, 55–60, 62–63, 65–68, 70–71, 74–75, 78, 80–81, 84–85, 98, 121, 130, 192, 210

Rome, 5, 7, 11, 19–20, 43, 80, 135, 156, 163, 265

Rouher, Eugéne, 15, 63, 77, 79, 87, 92, 113, 115, 117, 122, 125–26, 130, 137, 140–43, 149–51, 166, 171, 206, 249, 261–62, 264

Russia, 8, 19, 43, 123, 137, 147, 159

Saarbrucken, 50–52, 55, 57, 67, 121, 266

Sadowa, 39, 42, 44

Scandinavia, 147, 149, 154, 156–57

Scotland, 94, 268

Second Empire, 2, 7–8, 14–15, 17, 19, 23–24, 38, 40–42, 66, 82, 84, 97, 117, 154, 260, 264, 266

Sedan, 59, 63, 65–67, 69–70, 72, 78, 87, 96, 128, 141, 157, 250, 260, 281, 283

Simmons, Lintorn, 94, 111, 115, 126–27, 132, 152, 164, 169–70, 172, 174–75, 177, 181, 205–6, 257, 261, 266, 268, 279

Slade, Frederick, 131–32, 157, 162, 176, 186, 188, 246, 272

Solesmes, 281

Solferino, 20–21, 57, 66, 135, 137, 159

South Africa, 22, 27, 31, 37, 41, 148–49, 158, 161–69, 173, 180–81, 183–86, 189, 191–92, 194, 199, 205, 234, 240, 246–48, 250–51, 254–55, 259, 266, 270, 282

Spain, 19, 43, 65, 83, 90, 140–41, 150, 207, 249, 267, 280–81

Stuart, Marie, 29, 77, 151

Sweden, 11, 19, 154–56, 264

Third Empire, 136, 142–43

Thompson, Henry, 93, 95–96

Thyra, princess of Denmark, 147, 154

Trochu, Louis-Jules, 61–62, 73, 78, 81–82

Tuileries, 12, 19, 26–27, 29, 31, 33–34, 36–38, 40, 70, 72–74, 78, 82, 86, 88–89, 93, 123, 146, 281

Uhlmann, Xavier, 47, 79, 84, 103, 108, 121, 133, 169, 175, 177, 235–36, 261–62, 264, 266, 269, 279, 281

Utrecht, 148, 186, 188–89, 197, 201, 203–4

Victor Emanuel, king, 20–21, 63, 80, 135

Victoria, queen, 3–4, 6–10, 12, 14, 18–22, 25, 38, 78, 81–82, 89, 96–98, 100–101, 127, 131–32, 146–50, 172, 180, 191, 210, 230, 245, 247, 250–51, 253, 256, 258–61, 263–66, 268–69, 271–74, 278–79, 281–82

von Bismarck, Otto, 2, 40, 42–44, 66, 80–81, 92, 113, 119, 135

Wales,	10, 18, 78, 81, 86, 98, 123, 128, 145–48, 169, 191, 195, 261, 263–65, 271
Waterloo,	8, 10, 17, 68, 110
Willis, Robert,	213, 216, 219, 224
Windsor,	9, 34, 82, 86, 100, 278
Wood, Evelyn,	185, 187, 193, 196–97, 203, 205, 226–27, 258, 266, 270, 272, 276, 278
Woolwich,	20, 27, 35–36, 38, 94–96, 100–101, 103–4, 114–16, 120–27, 129, 131–32, 152, 159, 164–65, 193, 208, 261, 266, 271, 282
Zululand,	161, 165, 177, 180, 185, 187–88, 191, 193–94, 198, 200–201, 204–5, 208, 216, 238, 242, 246, 257–58, 262, 264–65, 272, 279
Zulus,	161–62, 166, 175–76, 182, 186–88, 194–95, 197, 199, 201–2, 207–8, 213, 216–21, 223–26, 231, 238–39, 243, 247–50, 254, 256, 259, 266, 269, 274–76